Wild Scots

Also by Michael Fry

Patronage and Principle, 1987

The Dundas Despotism, 1992

Adam Smith's Legacy, 1992

Scotland in the Age of the Disruption [with Stewart J. Brown], 1993

Land Reform and Liberty [with James Buxton], 1998

The Scottish Empire, 2001

'Bold, Independent, Unconquer'd and Free', 2003

Wild Scots

Four Hundred Years of Highland History

MICHAEL FRY

JOHN MURRAY

Copyright © Michael Fry 2005

First published in Great Britain in 2005 by John Murray (Publishers)
A division of Hodder Headline

The right of Michael Fry to be identified as the Author of the Work has been asserted by him in
accordance with the Copyright, Designs and Patents Act 1988.

1 3 5 7 9 10 8 6 4 2

A CIP catalogue record for this title is available from the British Library.

ISBN 0 7195 6103 5

Typeset in Monotype Bembo 10.75/13pt
by Servis Filmsetting Ltd, Manchester

Printed and bound by
Clays Ltd, St Ives plc

Hodder Headline policy is to use papers that are natural, renewable and recyclable products and
made from wood grown in sustainable forests. The logging and manufacturing processes are
expected to conform to the environmental regulations of the country of origin.

John Murray (Publishers)
338 Euston Road
London NW1 3BH

Praeterea sicut Scotorum uti diximus duplex est lingua, ita mores gemini sunt. Nam in nemoribus septentrionalibus et montibus aliqui nati sunt: hos altae terrae: reliqui imae terrae viros vocamus. Apud exteros priores Scoti sylvestres, posteriores domestici vocantur: lingua Hibernica priores communiter utuntur: Anglicana posteriores. Una Scotiae medietas Hibernice loquitur: et hos omnes cum insulanis in sylvestrium societate deputamus. In veste, cultu et moribus, reliquis puta domesticis minus honesti sunt, non tamen minus ad bellum praecipites, sed multo magis; tum quia magis boreales: tum quia in montibus nati sylvicolae pugniatores suapte natura sunt.

Johannes Major, Historia Majoris Britanniae (Paris, 1521)

And then just as we find Scots speaking two languages, so they have two ways of life. For some are born in the northern forests and mountains; these are the Highlanders. The rest we call Lowlanders. By foreigners the former are called wild Scots, the latter homely Scots. The former usually speak Irish, the latter English. One half of Scotland speaks Irish, and all these together with the islanders we assign to the society of the wild Scots. In clothing, religion and customs, they are more backward than the rest, the homely Scots, yet not less warlike, rather much more so – for they are more northerly, and because they are born in the mountains and live in the forests, their very nature is more pugnacions.

John Major, History of Greater Britain (Paris, 1521)

Contents

CONTENTS

Illustrations

Picture credits: 1, 2, 3, 4, 5, 7, 8, 9, 10, 16, 28 and 29, Scottish National Portrait Gallery, Edinburgh; 6, National Gallery of Scotland; 11, 17, 18, 19, 20, 23, 24 and 25, George Washington Wilson Photographic Archive, Aberdeen University Library; 12, 13, 14 and 15, National Portrait Gallery, London; 21, 22, 26 and 27, National Museum of Scotland.

Preface

The commission for this book I owe to my late agent, Giles Gordon. He won it for me not long before his untimely death in November 2003, and it is to his memory, in gratitude and in sorrow, that I dedicate my work.

But the period of its gestation goes back much further, more than a quarter of a century in fact, to my inaugural venture into Highland controversy. I was then a young recruit, doing my stint as a trainee leader-writer, to the staff of *The Scotsman*. Its old office on the North Bridge in Edinburgh, overlooking several of the city's monuments, must count among the most impractical buildings ever to have housed a newspaper. It rose ten storeys up one side of the Royal Mile, with three entrances on different levels and perhaps others I never found. This vertical warren contained about midway a leader-writers' corridor, where a pair of its many eccentrics nestled, men of a quality sadly vanished from today's cut-throat journalism. None could have been more endearing than James Vassie and Matthew Moulton.

The savouring of Vassie's memory will have to be left to some future occasion because it was Moulton, the chief leader-writer, that prompted my first foray into Highland history. He himself hailed from Caithness. If a slight figure, he showed the freckled complexion and the reddish-blond hair the Vikings had introduced to the gene pool of that distant corner of Scotland. Yet no man was milder, at least in outward demeanour. His one evident passion lay in the Scottish mountains, which he took every chance to climb right through the year. He might prepare his mind for an imminent editorial by a quick ascent of Arthur's Seat before he came on shift in the afternoon. He would at length die, aged over eighty, by falling off some inaccessible pinnacle. It was hard to mourn such a fitting end, much as I missed him.

I enjoyed having Moulton as my boss, for closer acquaintance revealed in him less obvious passions. The reader will find below some reference to the circle at the University of Edinburgh in the early 1930s that formed one of the seedbeds of modern Scottish nationalism. Moulton belonged to it and brought to it not the common-or-garden Marxism of most others but the doctrines of Charles Maurras, the French atheist who all the same espoused ultramontane Catholicism as an authoritarian rod for his own wayward nation's back. How all this had penetrated as far as Caithness I cannot imagine, but by the time I got to know Moulton he had long abandoned such asperity for tranquil juggling of the platitudes of Scottish public discourse. I was touched when, on my eventually leaving *The Scotsman*, he made me a present of his Vulgate, saying he had no more use for it.

Yet in a single particular Moulton remained prickly to the end of his career. He could not abide cutting his leaders. The editorial column as a rule contained three of them, and nightly practice soon trained the writer to pontificate to the right length, or pretty well. But occasionally there were only two leaders, when somehow in the composition their length became much more tricky to judge. I think I endeared myself to Moulton by suggesting perfect ways to fill the inches he might suddenly find still void as we were going to press. More often, though, we wrote too much, and something had to be cut. This was what happened one night in January 1977.

It was a slow Friday, with Edinburgh's climate at its foulest and only the pair of us on duty as a storm closed in. Moulton, for the sake of a quiet life, chose to ruminate on Africa. He left to me the other obvious subject of the night, the countess of Sutherland's resignation from the presidency of the Mod, the national festival of Gaelic arts. This had been forced by a ferocious campaign against her in the *West Highland Free Press* under its editor, Brian Wilson, later a Labour MP and Minister of the Crown. He waxed furious at finding the countess chosen to represent a culture that he claimed her ancestors had killed off by clearance. Although herself a champion of that culture, she felt she could not continue if her position was to cause discord and recrimination. I, however, gallantly sprang to her defence. My leader argued that guilt could not be transferred to people personally innocent. In any case, I added for good measure, 'the main motive of the Sutherlands, and of the many other landlords who followed the same course, was to improve the wretched condition of the people on their estates'. After the manner of leader-writers, I hedged my bets with pallid qualifications. Moulton, finding we were over-length by several lines, insisted on taking them out rather than prune his own sage sentiments. Otherwise he approved the tenor of what I had written: he a Highlander too.

What followed was extraordinary. For months afterwards readers' letters flooded in to the *The Scotsman* denouncing or, less often, defending the case I had set out. Its author remained, of course, anonymous. My editor, none too pleased at opinions in law attributable to him, imposed on me a monastic silence. But I had no need to intervene further. The apparently inexhaustible correspondence turned out the most lively and interesting I have ever read in any newspaper. It is recalled in Scotland even a quarter-century later, for example, by Dr James Hunter in introducing the latest edition of his own seminal work *The Making of the Crofting Community* (2000). He has wondered aloud who wrote the offending editorial. Now he knows. I will concede that at the time it rested on no great fund of expertise; but leader-writers have to be generalists. For me, at least, it was the start of a long process of deepening my knowledge of Highland history. From time to time, in other editorials and columns, I have given vent to the latest state of my researches and provoked the same wrathful reaction, for I have found no reason to alter my basic opinion, that the concept of clearance is inadequate to characterize the general course of modern Highland history. The time has arrived to present it here in more durable form.

One reason why the controversy of 1977 flared up so angrily was that it came at a crux between one dominant interpretation of Highland history and another. Hunter describes how he at the time sought consciously to supersede opinion among an older school of Scots historians, in essence chroniclers to the unionist establishment, that the clearances had been, if not quite a Good Thing, at least inevitable (like the Union itself). He argued the opposite to such effect that his line has today displaced the older received wisdom and itself become the dogma of a new establishment. Indeed, the Scottish Parliament re-established in 1999 has officially repented of the clearances, acknowledged the victimhood of Highlanders and in its legislation set out to find some redress. Far be it from me to split the difference. I do not much like either school of thought. If this book has a message, it is of regret that Highlanders have never been able to find fruitful expression for their spirit of independence. It may be too late now.

Dr Hunter and I later got on cordial terms. Indeed he is one of the people I have most to thank for stimulation and help during my writing of the present work, for freely giving of his reactions to my own points of view, however uncongenial to him: all this in the midst of his duties as chairman of Highlands and Islands Enterprise.

A second debt is to David Ross, Highland correspondent of *The Herald* (Glasgow). He again could scarcely disagree more with my general outlook on Highland history, yet he has never failed in generous response to my queries and arguments. Above all I have to thank him and his wife, Mary, for hospitality at their home in Cromarty, offered without stint over two decades, and for admitting me to the warm circle of their family and friends, including Mary's parents, Sorley and Renee MacLean. I am deeply grateful to the latter for permission to quote at length from her late husband's poetry.

I owe much also to one of the most distinguished Gaels of his generation, Dr Farquhar Mackintosh, for linguistic help and, once more, for hospitality – never lacking from Highlanders – both at his home in Edinburgh and at his croft on Skye. In particular he translated some of Mairi Mhòr nan Oran's poetry, not otherwise readily available in English, for me to quote in the text below. For his sake I had better add that he does not agree with my interpretation of Highland history either. The same is true of William Gillies, Professor of Celtic at the University of Edinburgh, for discussion and advice on a number of esoteric points. The same is true again of Dr Willis Pickard, who after retirement from journalism is in his turn on the way to being a Scottish historian.

For most poems quoted I have otherwise to thank Hugh Andrew at Birlinn Press for permission to use extracts from published translations by Meg Bateman and Ronald Black. My gratitude goes equally to Carcanet Press for permission to use the extracts from Sorley MacLean. It goes again to Hayden Murphy for acting as intermediary between me and his brother poet Seamus Heaney, who kindly gave permission for me to quote his translation into English of MacLean's 'Hallaig'.

For help with illustrations I am indebted to James Holloway, Director of the Scottish National Portrait Gallery, and more especially to Susanna Kerr, senior curator, who took such trouble to research many of the pictures I have used. For similar, generous services I thank David Forsyth at the National Museum of Scotland and in particular his colleague Helen Brunton, who gladly placed her knowledge of its collection of photographs at my entire disposal. Just as helpful was Craig Brown at Aberdeen University Library, which has charge of the immense collection of Victorian photography by George Washington Wilson.

More generally I have to thank every one of my Highland friends – whose numbers will, I hope, be not too much diminished by what they are about to read. Its faults are all mine.

Edinburgh, October 2004

Maps

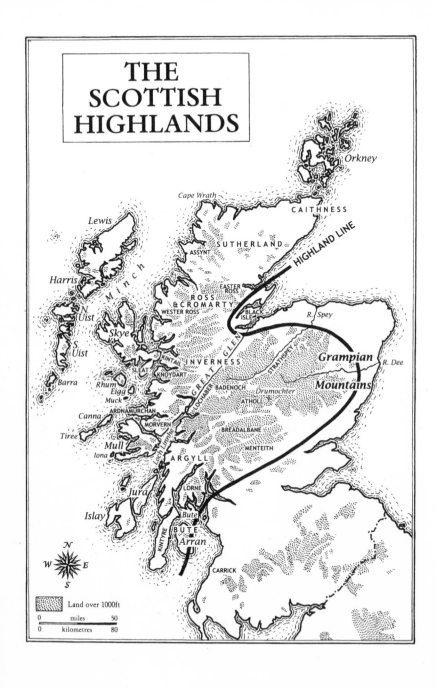

THE SCOTTISH HIGHLANDS

Orkney

Cape Wrath

CAITHNESS

Lewis

SUTHERLAND

HIGHLAND LINE

ASSYNT

Harris

EASTER ROSS

ROSS & CROMARTY

WESTER ROSS

R. Spey

BLACK ISLE

N. Uist

Minch

Skye

INVERNESS

STRATHSPEY

Grampian

R. Dee

S. Uist

KINTAIL

SLEAT

Barra

KNOYDART

Rhum

Eigg

Muck

Canna

ARDNAMURCHAN

MORVERN

Tiree

Mull

Iona

Loch Linnhe

GREAT GLEN

LOCHABER

BADENOCH

Drumochter

ATHOLL

Mountains

BREADALBANE

MENTEITH

ARGYLL

Jura

LORNE

Islay

Bute

KINTYRE

BUTE

Arran

CARRICK

N

W   E

S

Land over 1000ft

0   miles   50

0   kilometres   80

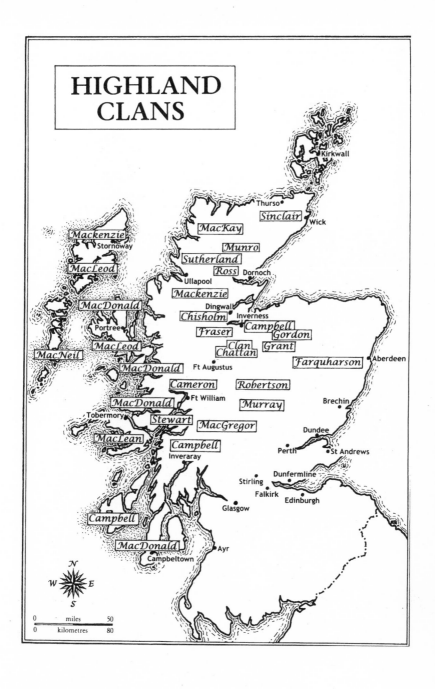

HIGHLAND CLANS

Kirkwall

Thurso
Sinclair
Wick

MacKay

Munro
Sutherland
Ross   Dornoch
Ullapool

Mackenzie
Stornoway

MacLeod

Mackenzie
Dingwall
Chisholm   Inverness
Campbell
MacDonald
Fraser   Gordon
Portree   Grant
Clan
MacLeod   Chattan
Farquharson   Aberdeen
MacNeil
Ft Augustus
MacDonald
Cameron   Robertson
Ft William
MacDonald   Murray   Brechin
Tobermory
Stewart   MacGregor
Dundee
MacLean
Perth   St Andrews
Campbell
Inveraray

Dunfermline
Stirling
Falkirk   Edinburgh
Glasgow
Campbell

MacDonald   Ayr
Campbeltown

N
W   E
S

0   miles   50
0   kilometres   80

A note on Gaelic pronunciation

Gaelic is like English in having a script that offers no sure guide to pronunciation. Some general principles are set out here, but there are many exceptions.

The Gaelic alphabet has five vowels: *a, e, i, o, u*. They are pronounced as in many European languages, such as Italian, for example. But Gaelic marks length by a grave accent: *athair*, father (short *a*); *màthair*, mother (long *a*).

There are numerous diphthongs, which the script records accurately enough, although the following spellings should be noted: *ao* in *caol*, a strait, like *ö* in German; *eu* in *beul*, crooked, like English *ai* in bail.

The Gaelic alphabet has thirteen consonants: *b, c, d, f, g, h, l, m, n, p, r, s, t*. These are often pronounced like equivalents in the English alphabet, but they may also be modified in one of two ways, by lenition or by aspiration.

Lenition occurs when the consonant comes next to the front vowels *e* or *i*. Think of the English 'ago' and 'eggy'; the *g* in 'ago' is articulated back behind the palate, while the *g* in 'eggy' is articulated further forward. In English this is an accidental and insignificant matter, but in Gaelic it is systematic and may mark difference in meaning. In the expression *deoch an dorais*, often garbled by English-speakers, literally a drink at the door, or 'one for the road', the *d* in *deoch* is pronounced like *j* in English, because of the *e* that follows it, while the *d* in *dorais* is pronounced as *d*, though the *s* is pronounced as *sh*, because of the *i* that precedes it.

Aspiration is the main method of marking grammatical variation in Gaelic, in ways too numerous to list here. For example, the masculine noun *ceann*, head, is declined with the definite article thus: singular nominative, *an ceann*, dative, *a'cheann*, genitive, *a'chinn*; plural nominative, *na cinn*, dative *na cinn*, genitive, *na ceann*. There is a different declension if no article is used.

Altogether, the root of the Gaelic noun can be modified in three ways: as in the Romance languages by an ending, as with *doras*, a door, *dorsan*, doors; as in the Germanic languages by internal modification of the vowel, as with *cat*, a cat, *cait* (pronounced like English 'catch'), cats; and then, uniquely to the Celtic languages, by aspiration of the initial consonant, *màthair*, a mother, *a'mhàthair*, the mother, with the *mh* being pronounced like an English *v*.

Gaelic has no word for Yes or No, answer being given to a question by repetition of the verb. Most verbs have no present tense, but convey the meaning of, for example, 'I come' by a construction akin to the English 'I'm a-coming', Gaelic *Tha mi a'tighinn*. The normal word order is verb+subject+object.

I

Bang it out bravely
The union of the crowns, 1603–1625

L ATE ON SATURDAY, 26 MARCH 1603, in bleak and blustery weather, a lone horseman came galloping towards Edinburgh along the high road from the south, and at nightfall found the entrance to the Palace of Holyroodhouse. The place was already locked up, and he had to hammer at the gate. He gave his name: Sir Robert Carey. The guards seemed to know, without his saying in his strange accent, who he was and what he wanted.

They led him to the private chamber of the King of Scots, who started up at the intrusion. Carey had a moment to take him in. James VI was an ungainly but typical Scotsman of thirty-six, of middle height, with short, sandy hair, a reddish beard, a ruddy complexion and blue, staring eyes, plainly dressed and slobbering a little in agitation: no regal figure to an English eye.

But Carey was already on bended knee, saluting him as King of England. The last of the Tudors, Queen Elizabeth, had died, aged seventy, at three o'clock in the morning of the previous Thursday at Richmond Palace, Surrey. Her minister, Sir Robert Cecil, as ever a model of cool, meticulous and devoted efficiency, had everything ready. At eleven o'clock the same morning James I was proclaimed in Whitehall. It remained to inform him as soon as possible, even before the official notification. This was what Carey had come to do, after thirty hours of breakneck riding, interrupted only by an ugly fall.

He was expected. There had been breathless excitement in Scotland during the Queen's last illness. James, seething with impatience, hardly left Holyrood in case of news from London. He was in touch with Cecil, had sent down a warrant to let all the ministers in London stay on for the time being as caretakers in their posts, and had vetted a draft of the proclamation to be made in Whitehall. Meanwhile the English government reinforced Berwick and Carlisle, along with other strategic garrisons, and arrested a few potential troublemakers. Carey reported all this to his new sovereign, who kept the bruised, exhausted envoy up far into the night with questions. When he let him retire, he asked how he could reward him. Carey said he would like to become a Gentleman of the Bedchamber, and James agreed. The English Privy Council would later refuse to confirm the appointment. The race is not always to the swift.

Among the other unforeseen consequences that had come swirling up the road in Carey's windy wake was the eventual doom of the Highlands. The Union of the Crowns in 1603 is as good a point as any to begin their doleful modern history. The date lies roughly half-way between 1493, when the Lordship of the Isles was forfeited, and 1746, when, after the Battle of Culloden, the Gàidhealtachd, the Gaelic-speaking area of Scotland, was wasted; between, that is, the end of the last real vestige or prospect of autonomy for Highlanders and their utter subjection to outside forces beyond their control.

History might have followed some intermediate, happier course – and still may do so. But the Union of the Crowns sealed the fate of the Gàidhealtachd in one crucial respect. It changed from being about one half of an independent kingdom to being the outlier of a composite, soon imperial, monarchy. Within Scotland the Highlanders, once brought into allegiance to the Crown, yet had to be accommodated, or at least the lords and chieftains who ruled them had to be accommodated: there was nothing else to do with leaders of great clans such as the Campbells or Gordons, who found welcome and flattery and reward when they came to Edinburgh. Within Great Britain no need of that existed; rather, there was an opposite imperative. The sovereign now sat in London and in the end could not afford, for the sheer security of his realm, recalcitrance in the north. It would take a long time, but the pressure on the Highlands mounted and at length they were to be subdued.

These facts of life emerged once James VI found himself amid the wealth and might of England. He had, however, already shown his distaste for the Highlands. It used to be the custom for the King of Scots after his succession to sail the circuit of his rugged coasts and, if he could, to address the Highland chiefs in their own Gaelic. The last to employ the language of Eden in this manner had been James IV, and the last to risk the perilous voyage had been James V. The same venture was proposed for James VI, yet somehow he never got round to it. He knew several ancient and modern tongues, but not Gaelic. In his ignorance he dismissed it, along with its intricate culture, as barbarous.[1]

Under his feared, formidable tutor George Buchanan, Europe's foremost Latin poet of the sixteenth century, James VI had grown into a learned man, steeped in the civilization of the Renaissance and the

Reformation. Like many intellectuals in politics, he was too taken with abstract ideas and impatient of those among his subjects who contented themselves with more humdrum concerns. If he had been a beacon to his brother Scots, he could only smoulder ineffectually among the alien English. He surely knew the verses by Joachim du Bellay praising 'France, mère des armes, des arts et des lois',[2] setting for that country a standard of national achievement that any modern monarch might strive to emulate. James patronized pageants, poetry and painting, while at every turn promoting good order in Church and state; only arms repelled him during his notably pacific reign. He had seen too much cold steel in his youth. Some said he had even sensed a horror of it while still in the womb of his mother, Mary, Queen of Scots, the night her Italian favourite David Rizzio was dragged howling from her presence in the palace of Holyroodhouse to be stuck with the daggers and swords of Scots noble thugs.

At any rate James espoused the ornate, formal culture that, across the courts of Europe, had flourished from the revival of learning over the previous century and more. Translated into a social and political ideal, it was often identified by him as 'civility'.[3] To contemporaries the term harked back, in a way it now no longer does, to the legacy of Rome, to civilian law, to civilized pursuits, to the security that might be claimed by a man who could say, 'Civis romanus sum'. Scotland, England and Europe in general still fell short of this ideal. To James's disgust, his barbarous Gaels seemed not to have the slightest inkling of it.

But James was wrong about their lack of culture. They belonged to the cultural continuum of a Gaelic world stretching from the southern tip of Ireland to the northern tip of Scotland. As a physical continuum it was not broken before James's own reign, with his plantation of English-speaking settlers in Ulster. The reality of that continuum had been seen at its most impressive under King Robert Bruce, a son of the Gàidhealtachd, who hailed from Carrick, was married to an Ulsterwoman and held lands on both sides of the North Channel. The culture in which he chose to live during his last years, with his toils and trials behind him, was the Gaelic culture. He settled down not in Edinburgh or Dunfermline or Stirling, but at Cardross on the River Clyde, open to the Highlands and the narrow seas linking them to Ireland. The cultural continuum might have proved of crucial importance to Bruce after his defeat of King Edward II of England at the Battle of Bannockburn in 1314, which secured the independence of Scotland. The following year Bruce circulated the Irish chiefs with a letter addressed to 'the inhabitants of all Ireland, his friends'. He reminded them how they had been 'free since ancient times'. Now he wanted to set about 'permanently strengthening and maintaining inviolate the special friendship between us and you, so that with God's will our nation may be able to recover her ancient liberty'. And by 'our nation', authorities agree, he meant Scots and Irish together. Bruce seems to have been proposing a grand alliance of Celts (perhaps even including the Welsh) to meet the Saxon on more equal terms.[4]

The continuum remained a reality, if now fading, 300 years later. Gaelic society on either side of the sea preserved immemorial forms. In Scotland it has become customary to describe it as organized in clans, from the Gaelic *clann*, which means 'children'. Since clans must play a big part in any Highland history, it is as well at the start to tackle the vexed question of their character in Scotland. No simple answer exists. The conventional view is that a clan consisted of people sprung from a common ancestor who held a certain territory. While a clan always had a chief, kinship gave its members a feeling of equality – especially in connection with its land, which they held to be a communal resource.

Clans of such a kind did exist in the Highlands of old, but all of those named in early sources had somehow vanished by the reign of James VI. The clans he had to deal with were a blend of that ancient Celtic tribalism with the feudalism imported by his royal ancestors from Europe, via England, to strengthen their power and capacity to defend their kingdom. Feudalism meant hierarchy. The king stood at the top, above the various ranks of vassal, reaching down to the peasantry at the bottom. The structure of Scottish clans came to bear some resemblance to this. The top rank of vassal was the chief, but he represented the weakest link in the chain of fealty to the king. As a matter of historical fact, many chiefs did not owe their position to any royal favour but had derived it in some fashion from the clan. Why, then, should they obey the king, unless they felt like it or he had something to offer them? Further down the chain the links became stronger. The chief relied on the heads of the cadet branches of his family, the *daoine uaisle* or gentlemen of the clan, to perform whatever tasks of military or agricultural organization needed to be done. They held authority over the ordinary clansmen and clanswomen, who fought for their chief or worked his land in return for his protection. Yet the chief could not afford to let the gentlemen of the clan get too powerful either, so he often weakened its primitive communism by exploiting the law of primogeniture: succession owed to anything other than the authority of the clan made him less accountable to it.

In practice, common ancestry was incidental to all this. Probably most Highlanders did not bear the same name as their chief. In fact, most bore for everyday purposes no surname at all, only a patronymic and a nickname, sometimes of an uncomplimentary kind. Genealogies could be recited, but they also left scope for embellishment or for glossing over past events when septs of the clan had been conquered or had sought asylum under the chief's family. While a true tribe of blood brothers may have had problems in assimilating incomers, feudalism found no trouble at all: they could be slotted in at a suitable level of subservience. In that case, common ancestry became a convenient fiction. Nor was there in reality anything permanent about the clans themselves. They warred with one another, the weaker being often broken up and absorbed by the stronger; at this point many clansmen might change their names. If Highland society arose out of a mixture of Gaelic tribalism and European feudalism, the result was unique not only to Scotland but also as between clan and clan: each, like a good whisky, became a distinct fusion of the particular elements that had gone into it. One generalization did hold: that while the feudalism of England and the Continent, by subjecting the ranks of vassals to a monarch, laid the foundation of modern nation-states, in the Scottish (let alone the Irish) Gàidhealtachd any attempt to erect a central authority had been fleeting.

In such a society martial values prevailed – the values of the conquering warrior, the noble hero. There had been ancient Irish laws, but the basic way in which this society regulated its greater affairs was by the blood feud. The carnage of the blood feud can be exaggerated: it had its own procedures and limits directed towards compromise, once a satisfactory number of skulls had been cloven and limbs lopped, or sometimes to avert such mayhem. Compromise won mutual consent because no other outcome could exist in a society without a central authority and judiciary to rule which party was right and which wrong.[5]

But this held true also of the Lowlands. The Borders had clans too: Armstrongs, Johnstones and so on. For most Scots kinship defined their place in the world or helped along those few who thought they might improve it. James VI himself in his little book about monarchy *Basilikon Doron* deplored how his countrymen, 'for anie displeasure, that they apprehend to be done unto them by their neighbours, take up a plaine feid against him, and (without respect to God, King or commonweale) bang it out bravely, hee and all his kinne, against him and all his'.[6] The practice of blood feud crossed the linguistic frontier in Scotland because all Gaels and nearly all Lowlanders lived in a kin-based society that relied for its livelihood on a system of agricultural subsistence, which made control of land vital. That is to say, on both sides of the linguistic frontier a feudal system blended with older, native elements, the differences being of degree rather than of kind. In that respect Highlanders and Lowlanders were not so far apart as they often imagined themselves to be, especially not at the level of the chief or the landowner.

On its age-old inheritance the Scottish state began to build in the sixteenth century, like other European states, more rational structures. It established the Court of Session in 1532, for example, as a central judiciary in Edinburgh. This effort was bedevilled by the heritable jurisdictions, the result of a sort of compromise between the medieval Crown and nobility by which the latter were given judicial powers on their own lands, if the monarch could not make his writ run there. The powers took various forms but at their highest were termed regalities – in other words, equivalent to a king's, with the notorious right of 'pit and gallows', to imprison and execute. This did little for Scottish justice but tended to make the nobles absolute masters of the people under them. For Lowlanders during the reign of James VI litigation in the courts more or less replaced other means of settling their differences. Highland chiefs stuck by the old ways. At once lords and judges of their clansmen, they had an admirable mechanism for exerting control of clans never quite secure against disintegration. Without that control, indeed, a clan could scarcely exist.

The saving grace of the Gaelic world lay in its arts. These depended on the patronage of its leaders. This was not a society that used money for its exchanges. Clansmen supplied in kind what the chieftain needed for hall and hearth. He kept in sufficient comfort a train of retainers for more refined services who, if they had nothing better to do, followed him round his territory or further afield, singing his praises. They would include at least a bard or historian, a genealogist or panegyrist to recite his noble ancestry as occasion demanded, a priest, a piper, a harper, a physician and a lawyer, and sometimes also an armourer or even a boatwright, should he have use for one. These formed the *aois dàna* ('learned orders'), in Gaelic society a separate, honoured caste, membership of which might be hereditary, not least among the priests: there was no scope for celibacy here. The culture was, after all, oral and best passed on from father to son or another close relation. Ceòl-mòr, for example, the highest form of music for the pipes, shows clear signs of having been composed for oral transmission in this way. The Beatons of Mull, guardians of a fund of Celtic-cum-classical medical lore, were the most famous physicians. But the greatest prestige attached to the bards, who were not only the masters of a labyrinthine prosody but also, by extension, the keepers of ancient wisdom, which could be turned into political advice to the chief. If he did not take it, and suffered as a result, they could still give the world an indignant rant on his unwisdom.

The poetry was the great ornament of the culture, which in Scotland drew on the same ancient sources as in Ireland. The earliest Celtic literature is the Ulster Cycle, which takes us back to the world of the Iron Age. It is in prose but shares with Homer a gruesome realism: war is necessary, yet also terrible. By the Middle Ages this tradition had given way to the less austere poetic lays of Finn MacCool, Deirdre, Ossian and other heroes, some of whose exploits are set in Scotland. Their memory persisted here until the eighteenth century, when James Macpherson collected the fragments, or said he had.

But all the while the poetic wellspring continued to flow. In both Scotland and Ireland the bards still composed in Classical Common Gaelic their formal syllabic verses, guided by the strict observance of traditional rules rather than by any impulse to imbue the finished work with their own interests or emotions. Such was the tyranny of these rules that it is sometimes hard to understand what attraction the poems may have had for anyone not a member of the learned order of poets. Yet George Buchanan, tutor to James VI, submitted himself to the same sort of discipline in his imitation of Latin models, and Buchanan, who came from Killearn in western Stirlingshire, may well have been a Gaelic-speaker. At any rate, by the time his royal pupil grew to manhood the old, learned practice of poetry was in its turn running down and being replaced by the originally non-literate tradition of song in vernacular Scots Gaelic, which survives, and is available in copious printed collections, to the present day.

It may appear inconsistent with this that in the same period the bagpipes became the favourite instrument of the Gaels, in place of the traditional clàrsach or harp; the harp can, after all, be easily sung to, unlike the pipes. Buchanan marked the change in his *History of Scotland* of 1582. The use of musical instruments was mutating in Europe. Instead of just accompanying the human voice, instrumental music attained an independent status. From no origin that can be traced in an oral culture, ceòl-mòr emerges in its fullness about 1600, with some tunes thought to date from much earlier. It had a learned order of its own, represented notably by the MacCrimmons, hereditary pipers to MacLeod of MacLeod. Tradition holds that they had founded a school of piping at Boreraig, on Skye, in the sixteenth century. Among early members of the dynasty figure Donald Mòr MacCrimmon (born about 1570) and Patrick Mòr MacCrimmon (born about 1595), composer of the wonderful 'Lament for Mary MacLeod' and 'Lament for the Children'. They established the lament as a typical Scottish genre. It cannot be said that the Highlanders were failing to keep abreast of the development of European music.[7]

King James would not have been impressed by this either, yet a subtler criticism than his might have shown that arts cannot easily be divided into civilized and barbarous. It passed for axiomatic in learned circles in the Renaissance that Homeric epics were civilized. This followed the opinion of the Greeks themselves, for whom a readiness to listen to and learn from those epics marked them off from barbarians. Yet the world of Homer, a thousand years older than the Athens of Pericles, is a barbaric world. Transmission of culture is oral. Regular metre and descriptive formulas help bards to remember their lines. As Troy is always windy or cloud-topped, so for the Gaels Edinburgh is *Dùn Eideann nan caisteal*, 'Edinburgh of the castles'. As a Greek hero is well greaved, so one Gaelic hero (of the civil wars in the seventeenth century) is Alasdair *nan geurlann guineach*, 'of the pointed sword-blades'. Homeric epic partook of the same values, the values of the ruthless conqueror, as early Irish epics: there is not much difference between Achilles and Cùchullain. This paradox of barbarism standing at the fount of civilization was to remain obscure for another couple of centuries, until it was faced by Adam Ferguson, one of the literati of enlightened Edinburgh – though also a Gael, the son of a minister in Perthshire. He pointed out amid the yet blander civility of the eighteenth century that the Classical ideals so admired by his fellows ultimately rested on the graphic grimness of Homer. The furore that then erupted over Macpherson's Ossian showed how even in modern Europe there was a public yearning to be sated by the passions of love and war. It is no sur-prise that Napoleon loved the Ossianic poems.

So what was the origin of the enmity felt by James VI for that half of his subjects in the Gàidhealtachd? It is odd that Lowlanders, while vaunt-ing themselves on the antiquity of their kingship, a Celtic one, should have agreed with him on the need to root out Celtic culture. Unruly the Highlanders were, but they did not dispute their fealty to him: it was enough for their conservative, aristocratic mentality that he traced his ancestry back to the royal line of Dalriada, a division of Scotland in the Dark Ages. King Robert Bruce, who united the Scots for good and all, had admitted no distinction among them. But in the nation he refounded, the Gaelic language went into retreat. In 1398 the Scottish Parliament endorsed the status of what it called 'Inglis', and what is now called Scots, by authorizing its use instead of Latin in legislative records. The implica-tion is that the men who carried on parliamentary business, lawyers, landowners from the counties and merchants from the burghs, did so in Scots, if they had no Latin. A century later 'Inglis' had become 'Scottis', the first language of the nation. Gaelic, in earlier documents called 'lingua

Scotica', had become 'lingua Hibernica', or 'Erse' in Scots. In other words, Lowlanders by then associated Gaelic with Ireland and thought it alien to them. In the confidence of their own independent nationhood they had broken with the ancient cultural continuum. But the Highlanders had not, and in Lowland eyes this stood to their discredit.[8]

There is a parallel in Scottish literature which may give us some insight into more popular Lowland views of the Highlands. The first comic Highlander in Scots verse, ancestor of many, appears in the *Buke of the Howlat*, written about 1450, where he is ridiculed as 'a bard owt of Irland'. It did not take long for the slapstick to turn tarter. The anonymous Bannatyne Manuscript contains a poem with the title 'How the first heilandman of God was made, of ane horse's turd in Argyll as is said'. One of its couplets runs:

> Quoth God to the Helandman, Quhair wilt thou now?
> I will doun to the lowland, Lord, and thair steill a kow.

The acid is found flowing at full spate a couple of generations later from one of the Makars, the classic school of Scots poets in the Renaissance. William Dunbar wrote a flyting, or exercise in round abuse, of his rivals, including Walter Kennedy, a clerical composer of religious verse. The interesting thing is that Kennedy came from Carrick, in the south-west of Scotland, a good way from the Highlands proper but at the turn of the sixteenth century still largely Gaelic-speaking. This was enough for Dunbar: with his Gaelic (even if only in addition to his Scots), 'cuntbittin crawdoun Kennedy' has acquired the vices of the far north. 'Thy trechour tung hes tane ane heland strynd,' remonstrates Dunbar, 'ane lawland ers wald mak a bettir noyis.' There follows much in the same vein, with particular aspersions cast on Kennedy's genitals – but Scots, then and since, are unembarrassed by physical function. The question arises how seriously all this is to be taken, for Dunbar was to mourn when Kennedy lay on his death-bed. In Scotland, where jocular insult easily flips over into something uglier, one can never be quite sure.[9]

From these instances it seems obvious that James VI was just concurring with fellow Lowlanders in the dim view he took of Highlanders. He turned their prejudice into policy because he wanted to run a modern state, and no modern state could stand for the chaos of the Highlands since the collapse of the lordship of the Isles. The lordship had been the victim of ill will from a Scottish monarchy that would no longer tolerate a rival but lacked the means to control the consequences of its elimination. The result was in fact to dissolve all restraint, in what was called *linn nan creach*, the 'time of forays'. Blood feud burgeoned not only among the clans but within them too; peaceful peasants were exposed to the oppressions of their own chief, especially to sorning, which forced them to provide free quarters to his military retinue. They suffered also from the ravages of so-called broken men, those who took to the heather in flight, either in revenge or because they had nowhere else to go. The Scottish state gradually improved its organization, leaving to posterity more copious documentation of the Highland lawlessness it abhorred. But it also grew more capable of concern about the causes. James VI had a double vision of clansmen, as creatures whom their chiefs now bade to a brutal banditry, now bent to a base bondage. The question was what to do.

The Scottish Parliament legislated emptily. With greater effect the Crown, unable to resolve the havoc, added to it by confiscating lands and assigning them to chieftains deemed more loyal. This could be a convenient fiction too, for these men wanted to expand at their neighbours' expense more than they wanted to be true to their king. (The two purposes were sometimes combined, but not always.) And the resulting frictions between legal possession of land by the chief of one clan and actual occupancy of it by members or descendants of another became the occasion of further violence. Anyway, with the help of the monarchy the Gordons, represented by the earls of Huntly, bullied Clan Chattan, while the Mackenzies of Ross-shire stretched a greedy grasp right over to the lands of the MacLeods in the Western Isles. Above all, the Campbells in Argyll, under the chiefs known in Gaelic as MacChailein Mòr, pressed forward with expansion from an original inland core of territory round Lochawe to acquire long stretches of the western coastline: first Kintyre and Knapdale, then Tiree, Morvern and Mull. They seized most of this territory, in the longest and bitterest of all the feuds, from the MacDonalds. These had held the lordship of the Isles, with the earldom of Ross, then Lochaber, Kintyre and other parts of the mainland. The land was lost either to the legal chicanery or, if that failed, to the brute force of the Campbells, a clan as crooked in the courtroom as it appeared to be unbeatable on the battlefield.

Still, a more profound and permanent change had meanwhile come over the life of the whole nation with the Reformation of 1560. Roman Catholicism was cast down, but Protestantism would take some time to rise up in its final Scottish form. For the Highlands the real problem was that, even before 1560, religion had been only fitfully organized through the region. Neither the see of Argyll nor that of the Isles had by then had a consecrated bishop for the best part of half a century. Highland parishes were enormous (as they remained into modern times), and could scarcely be ministered to even where they had a resident priest. Reports to King James V, who reigned from 1513 to 1542, said that many people in these remote parts were not baptized and knew nothing of the other sacraments, or of Christianity in general. That is to say, they were no better than pagans, and later descriptions by early travellers to the Highlands seem to show this would remain true for a long time yet.[10]

The Reformation first triumphed where it won support from the nobility. On the Campbells' lands it had that from the start. As early as 1556 the fourth earl of Argyll invited the reformer John Knox to preach before him. The earl and his heir joined the first band of reforming lords the next year. They promoted the Protestant cause notably through patronage of John Carswell, who had started his career as the priest of Kilmartin. In the new dispensation he became superintendent of Argyll, then bishop of the Isles. He organized reformed congregations as far away as Skye and Harris. His enduring claim to fame is that he translated Knox's Book of Common Order into Gaelic, as *Foirm na n-Urrnuidheach* ('Form of Prayers'). This volume, published in 1567, was the earliest ever printed in Scots or Irish Gaelic. Carswell had the type set in Edinburgh and apologized in a note for any mistakes made by a compositor who could not understand the copy he set. In fact that man, Robert Lekprevik, showed himself meticulous, and Carswell's linguistic skill as a translator makes of the work a literary landmark.

It was still not enough to win over the Highlanders to the Reformation. Carswell at least knew they had to be addressed in their own tongue if they were to be converted to the true religion, whatever the king might think. But, with his bardic education, Carswell could not bring himself to break away from using the Classical Common Gaelic, which was not always at once understood by congregations of the unlearned. His compromise between the medieval, oral culture of the Highlands and a modern Calvinist, reformed culture, with its requirement of universal literacy, remained awkward. He did, though, see the need for compromise if transition from one to the other was to be accomplished. He lived, however, in an age that found compromise on all questions of religion and politics virtually impossible. Gaels were not to receive sufficient spiritual sustenance until the foundation of the Free Church of Scotland in 1843.

Altogether, Highland problems, political, religious and social, reached a peak of complexity in the reign of James VI, not least in the way they worked on one another. This consciously modern monarch, in the vanguard of Europe's intellectual movements – and a contributor to them with tracts of his own – wanted apart from anything else to succeed at length to the English throne. He could hardly expect to do so if his homeland was submerged in anarchy emanating from the Highlands. All this prompted him to attempt a general settlement of the region.

In 1597 an act of the Scottish Parliament required the chiefs to produce a legal title to the lands they held. Sìol Torcail, the MacLeods of Lewis, could not find or had never had one. The king confiscated their lands and regranted them to a group of a dozen Lowlanders, the so-called Fife Adventurers. He seems to have entertained no doubt that they could turn rocky, boggy Lewis into a fertile, fruitful place, or that they could exterminate its natives and replace them with sturdy Lowland colonists. The Adventurers at once found the opposite to be true. In 1609 they felt fortunate to sell out their interest to Lord MacKenzie of Kintail, regarded as one of the more civilized chieftains by the king (who was to create him earl of Seaforth). James had also grown anxious to end the feud of Campbells and MacGregors, by simple dint of authorizing the earl of Argyll to exterminate his enemies. Early in 1603, just before departure for England, the king declared the very name of MacGregor to be illegal. The clan officially remained outlawed until 1775. It now lost lands it had held for centuries; those living off them became broken men, if they could not find refuge in the territory of their Irish offshoot, the Macdonnells of Antrim. With the plantation of Ulster too, the continuum of the Gaelic world was being rent. In Scotland, at least, the king's blithely genocidal policy represented a passing phase. For a poor kingdom it was too drastic, too difficult, too expensive.

Once James VI ascended the English throne, he conducted his vaunted 'government by pen',[11] sending instructions the 400 miles to dutiful privy counsellors left behind in Edinburgh. The departure of the Court from the capital is often thought to have been a huge blow to Scotland, but to these men it brought a welcome area of sensible discretion. Their king's blood-curdling orders continued to arrive. But they, supposed to find means and money for them, seldom could. Through procrastination they weaned him away from them.

James's most determined offensive against the Gaels came in 1608, after he realized he could not get his officials to do his dirty work for him. He sent a kinsman, Andrew Stewart, Lord Ochiltree, with a naval expedition to the Isles, including reinforcements from England. The aim was to execute laws and collect rents owed to the king in his capacity as lord of the Isles, all with sufficient rigour to overawe the Gaels. Ochiltree did so with panache and had a final trick up his sleeve. Riding off Mull, he summoned twelve chiefs to his ship. He obliged them to listen to a sermon from Andrew Knox, bishop of the Isles and commissioner of the king. Once they had heard him out, they were told they would not be allowed to leave the ship but would be sailed away captive to Ayr.

So far, so Jacobean, but then Knox wrote to his monarch to let him 'understand how easy it is to your Majesty . . . to establish and induce them all, without hostility or opening of your highness' coffers, to accept of such a solid order as may reduce them to a hasty reformation'.[12] The chiefs were left to languish in Lowland castles for several months. Then in August 1609 came an offer to release them, on condition of their attendance at another meeting with Bishop Knox, this time on Iona. Nine of them went there: MacDonald of Dunivaig on Islay, MacLean of Duart and MacLean of Lochbuie on Mull, MacDonald of Sleat and MacKinnon of Strathardle on Skye, MacLeod of Harris, MacLean of Coll, the Captain of Clanranald and MacQuarrie of Ulva. They cannot have expected it to be an enjoyable occasion, but at least it turned into a memorable one, as Knox revealed to them what he had had in mind with his letter to the king. His nine Statutes of Iona, as they came to be known, are often seen as the first act of general legislation for the Highlands.

These statutes set on the surface a strange order of priorities and displayed other eccentricities, not to speak of a certain ignorance about Highland society. The first required the Church to be maintained and for its regular disciplines to be established – for example, on marriage (where it banned a Gaelic custom of wedlock for a fixed term of years which did not in fact exist). The second called for inns to be erected in the Highlands. The third demanded a limit on the military retinues of the chiefs. The fourth abolished sorning. The fifth banned the sale of wine and whisky. The sixth said the chiefs and leading clansmen should educate their sons, or even their daughters if they had no male heir, in the Lowlands. The seventh forbade the carrying of firearms. The eighth proscribed Gaelic bards. The ninth provided a means for all the other articles to be enforced, namely for the chiefs to arrest offenders and hand them over to the national authorities. On Iona the chiefs accepted the statutes rather more promptly than did the king in London, once Knox told him about them. But when he did, his consent represented a victory for his sensible counsellors.

The statutes have aroused debate among historians because they are so hard to interpret as a coherent whole. The first, on the Church, is fair enough, and an obvious priority for Knox, as for his king. But it is not clear why this pair thought the Highlands should be dotted with inns, especially if the inns could not sell wine or whisky. The answer lies in the fact that any payment for hospitality was deeply unCeltic: a chieftain offered an abundance of food and drink to visitors as long as they wished, and liked to hear they were getting more from him than from his rivals, though he might resort in the end to certain sinister heavy hints to those outstaying his welcome. So this statute is an attack on the power of chiefs to offer largesse and with it demonstrate their wealth and might – an attack on their prestige, not just on the drunkenness of their followers. However that may be, no inns were built and Gaels continued consuming alcohol with as much abandon as before. The proscription of the bards could have been expected to exert a similar effect on the Gaelic way of life by depriving the chiefs' castles of their greatest cultural ornament. The learned order of poets was in decline anyway, though it did not finally disappear for a century or so; but there is no evidence that the relevant statute had any effect on the process. At the same time, this statute connected with the aim of another, to anglicize at least the leading cadres of Highland society, whose offspring would be brought up speaking English and have no time for obscure syllabic poetry. The provisions against military retinues, their arms and their uses of them, were meant to limit chiefly practice in its more arbitrary and destructive forms, serving law and order in general as any state would wish. By the same token, a chief could find favour and so maintain his authority if he obeyed the statutes and co-operated with the government.

The Statutes of Iona should be seen not as making law in the way an act of Parliament makes law. They rather announced that the sins of the Highlanders would be viewed differently in future, much as the Scottish Parliament, once restored in 1999, declared its disapproval of drinking, smoking, smacking, hunting, singing, bingeing and other obnoxious habits of the Scots people. The statutes were also an offer to the chiefs, which they could take or leave but would be unwise to refuse. This reading raises the question of whether anyone ever tried to enforce them. The statutes offered the chiefs a way to come in from the cold of the chaotic Highlands and to warm themselves at the hearth of a modern Scottish state, on condition that they showed a minimum of good manners as defined by this state. Its rules admittedly did not stop there. From 1610 the chiefs were required to present themselves once a year in Edinburgh, to be praised for good behaviour or browbeaten for bad and to hear what further plans lay in store for them. In 1616 they were lured into an agreement that included an overt assault on the Gaelic language as such. The Act for the Settling of Parochial Schools passed by Parliament that year, the first educational legislation since the Reformation, ordained 'that the vulgar Inglishe toung be universallie plantit, and the Irishe language, whilk is one of the cheif and principall causes of the continewance of barbaritie and incivilitie amongis the inhabitants of the Ilis and Heylandis, may be abolisheit and removeit'.[13]

But if the chiefs could put up with the insult to their culture and concede the ascendancy of Lowland values, they might ally themselves with the Crown and be received into the wider political class of Scotland or even of Britain as a whole. They might go to Court and adopt airs and graces. They might grow rich from official favour. They could play intelligent politics rather than indulge their bloodlusts. In different times and places, according to diverse circumstance, with contrasting degrees of enthusiasm and at variable speeds, most chiefs did accept the offer and guaranteed a future for themselves. The chiefs of the Scottish Gàidhealtachd are, after all, still in existence today, whereas their Irish counterparts have vanished.

Finally it is appropriate to acknowledge, if not exactly admire, the achievement of a remarkable monarch, James VI and I. He was by common consent one of the best kings of Scots, yet his repute as king of England is dismal. 'The wisest fool in Christendom',[14] he appears to have attempted more than he could ever accomplish, to have rubbed up the wrong way too many of his new subjects south of the border, and to have aimed at an absolutism that sowed a whirlwind reaped by his son Charles I. Yet James must count as a far more committed and energetic founder of the British state than his lethargic great-granddaughter Queen Anne, even though it was under her that the state came formally into being in 1707. The vision of Scotland and England united belongs to James, far ahead of its time though it was. In 1603 neither Scots nor English felt ready for it, yet the idea was planted in their minds and in the course of a century it came to appear as a solution to problems between them not to be remedied in any other way. The solution also had the effect of marginalizing the Highlands. That was no doubt the king's intention. If the details of his project could not always be realized in the circumstances of the age, success on a greater scale would in the end be his.

2

Jesus and no quarter

Civil war, 1625–1660

INVERLOCHY, ON THE outskirts of the present-day Fort William, stands at one of the most strategic sites in the Highlands. In medieval times a huge castle was built there, commanding three routes: north, up the Great Glen to Inverness; west, along Loch Eil towards the Hebrides; and south, down Loch Linnhe to somewhat gentler terrain and to the sea linking Scotland and Ireland, the crossroads of Gaelic civilization.

Only to the east of Inverlochy are all ways barred by a long, steep wall of mountain. The castle lay in the shadow of Ben Nevis, at over 4000 feet the highest peak in the British Isles. Nobody could come or go on that side unless they knew the narrow glens and high passes of the massif beyond.

Yet it was here that the fighting men of Clan Campbell, encamped with their Lowland allies in the army of the Covenant, saw to their astonishment a hostile vanguard appear in the gloomy twilight of 1 February 1645. Pickets exchanged shots, but the chief of the Campbells, the marquess of Argyll, MacChailein Mòr to his men, could not be sure who was mustering on the braes above him or why. In the night, under a full moon, their numbers grew. Somehow an army had come over the trackless hills through the ice and snow of winter.

Dawn revealed the truth. It was the army of the marquess of Montrose, which in the name of King Charles I had ravaged Scotland for the better part of a year. Argyll had no choice but to stand and fight. From a galley in the loch whence he could observe the field, he deployed his forces, the Lowlanders on the wings and his own clansmen in the centre.

After some preliminary skirmishing two moves decided the encounter. The Campbells fired a volley. The warriors along the whole royalist front answered with a Highland charge, a terrifying tactic that brought them hurtling down the slope swinging their claymores and screaming their war-cries. They were used to seeing their enemies take to their heels at this point. But the Campbells, proud of their traditional valour, stood their ground. Even so, they held for only a while. From ferocious hand-to-hand combat they at last broke and fled. Some tried to swim out to their chief's galley, but he made away and left them to their fate. Others sought refuge in the tower of the old castle. The rest ran away down the shores of the loch. There, in the usual conclusion to battles of the Scottish Civil War, they were butchered by their pursuers.

Montrose did not like waging war in the savage Highland fashion. His ultimate aim was to restore the country to the king, which counselled at least a measure of humanity. This time he managed to insist that the Lowlanders should be given quarter. But the Campbells could expect none and found none from rival clans. Their commander in the field, Sir Duncan Campbell of Auchinbreck, was captured and brought before Montrose's right-hand man, Alasdair MacColla MacDonald, him of the pointed sword-blades celebrated in poetry. MacColla jested with his captive. Did he want to be made longer or shorter? Did he want his neck stretched by the rope or his head severed by the sword? It was not much of a choice, replied Auchinbreck, at which MacColla settled the matter by striking off his head (or, in one macabre account, the top of it) with a single blow.

War, as ever, set the bards singing. Iain Lom, the greatest Gaelic poet of the seventeenth century, was an eye-witness to the Battle of Inverlochy. He himself had brought word to Montrose, marching away up the Great Glen, of Campbells concentrating in the rear, and returned with the royalist army to watch the fighting from the hill above. Lom was a young man who had trained for the Catholic priesthood in Spain, before succeeding as hereditary bard to MacDonald of Keppoch; Christian charity was anyway not his strong point. In the traditional manner he saw his prime task as political, to glorify the deeds of the clan. Yet in a long poem on the battle he displays no interest in the wider matters at stake, neither in the Scottish conflict of king and Covenant nor in the parallel struggles of England or Ireland. To him Inverlochy is simply a fight between MacDonalds and Campbells. He praises MacColla – *creachadh, losgadh agus marbhadh* ('burning, killing, wreaking destruction') – yet never so much as mentions Montrose. And while Iain Lom has the gruesomeness of a Highland Homer, he shows no sense of the pity of war such as otherwise dignifies verse of this genre. On the contrary, he uses deliberately sickening images. The ground round Inverlochy has received a fine manuring:

> *Chan inneir chaorach no ghobhar*
> *Ach fuil Ghuibhneach an dèidh reodhaidh.*

> Neither with sheep-dung nor goat-dung
> but with Campbell blood after congealing.[1]

This was Scotland twenty years after King James VI had departed from her in peace, now not governed by the pen but terrorized by the sword. The relative prosperity and tranquillity in the first quarter-century of the Union of Crowns had been ended by two powerful, connected forces: religion and nationalism. While James had known how to handle them, he cannot be absolved from blame for the way they wrought havoc following his death. It was he, after all, who sought to bring the Church of Scotland to heel under an Episcopal rather than Presbyterian regime. While his effort proved unpopular, it was not fatal to his government because in his hands it could not readily be pilloried as an anglicizing measure. Authority in the Kirk had been a subject of debate since the Reformation. James grew up with that, knew all the arguments and deployed them as skilfully as any clerical opponent. His countrymen's penchant for disputation soon drove them onwards to the finer points, such as whether or not to kneel at communion. There James could by and large leave them.

His son Charles I, on the other hand, knew nothing of Scotland or the Scots, despite having been born at Dunfermline in 1600, before the Union of the Crowns. He had grown up an Englishman, assuming that Scotland ought always to follow the example of England. From his religious policy Scots drew the simple conclusion that he wanted to make the Church of Scotland an Anglican one – and of a type, with smells and bells, especially obnoxious to them; in other words, a high Church as promoted by his favourite, William Laud, archbishop of Canterbury.

When Charles returned to Scotland in 1633 to be crowned, it was with rites that most of his people abhorred as popish. In 1637 he ordained for the Kirk a new prayer book which not only took kneeling at communion for granted but babbled on about ornaments in church and celebration of saints' days. When used for the first time at St Giles in Edinburgh, it seemed to the citizens the last straw, the climax of a long campaign against the Kirk, quite likely heralding a reversal of the Reformation. According to legend, it was at any rate too much for Jenny Geddes, who sold herbs by the Tron, in one of the city's markets. In St Giles she started up angrily and shouted at the dean: 'Out, thou false thief, dost thou say mass at my lug?' Then, snatching the stool on which she always rested her old bones in church, she hurled it at the head of the bishop of Edinburgh. A riot ensued, and such widespread unrest in the capital and the country that within a week the government had to announce the abandonment of the prayer book. Modern historians have decided that Jenny Geddes never existed. In that case, however, it was necessary to invent her: she represented a people who would put up with no more corruption of their religion. Revolution followed.

The revolution arose out of Lowland sentiment, hardly of interest to distant Highlanders: since the Reformation had as yet hardly arrived among them, they were unlikely to be upset by its reversal. Yet they too would be drawn into the great religious and political upheaval that followed, not least because the clans held the country's biggest reserves of manpower accustomed to war. The leaders of Scotland signed in 1638 the National Covenant, pledging themselves to her reformed religion, and sent copies of it to be subscribed all over the country. By 1639 the Scots were in arms against their king, in a conflict that developed into what has justly been dubbed by modern scholarship the War of the Three Kingdoms, as it spread over England and Ireland as well.

It was a long, costly war of daunting complexity. Various parties tried to unite the three kingdoms, or rather impose uniformity on them. But this only served to show how far from unity they remained, divided as they were by religion, politics, language, culture and level of development, not only one from another but also within themselves. In the end these struggles petered out in exhaustion, and some semblance of the status quo ante was restored. In reality, though, relations among the nations and regions of the British Isles had been broken and reforged, directing their peoples towards an unforeseen future. Nowhere did this prove truer than in the Scottish Highlands.

The succession of Charles I in 1625 had not in itself much affected the Gàidhealtachd. At first Charles merely continued to follow his father's jaundiced views. From London in 1626 the new king signed orders for 'the better civilizing and removing of the Irish language and barbaritie out of the heighlands'. A small difference was that he had inherited with his throne a precarious Scottish colony in Nova Scotia. In 1629 he reached an agreement with a few Highland chiefs for dumping in the New World their more unruly followers, to fight each other or the natives to their hearts' content, or at any rate 'for debordening that our kingdome of that race of people, which in former times hade bred so many troubles ther'.[2]

It was an early sign that some chieftains might be giving up an unconditional commitment to leadership and patronage of their clansmen, who instead were to be bargained away for political or material gain. One that signed up to this scheme, which came with a baronetcy for its sponsors, was Sir Lachlann MacLean of Duart on Mull. His bard, Eachann Bacach, respectfully reproached him for spending his time at the gaming tables of Edinburgh, while his islanders always stood ready to rally round his standard:

An Dùn Eideann nan caisteal
Tha ceannard truen na mòr aitim;
'S ann de d'bheus a bhith sgapadh an òir

Is nach b'urrainn do d'dhùthaich
Chur ad ghlacaibh de chùinne
Na chosgadh to chrùintibh mun bhòrd

In Edinburgh of the castles
is the chief of the great people:
one of your customs is the dispensing of gold;

Though never could your country
put in your hands the coinage
that you would gamble in coins at the board.[3]

The projected plantation or transportation of Highlanders to America was a presage of the future but came to nothing for the time being. Charles surrendered Nova Scotia to the French in 1632 after another set-back to his always ill-judged foreign policies. By now he was losing interest in forcing civility on the Gaels: just as well, for soon they would become his most ardent supporters.

Instead, Charles set out on the suicidal course that would lose him the loyalty of Presbyterian Scotland, then prompt the Parliament at Westminster to assert itself and drive England too towards civil war. After the National Covenant a general assembly of the Kirk was called, the first for many years. At its meeting in Glasgow, it banned the king's prayer book and for good measure abolished episcopacy, an act confirmed by the Scottish Parliament in 1640.

The leader who emerged from this defiance came of Clan Campbell, bastion of the Reformation in the Highlands. He was Archibald, eighth earl of Argyll: close, cunning, cast-eyed. He had moved cautiously at first for he owed a debt to the king, who was making the seventh earl, a dotard convert to Catholicism, turn over his estates to his son and leave the country. The greybeard wrote to his sovereign: 'Sir, I must know this young man better than you can do. You may raise him, which I doubt not you will live to repent, for he is a man of craft, subtlety and falsehood, and can love no man, and if he ever finds it in his power to do you a mischief, he will be sure to do it.'[4] Someone other than a bitter parent might rather have praised the new chief of Clan Campbell for his acumen and artfulness. At the General Assembly he anyway placed himself at the head of the opposition to the king. He was then in a position to lead the Covenanting government which took control of the country, at first depending heavily on the military prowess of the Campbells and allied clans.

Despite its reputation for Calvinist fanaticism, the Covenanting government actually turned out to be a good one. It was parliamentary, it proved reasonably regular and efficient, and it united the aristocracy with the Lowland middle class. For several years it maintained the peace and defended the nation, with buffer zones beyond the borders up to the River Bann in Ireland and to the River Tees in England. Charles soon found himself obliged to come to terms with this government when, in 1639, it sent an army towards England.

Among its commanders was James Graham, earl of Montrose, whose lands lay along the Highland line, in Stirlingshire, Perthshire and Angus. He showed how deeply the Covenant had at first struck home in the hearts of Scots. Montrose was an aristocratic royalist devoted to a sovereign he felt had erred. He took his stand for both King and Covenant, for a Scottish monarchy that governed Church and state through general assemblies and free Parliaments. As ever, the sensible line proved the least feasible in troubled times, partly because Montrose showed no moderation at all in pursuing it. He was a man of contradictions in a world of contradictions, through which he found his way by a high and mighty egoism. Never that interested even in carrying his peers with him, he learned how to conquer by means of such elemental violence that his soldiers quite forgot his prior professions of humanity to foes of a different sentiment. For valour and fidelity to his sovereign (once he had made up his mind where his loyalties lay) Montrose was no doubt deserving of the heroic status he won in his life and of the royalist cult that built up around him after his death. He has often been contrasted too favourably with Argyll, his superior in stamina and patience, who achieved more of what he wanted but without brute force. In the contest between these two the fate of Scotland in the civil war was anyway played out, and played out largely in the Highlands.[5]

Montrose, though a Presbyterian himself, could only act to any effect for the king because, even now, Scotland was not yet wholly Presbyterian. Beleaguered Catholic remnants could be found in the north-east and in the Highlands, notably among the shattered Clan MacDonald, where it yet clung on against the Campbells, who had conquered and dispossessed it. It had to look for a saviour to the head of its offshoot in Ulster, Ranald MacDonnell, second earl of Antrim. From across the water he made clear, and on behalf of the Scottish MacDonalds too, his enmity to the Covenant and his allegiance to the king. This stood him in good stead as unrest spread from Great Britain to the sister isle.

In 1641 the Gaels of Ulster copied the Covenanters and revolted to extract concessions from the English government, especially a guarantee of toleration for their Catholic faith. They started by attacking Protestant settlers who had taken over native lands during the plantation of the province. Many died in massacres. The leaders of the rising created a Catholic Confederacy which at length set up its headquarters at Kilkenny. They were frustrated in their aim of dominating Ireland when the Covenanters sent over an army to defend their compatriots in Ulster, while the English reinforced the garrison in Dublin. This was the start of a long agony for the Irish.

But for now the rising brought to light a survival of cultural continuum among the Gaels, as those in Ulster received help from those in the Highlands. Alasdair MacColla had been brought up on Colonsay, from which his family was expelled by the Campbells in 1639. He fled to Ireland and joined the Catholic rebellion, taking over a command. On 11 February 1641 he fought the Battle of the Laney against a unit of Protestants on a sortie from Coleraine. It was a minor engagement, but one that gains historical importance with hindsight because it was here that the Highland charge is supposed to have been invented.

In this period combat often began with volleys from the muskets of the opposing forces. It would continue until one side saw some other advantage to exploit, with the soldiers slowly and laboriously reloading their unwieldy weapons in between each exchange. At the Laney, however, MacColla ordered his men to drop their guns after the first round had been fired, pick up their swords and targes (the small, circular shields of the Highlanders) and run down screaming their war-cries on the Protestants, who were still fumbling with gunpowder, ramrod and shot. These then had the choice of standing and fighting at a disadvantage, with sword alone against sword and shield, or of taking to their heels. So much for modern technology. At the Laney the Protestants must have stood and fought because the majority, several hundred of them, were killed. Later forces facing the Highland charge frequently preferred to run away before it slammed into them. The Gaels were the only part of the British population for whom instruction in war was a normal part of their upbringing, and practice of war a normal part of their way of life. This further refinement in military technique brought repeated success to their arms right up to the Battle of Culloden in 1746.[6]

Meanwhile across the three kingdoms the situation remained confused. By the summer of 1641 the king, seeking allies against the English Parliament where he could, came in person to Edinburgh to ingratiate himself with the Covenanters. (He elevated Argyll to a marquess, not that this made any difference.) Montrose had meanwhile, after an alleged plot, spent a spell as a prisoner in Edinburgh Castle, courtesy of Argyll – a big mistake on the latter's part, for it helped to crystallize the opposition to him. It also prompted Antrim to envisage a means of connecting three wars that until then had been almost separate, so supporters of Charles I might unite and defeat his enemies: the king should make his peace with the Catholic Confederacy in Ireland and sound out the Scottish dissidents.

Montrose had watched with dismay the mounting conflict all over the British Isles, the threat to the monarchy in England and the growth of Argyll's power in Scotland. His power reached its peak in 1643, when his government persuaded the Parliament at Westminster to join in the Solemn League and Covenant. Presbyterianism was to be made the religion of England, a provision never fulfilled. In return, another Scottish army marched south, where it would play an important part in crushing the royalists at the Battle of Marston Moor the following year.

At this point Montrose broke with the Covenant. He made his way to Oxford, the king's headquarters, where Antrim had also arrived. Now he could try to put his master-plan into action. In the only part of it to achieve anything he commissioned none other than Alasdair MacColla to lead an army from Ireland to Scotland. About 2000 men, some Scots as well as Irish, sailed in June 1644 from Wexford to Ardnamurchan, the remote peninsula that ends in the westernmost point of the Scottish mainland, formerly belonging to the MacDonalds but now held by Campbells. At first the expected support from restive chiefs in the surrounding area did not materialize – they thought the venture insane. MacColla had to raise clansmen by force for his army as he struck inland. In Atholl he made a rendezvous with Montrose, arrayed in Highland dress, who had received the king's commission to command the army and a marquessate to boot. For over a year they were to rampage more or less at will all over central and eastern Scotland, gathering support as they went, though many clans still kept their distance. These, along with Lowland Scots, seem to have regarded this as in essence an Irish invasion.

At any rate, the Highland charge carried everything before it. At Tippermuir, just outside Perth, Montrose's 3000 men, some armed with nothing better than stones, routed Lord Elcho's 7000 Covenanting troops with 'Jesus and no quarter' inscribed on their banners. It was they who got no quarter: a dozen died in the battle, but 2000 were hacked down in the pursuit. The Highland charge again broke the defenders of Aberdeen, and the city was sacked amid the butchery of civilians.

With the campaigning season advanced, Montrose wanted to winter in the Lowlands, but MacColla argued that this was just the moment for an unsuspected assault on the Campbells' heartland of Argyll. First and last a warrior of Clan Donald, he saw here the chance to reverse the history of a century and restore the land to its rightful owners. The royalist army achieved complete surprise and overran large areas against little resistance. It showed no mercy to the Campbells. Men of military age were killed in cold blood: Niall MacMhuirich, the bard of Clanranald, rejoiced that nearly 900 died without ever a battle being fought. Their houses were burned, and their wives and children left to freeze and starve.

There is a poem attributed, though without certainty, to Florence, sister of the Auchinbreck beheaded at Inverlochy and wife of MacLean of Coll, that gives some picture of these horrors from a Campbell's point of view. Not only has she suffered the loss of all her male relations but now she too has been captured, robbed, humiliated and shackled, with nobody left to defend her:

> Chaidh iad don t-searmoin Di-Dòmhnaich
> 'S dh'fhàg iad san taigh bhàn mi am ònar
> 'S an tubhailte chaol ma m'dhòrnaibh
> 'S mi an ceangal am fuil gu m'bhrògan,
> 'S gum b'e fuil mo bhràithrean òga.

> On Sunday they went to the sermon
> and left me alone in the deserted building,
> my wrists bound with the fine-woven towel,
> down to my shoes in blood, fettered,
> and that was the blood of my young brothers.

While it is a moving lament, even this illustrious lady cannot forbear, as an envoi, to wish she could see her foes roasted like pigs or gutted like chickens, which detracts from the noble fortitude of what has gone before. Unsparing physical detail naturally belongs to the poetry of war and deepens the impression of sacrifice which is heart-breaking yet somehow consoling. It is as well to interject that more often a different convention prevails in Gaelic poetry, of winning through adversity to a certain peace of mind or even joy. This can be true of elegy: *Air a bhròn sin cuir-sa smachd – deònaidh Dia dhuit mac a' rist* ('On that sorrow keep constraint – God will grant you a son again'), wrote Donnchadh MacRaoiridh, bard to the earl of Seaforth, who had just lost his heir. It can assuage the pains of love, as in a poem by Cathal MacMhuirich:

Nar chualais riamh do rò gràidh
ò thùs tochta an domhnàin –
's è dà ràdh riamh mar oideacht –
nach biadh cràdh 'na chomhuideacht?

Heard you not this about excessive love –
recounted ever as a caution –
that as long as the world has existed
love has been accompanied by agony?

This convention can be a comfort amid the misery of war too, as a lady of
Clan MacLean sang amid defeat and despair:

Gu bheil m'inntinn-se fo smalan
Is mo shùilean gu bhith galach
Gus am faic mi ris an latha
'Sam bi dol suas air sìol mo thaighe.

My spirit is sore and dejected
and my eyes will keep on weeping
until once more I see the day when
the people of my house will triumph.

In the brutality of the civil wars this strain of consolation could be too often
overborne by the urge to see enemies degraded and dishonoured. But these
were unforgiving times in an unforgiving country. The Battle of
Inverlochy marked their horrible climax.[7]

Triumph though it was for the royalists, the Battle of Inverlochy also
exposed a certain weakness in the personal position of Montrose. He never
wanted to be drawn into the clansmen's feuds, yet he found himself unable
to curb the bloodlust of MacColla and other chiefs. The impression is hard
to resist that it was they rather than he who called the tune, or at least that,
while content to leave the grand strategy to him, it was they who took
charge of the cut-throat tactics. At any rate, with the Campbells crushed,
Montrose took the field again in the spring of 1645. In May he fought off
and defeated a superior force that sought to surprise him at Auldearn, near
Inverness. In June he destroyed another Covenanting army at Alford in
Aberdeenshire. With success swelling his ranks he hurried south and in
August won again at Kilsyth, not far from Glasgow, his biggest battle of all
in terms of numbers engaged, decided by a Highland charge which
MacColla ordered without waiting for orders from his commander. In each
case the routine massacre of the defeated followed.

The Lowlands now lay prostrate and trembling before Montrose. From
Kilsyth, which commands the central valley between Forth and Clyde, he

could have moved east or west: there was no army left to oppose him. The natural target for him would have been Edinburgh, whence Argyll had fled into England, leaving the Covenanting government in temporary collapse after seven years of holding Scotland in its grip. But, to cap everything, the capital was visited by the plague and had to be avoided. Montrose in fact found himself robbed of a supreme triumph. It would have seen him installed in Edinburgh at the head of a royalist government, which might have changed the outcome of the war. Instead, the flaws in his position came to light.

During the whole era of Highland military superiority in the late seventeenth and early eighteenth centuries, there was yet a constant problem of keeping the armies together. The chiefs, let alone their clansmen, had no discipline and, more to the point, were often uninterested in any role they might be playing in British politics. After a victory they wanted to return to their mountains with their booty, to lounge around consuming it or, as the case may be, to carry on their local feuds. While Montrose sought, after subduing Scotland, to bring succour to the king in England, MacColla preferred to go back and kill more Campbells. So he did, until Argyll raised a fresh force and cornered him in Kintyre. MacColla then escaped to Ireland, where he met his death at the Battle of Knocknanuss in 1647, executed after he surrendered: he would have expected no less.

With diminished strength Montrose meanwhile had indeed set off southwards, only to be surprised in September 1645 at Philiphaugh, near Selkirk, and see his entire army cut to pieces, together with its camp-followers. The Covenanters slaughtered them, women and children too, with all the more godly zeal for having themselves been so often slaughtered. Montrose only just escaped. He fled back to the Highlands, hoping yet to continue resistance. Charles I forestalled this effort, once he had thrown himself the next year on the mercy of the Scottish army in England. One price exacted was that he should order the remaining royalist forces in Scotland to be disbanded. Montrose obeyed and went into exile in the Netherlands. He stayed there until after the king was executed in 1649, then staged the first invasion meant to put Charles II on his father's throne. It was a hurried, hopeless affair. Montrose landed in the north of Scotland and was easily defeated at Carbisdale in Easter Ross in April 1650. He escaped again, only to be betrayed and taken prisoner to Edinburgh. In May he suffered the demeaning fate of being hanged and dismembered like a common criminal.

After hearing his sentence, Montrose consoled himself by writing a poem. It is hard to damn a man who seeks solace from a frantic life and a wicked world in poetic composition. He seems often to have done this, though only fragments of his *oeuvre* survive. This piece he is supposed to have scratched with a diamond on the window of his cell in the Tolbooth, though the story cannot be true. Quite apart from the question of whether he had managed to keep a precious stone about him, the windows of the Tolbooth had no glass. In any event, he does not spare himself thoughts of the grisly morrow, yet reconciles himself to his fate in serenity:

> Let them bestow on every airth a limb;
> Open all my veins, that I may swim
> To Thee, my Saviour, in that crimson lake;
> Then place my parboiled head upon a stake;
> Scatter my ashes, throw them in the air:
> Lord (since Thou know'st where all these atoms are)
> I'm hopeful, once Thou'lt recollect my dust,
> And confident Thou'lt raise me with the just.[8]

With the defeat and death of Montrose the Highlands ceased to be a major theatre in the War of the Three Kingdoms. Of peace there was little enough, but the region's strategic importance vanished. Nobody could or would use it again as a base for the prospective conquest of Scotland, let alone the rest of Great Britain. Rather, the tables were turned.

The execution of Charles I cleared the way for Oliver Cromwell to govern England, yet it lost Cromwell his Scottish allies. Scotland remained unaware of her monarch's doom until too late. He was only condemned on 27 January 1649 and died on 30 January. His fate became known in Edinburgh the following weekend. Nothing could be done on the sabbath, but straight away on the Monday morning the Chancellor, the earl of Loudoun (a Campbell), proclaimed Charles II at the market cross.

Charles I had been a bad ruler, who tried to oppress, who sought to dupe, who made war on the Scots. They steadfastly opposed his excesses, endured his duplicities, scattered his armies. Yet they retained throughout a sort of desperate loyalty to him, as their lawful sovereign, as a Stewart sprung from their own immemorial line of kings and as a born Scot. What they wished was for him to see the error of his ways, to grasp the distinction they drew between the office of monarchy and his personal conduct. They resisted him because they wanted a godly Scotland, and his laws were ungodly. It was not in Scots' eyes legitimate to kill the sovereign. If the English thought otherwise, they might have borne in mind that he was King of Scots too. He could surely not be disposed of without a thought for Scotland. Yet that was what had happened. The English were being their usual arrogant selves.

So a wave of revulsion and outrage greeted news of the execution, together with an upsurge of loyalty to the dead king's son, a boy of eighteen. In this the government of Scotland did not differ from the people, militantly Covenanting government though it remained. Still led by Argyll, it was therefore not only Covenanting but also calculating. When in May 1650 it sent envoys to Charles II at The Hague, they carried, along with their promises of allegiance, demands that he should take the Covenant, in which he did not believe, and repudiate the then captive Montrose, who had been more faithful to him than anyone else. The king agreed, since he saw no choice. He was for ever after to rue it.

Charles II landed in Scotland more or less the pawn of her rulers. To gratify them he sat through eternal sermons by Presbyterian ministers who often took his own sins for their subject. Even Argyll pitied him the ordeal. A coronation was hastily arranged at Scone on 1 January 1651, with the marquess himself setting the crown on the king's head. The ceremony had to be performed at Scone because Cromwell was already in occupation of Edinburgh, after leading his forces across the border and smashing the Scots at the Battle of Dunbar. He now did what none of them had been able to do and united the Highlanders with the Lowlanders in a common national cause. Gaels who had taken up arms for Charles I were admitted to the Covenanting army, and enhanced its fighting qualities. When Cromwell in July sent a force across the Firth of Forth, it was turned back at the Battle of Inverkeithing.

This victory prompted Charles II to march south, in the hope of rallying the English to his cause. Argyll advised him against it but was ignored; he washed his hands of the whole business and withdrew to his castle of Inveraray. The soldiers set off, heartened by the wild music of the Gael. The king of pipers, Patrick Mòr MacCrimmon, was brought before the King of Scots, and on the spot composed a tune still played today, 'Thug mi pòg do làimh an righ' ('I got a kiss of the king's hand'). The royalist army was dogged by Cromwell. It got as far as Worcester, where on 22 August 1651 he destroyed it. The Highland contingents suffered especially heavy losses. Prisoners were transported into white slavery in the American colonies and the West Indies. The story of the king's escape from the battlefield into exile, trusting simple countryfolk, living in Catholic priest-holes, hiding in an oak tree, became the stuff of legend and stood him in good stead when the time for his restoration came.

Scotland now lay at Cromwell's feet. A hasty Union sent Scottish members to Westminster for the first time, most of them English military officers. The clans were ordered to disarm. Several had seen their territories

devastated as vengeful armies marched back and forth across them. With
clansmen killed or fled, townships burned, livestock stolen and crops laid
waste, chieftains found themselves lording it over little, and still with a train
of followers to maintain. Peace came, but it was the peace of a desert, of a
ravaged, exhausted and helpless nation. Iain Lom wrote:

> Mar a bha Cloinn Israel
> Fo bhruid aig rìgh na h-Eiphit,
> Tha sinn air a'chor cheudna:
> Cha èigh iad ruinn ach 'Seoc'.

> Like the Children of Israel
> In bondage to the King of Egypt,
> We have the same standing:
> They call us only 'Jock'.[9]

That anything worthy of the name of culture could survive in such conditions is a wonder. Yet, beside the lamentations of poets, the synod of
Argyll, successors to John Carswell, continued a modest programme of
Gaelic publication under the protection and patronage of the marquess. He
had apparently gone into complete retirement at Inveraray and come to
terms with the English regime, 'my duty to religion, according to my oath
in the Covenant, always reserved'.[10] The synod's activity fulfilled one side
of that duty. Before the political storms ever broke over Scotland, in 1631,
it had published a Gaelic translation of John Calvin's Catechism. In 1649
it started work on a translation of the General Assembly's Shorter
Catechism, which came out in 1653. This was reprinted in 1659, along
with the first fifty of the metrical psalms (albeit set to Lowland tunes out-
landish to the Gael), in the earliest appearance of any section of the Old
Testament in the language of Eden. The Church of Scotland accepted the
need to work with the people in their own tongue, whatever aspersions
had been cast on it in the past. But, like everyone and everything else in
the Highlands of these years, the Kirk struggled to subsist.

Perhaps the best advice to any Gael, or any Scot, was to stay at home
and pray. Nothing else stirred, except once when a half-hearted insurrection was launched by the earl of Glencairn, together with a good number
of chieftains, Cameron of Lochiel, MacDonell of Glengarry and Lord
Lorn, Argyll's heir. The marquess merely looked on: in the endless troubles of the next century Highland families were often to insure themselves
by having different generations pursue a different political line. Cromwell's
lieutenant, General George Monck, put an end to the rising with
admirable restraint. He had no trouble dispersing the rebels in July 1654 as

they tried to cross the Pass of Drumochter, on the watershed between the north and south of Scotland. He issued an amnesty and ordered his soldiers not to massacre the clansmen, only to destroy their stocks of food: it was 'better to pinch their bellies than to shed their blood'.[11] He built military bases at Inverlochy and Inverness to overawe the Gaels. He was the first to show how a firm military hand could pacify even the Highlands.

Charles II came back from his second exile to reclaim the throne of his fathers on 25 May 1660. Waiting for him on the beach at Dover was Monck. At the turn of that year he had taken advantage of the reigning political confusion in England to cross the River Tweed with the parliamentary army entrusted to him for the occupation of Scotland. This at length clinched the restoration of the monarchy. An insubordinate gamble paid off, and now Monck handed three kingdoms back to his monarch.

In those kingdoms wild popular rejoicing went on, perhaps most of all among the Scots, now that the royal line of Stewarts enjoyed its own again. Their emotion was wasted on Charles II. He made straight for London and stayed there. He had vowed never again to set foot in Scotland, to him a land of endless sermons from insolent ministers, after his searing experience of discord and defeat in 1650–1. The Scots, left entirely to their own devices in the months since Monck's departure, had to go south to find out what was to happen to their country. It would regain independence, but so little account of it did the English take that nobody bothered to say so. There was no royal proclamation, no dissolution of the Cromwellian Union, nothing.

Among the crowd of Scots who flocked to attend Charles II in his palace of Whitehall, some were to be selected for royal favour, while others – unknown to themselves – had been marked down for death. Argyll approached the Court with caution. He sent ahead of him his son, the loyal Lorn, with a letter for the king. According to one report, Charles II 'returned an answer that had a show of encouragement in it, but a little too equivocating for a prince'. When the marquess himself arrived in July 1660, he found waiting for him not an audience with his sovereign but a warrant for his arrest. He was thrown into the Tower of London.[12]

Argyll pondered escape. Friends hatched a plot. They sent a sedan chair to his prison, where he was waiting in women's clothes to step into it. But at the last moment he could not: he feared that he might be caught, and that this would confirm his guilt. People sniggered, saying he had always been a coward. They recalled how at Inverlochy he had fled by water while hundreds of his clansmen were butchered. He was sent back to Edinburgh for his trial, which in the event went not too badly for him at first. It proved hard to make the charges stick. His lawyers began to speak of acquittal. Then a spectre from the past struck with a vengeance. Monck dug up some old letters that the marquess had written to him during the occupation, pledging support to Cromwell in fulsome terms. When the prosecution read them out, there was nothing else to be said for MacChailein Mòr. The Scottish Parliament found him guilty and sentenced him to be beheaded.

Coward or no, on the day of his doom, 27 May 1661, he was calm, brave and dignified. In Edinburgh executions took place in public in the early afternoon. The victim had time for a last meal, and Argyll cheerfully lunched off a partridge. On the scaffold he spoke for half an hour, first denying any complicity in the death of Charles I, then urging the people of Scotland to stand by the Covenant, before finally forgiving his foes and submitting to his fate as the will of God. 'The king whose head I crowned', he said, 'now sends me to a crown higher than his own.' After prayer he was strapped to the board of the Maiden, a sort of guillotine, and the blade severed his head. As a spectacle to the populace, this was then placed on the same spike from which Montrose's skull had just been removed.[13]

While awaiting his fate, Argyll wrote a little book by which his son Lorn could remember him. He was no poet like Montrose, but the relative art-lessness of his style is as good a pointer to his mind. On one page he tried to explain what had possessed him in the time of tumult after the execution of Charles I:

> By that confusion my thoughts became distracted and myself encountered so many difficulties in the way, that all remedies that were applied had quite the contrary operation; whatever, therefore, hath been said by me or others in this matter, you must repute and accept them as from a distracted man of a distracted subject in a distracted time wherein I lived.[14]

Montrose and Argyll left us with archetypes of the Highlander, or indeed of the Scot in general. Argyll was cautious, furtive and scheming, yet showed a steely commitment to ends higher than his own, the Covenant above all. Montrose was not really a Highlander but, brave, dash-ing and debonair, he displayed qualities that won the devotion of the Gael and harnessed it to his own baroque form of idealism. When the end came for each of them, they could cast a cold eye on lives lived amid events greater than any mortal could compass, even they as leaders of men, and settle their accounts.

3

Powerless before the Campbells!
Restoration and revolution, 1660–1692

THE SOLDIERS HAD already shot a man dead, a poor fellow who started away from them in terror, by the time they reached Polveig, the house of Alasdair MacIain MacDonald of Glencoe, chief of his clan. It was just after five o'clock in the morning of 13 February 1692. A blizzard shrouded the glen and the mountains brooding round it. Deep snow would not halt for a moment the work of death on which the troops were set, a company of the earl of Argyll's regiment under Lieutenant John Lindsay.

After arriving at MacIain's door, Lindsay woke the servants and said he had come to take leave of their master. He wished to express his thanks for the hospitality he and his men had enjoyed during their fortnight or so of being quartered in Glencoe, supposedly on their way to military operations further north. It was an odd message to deliver before dawn in a snowstorm. It must have come as all the more of a surprise to the chief, a man with manners refined by an education in Paris, because he had invited Lindsay and other officers to dine with him that very evening. If MacIain had stopped to think, he might have recalled a moment three years earlier, while he was fighting for King James VII in Strathspey. Then a man with the second sight had saved him by warning him in time of the approach of Whig dragoons, but pronounced his doom, that he would die in his own house at night.

Instead, MacIain sprang without hesitation to the duties of Highland hospitality. A huge patriarch of a man with flowing white hair and long beard, he got up and began to dress, calling for whisky to warm his guests for their onward march. At once they were in his chamber, armed to the teeth. They fired point-blank into his back as he fumbled with his garments. He lay on his sheets weltering in his own blood. His wife threw herself on him, but the soldiers pulled her off. They stripped her naked and yanked the rings from her fingers, gnawing with their teeth at those which would not shift, yet they did not kill her. Others took hold of her husband's corpse and dragged it outside. Before the house already lay the bodies of his servants.

Captain Robert Campbell of Glenlyon had the previous night played cards with MacIain's sons Iain and Alasdair at another house, where he was lodging. Before setting out in the morning, he had ordered his host's whole family to be bound and gagged in the byre, lest they give anything away. Now they were hauled to the midden outside, shot or bayoneted and left fouled in the dung of their cattle. Campbell was an old enemy of the MacDonalds, ruined by their depredations, but he still did not like this work. Twice he tried to spare victims, a youth and a boy, but his fellow captain, the thuggish Thomas Drummond, had them shot – the boy with a brutal jest that a nit spared would grow into a louse.

Up the glen less trustful clansmen took alarm from all the tramping about in the dark, so the soldiers found it hard to achieve surprise. Sometimes they kept silence and saved bullets by braining their victims with the butts of their muskets. They managed to shoot a few men still asleep. In the military way of things, though, they also missed sitting targets. A platoon under a sergeant went to the farm of Achnacone, where the tenant, his brother and seven others were warming themselves round a big blaze in the open air. The soldiers opened fire and killed five of them, but the wounded got away. The volleys, which the weather could not muffle, alerted everybody else to their peril. MacIain's sons fled their houses in time and met on the hill, though they had been marked down by name for murder. When the able-bodied eluded the troops, these turned on the very young and, contrary to their orders, on the very old.

The bloodbath went on until thirty-eight MacDonalds lay dead, although it is not certain whether the count included women and children. Survivors climbed up slopes that towered 3000 feet above them. They crouched shivering with cold and fear in what shelter they could find. MacIain's widow, after her sons had found and helped her, was one of several women to die of exposure. At daybreak those still alive made their way on as best they could to seek refuge in their sheilings or with kinsmen further off.

This was the Massacre of Glencoe.[1] Of all the infamous happenings in the Highlands it has gone down as the most infamous, even if in the bloody history of the Gaels it ranked as quite a small massacre, with not many dead. After battles of the Civil War and long before, hundreds had been slaughtered, in combat and then in butchery of prisoners as they surrendered or tried to surrender. To clansmen in arms it was routine. The MacDonalds of Glencoe, however, despite their notorious reputation as marauders and thieves, had been at peace on that winter's morning in 1692. Treachery took their lives. It went down in legend as the treachery of their hereditary enemies the Campbells, but it was much more the treachery of their nation's rulers, the servants of William of Orange, King of Scots.

A long train of events had led here. On the Restoration of Charles II in 1660, clansmen were in an unaccustomed position. This king did not see in them just a horde of savages. In the Civil War clans best known for fighting one another had taken up arms for the Stewarts and won glorious victories under the marquess of Montrose. Charles II had come to hate Lowlanders, but he found every reason for gratitude to Highlanders. Not that they were reformed characters: most still followed straightforwardly tribal interests. They had been cowed while Oliver Cromwell's troops were occupying Scotland and standing for no nonsense. Then, it would be recalled, a stray cow could wander unmolested into Lochaber. Despite any such fond memories, from 1660 the Gaels destroyed law and order in the Highlands. English soldiers went home after demolishing their forts. Ministers in Edinburgh trying to remember how Scotland had ruled herself might have been glad of these strongholds. They remained symbols of subjection to England, however, and Highlanders joyous at the king's return, burning their passes to travel and retrieving their claymores from the thatch, were not going to tolerate any more garrisons. The glens again became havens of impunity.

In particular, cattle-raiding flourished. It was an easy, parasitical way of life, but it also had a historical function, which now changed and expanded. The first Gaelic literature, the Ulster Cycle, celebrated cattle-raiding, which was celebrated yet in song and prose as worthy of a Highland warrior. It seemed not so sensible, however, once cattle became the main, if not sole, motor of economic growth in the Highlands, through a new trade to the Lowlands and even England. It gave those able to exploit it at last a chance to rise above the miserable subsistence yielded by their glens. They won scant praise. The first MacDonald to take up droving on Skye in the late sixteenth century had been Donald MacIain of Castle Camus, the clan's fiercest warrior, famous for his great sword Cuig Mharg. His kin despised his commercial venture: Donald's own son-in-law derided his wife as *Nighean àireach liath nam bò* ('daughter of the grey-haired herdsman').

A century on, and gentlemen of the clan were directing the movements of vast droves which swam, nose tied to tail, from island to mainland. The raiding followed them, though without fatal hindrance to such a burgeoning trade. Already important on the fringe of the Highlands before the Civil War, it later spread northwards. The signs of it were the huge trysts or cattle markets, which for the convenience of customers spread southwards, from Muir of Ord to Brechin to Crieff and finally, in the eighteenth century, to Falkirk. They were useful also for introducing money into the Highland economy for the first time on any scale. The profits became vital for purchases of grain and meal in a region barely able to feed itself. Once cash arrived, it might be used in other exchanges among Gaels, such as dowries or rents. It also encouraged gentlemen of the clans to take out written leases on fixed terms. (Such leases were known in Scotland as 'tacks', and those holding them as 'tacksmen'.) Money follows money, and to chiefs who had some, or could lay claim to some, Lowlanders might extend credit. So it was possible to enjoy from cattle a stream of income, something rare and precious to a chief. It could help him to realize opportunities opening up in the Scottish state. He might enjoy himself in Edinburgh, or even in London, and follow more familiar, if sometimes treasonable, paths to Europe. Angus MacDonell of Glengarry found it handy to acquire a second home in the Lowlands. All the chiefs coveted elegant clothes and other seductive luxuries which even noblemen there could hardly afford. It was, in other words, rather too easy to spend the new income and more.

The net effect on most chiefs was to increase their debt, which had mounted in wartime. Further deficits followed from taxes, whether imposed with relative justice and efficiency by Cromwell or with neither by Charles II. The one way to raise large sums of money at a stroke was for a chief to feu out part of his estate and create further vassals' holdings on it. The sharp-set earl of Argyll and Sir John Campbell of Glenorchy did this in order to finance yet more purchases of land. Yet they had to exert themselves to maintain political control over the ensemble of their estates, and for clans smaller or weaker than the Campbells the necessary effort proved a deterrent to imitation. Elsewhere meagre farming returns were still paid in kind. Other commercial possibilities could not be realized because of the overriding need to keep fighting forces on the land. The logic of this was for an estate to house as many clansmen as might be carried just above subsistence. For them it remained each year a struggle to scrape together a surplus against starvation, in a relentless cycle ending with hunger in the last of winter, when some slight misfortune might bring death. A chief could not, within reason and justice, squeeze much more out of his people, whose hard lives already contrasted with his own relative comfort, as his bard might remind him.

So most chiefs lived with their debts, as they could usually manage to do unless they ventured to the southern fleshpots, where they might be pursued by creditors. The privy council, which liked to see them once a

35

year, had to issue them with passes against arrest. This only prompted them
to live it up with all the more gusto in Edinburgh. Seldom did a shrewder
chief such as Iain Breac MacLeod of Dunvegan manage to improve his
finances while missing none of the fun. He cut a figure in the capital as
well as making his castle on Skye a mecca of Gaelic culture with music,
poetry and hospitality. He patronized, among others, the Blind Harper,
Ruaidhri MacMhuirich, whom he brought over from Lewis and settled on
a nearby farm. By good husbandry Iain Breac yet paid off most of his debts.
He need not have bothered: in a few years of Lowland prodigality his son
doubled them again. After the father's death in 1693, the Blind Harper
addressed the echo that was all he found left in the great hall of Dunvegan:

> *A Mhic-alla 'n seo bhà*
> *Anns a bhaile 'n robh gràdh nan cliar,*
> *An triath tighearnail teann,*
> *Is an cridhe gun fheall na chliabh –*
> *Ghabh a tlachd dh'a thir fèin,*
> *'S cha do chleachd e Dùn-èideann riamh.*

> O Echo that was in the hall
> Where dwelt the love of poet-bands,
> The solemn stately chief
> With the guileless heart in his breast –
> In his own land he took delight,
> With Edinburgh he bothered not at all.[2]

Yet even at his most prosperous Iain Breac's land belonged in law, under
an apprising, to creditors who creamed off from it an annual rent or interest. Since safe investments were hard to find in Scotland, the device satisfied
all concerned. Such expedients at least gave the chiefs a modicum of interest in the rule of law, or rather in robust rights of property. They could
wield an interdict, not just a claymore, and do more damage with it. The
culture of violence was modified by a culture of litigation, yet no more in
the Scotland of the Restoration than in the United States today did this
guarantee justice. It also tended to obscure the fact that most Highland
estates just could not bear the rising social and legal outlays of their chiefs.
The debts that built up in this period weighed on many like a curse pronounced by some Highland hag, and were passed from generation to generation until the family finally went bankrupt or resorted to clearing the
clansmen off its land.

Chiefs pursuing their causes in court were not inhibited from conniv-
ing outside at daylight robbery. The privy council could do little about this

amid the general Highland mayhem. If it wanted to punish crime, it had to rely on granting ham-fisted commissions of fire and sword from the Crown for one clan or sept to wreak retribution on another. Justice was then no longer blind: in effect, self-interested private parties could decide between war and peace in the Highlands. From such situations the Campbells especially had often profited. Archibald, ninth earl of Argyll and son of the marquess martyred in 1661 (the higher rank was then forfeit), now tested the system to the limit. Much of the southern and western Highlands and Islands formed a regality, with him as its hereditary justiciar. He could use his own courts for protection from his own creditors, which left him, saddled with huge debts as he was himself, free to pursue his debtors. In consequence he gained, regained or had confirmed his feudal superiority over Glenelg, Knoydart and Moidart. Against the MacLeans of Duart he waged war, and seized their lands on Mull in 1674. Mairghread nighean Lachlainn, a *bean tuiream*, or professional mourner, wrote:

> *Ach cò e an neach a tha gun mhùtha,*
> *Mar an nialaibh air an aonach?*
> *Cinne làidir nan lann rùisgte*
> *Bhith mar tha iad roigh na Duibhnich!*

> Who is the person time does not alter,
> Like the shadows of the clouds in the mountain?
> The strong tribe of swords unsheathed
> Standing powerless before the Campbells![3]

Sure enough, as an observer noted of Argyll, 'his ambitious grasping at the mastery of the Hylands and Western Ilands of Mull, Ila etc., stirred up the Earl of Seaforth, Marquis of Atholl, Lord MacDonald, Glengarry, McLoud and other clans into a combination for bearing him down.'[4] And bear him down this formidable crew did. In 1681, on a frivolous charge, they set about the prosecution that would drive him to exile, rebellion and death. Like his father, he was executed by the Maiden in Edinburgh, on 30 June 1685. If law and due process could do this to MacChailein Mòr, who was safe?

Luckily, most chiefs just had cattle-raiding to deal with. This was now usually the work of broken men, called in this guise *caithernaich*, anglicized as 'caterans'. The droves moving south every autumn offered a new target to the lawless and a chance for them to penetrate the Lowlands disguised as drovers. Raids occurred even in an area such as Menteith, almost within sight of the tryst. But then, according to Glenorchy, there were three clans that, beside sheltering caterans, themselves raided cattle. The MacDonalds of Keppoch did this, and with dire consequences. After the Restoration their chief Alasdair and his brother returned from school in Rome. Their uncle Alasdair Buidhe had acted as Tutor of Keppoch, that is, guardian of the clan's interests, which gave him control of it. He wanted to keep it. Young Keppoch rashly made enemies of the MacDonalds of Inverlair, a defiant sept given to cattle-raiding, which he sought to curb. With these the sons of Alasdair Buidhe banded together and gorily slew chief and brother in their own house. Their bard, Iain Lom, denounced the crime and appealed for justice to Glengarry, self-styled head of Clan Donald. He did nothing. Nor could other MacDonalds care less: a chief who hindered raids was no use to them. Indeed they chose Alasdair Buidhe as their new chief. Iain Lom was the one who had to make himself scarce. From a safe distance he sought aid from Sir James MacDonald of Sleat, former foster-father to the two dead boys. Sleat at length got a commission of fire and sword and sent in a gang to kill six clansmen of Inverlair. The avengers waved the severed heads in Glengarry's face, as a reproach to his indifference, but the wicked uncle remained chief, and his son Archibald, though implicated in the murders, smoothly succeeded him; on moving into Keppoch House, they furnished it with hiding places. Such were the troubles a cattle-raiding clan could bring on itself. But this did not deter the second such clan named by Glenorchy, the Camerons of Lochiel. Nor did it deter the third, the MacDonalds of Glencoe.[5]

Into these conditions the government of Charles II could bring only rough justice. He treated MacLeans and MacLeods with disdain, MacDonalds and MacGregors with favour, if not as much of it as they hoped. Up to the revolution of 1688 the nation's rulers would now and again toy with blueprints for imposing law and order on the Highlands, starting with re-establishment of a garrison in the ruined castle of Inverlochy. But the royalist government could not even get as far as the republican government before it (which did garrison Inverlochy). The test was whether the chiefs would put up with new restraints, and those they did tolerate proved no more effective now than ever before. Still, one way or another the restored royalist regime could count on a fresh factor in Scottish politics, the loyal clans, those which had once tried to reconquer the Lowlands for Charles I and, more to the point, would police them now for Charles II. In contrast to some other Scots, Highlanders seemed almost innocuous; disorderly, to be sure, but with each man of them knowing his place in the hierarchy of his clan. Chiefs of loyal clans were thus welcome in Edinburgh and eagerly accepted its hospitality.

A chance existed for Gaelic culture to fare better out of these chiefs' assimilation into the national élite than it had done earlier, when they were still too alien, or would do later, when they became too anglicized. Of course, they could not afford to lose touch with the source of their power, the fighting men, who in the majority spoke Gaelic. Some chiefs still had the language of Eden as their mother tongue – notably the third earl of Seaforth, Coinneach Mòr (said also to possess the second sight), who succeeded his exiled father as chief of the Mackenzies while studying at Aberdeen, but despite a Lowland education preferred to tarry in his lands on Lewis. The usurping chiefly line of Keppoch carried Gaelic poetry in its genes in the form of smug young Archibald MacDonald, a eulogist of the bagpipes, then in his daughter Sileas, who wrote Jacobite elegies. Still, most chiefs now spoke Scots as their first language and, like Lowlanders, referred to Gaelic as Irish. Even so, they took care to have it taught to sons who might need it in a crisis to appeal to their clansmen's loyalty, or indeed to lead them in battle.

In contrast to its politics of absolutism, the culture of the Restoration showed a free spirit presaging the Enlightenment. It embraced both Anglo-Scots such as Sir Robert Moray, the king's friend and first president of the Royal Society, and home-based Scots such as Sir Robert Sibbald, leader of intellectual life in Edinburgh, familiar of antiquarians and natural philosophers at home and abroad. He found Gaelic civilization absorbing, not pitiful. He was indirectly responsible for a survey of the Hebrides, through his patronage of Martin Martin, author of *A Description of the Western Isles of Scotland;* Martin was himself a Gael, tutor to MacLeod of Harris.

The culture of the Restoration embraced other Highland gentlemen and scholars. None would have been finer than the polymath Sir Thomas Urquhart of Cromarty, had he not died laughing at news of the Restoration. One who long survived it was Sir George Mackenzie of Rosehaugh, kinsman of Seaforth and Gael as well. He adhered to the Episcopalian nationalism that emerged after the Restoration, which was anti-English but not populist in a Scottish sense; rather the reverse. He made his name as advocate for the marquess of Argyll at his trial in 1661: since MacChailein Mòr was going to die anyway, this did not hold back Mackenzie's rise in law or letters. He was a fecund writer on everything from legal codes to history to moral philosophy to pastoral romance. He had a hot temper but not a harsh temperament: he favoured religious toleration and in his profession demanded better proof than was usual for charges of witchcraft. Modern Scots have reason to be grateful to him too, as founder of the Advocates' Library, now the National Library of Scotland. Yet this cultivated man lived in an age that saw in him above all the Lord Advocate that persecuted the Covenanters, Bluidy Mackenzie.

The only Scots so far eager to expand the scope of Gaelic by translating religious texts into it had been Highland Presbyterians, notably the synod of Argyll with the fifty metrical psalms published in 1659. This literature received Episcopalian additions. In 1684 the minister of Balquhidder in Perthshire, Robert Kirk, brought out a complete Gaelic psalter. He took over the first batch of psalms from the synod but translated the remaining 100 by himself: a stupendous labour, continuing the work of four men who had burned the midnight oil for six years. Balquhidder lay on the lands of Campbell of Glenorchy, another Episcopalian, ennobled in 1681 as earl of Breadalbane. Known to Gaels as Iain Glas ('Grey John'), he was a pious man despite his penchant for political plots. He appointed to his household a chaplain, James Kirkwood, who on his arrival from East Lothian felt shocked at the spiritual destitution of Highlanders. One remedy would be for them to read the Bible in their own language. An Irish Bible appeared in 1685, which put between two covers a translation of the New Testament by Nathaniel Donellan and a translation of the Old Testament by William Bedell, bishop of Kilmore, publication of the whole being financed by Robert Boyle, aristocrat of County Cork, a member of the Royal Society and the father of modern experimental chemistry. He had an extraordinary devotion to scripture and studied it intensely, beside spending his own money on translations of it into a range of languages, from Welsh to Turkish to Malay.

In 1687 Kirkwood got in touch with Boyle and suggested that any left-over copies of Bedell's Bible, as it was generally known, might be distributed in the Highlands. The next year 200 of them arrived in Edinburgh. The problems only started there. The language of this Bible was little different from the prestigious Classical Common Gaelic used by John Carswell and the synod of Argyll, but on the page it looked funny. The book was printed in type derived from the old Gaelic script, a medium of writing for centuries in both Scotland and Ireland. It had six letters and various spelling conventions that differed from those of the Gaelic printing in Roman type used in Scotland. It put readers off. Robert Kirk heroically agreed to revise and transcribe the whole lot into Roman type. The result, the first complete Gaelic Bible ever printed, appeared on 1 April 1690 – just in time for the Episcopalian Church to be disestablished in Scotland, after the revolution that brought William of Orange to the throne.[6]

A revolutionary period is not the best in which to bring out bibles. Nor did Highland conditions afterwards favour their distribution. Yet the logistics were probably not the real obstacle. The Church of Scotland now took on the Presbyterian constitution that it retains down to the present day. The new establishment wanted to train and deploy Gaelic-speaking ministers, but on its own terms. Episcopalians remained suspect, along with anything done by them. It was ruled that Bedell's Bible could not be sent on to the Highlands until the General Assembly had given its approval. Even by 1699, when Kirkwood made his last effort to shift the stock, only 100 volumes had left the capital for northern parishes. Presbyterians took the view that if Gaelic texts bore an Episcopalian taint, then spiritually bereft Highlanders would have to do without them. The presence of dogs in the Church of Scotland's manger is betrayed also by the way poor Robert Kirk's translation of the psalms was spurned in favour of a version commissioned by the General Assembly in 1694. None of this did much for the shifting and tangled, but above all beggarly, state of religion in the Highlands. In particular, the region lacked enough ordained clergy of whatever persuasion, without whom Gaelic texts could not be read even if they existed.

The strength of that Presbyterian reaction can in turn be traced back to 1660 and the return of an Episcopalian regime to the Church of Scotland. Matters did not stop there. Charles II at length committed himself to continuous confrontation with the Covenanters, no longer a national movement but reduced to a sect concentrated in the south-west. One of them, Richard Cameron, led a band that in 1680 drew up the Declaration of Sanquhar, affixed to the market cross of the town, telling Charles he was no longer a lawful king. Cameron soon met his death, but his followers, the Cameronians, remained stubborn enemies of the state. By challenging the monarchical society of the Restoration they provoked a persecution as extreme as themselves. For the dirty work of hunting them down, in what became grimly known as the Killing Time, loyal clans were ideal.

The worst phase of persecution opened after the so-called Highland Host was quartered on the western counties in 1678. It came under the command of John Graham of Claverhouse. A man striking for his almost feminine beauty, he yet had a heart of flint, indifferent to others' sufferings. A pact with the devil was suspected by contemporaries; today's reader of his letters will be struck rather by his dog-like eagerness to obey orders from on high, his amazement at the obvious and his focus on the trivial. Like his late kinsman Montrose, he could not count as a Highlander since his home overlooked Dundee, but he knew how to handle fighting Gaels in the sort of shambles they enjoyed, and this won him the nickname of Bluidy Clavers. Bluidy Clavers pursued the Covenanters to the hills and glens, just as Bluidy Mackenzie pursued them to the courtroom and gallows. Lowlanders had for the first time to accept Highlanders as participants in the affairs of the Scottish state, and in a most uncongenial fashion.

The Highland Host looked all the nastier to Lowlanders as many of its soldiers were papists. Catholics had shrunk to a remnant in Scotland, but concentrated north of the Highland line. The MacDonalds were the one clan whose religion dated back to before the Reformation. The leader of their offshoot in Ulster, the earl of Antrim, did what he could to promote the Counter-Reformation by setting up a friary on his lands, from which Franciscan missionaries infiltrated Scotland. This patronage was inseparable from his ambition to regain lands MacDonalds had lost to Campbells, though Alasdair MacColla's preference for genocide as a means to the same end was hardly an advertisement for it.

After the Restoration, when their religion still attracted unkindly political attention, some MacDonalds found it expedient to leave off an unequal struggle with persecution. A chief did not need to renounce his faith and imperil his immortal soul. He could hand the risk over to his son by giving him a good Scottish education and letting him succeed as a Protestant. Alasdair Buidhe of Keppoch did this for his heir, Archibald: both being under suspicion of the previous chief's murder, it can have made little difference to their posthumous destination. But a greater chieftain, Glengarry, did the same. Otherwise heirs might have to go to Europe for schooling, as the unlucky brothers of Keppoch did to Rome and as MacDonald of Glencoe did to Paris. This underlined how Scottish Catholicism could make up for the blood it was losing only by transfusions from abroad. These proved just enough to prick Presbyterian complacency. The Catholic mission to Scotland was quite aggressive, considering the paucity of its resources. Gaelic-speaking priests had usually to come from Ireland, and they seldom endured Highland hardships for long. Even so, they could boast of some successes, among the Chisholms of Strathglass or the Farquharsons around Braemar. The 'increase of popery' remained an obsession of the Church of Scotland through the seventeenth century and into the eighteenth.

It also, of course, justified the overthrow of the Catholic James VII and II by William of Orange in 1688. William's wife and James's daughter, Mary, ascended the throne with her husband, so the succession of Stewarts was maintained in some sort. But that all happened in England, where the events became known as the Glorious, or even Bloodless, Revolution. For Scotland the epithet is risible. War followed, with the Massacre of Glencoe as a closure to it.

One immediate result of the Revolution was the emergence of the

Jacobite movement. It remained loyal to King James until his death in exile in 1701, then to the son born to him just before his deposition, also James, the Old Pretender, and then to his son Prince Charles Edward Stewart, or Bonnie Prince Charlie, the Young Pretender, who died in 1788. A hundred years after the legitimate line of Stewarts had lost the crown, men in remote parts of Scotland still refused to take an oath of allegiance to George III, as they had to do, for example, if they wanted to cast their votes at a parliamentary election. A trifling remnant even transferred their allegiance onwards to Charles's brother, the so-called Henry IX, a camp Roman cardinal with whom Jacobitism was laid to rest in the vaults of the Vatican in 1809. For the century and more that the movement lasted, its main strength, above all its military strength, lay in the Highlands.

At first its support was not so confined. In Scotland the moment of Jacobite emergence can well be dated to 18 March 1689. A Convention of the Estates (something short of a full Parliament) was meeting to settle the affairs of the nation, guarded by a thousand Covenanters. But royalists attended too, for they still hoped to sway the outcome. All listened to letters from the two claimants to the throne. King William wrote a message friendly but vague on matters of substance, except the security of the Protestant religion. King James sent a crass diatribe, an essay in outraged absolutism threatening anyone who refused him immediate submission. It threw away any chance he had of restoring himself by winning the convention over.[7]

But up in Edinburgh Castle the duke of Gordon still held out for James. Also hanging round the capital, guarded by fifty dragoons, was Claverhouse, now Viscount Dundee. On that 18 March he approached the castle from a secluded spot on the northern side away from the city; a plaque now marks it. He climbed to a postern-gate, where he consulted with Gordon. What passed between them is unknown, except they agreed James had bungled. Gordon is supposed to have asked Claverhouse where he was going. 'Wherever the spirit of Montrose shall lead me', came the reply. This meant first going home. There Claverhouse kept his counsel for some weeks, but the convention declared him a rebel.[8]

Thus did Jacobitism emerge. Everyone in Scotland judged, rightly, that Claverhouse left Edinburgh to organize resistance to the Revolution and bring back King James. His prospects were not hopeless. Some clans, MacDonalds and Camerons, would fight for the Stewarts in any event. Even the self-serving Campbells seemed this time divided: Breadalbane, head of their main cadet branch, sought to keep in touch with the elusive Claverhouse. Gordon, if forced to surrender Edinburgh Castle in June, remained the greatest magnate of the north-east. In his anti-Presbyterian region the religious settlement of 1690 made Jacobites of many among its aristocracy, gentry and clergy. In the Lowlands, too, there were Jacobite lairds. Nevertheless, Jacobitism put down its deepest roots in the Highlands. Here was a society founded on nobility. A revolution that deposed a dynasty two thousand years old, according to contemporary myth, struck at the heart of nobility.

Claverhouse set out for the north, then. He worked hard to redress his weaknesses, not without success. During the summer of 1689 he raised more than 2000 men – quite enough, given the modest scale of Scottish warfare, to launch a rising. He received also a small reinforcement from Ireland, where King James seemed to be restoring his authority. Claverhouse, having ranged round the north-east and down the Great Glen, was by the end of July moving south. He crossed into upper Strathspey towards the Pass of Killiecrankie, which would lead him into the Lowlands. Marching in the opposite direction came a force loyal to King William, under General Hugh Mackay of Scourie. Mackay was a Gael from a far northern clan – its lands included Cape Wrath – the only one to have switched sides during the Revolution. He brought about the change of heart himself, when he returned home after a long mercenary's career in Europe.

Mackay did not know or did not believe that royalist forces had mustered so fast. So when, on 27 July, he was advancing through the pass, he remained unaware of their approach from the other side. Claverhouse could and did read the situation. Leading his troops at a run in the heat of summer, he mounted a hill above the pass. An astonished Mackay turned his regiments to face them, suddenly aware of his great peril. For a couple of hours the two sides skirmished, each meanwhile trying to extend its lines and outflank the enemy. Claverhouse suddenly resolved matters at seven o'clock in the evening, when the sun was no longer in his men's faces. He ordered a Highland charge down the braes of Killiecrankie. It smashed Mackay's thin, stretched lines. Mackay's troops fled back along the pass, and were cut down as they ran. In this moment of supreme triumph Claverhouse, rising in the stirrups to rally his irresolute cavalry, was shot under the left arm and fell dying. During the night, before he was to be laid in an unmarked grave at Blair Atholl, some Camerons from his own army stripped and robbed his body.

The first Jacobite rising had won a great victory, but its leader was no more. The scale of the loss could be gauged a few days later, when the clansmen tried to debouch into the Lowlands. At Dunkeld, guarding the southern end of the pass, they were stopped dead by the Cameronians, a regiment raised from extreme Covenanters to defend the Revolution. These, outnumbered three to one in fighting round the cathedral, would not yield even when their commander, Colonel William Cleland, lost his life.[9]

Over the rest of the country the conflict descended into guerrilla warfare. Jacobites raided where they could marshal enough strength, while the government's garrisons struggled to contain them. In May 1690 King William's forces did, however, disperse a larger Jacobite force at Cromdale, on the River Spey. In July, after he had beaten King James at the Battle of the Boyne in Ireland, William decided the time had come to pacify Scotland too, so he could move troops from there to Flanders and carry on the one struggle that counted for him, against the French in Europe. He needed somebody to show him how to wind down this messy little Highland war. He found that man in Breadalbane, who, like many Scots, had been hedging his bets and waiting to see what course the post-revolutionary nation would run. He lurked in his houses near where Claverhouse and Mackay were to encounter each other, without supporting either. He could not be provoked even when MacDonalds of Glencoe, along with other Jacobite clans drifting back from the Battle of Dunkeld, burned his castle of Achallader, on the southern edge of Rannoch Moor. In his own good time Breadalbane made contact both with King William and with the rebels still in arms about the Highlands. He had a plan for peace to break the military stalemate and at the same time benefit himself, perhaps with the reward of a lucrative office.

In June 1691 Breadalbane summoned the rebellious chiefs to a conference by the ruins of Achallader. Quaking, MacDonald of Glencoe came along too but soon left, saying he feared nothing so much as a Campbell's mischief. To the rest Breadalbane laid it on the line that, unless a settlement was reached here, William would harry the Highlands in person. There was an offer: £12,000 from the government, to be divided among the chiefs in return for a truce. They quibbled, in jealousy, and greed. Breadalbane played along, refined his terms, sought to save their faces for the semi-surrender he wanted of them: he conceded, for example, that they might ask King James's permission to give up fighting for him. Within a week Breadalbane had a deal.[10]

Members of the Scottish government, in the dark about the conference at Achallader, showed themselves, when it came to light, if anything less reliable than the chiefs. Some suspected the truth about Breadalbane: that he was a covert Jacobite. To them his work had to be read in terms of the good it did his cause. That seemed obvious: it took pressure off disloyal chiefs and let them regroup for continued insurrection. Perhaps, then, it was better to undermine the truce. Several great men sought to do so. One was the tenth earl of Argyll, jealous of a cadet's achievement. The duke of Hamilton, leader of the Lowland Whigs, feared for his own influence if a Highland compromise worked. The Secretary of State, Sir John Dalrymple, Master of Stair, saw Breadalbane's bargain as proof of his Jacobitism. Dalrymple had the experience to judge of this, for he himself had served James VII as Lord Advocate before ditching him to play a role in the convention that offered William and Mary the crown; Dalrymple was then rewarded with his old job back, before becoming Secretary of State in 1691.

But it was on William, campaigning in Flanders, that everything depended. Breadalbane went to see him and pleased him with an account, touched up for the occasion, of what had passed at Achallader. The king decided the best way forward was to set a deadline of 1 January 1692 for the clans to swear an oath of allegiance to himself. This reckoned without his own ministers' wish to sabotage the deal, and without the craziness of King James, who ordered the chiefs to carry on fighting when, as agreed with Breadalbane, they asked him if they could stop. As the winter of 1691 approached, peace in the Highlands seemed no nearer and tempers frayed on every hand.

In fact, the chiefs were weighing matters up. Gestures of intransigence came yet from a few, especially Glengarry, who thought to throw a spanner in the works by denouncing Breadalbane as a traitor to King William. The rest, when they looked at what was by any standards a reasonable offer, and at the harsh realities of the Highlands in which they lived, decided the government meant what it said. As the deadline approached, they all at once fell into line. One of the last to do so, MacDonald of Glencoe, arrived not until 31 December 1691, at Inverlochy, now rebuilt as Fort William. He presented himself to the governor, General John Hill, only to find he had come to the wrong place. The oath had to be administered by a civil, not a military, officer: in this case by the sheriff-depute of Argyll, Sir Colin Campbell of Ardkinglas, 50 miles away at Inveraray. In fear and trembling MacDonald set off through the snowdrifts and got there on 3 January. But Ardkinglas had gone home after the deadline, and a storm hindered his return for three more days. Even then, MacDonald was reduced to pleading in tears before his oath was accepted. When Ardkinglas went to Edinburgh with the certificate of all the oaths from Argyll, he was obliged by the clerks of the council to erase the name of MacDonald of Glencoe, as one who had sworn too late.

Dalrymple was behind this. He had already drawn up orders against the chiefs holding out: 'I hope the soldiers will not trouble the Government with prisoners.'[11] But it was fantasy to think of a punitive campaign in a Highland winter. In fact, talks with the refractory continued behind the scenes well after the deadline. It occurred to Dalrymple that he could show he meant business by picking on Glencoe: 'if MacIain of Glencoe, and that tribe, can be well separated from the rest, it will be a proper vindication of the public justice to extirpate that den of thieves.'[12] By 23 January the message got through to Sir Thomas Livingston, commander-in-chief in Scotland. Taking his cue from a political superior, he wrote to an officer at Fort William:

> I understand that the Laird of Glencoe, coming after the prefixed time, was not admitted to take the oath, which is very good news here, being that at Court it's wished he had not taken it . . . So Sir, here is a fair occasion for you to show that your garrison serves for some use . . . Begin with Glencoe, and spare nothing which belongs to him, but do not trouble the Government with prisoners.[13]

This was, in effect, the formal order for the massacre.

After 13 February the next reference to the MacDonalds of Glencoe mentions their hanging about the country as submissive refugees, begging a little meal to keep from starvation. They were pitied by those that had last dealt with them, General Hill and Campbell of Ardkinglas, who offered security for their good conduct and appealed to Edinburgh for them to be received into mercy and resettled. This happened in August. Two years later MacIain's sons and others gave evidence to the official inquiry, which produced a standard official whitewash of the affair.[14]

4

'I am no stranger to misfortune'

The Jacobite rising of 1715

IT IS IMPOSSIBLE to say quite what happened at the Battle of Sheriffmuir on 13 November 1715. The fighting took place over a dreary stretch of moorland in southern Perthshire, near Dunblane, up against the Highland line. Confusion and clumsiness marked the conduct of the commanders. On one side was the 37-year-old John Campbell, second duke of Argyll, who from Stirling deployed 3000 Scots and English troops to fight for George I, King of Great Britain and Elector of Hanover. On the other side was the forty-year-old John Erskine, earl of Mar, coming from Perth with more than 4000 Highland and Lowland Jacobites in the cause of the Old Pretender, James VIII and III.

No coherent account of the clash survives from any of such men on the ground as might have been capable of writing up their experience. A few historians have constructed narratives that seem deceptively logical. Without doubt it was a messy day of military muddle and meaningless manoeuvre. One thing known for certain is how it ended, as early night-fall obscured the terrain. Most Hanoverian units had taken to their heels at the first Jacobite attack, but 1000 men stayed with Argyll to make what he must have feared would be a last stand. MacChailein Mòr was a competent and courageous general who had distinguished himself in European wars. He possessed both the staunchness of a noble family that for a century and a half had stood up for Protestant Scotland and the valour of a chieftain of the Gaels, who gave him the heroic epithet Red John of the Battles. At Sheriffmuir he had an off-day, though the engagement hardly tested him.

In the dwindling light Argyll ordered his soldiers to dig up fails of turf and build crude breastworks. Behind these they awaited Mar's final onslaught out of the dusk. If they had to die, it would be with honour. Hours of bewildering battle had left the Jacobites in some disorder too, though Mar probably retained effective command of the bulk of his force. Yet he never came. He just withdrew, and nobody knew quite why. The first armed attempt to break the Union of 1707, sustained largely though not entirely out of Highland hostility to it, faded away into the oncoming night of the north.

These goings-on arose from politics as murky as the winter's eve over Sheriffmuir, and the two commanders typified it. That Argyll appeared here as defender of the Union was no wonder. He had been born on the leafy banks of the River Thames in Surrey, where the Anglo-Scottish gentry of the Restoration clustered, and schooled at Eton. Even so, he remained a great lord of the Gàidhealtachd. Many Gaels hated the Union, but his house had since the Reformation stood at the head of those Highland interests which helped to unify the nation, on their own terms, and find a way forward from the trammels of its past. On the strength of that, they could fairly be called patriots. Their work meant accommodation with the Lowlands in politics, religion and culture, and it was the Presbyterian Lowlands that gave the Union its strongest support. Argyll's personal standing relied not least on the fact that his family had offered martyrs for Presbyterianism. The Union was intended to secure the Protestant succession to the throne of a new United Kingdom. This came with George I, on the death of Queen Anne in 1714. It had now sparked off a fresh Jacobite rebellion intent on passing the Crown back to Anne's half-brother James. This was what took Argyll to Sheriffmuir. Before he set out, an aunt had reproached him for opposing the legitimate line of Stewarts. He replied: 'That family, Madam, owes me and my family two heads, whereof your father was one; and it becomes you ill to propose this question.'[1]

Mar the Jacobite was by contrast a Lowlander – or rather, he belonged both to the Lowlands proper and to the debatable land around the Highland fringe that gave several leaders to movements of the clans. The estate from which he took his title lay by the head of the River Dee beneath the Grampian Mountains at the far western end of Aberdeenshire, a Gaelic-speaking district, poor and unprofitable. It was from other lands in Clackmannanshire, just north of the Firth of Forth, that he derived the income befitting a peer. Here he was a progressive and enterprising landlord. He took a special interest in industrial development, whether of his seams of coal, which he tried to exploit with elaborate water-powered machines, or of manufacture of glass, which he was to direct from his later exile.

More remarkable was that Mar had been in 1707 a champion of the Union, after playing a large part in its preliminaries. As Secretary of State for Scotland from 1705 he probably produced the first drafts of the treaty between Scotland and England. As a commissioner for negotiating its terms he arranged bribes for nationalist noblemen to abandon their opposition to it. While he remained afterwards a confidant of Queen Anne, that did not stop the Union getting off to a terrible start through English arrogance and bad faith, though with much help from Scottish squabbling. This fatal combination brought about the abolition of the Scottish privy council in 1709. It had been expected to remain in being and provide a sort of devolved administration. For its undoing there was nothing to be said. Less direct government stored up huge problems, not least through a loosening of control over the Highlands. In the previous century the council had done what it could to maintain that control, which was often not much. At least it could do more than the English privy council. Without it, nothing was done at all. In their other, mainly economic, interests Scots found themselves neglected, if not insulted. Among their representatives at Westminster a rapid process of alienation set in, until they moved for repeal of the Union in 1713.

Mar's woes matched the nation's. When in 1709 a new job of Secretary of State 'for Great Britain' – in effect for Scotland – was created, he did not get it. It went to the duke of Queensberry, and after he died in 1711 it was just left vacant. Mar won it when it was filled again in 1713, after a general election, but his comeback lasted less than a year. Queen Anne died, and Whigs pushed through the Hanoverian succession. When Mar sought an audience with George I, the king turned his back on him, having been told that he harboured Jacobite sympathies. Since Mar could expect nothing of the new regime, he had to recur to an older one. He sailed in disguise from London, landed in Fife, rode for the north and on 3 September 1715, at Braemar in his own Aberdeenshire, raised the Pretender's standard.

So it was not as one of a persecuted minority that Mar assumed leadership of this rising, but rather as a fully paid-up member of the Scottish establishment. That he of all people turned against the Hanoverian succession was a measure of how far Scots had been disillusioned since 1707. Among the Jacobite rebellions the sole one that ought to have succeeded was the '15. The Hanoverians had had little chance to dig in. The government in London was caught off guard because no foreign power fomented revolt, so that warning signs in diplomatic disputes or military preparations were lacking. Jacobitism arose this time as a popular movement, prompted not only by Scottish dismay but also by a good deal of English restiveness at, among other matters, the change of dynasty to a German one.

Mar's faint heart at Sheriffmuir was the first of fresh betrayals, the more miserable because his prospects after a victory would have been glittering. If he had crushed Argyll, he could have swept down and cowed the hostile Lowlands, crossed the border, then roused the north of England while daunting the south with his clansmen. By the time he reached Derby he might have rallied 20,000 men, with an open road to London before him. George I would surely have scuttled back to Hanover. Mar would have won his place in history, not least as the man who restored independence to Scotland after eight dismal years of Union.

As it was, the rising fizzled out. On the day of Sheriffmuir a southern Jacobite force, Scots and English, was surrendering in the streets of Preston in Lancashire. The northern Whigs stormed Inverness, captured by rebels two months before. With no stronghold left, Mar's soldiers had to cast themselves on the meagre resources of mountain and moor in a bitter winter.

Not even the belated arrival of James VIII could save his cause. Landing at Peterhead just before Christmas, he brought no French troops or other aid with him. The Hanoverians were meanwhile regrouping. Argyll advanced through the snowdrifts of a Perthshire that the Jacobites otherwise left behind them as scorched earth. James paused to be crowned at Scone on 23 January 1716, the last such ceremony in Scotland, though so slapdash as to be barely valid by the old traditions. Six weeks after setting foot on Scottish soil he was gone again. On 4 February he slipped away by night from Montrose with Mar and a handful of others. James had hardly impressed the Scots: his mournful parting comment, 'I am no stranger to misfortune', summed up to them his phlegmatic dulness. As for Mar, they dubbed him Bobbing John for his alacrity in changing sides.[2]

Worse yet was that the leaders abandoned fighting men who had risked all to join them. From that desertion Jacobitism could not recover, although it staged further rebellions, the last of them thirty years later. There was never again a chance that the majority of Scots would place faith in the Stewarts, any more than the Stewarts would in them. The ancient royal line of Scotland threw away its last opportunity to win over the many subjects of every persuasion who fared badly out of the Union. The Hanoverian regime secured itself: nothing reinforces a government so much as failed revolt against it. Support for the Jacobite cause would afterwards remain largely confined to the Highlands, and even then not the whole Highlands. An unhappy association between the two, incomplete as it was in reality, would do nothing for the fallen dynasty but was to doom a traditional society and culture.

The contradictions in the behaviour of the two generals at Sheriffmuir presaged this development. If Bobbing John could not decide on which side of the Highland line he stood, the Campbells were in their divisions more typical of the Gàidhealtachd. A large clan lording it over the southern Highlands, with an outlier in Nairnshire, they all claimed descent from Diarmaid, a hero of the ancient Irish epics. The myth of common ancestry did not keep them together. Their most important sept was the one represented by Argyll, its allegiance to Reformation and Revolution no doubt bolstered by the elevation of MacChailein Mòr to ducal dignity in 1701. Next were the Campbells of Glenorchy, headed by the earl of Breadalbane. Iain Glas still lived in 1715. Although he had brokered a peace between King William and the clans a quarter-century earlier, Breadalbane remained at heart a Jacobite. Now, at the age of eighty, he all but joined the rebellion while brandishing bits of paper from his doctor and his minister testifying he was too decrepit to do so. His men did serve with Mar, but under Campbell of Glenlyon, a cousin once removed. Two battalions from Breadalbane went to Sheriffmuir. There, in other words, Campbells stood in the Jacobite ranks.

That was just one instance of members of the same clan, or at least men bearing the same name, taking opposite sides in these turbulent times. Another magnate on the southern fringe of the Highlands was John Murray, duke of Atholl. He remained a Hanoverian Whig, while his heir, William, marquess of Tullibardine, joined the Jacobites. The duke had several sons, whose conduct he found hard to control. The eldest, John, had been killed fighting the French as colonel of a Scots-Dutch regiment at the Battle of Malplaquet in 1709. William, successor to the courtesy title, was an officer in the royal navy, but that did not stop him, along with his brothers in the British army, George and Charles, rallying to the Pretender's standard. They brought 1400 fighting men with them, formed into the Atholl brigade of four regiments, respectively commanded by the three brothers and their uncle Lord Nairne. Tullibardine, for his pains, lost his inheritance and went into exile to become the shadow Duke William of the Jacobite peerage, while Duke James, his father's fifth son, enjoyed the legal succession.

This penchant for placing members of a family on both sides in civil wars was reinforced by memories of disasters for clans that had made the wrong choice – a choice never easy. Highland feudalism often dragged hapless vassals into doomed causes, and a crude system of insurance was understandable. During the rebellion of the ninth earl of Argyll in 1685, many families of Campbells had their first sons with him and their second with the forces of King James VII. Sir Ewen Cameron of Lochiel was the foremost chief to follow Claverhouse in 1689 and led his clan's charge barefoot at the Battle of Killiecrankie (he did not want to slip on the grass of the braes); but he had a younger son in King William's army.[3] An alternative was for clans just to ignore their feudal burdens, even at a cost to a cause they were inclined to favour. The Farquharsons long bragged of their cleverness in maintaining a loyalist reputation while evading orders from their superiors the Erskines to join the army marching to defeat at the Battle of Worcester in 1651. Such tales contributed to a cynical streak in Highland culture that, if less salient than the usual hero-worship, was often of greater force. Chiefs vaunted themselves on successful ruses and, according to one reproach, repeated 'their scurvy, ungenerous, dishonourable maxims by way of vindication and showing their parts and dexterity'. But the fury this aroused outside the smug club of Highland narcissism could be just as canting: that reproach to the Farquharsons came from James Erskine of Grange, Mar's brother, who had his wife, Rachel, kidnapped and imprisoned in the Western Isles until her death. In any case boasting belonged to the repertoire of Gaelic self-expression. Breadalbane and Glengarry were both notorious for it and talked up what they were doing or had done during the pacification of the Highlands in 1691. They found not so much to boast about – it is to be hoped, at least – when the Massacre of Glencoe resulted.[4]

Such fickleness underlines the absence of a strict identity between the Highlands and Jacobitism. Nor is it wise to see in the risings and other disorders of the eighteenth century an Armageddon of Gael and Saxon, a final, fundamental, implacable clash between two cultures: the one modern and soulless, the other archaic and honourable; the former bound to win, the latter doomed to fail. The idea has fed legends but can never represent the complexity, not to say the instability, of Highland society.

Of course, loyal clans still existed. Some, if a minority in the whole Highlands, stayed true to the Stewarts from the moment they took up arms for Charles I until the time came to lay them down for good after the defeat of his great-grandson and namesake at the Battle of Culloden a century later. Broadly speaking, they occupied a swath of territory across the middle of Scotland from the Gordons in the Grampian mountains to the MacDonalds in the Hebrides. Their chiefly families were Jacobites in culture as well as in politics, but this culture had a dynamic of its own, and was not just atavistic. It upheld values of hierarchy, dignity and ceremony in Church as well as state and, of course, inside the clans too. Sileas, daughter of MacDonald of Keppoch and wife of a Gordon in Banffshire, wrote a poem on the Battle of Sheriffmuir where she remarked that:

A liuthad cùbaid tha an dràsta
Fo chùram na gràisge,
Agus easbuig fo àilgheas nam biasd.

There is many a pulpit now
In the care of the rabble,
And many a bishop under the heel of the beast.

She means the takeover of the Church of Scotland, as a result of Whig
policy, by vulgar Presbyterian ministers and the great unwashed whom
they inflamed with rants about hellfire. Jacobitism could be an angry movement, too, given to political or religious polemic of this kind. But it had a
telling point in its reproofs of extreme fundamentalism and of unprinci-
pled government.

It was in religion that the ideology took its purest form. Pious Jacobite
writers espoused a cult of mysticism that owed most to saints of the Middle
Ages and the Counter-Reformation, to Thomas à Kempis, Teresa of Avila
and John of the Cross, known through the chiefs' connections to Europe.[5]
The attitude to the fallen world was quietist: Christians could only expect
to suffer in it, and should accept their fate while looking into their own
souls and, for the rest, submitting to powers that be, whether good or evil,
as Jesus and his disciples had done. Jacobitism developed a powerful
iconography that drew on these sources, but in the language of Eden it
found above all, as ever, poetic expression. Chiefs of the MacLeans,
MacLeods and Stewarts were among those who patronized verse of this
kind. Iain mac Ailein's 'Trodan ris an Fheòil' ('Struggling with the Flesh'),
is cast in the form of a dialogue between two sisters, one a woman of easy
virtue, the other a bride of Christ. The latter seeks and finds pleasure in
her own way:

Far a bheil mo thasgaidh-sa
Tha glasan air do-leòint',
Gum beil mo stiùbhart saidhbhir,
'S bheir e làitheal domh mo lòn.

Where my treasure lies
It has locks on it undented,
Yet my steward is a rich man
Who feeds me every day.[6]

Still, the virtuous maiden's path is stony and she wonders if she might be
tempted to wander off it and follow her wayward sister. Indeed, Jacobites
maintaining a doctrine of passive obedience joined the rebellion of 1715,

but they lived in a vale of tears where every road was crooked and no destination certain.

Given this religion of resignation to worldly woes, the nature of Jacobite politics is harder to pin down, politics being a worldly business. Of course, the foundation of it lay in the indefeasible right of hereditary monarchy: if that foundation should be broken, the whole fabric of society might crumble. The idea appealed to Highlanders used to seeing chiefs as fathers of their clans and, by extension, to seeing the king as father of the nation. Beyond that, matters were not so simple. Jacobitism also rested on Scottish nationalism, and the Pretenders forever promised to undo the Union of Parliaments. But that would have returned Scotland to the Union of Crowns – the worst of all worlds, worse than the perils and poverty of independence, worse than incorporation with a larger, stronger neighbour where Scots were at least entitled to a say. For too long the English would not listen, but that did not alter the fact that the Union of Crowns had itself created, and done nothing to solve, the problem of the marginal Highlands under a distant British kingship.

One great Whig complaint against the legitimate line of Stewarts had been that their arbitrary absolutism subverted rights of property. Yet it cannot be said that Jacobites felt any less attached to rights of property. A whole history of the Highlands could be written in terms of such rights, especially in the late seventeenth century, when they began to replace the rights of conquest prevalent before, prompting Scots law to take flight into metaphysics as it set about reconciling natural with Roman with feudal principles. After the rebellion of 1715 and the renewed military occupation of the Highlands, the government in London attainted prominent Jacobites so as to deprive them of their titles and lands and to destroy their social standing. These included Lords Nairne and Sinclair, the earls of Airlie, Panmure, Perth, Seaforth and Southesk, to name just the peers among them with estates in the Highlands or on its fringes. The attainders met with opposition from Jacobites and Whigs alike.

The principal officer of Scottish government after 1707 was the Lord Advocate. Two successive holders of that post, Sir David Dalrymple, brother of the culprit of Glencoe, and Robert Dundas of Arniston, whose family later went on to conduct the public affairs of enlightened Scotland, now did what they could to hinder forfeitures they considered socially or politically damaging. These lawyers were Lowlanders through and through, but they won general support from a landed class that showed a patriotic *esprit de corps* and a bottomless suspicion of carpet-baggers eager to snap up confiscated lands. The main butt of this suspicion was the York

Building Company of London, which seemed intent on buying estates just to strip them of their assets. So long as matters remained in limbo, means were found to continue paying rents to exiled chiefs and gentlemen of the clans. When the government in London decided to get tough in 1721 and sent troops to collect rents from the estate in Wester Ross of William Mackenzie, fifth earl of Seaforth, his factor called out the clansmen and put the intruders to flight with an ambush in Kintail. After six years of such civil or not so civil disobedience the government settled for restoring the forfeited estates in return for sureties of good conduct. The point is that all Scots upheld the same rights of property against a high-handed British state. It is idle to ask whether a Jacobite or a Whig, a Highland or a Lowland principle, was at stake.

Nor is it convincing to construct some more general equation of Whigs with progress and of Jacobites with reaction. Again, all Scots were moved around the turn of the eighteenth century by a frustrated urge for what they called improvement. Mar enjoyed far more success with his businesses than he ever did with his politics or leadership of the clans, but the first Highlanders to promote new economic development had been Breadalbane and Lochiel, the one an equivocal Jacobite, the other a steadfast one. Breadalbane financed his numberless intrigues out of sawmills, worked by his clansmen's forced labour, to which he floated timber down river and loch, then sent the finished product on to Lowland towns or even to shipyards of the English navy. When Cameron of Lochiel marched off to join Claverhouse in 1689, he left behind at his estate of Achnacarry on Loch Arkaig a blast furnace that made and sold good iron; it was destroyed in the subsequent warfare. This kind of enterprise proved to be too far ahead of its time so long as the Highlands remained inaccessible, at least over land. Still, through a commodity that could solve the problem of transport by moving itself, namely cattle, the region steadily connected itself to the Lowland and English economy.

So the Highland economy grew, perhaps for a while faster than the economy of the rest of Scotland. This went into depression after 1707, as fledgeling industries fell to competition from cheaper and better English manufactures. This depression did not lift until the mid-eighteenth century. By contrast, the Highlands were probably making better use of their resources, putting to work hands that had often been idle in a system of bare subsistence. Chiefs such as Cameron of Lochiel could carry on sending cattle to the trysts, indeed sending more and more of them from year to year. Cameron stood also at the forefront of progress with his investments in American and Caribbean colonies, where he gave jobs to some of his close kin. In 1734 a grandson, Ewen, sailed from Fort William to the West Indies with a cargo of people, one of the earliest Highland emigrations of which a record survives.[7] A Jacobite commitment put up no bar to taking a keen part in the free trade opened up by the Union across Great Britain, or in the further imperial expansion to which Union was a key. The fate of the Stewarts proved irrelevant to all this.

So an ideology of property and progress cannot be ascribed on the one hand to Whiggery or Jacobitism, or on the other hand to Lowlands or Highlands. In politics Scots were divided not by ideology but by personal convictions or circumstances, not to speak of cranks and whims in a feudal aristocracy that did not scruple to use its powers of pit and gallows. But if ideals were to be found in this bedlam, one of them rested on outrage at abuse of Scotland in the Union and the shock thereby dealt to Scots who had promoted and accepted it as a patriotic option.

These were matters on which not only unreasonable but also reasonable men could differ. So it is no surprise to find at the opposite end of the spectrum some Highland families consistently Whig, from the Campbells of Argyll to, beyond Inverness, the Sutherlands, Rosses, Munros and (from 1688) the MacKays. In fact these clans, which occupied much of the northernmost peninsula of Great Britain, were to be counted on as steady foes to Jacobitism, so no equation of remoteness with it may be supposed either. Again some clans preferred neutrality, notably the MacLeods, who cried a plague on all houses once they found the restored Charles II heedless of their interests. Others were divided, such as the confederal Clan Chattan, which possessed no central authority to enforce a single political line on every one of its septs. Yet others switched, perhaps several times, as a new generation of leaders followed an old, or within a single generation as one pursued purposes of his own with greater or lesser astuteness.

The Whig MP for Caithness in 1715 was a fatherless slip of a boy, the nineteen-year-old Robert Gordon of Gordonstown, wangled into Parliament as a minor by friends of his family, the Sinclairs of Ulbster, who controlled the county. (Highland gentlemen did not worry how the English defined the age of majority.) In the rising the Sinclairs were split, but Gordon dashed off to join it and fight at Sheriffmuir with the Master of Sinclair, whom he regarded as a big brother. He made a bad choice of role model: Sinclair was said to have been 'prepossessed with the same folly that most young men are' when he signed up with the British army after the Union. During a short military career in Flanders he killed two men in illegal duels and had to depart in haste for the Prussian service instead. Although Sinclair said he found Gordon 'of great fire, courage and good sense', the opposite seems to be truer.[8] Still, Gordon was rescued from his puerility (unlike Sinclair, who spent ten years in exile) by an indulgent Argyll. After the Jacobite defeat the duke got this sullen pup off scot-free, probably with a view to turning him into a political pawn. After a single term at Westminster, however, Gordon had had enough and retired to his estate to oppress his tenants; he once imprisoned an old lady for stealing a fish head from his midden.

The most blatant of all such trimmers was Simon Fraser, who, born into a cadet branch of his family, stopped at nothing in pursuit of his ambition to be recognized as chief of his clan. For this he had to succeed to the feudal superiority of Lovat, which carried the chiefly dignity with it and fell vacant in 1697. Fraser adopted the simple expedient of kidnapping and forcibly marrying the widowed Lady Lovat, whose screams were drowned out by his pipers as he then had his evil way with her so as to render the transaction irrevocable. It did not matter to the new laird of Lovat that she was a daughter of the mighty house of Atholl, but it did to the duke. Fraser had to go into Jacobite exile, from which, changing sides, he returned to join in the recapture of Inverness from the Pretender's forces in 1715. In fact he afterwards announced to the world that he, rather than the northern Whigs who raised the necessary forces, ought to be credited with this important operation. Neither the politics of Jacobitism nor that of Whiggery was pretty to look at, but Fraser in his utter lack of scruple shows himself as one of nature's Whigs. So he now remained for three decades until the final Jacobite rebellion brought out once again the turncoat in him, and he finished up at Tyburn in 1747.

It seems only natural to conclude that in 1715 Scotland split not as between Highlands and Lowlands but for a variety of reasons, good and bad, which on either side of the Highland line were much the same. At their best they represented a wronged nation, and one wronged on grounds that, for all their cynicism, were trivial. After 1707 England had to do nothing more than honour a treaty freely entered into, yet provisions constructed with care so that Scotland could undergo a smooth transition into the Union were broken with no thought. Scots had compromised much for this mess of pottage, not least their national sentiment and their pride in an ancient dynasty. Wanting to enjoy some peace and prosperity at last, and deciding they wanted these blessings more than anything else, they had let their heads rule their hearts. They still regarded themselves as patriotic Scots, but they became, with distressing speed, malcontent Britons. Force then seemed to many the quickest way out of a Union that had betrayed them. If the reaction appeared more Highland than Lowland, this was because the chiefs, unlike the lairds of a more settled region, could call on the reserves of fighting men they maintained on their estates. From far away the Stewarts stood ready to rally the loyal clans once again through the call of the blood and the skirl of the pipes; but it would be wrong to think that the '15 had at its heart a dynastic rather than domestic inspiration.

A final incident may define the matter so far as it affected the clans. During the campaign before the Battle of Sheriffmuir, one Jacobite offensive struck at Inveraray, the tiny burgh on Loch Fyne beside the huge castle of the duke of Argyll. About a thousand Campbells were besieged there by twice their number from other clans – mostly Camerons but also including some Campbells of Breadalbane. The siege saw more talking than fighting, and while the parleys went on, the bored commander of Breadalbane's men, Campbell of Glenlyon, rode off to seek Jacobite recruits in the district of Lorne. In his absence the siege was raised. A party then set out in pursuit, led by Alexander Campbell of Fonab, one of the rare survivors of Scotland's catastrophic attempt to establish a colony at Darien on the isthmus of Panama in 1698–1700; Fonab had been its military commander and won for an independent Scotland her last victory in the field, over the Spaniards at Toubacanti. When the two captains, each in the service of a different king, met amid the hills of home, they ought no doubt to have committed themselves to battle. They did deploy their forces as if they meant to, but then they preferred to strike a bargain, for to both it seemed wrong for Campbell to fight Campbell just because a prince in France and a prince from Germany were contending for the Crown. The men from Breadalbane laid down their arms in return for a safe passage out of Argyll into their own country.[9]

This incident reveals much about the uncertain relations between the Highlands and Jacobitism. What it argues above all is the resilience of the clan in an era of upheaval. Brothers took opposite sides because they wanted their clan to survive, whether as a social, cultural or religious community, much more than they favoured the succession of one dynasty or another to the throne of the United Kingdom. Equally, kinsmen could come together again to promote the same end. In the Gàidhealtachd, with national independence and the native dynasty gone, the clan remained as the highest entity to which a man could give his allegiance. At any rate the British state, quickly hatching its own suspicions of the clans, was no match for them.

Still, other forces of modernity had a greater effect in picking at the fabric of Highland society. The chiefs' growing refinement forbade them to condone delinquencies done in their name: Fraser of Lovat was one of the few real reprobates left. Most would rather now bargain among themselves and protect their interests by keeping the peace. The tacksmen turned from a warrior caste into a middle management of clans that had abandoned feuds and no longer seized land from one another by force. While there was still much lawlessness, it came more often from the caterans rather than from the clans as such.

It is striking, for example, how little trace remained of an earlier consistent pattern of internecine hostility when coalitions of lesser clans tried to gang up on the Campbells, if only in riposte to Clan Diarmaid's aggressions against them. The Campbells were themselves divided in 1715. More to the point, the duke of Argyll rode on the back of the victory he claimed at Sheriffmuir to a Scottish political ascendancy that gave him enough weight to get his way in London too. He made himself the focus of a new system based on the distribution of British official patronage by a manager of Scotland who mediated between his supplicant countrymen and the government. That demanded of this old soldier a novel dexterity, not with the claymore but in back-slapping, glad-handing and palm-greasing. In principle anyone likely to matter to the manager's control could find a niche in the system, although the imperious Argyll did shut out some families foolish enough to have rubbed him up the wrong way, and he always made sure that the Campbells got their cut. But the whole fitted in well with the more amiable traditions of clanship. For a while it was possible the clans might become a force for stability rather than instability.

At least some of this change arose from the capacity of the clans, or more especially of the chiefs, at last to reform themselves. London had no interest in the Highlands, except in the extreme circumstances of rebellion or invasion, and not even always then: a farcical Spanish landing at Glenshiel in 1719 was repelled by nothing more than a route march by the garrison from Inverness. Over much of the region the British government's writ anyway did not run. As we have seen, it failed to impose its will on the estates of the earl of Seaforth, in a fine example of how resilient a clan could be with its back to the wall and its chief facing destitution. The government was serious about making Seaforth, a Catholic under attainder, lose his lands, but they lay in Ross, beyond the limits of its power. The gentlemen of the clan and the ordinary clansmen stood ready in the last resort to put up a fight for the inheritance of Clan Mackenzie. There was nothing anyone in London could do.

War might, though, be pursued by other means. After the '15 the government appointed a Commission of the Forfeited Estates to dispossess leading rebels. The process got hopelessly bogged down in legal technicality. It began with ascertaining title to a chief's estates. This may have looked easy enough to the commission's surveyor-general, Patrick Strachan of Glenkindy, but when he came knocking at Lord Sinclair's door to ask about the property of the Master of Sinclair, now in exile, he was told first that his lordship felt ill, so could not receive Strachan in person, then that back in 1712 the Master's property had anyway been passed on to the second son, James (who thus gained the means for a distinguished career as a British general, MP and diplomat). Full documentation could be provided if Strachan wished, but he would be wasting his time. He was stumped.

If Strachan had got past the first stage of his inquiry here, he would have gone on to ask about the rental together with the location and value of movable property belonging to the forfeited person. Against all this, however, he was legally obliged to set the claims of legitimate creditors owed money by the estate at the time of forfeiture. Since the late seventeenth century Highland estates had been sinking under their debts, so creditors turned up before the commissioners in great numbers. Most of their claims may even have been genuine. The cumulative effect was often that the estate, in its net value, had little left to confiscate, or else, if claims were to be rejected, that the government would make more enemies than friends, which was not the aim of its Highland policy. Those blatant rebels the Camerons of Lochiel escaped through such a morass of detail, deepened by obscure testamentary manoeuvres within the chiefly family itself, from any serious threat of forfeiture. And even if confiscation could be enforced, it might in effect be soon reversed. Deprived of his property, Chisholm of Strathglass, also a Catholic under attainder, had his lands passed first through a lawyer in Edinburgh, then through a friendly Mackenzie to his younger brother, who entailed them on his elder son.[10]

As in the period of the Restoration, creditors were fair-weather friends to a chief, but by the eighteenth century he could find more of them. A problem for the Highland economy lay in the introduction into it of money, along with new commercial values, without means to ensure a sufficient supply of the stuff. Chiefs were the only Highlanders who ever saw much of it, but it was needed by wider circles in the region as markets came into being. No banks existed in the north before one was founded in Aberdeen in 1749, then another in Perth in 1765, and neither lasted more than a few years. Breadalbane's factor, John Campbell, was chief cashier of the Royal Bank of Scotland for four decades from 1734, but he probably extended rather than modernized a system under which chiefs took on banking functions for their clans, or at least created credit within them.

Chiefs could still get by with little cash, but sometimes they had to have more than came from their rents or from the sale of what was paid to them in kind. Certainly if they wanted to emulate the agricultural improvements now being started in the Lowlands, they would need more money. It could be raised in the form of wadsets or mortgages. These, secured against the estate, might also be used by the creditor as a form of negotiable security; on Wall Street they call this a derivative. The effect was to increase the money supply in an economy always short of gold and silver – and it amounted, on yet scarcer resources, to no more than was being done in the Lowlands by the old Scottish banking system with its invention of paper money. In theory an estate ought not to have been mortgaged beyond its real value, yet there was no way of stopping a landlord from building up other kinds of debt to any level his creditors would tolerate.

The chartered Scottish banks developed a self-regulating mechanism that suppressed inflation and prevented failure. There were no such safeguards in the finances of the Gàidhealtachd. Some people inevitably lost their bearings and ran into rough waters. The less seaworthy Highland gentlemen began to vanish over the brink of bankruptcy. A case in point was the Mackenzies. In 1724 the chief of the clan, John, second earl of Cromartie, went bust, owing not least to the efforts of his wife, Lady Elizabeth Gordon, who contracted large debts for 'meat, drink, clothes, abulziments [outer garments], rings, bracelets and jewels of great value'.[11] In 1727 a connection by marriage, Alexander Urquhart of Newhall, followed. In 1741 another senior member of the clan, George Mackenzie of Cromarty, sank too. Here came an example of war carried on by other means: much of the property released was snapped up by the Gordons of Invergordon, Whig lairds who had a daughter married to George, third earl of Cromartie, and were besides among the Mackenzies' main creditors.

Like other fair-weather friends, debt demoralized in the end. Norman MacLeod of MacLeod was born posthumously to his chieftaincy in 1706, well connected to other high aristocrats of Gaeldom, to Frasers of Lovat and MacDonalds of Sleat. During his minority his tutor, John MacLeod of Contullich, performed as agent both for the estate and for the Jacobites; he even got a peerage from the Pretender for his young charge, which at least came cheap. On attaining his majority, the chief soon found himself short of money for his expensive drinking and gambling habits. With Sleat he worked out a scheme for deporting their surplus tenants on Skye to be sold in the American plantations. The pair faced prosecution when it was found that these wretches, many of them women and small children, had not been convicted of crimes punishable by transportation. MacLeod appealed to the Lord President of the Court of Session, Duncan Forbes, no less:

> You know better than I that were we never so innocent, a prosecution would be attended with a multitude of inconveniences, and ought in my weak judgment to be shunned if possible. You not only know best if it can be shunned but likewise the proper means how to shun it and are the only person in earth we would mostly, nay entirely, rely on, do therefore in God's name what you think best for us.[12]

Forbes, a sainted figure in the annals of Scotland, omitted to prosecute the guilty. On the contrary, he saw here a chance to draw MacLeod into the network of patronage he was helping Argyll to weave. In 1741, with help from Fraser of Lovat, Forbes made MacLeod MP for Inverness-shire. By now Fraser had tired of Whiggery and, together with Erskine of Grange, Mar's brother, was angling for French support to restore the Stewarts. They told Cardinal Fleury that MacLeod was one Highland chief bound to back a fresh rebellion. Yet he refused to see Bonnie Prince Charlie in 1745 and evaded any commitment to him. After Culloden, MacLeod could not live on Skye because of the people's hatred for him. He was a ruined man when he died.

5

The little fire!

Highland Calvinism in the eighteenth century

JUNE 1727 WAS freezing, nowhere more so than in the Highlands. But the citizens of Dornoch had a different reason for lighting a big bonfire one day that month on the open space that passed for their market-place.

Theirs was a miserable little town, a mere huddle of turf huts. According to its minister in 1791, the Revd John Bethune, writing in the *Old Statistical Account of Scotland*, it lay in 'in the last stage of decay', with no more than a hundred dwellings and 500 people; it must have already been well on the way downhill in 1727. The main reason Dornoch existed was as the seat of a bishopric, but bishops had been banished from the Church of Scotland. The castle where they used to reside had been besieged and slighted during the Reformation. Its massive walls, restored as a hotel today, still stood open to the sky. Opposite, the cathedral, partly ruinous too, had become for all its medieval grandeur a humble kirk. Bethune said it was 'a very incompetent house of worship, being extremely cold, and beyond the powers of an ordinary voice'. The churchyard doubled as market-place, with the road to the north running through.[1]

It was the scene of such public events as Dornoch ever saw. Although crumbling and destitute, this remained the head burgh of Sutherland, where magistrates and ministers met to deliberate, in English, about good order and sound doctrine among the county's Gaelic-speaking peasants. Sometimes they had to set a stern example: hence the bonfire. They lit it to burn a witch.

Under lowering skies they brought Janet Horne to the place of her execution. She had been held in little comfort, so she felt chill. Her face brightened as she approached. '*An teine beag!* – the little fire!' she mumbled in pleasure, giggling like a child and rubbing her hands at the flames. The crowd noted with interest her choice of adjective. If she had exclaimed '*An teine mòr!*', they would have said she had a premonition of hell-fire. She sat 'very composedly' while other instruments of her death were prepared. By normal procedure the witch would be tied to a stake and strangled. Her body would be covered in pitch, or shoved in a barrel of pitch, and consumed on the pyre.

Janet Horne hailed from the parish of Loth, further up the high, wild and windy coastline of Sutherland. She had been tried with her daughter, who, however, was acquitted as an unwilling accomplice. The crime laid to the mother's charge was that she had maimed the girl by turning her into a pony, summoning the devil to get her shod her with horseshoes, then riding on her to a witches' sabbath. The sole fact amid this farrago of nonsense was that the girl had crippled hands and feet. Since she later bore a son with the same deformities, some unfortunate genetic defect must have been to blame.[2]

This was the last burning of a witch in Scotland. It does not cast the nation in a good light to find such a thing going on when Newtonian physics had been introduced at the University of Aberdeen, or when students at Edinburgh were debating the philosophies of Bishop Berkeley and John Locke. Yet in a strange way belief in witchcraft was a facet not of the ancient Scotland, but of a more modern one. It had not become a criminal offence until 1563. There had been witches before, so called by themselves or others, but they were seldom persecuted or killed.

To the still half-pagan mind of the medieval Scot the air was full of good and evil presences, from saints to sprites. Any effort to get rid of them would be at once perilous and futile, likely to open a supernatural Pandora's box. The best thing was appeasement, with little gifts left out overnight or something of the sort. Highlanders, as opposed to Lowlanders, remained in this state of mind. In his *Description of the Western Isles of Scotland* Martin Martin writes about a custom of carrying fire around a woman before she first went to church again after giving birth. People 'told me the fire-round was an effectual means to preserve both the mother and infant from the power of evil spirits, who are ready at such times to do mischief, and sometimes carry away the infant'. A similar heathen rite was performed by sailors or by those worried about their welfare:

> Some are very careful when they set out to sea that the boat be first rowed about sunways; and, if this be neglected, they are afraid their voyage may prove unfortunate. I had this ceremony paid me (when in the island of Islay) by a poor woman after I had given her an alms: I desired her to let alone that compliment, for I did not care for it; but she insisted to make these three ordinary turns, and then praying that God and MacCharming, the patron saint of that island, might bless and prosper me in all my designs and affairs.[3]

Even islanders protected by such a genial saint as MacCharming could not withstand a Reformation that drove witchcraft underground and made death the normal punishment for it, on the authority of the Mosaic text,

'Thou shalt not suffer a witch to live'.[4] To root out witchcraft became one of the Scots' missions as a chosen people, part of the grand design for a reformed, godly nation. Now they were wholly christianized for the first time and taught to govern their personal conduct according to orthodox belief. This was why the Kirk set such store by literacy and by the sermon, the most potent new mode of expression. Simple peasants, who had little other contact with the outside world, were browbeaten every Sunday by their minister's ferocious eloquence, his lurid images of hell and the devil, his message of predestination, that it was in vain for any of them to try redeeming himself. Again this came to the Highlands well behind the rest of the country. The region had always been ill supplied in religion, and a good many chiefs remained Episcopalians or even Catholics, not Presbyterians. It was several decades before the religious settlement of 1690 took full effect in the Gàidhealtachd. Episcopalian ministers often continued to serve their parishes and preach their gentler doctrines until orthodox substitutes for them could be obtained.

Since the Reformation the Scottish state had joined the Church in efforts to enforce higher moral standards on the people. The state underwent a revolution too, especially in its jurisprudence, through the College of Justice already established in Edinburgh as a central court for the nation in 1532. Before then most courts, where they existed, had been local, concerned with righting wrongs done to individuals; and where the courts did not exist there was always the feud. Now, in place of this casual and ramshackle structure, justice became majestic, retributive, a means of attacking deviance and imposing general, abstract laws. Feudal justice did not at once disappear. It was still dispensed in so-called regalities, where noblemen held kingly powers over life and death on their own lands. Only two crimes could not be alienated to regalities, but had to be tried in the central system. One was treason, the supreme offence against the king. The other was witchcraft, the supreme offence against God.

In Scotland from the Reformation onwards, witch-hunts rose and fell in waves. Perhaps they followed this pattern because they were so repulsive even to Scots at their most touchy and violent. A woman denounced as a witch had the option of making a confession, advisable in view of what would happen to her otherwise. If not, evidence had to be extracted under torture before she went to trial. This was often the task of an expert witch-pricker. He would blindfold the woman and start sticking needles in her. If he found a spot, usually a mole or birthmark, that did not make her cry out in pain when pierced, this was taken as absolute proof that the devil had touched her there.

The most hysterical and sadistic witch-hunt came in the 1660s, after the Restoration, when Scottish national neurosis was acute. Sir George Mackenzie of Rosehaugh then embarked on his prominent legal career. His personal culture was aristocratic, with little time for the people and their Presbyterianism, which he condemned in his book *Religio Stoici* for its violence, rebellion and disloyalty. Bluidy Mackenzie never hesitated to use the full rigour of the law, but he must have had a heart, for he was moved to pity by a helpless old woman awaiting her fate:

> She told me under secrecy that she had not confessed because she was guilty, but being a poor creature who wrought for her meat and being defamed for a witch, she knew she would starve, for no person thereafter would either give her meat or lodging, and that all men would beat her, and hound dogs at her, therefore she desired to be out of the world. Whereupon she wept bitterly and upon her knees called God for a witness to what she said.[5]

Mackenzie effected a change in the practice of suppressing witchcraft. Scottish government at the time was authoritarian and cracked down on all popular disorder, even if directed against the devil. Mackenzie and other lawyers did not doubt the existence of witches, but still wanted to make sure they would be dealt with by due process. They introduced safeguards – modest, but enough to halt the great witch-hunts.

Odd trials and executions still took place, and spread to the Highlands, which until now had been almost free of them – perhaps a sign that this region, too, was at last leaving behind its half-pagan past. On 5 March 1719 the Lord Advocate, Robert Dundas, wrote a snooty letter to the sheriff of Caithness. He had reports from there of 'very extraordinary, if not fabulous, discoveries of witchcrafts'. He pointed out that 'it is the part of every sheriff, when things of that kind fall out, to transmit ane account of it to those whom His Majesty is pleased to employ to look after these matters, it being our duty'. He pulled the sheriff up and warned him not to proceed with a certain case on his own authority, because it was 'above the jurisdiction of an inferior court'. But nothing in the letter reveals any doubt in Dundas's mind about the reality of witchcraft.[6]

As a Presbyterian, Dundas probably did believe in witches, along with other teachings of the Kirk. What was happening to it worried people like him. They knew that, despite the religious settlement of 1690 and guarantees for the Church of Scotland in the Treaty of Union, the Parliament in London still disliked Presbyterianism. It had clipped the Kirk's wings with the Patronage Act of 1712, robbing congregations of a right to call their own ministers. Presbyterians had to remain on guard against further arrogations by the British state.

Dundas numbered among his friends the Revd Robert Wodrow, minister of Eastwood, famed as a preacher and active in the politics of the Kirk. He had belled the cat at the Hanoverian succession by asking King George I for repeal of the Patronage Act. Wodrow got nowhere, but colleagues often asked him to position himself so as to bring his influence better to bear, to accept a charge in Glasgow or Edinburgh and to serve his turn as moderator of the General Assembly. Yet he preferred to stay in rustic Renfrewshire, for he had a big writing project on hand. In 1721–2 he published his monumental *History of the Sufferings of the Church of Scotland from the Restoration to the Revolution,* in part a riposte to Mackenzie's attacks on Presbyterians. The Covenants, Wodrow countered, had to be understood in context, as an effort 'through so much blood and suffering' to preserve Protestant liberties. It was a reasonable view, though not quite what the remaining Covenanters would have said. Wodrow in effect apologized for their forefathers and tried to make them respectable for a new, less fraught age.[7]

Wodrow also kept a commonplace book, which he called *Analecta,* things picked up on his daily round. It is full of rumours of Jacobite plots, and often remarks on the 'terrible increase of popery' (in fact, Scottish Catholicism was now going into sharp decline). Ever present in its pages is the second duke of Argyll, victor over the Jacobites in 1715, rising on the back of that to political mastery of the country, as one of the few among his compatriots whom the English trusted: he was, after all, an Old Etonian. Wodrow trusted him not a bit. He noted down for future reference how the duke was a secret Jacobite, or had introduced the Prince of Wales to the whorehouses of London. Argyll's ancestors had fought and died for the Covenant, yet he himself seemed to be an agent of servitude and corruption.[8]

Why else, Presbyterians asked, did the duke pack the General Assembly with his minions? In 1726 Wodrow recorded in horror the presence of a blue-blooded young advocate from the north, George Ogilvy, whose father, the earl of Findlater, was serving the same assembly as Lord High Commissioner, or representative of the Crown. (He must have been nominated by Argyll.) Of Ogilvy, Wodrow says that 'one who does not look as if he were 20 or 24 was designed to be chosen ruling elder from the burgh of Cullen to this Assembly. His reputation is not entire. He is alleged deistical in his principles. He fell into fornication.' Here was the threat made flesh, in false doctrine and evil habits.[9]

After the Revolution of 1688 Presbyterians had broached a new and temperate path in keeping with their custody of an established Church. So what was to be done about this blatant subversion? One course, perhaps, would be more zeal in matters of lesser political import, in order to display the Kirk's authority and its command over the minds of Scots. Witchcraft could serve. Wodrow doubtless believed in witchcraft too: at any rate, people thought it worth bringing cases to his attention, and one of his junior colleagues urged him to publish a treatise on the subject. The flatterer was another fresh face at the General Assembly of 1726, a young minister from Ross, the Revd James Fraser, son of a Covenanting manse whose father had been banished to America by James VII. He even suffered a bit himself. Episcopalian parishioners had resisted his induction at Alness that spring, as they were sometimes still numerous enough to do in Highland parishes: they locked up the kirk and obliged him to preach in the graveyard.

The year after their first meeting at the General Assembly, in April 1727, Fraser wrote to remind Wodrow of his suggestion for a tract against witchcraft. He was prompted to do so by the discovery of a witch among his own flock, and then by this: 'There has been a great noise in the parish of Loth, in Sutherland, by which the minister is said to have suffered. He is not yet recovered, however, the case has been examined into, and the women were, I know, before the presbytery.' The minister was the Revd Robert Robertson, of an age with Fraser, and presumably acquainted with him, who may anyway have been in poor health because he was to die young. Wodrow recorded the item in his commonplace book, in rather garbled form, and added a tale about a minister losing the sight of one eye through sorcery.[10]

Just what was going on at Loth? The parish probably held to Calvinist orthodoxy. It was one of those in the north with a strong and early Protestant tradition. Its people had stood for the Covenant and its soldiers had fought against the Stewarts in every war since. The minister who later wrote the parish up in the *Old Statistical Account*, the Revd George McCulloch, boasted there was not a single religious dissenter among them, but he also found a spontaneous evangelical life so ardent as to unnerve him: 'Though there be no open schism to divide them in public worship, they have their lay leaders, some of the boldest and most conceited speakers at fellowship meetings, whom they implicitly believe.'[11]

Here the scene was set for Scotland's last burning of a witch. In the background stood a christianized peasantry bent on rooting out deviance: McCulloch said of Janet Horne that 'the common people entertain strong prejudices against her relations to this day'. In the foreground stood a sick minister, and in his paranoid presbytery ready ears for malicious gossip. Then there was a confused and senile old woman, who when brought before her clerical accusers grinned and winked at them before agreeing with all charges they laid against her. She was passed to the civil power, to a sheriff who must be presumed by the precedents to have got permission to proceed from the Lord Advocate. Then came a trial and a jury, over-awed by the combined forces of Church and state, pronouncing a verdict of guilty. Lastly there was the sentence of death. But behind the scenes some very long fingers may have reached out to choke the life from Janet Horne on that dreich day in the summer of 1727.

Seven years later the law against witchcraft of 1563 was repealed, though not on any Scottish initiative. The English wished to repeal their law, and somebody in the House of Lords thought to bring Scotland in by an amendment. The next year Parliament passed a new Witchcraft Act, which admitted only the crime of pretended witchcraft and set a sentence for it of a year in prison and the pillory on quarter-days. No Scot was ever prosecuted under the act, which could not be applied in Scotland since it had no prisons, no pillories and no quarter-days. Still, Presbyterians long protested that this reform was 'contrary to the express law of God'.[12]

The pathetic fate of Janet Horne illustrates how in one respect civilization as defined by non-Highlanders was penetrating the Highlands. A vital part of the process lay in the region's conversion to orthodox Calvinism, with all that implied for a graduate ministry and literate populace, brought up in a public system of education, accepting a morality set forth and enforced by the Kirk as best it could, even against the wiles of witches. This had become a reality in much of the Lowlands, though, of course, never perfect and often precarious. It was much harder to make a reality of it in the Highlands.

The Scottish state had started with education. First came the Statutes of Iona (1609), ordering sons of Highland chiefs to be instructed in English. General legislation followed with the Act for Settling of Parochial Schools (1616), which had the Kirk run a school in every parish and appoint a schoolmaster, often an aspirant minister or a failed one. That act also defined Gaelic as a cause of Highland barbarity and incivility, so it set the aim of abolishing and removing it. The lack of progress may be gauged by the fact that the act was in effect passed again in 1646 and again in 1696, augmented by machinery for its enforcement.

Evidently the Lowland system of public instruction had not yet come to the Highlands. Here, if anything, formal education reached a nadir about the turn of the eighteenth century. What existed earlier had disappeared, and nothing replaced it. That is to say, the hereditary élite of Gaelic learned orders faded away, while there was as yet no new notion of school and college for the people, as in the Lowlands. A few bards still haunted chiefly halls: Iain Dubh Mac Iain mhic Ailein hymned the MacDonalds of Clanranald, Iain mac Ailein honoured the MacLeans, and Murdoch Matheson lauded the Mackenzies. Not before the end of the eighteenth century would their courtly strains quite die away, but by then the bardic tradition had become a self-conscious indulgence in antiquarianism. When Sir James MacDonald of Sleat made John MacCodrum his personal poet, or Alexander MacDonell of Glengarry did the same for Allan MacDougall, they acted not out of hereditary obligation but after reading in their Ossian that it was the sort of thing a Highland chief ought to do. Nor, by this stage, did the bard perform any social function for the clan at large; he merely tickled his employer's fancy.

Even the most useful learned order, the physicians, sank into oblivion. One aim of Martin Martin's work in 1695 had been to add to the pharmacopeia, for his patron Sir Robert Sibbald in Edinburgh, information about properties of curative herbs known – in an age when useful knowledge was often assumed to be esoteric – only in faraway places. Martin retrieved much lore, but in general he just gleaned it from people he happened to meet and came across mere remnants of the learned order that had guarded such knowledge. He mentions Fergus Beaton in South Uist, who owned Gaelic medical manuscripts of Hippocrates, Avicenna, Averroës, Joannes de Vigo and Bernardus Gordonus. Martin also found a quack on Skye, Neil Beaton, 'an illiterate empiric without the advantage of an education', who claimed to have been taught his skills by his father.[13] In the Victorian Hebrides there were still botanizing Beatons, but anything resembling medical science vanished by the end of the eighteenth century, when in the whole southern Highlands the sole doctor lived at Inveraray. The decline even of the sort of medicine gleaned from dusty tomes or oral traditions meanwhile fostered superstition and the use among the people of charms and incantations, some of them preserving vestiges of pagan or Catholic belief.

Without learned orders and without new schools Gaelic culture was transmitted at this informal popular level, above all through the ceilidh. It is an institution that survives today, of which a continuous history has been traced by Alexander Carmichael in his introduction to the *Carmina Gadelica*.[14] In its modern form it has become a sort of sit-down party, with song or instrumental music performed to an audience which may join in and, as the evening wears on, is often moved to do so by the amount of drink taken. More or less anything can prompt a ceilidh. The first ever attended by the present writer was on Skye thirty years ago, to mark the inauguration of a postal bus service between Broadford and Elgol. Martin must have just been to something of the kind, though with no whisky, when he wrote three centuries earlier: 'The natives are generally ingenious and quick of apprehension; they have a mechanical genius, and several of both sexes have a gift of poesy, and are able to form a satire or panegyric extempore, without the assistance of any stronger liquor than water to raise their fancy.'[15]

The ceilidh once had a broader purpose than occasional celebration. Within humble homes on a winter's night Gaels gathered to hear tales told, news or gossip exchanged, memories swapped, riddles posed, games played and debates pursued, quite apart from the musical element. It is easy to paint a romantic picture of the people of a township, free for an hour from their hardships, nestling round a peat fire while the wind howled and rain beat down outside. Still, with men and women of all ages gathered in the warmth, soft light and sweet odour, the ceilidh must have been for the young the main method of acculturation to the Gaelic world, and a delightful one. The contrast with later times, when children were thrashed for speaking their mother tongue, is with hindsight not too pointed. In such homely surroundings the culture could readily branch out.

The whole tradition of Highland music for the fiddle is probably a product of the ceilidh. The Gaels' favourite instrument had once been the clàrsach or harp, superseded in the seventeenth century by the bagpipes. The violin may first have been preferred in the eastern Highlands, in Strathspey, which gave its name to one of the basic styles of tune, slower than a reel. Here families of fiddlers are known from early on, Browns of Kincardine and Cummings of Freuchie. Also the most famous deerstalker of his day, Lachlan MacKinnon, is said to have been master of both violin and harp. Martin Martin wrote: 'They are great lovers of music; and when I was there they gave an account of eighteen men who could play on the violin pretty well without being taught.'[16]

Ceilidhs also offered remote communities an opening on the outside world. Martin would have been readily invited to them: a frequent excuse for one was the coming of a stranger to a township, and a man who told his tale until dawn would be heartily welcome. Ceilidhs offered these communities an opening on their past too. In the central Highlands the stranger was asked as soon as he appeared, '*A bheil dad agad air an Fhèinn?*' ('Do you know anything of the Fianna?'). In the medieval lays the Fianna had been the semi-regular militia of Finn MacCool, performing fearless feats in athletic defence of the underdog when not too busy with erotic entanglements or with discussions in elegant and complex poetry on the relative merits of the active and the contemplative life. If the stranger coming to the township could add any good stories or verse about the Fianna to those already known there, he was invited to do so that night at a ceilidh. James Macpherson, visiting Uist in 1760 in search of poems of Ossian, got little reward when he reversed roles and asked the question of John MacCodrum, since it can also mean: 'Do the Fianna owe you anything?' No, said MacCodrum, '*Chan eil, 's ged a bhitheadh, cha ruiginn a leas iarraidh a'nis*' ('and if they did there would be no point in my looking for it now').[17]

The ceilidh was a late development of an oral culture that, as in Homeric Greece and other preliterate societies, listened to all its muses, whether the Calliope of poetry or the Clio of history, and did not distinguish between arts and sciences. Modern anthropologists have often been astonished to find in surviving societies of this sort how much exact knowledge is imparted not by reading and writing but by oral communication through the power of memory. Absence of material written or read seems to strengthen the memory, so that a tune might be recalled after one hearing, a poem after two, a complete story after three. And the power can be extended to fact as well as fiction. When literacy supplants strong memory and oral communication, there are gains but also losses. Reading and writing are the powerful tools of a literate culture, yet they may also impair it by introducing an internal division between the learned and the popular; this problem does not exist in preliterate societies. Perhaps the ideal would be somehow to marry the two.

A union of opposites happened, after all, in Gaeldom with the sacred and the profane. Archibald Grant, the bard of Glenmoriston, says it was 'the common habit to tell stories of the Fianna after the reading of the Bible was over'. This combination seems to have given rise to a feature of religious practice that survives right down to the present day. An apparent derivative of the ceilidh is Latha na Ceiste, the Day of Questions, part of the celebration of Presbyterian communions. In the Highlands such days are held infrequently and so all the more elaborately, often lasting over a long weekend. Nowadays they represent an accretion of several different features, some of obscure origin. Latha na Ceiste seems to date from times when there were few ordained ministers to still Highlanders' hunger for the true faith. These always felt anxious to put themselves in a proper state of mind for receiving the sacrament. So beforehand they raised points troubling them with godly laymen, itinerants who took it on themselves

WILD SCOTS

to 'discuss and resolve cases of conscience' in a sort of 'spiritual clinic'.[18] This was the same learning process as employed for secular matters at a ceilidh.

The Revd George MacCulloch who wrote, in the *Old Statistical Account*, how proud he felt of the orthodoxy of the people of Loth, also remained uneasily aware that it might not all have been due to him, their minister. He added:

> Of late they have begun to keep fellowship meetings amongst themselves, without the presence of a minister. To these meetings they convene at certain fixed periods from different parishes, propose questions in divinity, explain scriptures and give a sanction to any doctrines or opinions that are considered as orthodox by the presiding saint.[19]

By his last gibe MacCulloch means the lay leaders he had mentioned earlier, in whom he found 'high pretensions and affected sanctity, by which they impose upon the people, and frequently mislead them'. Some were not above claiming clerical authority without ever having been ordained. So at a certain stage, in order to prevent sectarian fragmentation, ministers must have got themselves by hook or by crook invited to Latha na Ceiste in place of the 'presiding saints', and brought the fellowship meetings within the fold of the Church. This still did not stop laymen going round to pray and preach and generally bring the solace of religion to anyone needing it, sometimes in defiance of the Kirk. These figures were given the Gaelic epithet of *Na Daoine*, which translates simply and unhelpfully as 'the Men'. They would retain a central role in Highland religion for a long time.

In present practice Latha na Ceiste is one of the days leading up to the celebration of communion. On that day the minister of a parish presides over discussion among his flock on some portion of the Bible. After leading prayers he comes down from his pulpit and chairs the meeting from the floor. He asks for a 'question' – a suitable verse of Scripture to be proposed by any intending male communicant present. He has no warning of the chosen text and, while he may reject it, he usually accepts it as a point of honour. He preaches on it so as to turn it into a question suitable for debate, then he calls on members of the congregation to speak to the question. They enliven their remarks with anecdotes from their own experience, and by the tradition on Lewis they give a spiritual autobiography, often well worn. Afterwards the minister deals with interesting points made and clarifies doctrinal matters arising, before the meeting closes with more prayer. This may sound solemn, but it is also an opportunity for quips, scoffs, taunts, wiggings and wisecracks, which are appreciated all the more if they wield Holy Writ to deadly effect. It is also a chance to let off steam at moments, still frequent, when the Highland churches face schism. Here, transformed by the passage of time, is a development of the original ceilidh giving something of its old flavour.[20]

It is an example also of one of the most striking features in the Gàidhealtachd even of the twenty-first century: the peculiar intensity of a religious life embedded in the culture and in the everyday experience of the people. Highland religion of the seventeenth century had been lackadaisical: the people accepted whatever ministrations were available. In the next century three influences may have joined to replace laxity with fervour. There was Jacobite mysticism; there was the Calvinist demand for orthodoxy; and there was a more general effect of the irruption by new forms of observance into a country where religion had been neglected, deficient or even forgotten for a couple of centuries. Now it revived almost with the force of the Apostles who had first spread the Gospel, or of the Scottish missionaries who later went into Africa and found, if only after much frustration, the right message, of salvation for natives with no previous inkling of it, and the right medium, the local vernacular. The result here in the Highlands was a spiritual hunger that created the intensity of religious life, now in the people rather than in the élite, and as a matter of evangelical exhibition rather than of quietist introspection.

The vernacular was the key. The use of Gaelic made religion comfortable to the people, if less so to an established Church dubious of a language balefully linked to barbarism and popery. The Kirk did use Gaelic, but still paid lip-service to the wishes of a Scottish state aiming to extirpate it. The state had reached for what turned out to be the feeble tool of education, a responsibility of the Kirk under the act of 1616 requiring it to set up a school in every parish. But its educational policy became bedevilled by confusion between two issues, the provision of public instruction and the language of public instruction.

Provision in the Highlands remained poor. The General Assembly ordered an inquiry a few years after the act of 1696 and found a single school in Sutherland, two in Caithness and not many more in Argyll, where Presbyterianism had strong roots. Even places with a school replied that their needs had not been met, since, given the size of Highland parishes, there were large areas where children could not get to it. The Church had no authority to provide anything beyond the minimum of one school in each parish. The General Assembly of 1704 responded by calling for subscriptions from 'gentlemen and other charitably inclined persons within their paroches'. The aim was to set up so-called charity schools. The label did not sound patronizing to contemporary ears but defined schools to all intents and purposes like those in the national system, but financed by different means: private donations, legacies and the like.[21]

The Kirk lacked the powers to offer firmer leadership and preferred giving a sanction to external efforts. For example, a Society for the Reformation of Manners had been formed in 1699 by a circle of Presbyterians in Edinburgh who, as their chosen name suggests, were concerned generally with morals public and private. Beside hoping for mutual self-improvement through discussion, they sought ways to stop Scots swearing in the street or picking fights in pubs, the sort of thing the Scottish Parliament is still trying to ban three centuries later. They also took an interest in education. They went so far as to aid what seems to have been the first charity school, in the Catholic area of Abertarff in Inverness-shire. They received an appeal from its teacher, Daniel Cameron, 'who has begun a school amongst the Wild Highlanders for teaching the English language. These letters contain very comfortable accounts of the wonderful success thereof. All present subscribed to give what everyone thought fitting towards the encouragement of the undertaking.' Here was a model that might be extended on a greater scale.[22]

These reformers of manners came into contact with James Kirkwood, now retired to East Lothian, the Episcopalian minister who two decades earlier had imported the left-over stock of Bedell's Bible from Ireland in a vain attempt to evangelize the Highlands. This also brought the Presbyterians up against the linguistic question, for Kirkwood had never ceased to argue two points. His first was that the Bible should be made available to Gaels in their mother tongue – so as to follow, apart from anything else, a basic principle of the Reformation. If in Scotland it was to be defended from a papist, rebellious Gàidhealtachd, reformers of manners ought to recall the reproach against Rome that it had enforced use of the Vulgate and burned biblical translators. Kirkwood was still trying to arrange for another printing of Bedell's Bible as revised by his long-dead colleague Robert Kirk, but got nowhere because of Presbyterian suspicions of a couple of Episcopalians. Kirkwood's second point was that Gaels had to be made literate in their own language before evangelization of the Highlands could succeed. It was unchristian, indeed impractical, to place a higher, political priority on extirpating Gaelic: Christianity would work faster than the English language to end Highland barbarism.

Kirkwood also had advice on provision of schools. He was Scottish corresponding member of the Society for Propagating Christian Knowledge, recently founded in England. In 1705 he proposed an equivalent for his own country. It was set up in 1709, after much toing and froing to win what was reckoned the essential approval of the General Assembly and establish the society's loyal, orthodox credentials. The aim was the 'the further promoting of Christian Knowledge and the increase of piety and virtue within Scotland, especially in the Highlands, Islands and remote corners thereof, where error, idolatry, superstition and ignorance do mostly abound, by reason of the large- ness of parishes and scarcity of schools'.[23] The foundation of charity schools in the Highlands became the principal activity of this Society in Scotland for Propagating Christian Knowledge.

Kirkwood was one of the inaugural directors of the society, a tribute to his untiring efforts and to his influence even with Prebyterians – although as an Episcopalian he had, of course, no standing in the deliberations of the General Assembly. Little time remained to him, unfortunately, to carry his work forward. By April 1710 he was dead, and that month his fellow direc- tors took delivery of a collection of books he left them. All the same, they spurned his advice on linguistic policy. Having gone to such lengths to keep on the right side of the Kirk, they were unlikely to query its leaders' political prejudice against Gaelic. Those leaders had ever since 1690 remained indifferent or hostile to circulation of the Irish Bible and done nothing to encourage translation and publication of Gaelic scriptures. There is no sign in the society's minutes of directors dissenting from the view that charity schools in the Highlands should teach English alone – in other words, that anglicization ought to be the first aim of the education they provided.

So without Kirkwood the society acquiesced in the official hostility to Gaelic. In 1713 it ruled that the children in its schools should not be taught to read their own language. For good measure, all the masters it employed were to subscribe to a formula against popery and to undertake to 'dis- charge their scholars to speak Erse', even though most children would come into the schools able to speak Gaelic only. The society flourished all the same: by 1715 it had set up twenty-five schools in the north (one of the first was on St Kilda). By 1750 it was running 150 schools and by 1800 more than 300, but it missed a crucial opportunity to transform Gaelic cul- ture into a literate modern culture: bad for Gaelic, yet not good for the religious establishment either. For a long time yet, ministers had to preach in Gaelic just so that their flocks could understand them, but the rising generation, as taught in school, was expected to associate Christianity with English. As a matter of fact, many still did not. This contributed to two lasting effects which eventually clashed: weakness in an established Presbyterianism unable to enforce its linguistic policy, and the vigour of popular religion in its vernacular intensity.[24]

Of this intensity there can be no doubt. It is illustrated, for example, by the case of Mary MacPherson, Bean Torra Dhamh. She was born in 1740 at Laggan in Badenoch, the daughter of the schoolmaster, who probably taught first in a charity school, then in the parochial school. He gave her a good education in both Gaelic and English; in the one she was to compose vibrant verse and in the other plain, pellucid prose. She married and had children, but the family was poor: her husband worked a barren smallholding above Glen Truim. As a young woman she loved music and dancing, until one day she fell and broke her leg. 'I have been of a very bad and wicked disposition,' she wrote, 'therefore, the Lord was obliged to break my leg, which was the first means of bringing me to think of my sinful and lost condition.' The fracture did not set well and for the rest of her days she had to hobble about on crutches or sticks.

Mary MacPherson's affliction converted her to orthodox Calvinism. This must have happened before 1785, for her autobiographical hymn *M'anam, imich thusa sàmhach* ('O my soul, go quietly on') was published then. The gift of poetry also came to her first in English, but her husband persuaded her to switch to Gaelic, which he and his neighbours better understood. For inspiration she searched the scriptures, 'browsing in the Bible in the hope of finding mouthfuls of comforting mercy'. She found them, for example, in Isaiah 54: 7–8, where God says: 'For a small moment have I forsaken thee, but with great mercies will I gather thee. In a little wrath I hid my face from thee for a moment, but with everlasting kindness will I have mercy on thee.' Her poems primarily present this religious experience of passing through pain to gladness. They may have struck such a chord with Gaels because they drew on conventions of the older poetry familiar to them, whether of love, praise or remembrance. Mary MacPherson addresses God with the same devotion as a bard might laud his chief or with the same ardour as a swain might sing to his sweetheart, and finds in her rapture a relief from suffering.

Mary's husband died young, and her children left home. She lived in poverty but was borne up by her faith and by a traditional Highland community cherishing and supporting her. She never complained. Anecdotes stress her joy:

> The catechist of the parish, while on his way to church on a Sabbath morning, heard unusual sounds as he approached her door, as of the quick movement of her crutches. On going in he found her as on other occasions, but

before he left she reluctantly confessed that though it was the Lord's Day, her soul was so happy in the overflowing fulness of the Lord's mercy and love to her that she had been enjoying a dance all by herself. She was really imitating David dancing before the Ark.

The most famous anecdote is of her answer when asked, with communions due to take place at Laggan, how many visitors she could put up. '*Tha sabhal agam a chumadh fichead agus cridhe a chumadh ceud*', she said; 'I have a barn that would hold twenty and a heart that would hold a hundred.'[25]

6

Run, you cowardly Italian
The Jacobite Rising of 1745

A T THE BATTLE of Culloden, on 16 April 1746, Prince Charles Edward Stewart felt sure right up to the final rout that a Highland charge would carry the day for him. When the clansmen attempted this and were brought rather to a halt, then forced to flee for their lives from the fire of the duke of Cumberland's artillery, as from the encircling movements of his cavalry, the prince burst into tears. He rode among his soldiers and sought to rally them for a last, defiant stand, but his aides insisted on his leaving the field. One seized his bridle, and a detachment of lifeguards led him away. Their commander, Lord Elcho, shouted after him: 'Run, you cowardly Italian'.[1]

In flight a few Jacobite units still held together. These had the best chance of making good their escape if they headed south and crossed the River Nairn into the hills beyond. Those running west towards Inverness, a mile or two away, survived only by luck or fleetness of foot. They jostled with terrified townsfolk who had come out to view the battle, and all fled pell-mell from Cumberland's horsemen. The road was soon littered with corpses, of rebel soldiers and of civilian men, women and children. Even after reaching Inverness the dragoons killed some fugitives. Behind them the royal infantry crossed Drummossie Moor, the bleak stretch above Culloden House where the actual fighting took place. With a roar of triumph they grounded arms where the Jacobite army had been arrayed that morning.

Not a year had passed since Charles conquered Scotland by dint of walking to Edinburgh from Glenfinnan, where he first raised his standard. While the British government's incompetence made that easier for him, it was still a remarkable feat. On his arrival in July 1745 Scots did not feel pleased to see him. He came with seven companions and none of the foreign forces or arms that might have given his rising a prospect of success. He was obliged to find everything from scratch in Scotland, and in a Scotland that had been at peace, more or less, for thirty years. The prince ignored all this and simply demanded unconditional obedience of known

Jacobites; he assured them that any Hanoverian army sent against him would run away. It says much for his force of character that his appeal proved so irresistible. But if, right at the outset, he had not won over a couple of crucial figures, such as Donald, the Gentle Lochiel, chief of Clan Cameron, Charles would have had to turn round and go back to France.

It is piquant to look at the different response the prince received, at a distance, from the leaders Scottish Jacobitism had thrown up before the '45 – the two wicked old men and one wicked young man who had been conspiring with the French to restore the Stewarts. General European war was brewing and they calculated that, while the Hanoverians faced it, a Scottish insurrection would have more chance. The two wicked old men were Simon Fraser, Lord Lovat, and Sir James Erskine, brother of the earl of Mar, leader of the '15; Erskine bore, as a Senator of the College of Justice, the title of Lord Grange. The wicked young man was Norman MacLeod of MacLeod.

Grange, 'a good lawyer, a ready and forcible speaker', made an unlikely Jacobite. He had served in the General Assembly of the Kirk and he believed in witches, the hallmark of an orthodox Presbyterian. Another such hallmark is hypocrisy: people said Grange was a secret libertine. He himself stayed out of the '15, then set about recovering the forfeited estates of Mar. He latched on to the duke of Argyll's political machine by truckling to Lord Ilay, the duke's brother and electoral manager. Holding out hopes of full pardon, Ilay got leave for Grange to buy back the estates on behalf of his nephew, Mar's eldest son, Thomas, Lord Erskine. Their affairs remained tangled. In 1728 Erskine asked Grange to save his lunatic mother from being taken into legal custody by her sister Lady Mary Wortley Montagu, as this would cost a penniless Mar her annual jointure of £1000. Grange kidnapped Lady Mar and set off with her for Scotland, to be stopped on the way by Lady Mary brandishing a warrant from the Lord Chief Justice of England. Grange had more luck with his harridan of a wife, whom he abducted in 1732 and cast away on St Kilda. By then Mar was dead and Grange had given up on Ilay's promises of reversing the attainder on the family. For the general election of 1734 Grange joined the opposition. After resigning his gown, he won election in Clackmannanshire, but the new Parliament saw Argyll, under Sir Robert Walpole, at the height of his power. Opposition was frustrated, and Jacobite plotting a product of this frustration. In June 1745 Grange told the Old Pretender that, with the government divided and its army abroad, 'there never was and never can be such a favourable opportunity to attempt your Majesty's restoration'. Yet when he heard that the Young Pretender, tired of the dilatory French, might come to Scotland alone, Grange thought it 'very weak and rash' and forecast that 'some great misfortune will ensue'. He stayed in London through the rebellion, in close touch with English Jacobites. Afterwards he went straight over to the government.[2]

MacLeod of MacLeod had seemed one of the most committed to Prince Charles when, by the autumn of 1744, it appeared he might have to risk a rising without foreign help. In anxious conclaves of Scottish Jacobites MacLeod stood out as one chief ready to raise his clan come what way. Indeed he had authority from the prince to rally others. In May 1745 he already knew of Charles's impending arrival, and posted watchmen to await signals from his French ships. But MacLeod was a double agent. In June he wrote to Duncan Forbes of Culloden, Lord President of the Court of Session and the government's factotum in the north, with rumours of Charles's approach: the watchmen were in Hanoverian pay. When the prince did land in July, he sent for MacLeod, who played for time and asked if 'the Prince had a power signed by the King his father'. Charles said he did, and bade loyal subjects of James VIII and III to follow him. MacLeod told Forbes that he and Sir Alexander MacDonald of Sleat 'not only gave no sort of countenance to these people, but we used all the interest we had with our neighbours to follow the same prudent method; and I am persuaded we have done it with that success that not one man of any consequence benorth the Grampians will give any sort of assistance to this mad rebellious attempt'. Later, as other chiefs did join the rising, MacDonald added on behalf of MacLeod and himself: 'You may believe, my Lord, our spirits are in a good deal of agitation and that we are much at a loss how to behave in so extraordinary an occurrence. That we will have no connection with these madmen is certain, but are bewildered in every other respect.'[3]

Not until after the Battle of Prestonpans, on 21 September, which was by a Highland charge and secured Jacobite control of Edinburgh, did the second wicked old man come into the picture. The prince gathered forces to invade England. He sent again to MacLeod, and to Lovat. The latter had for two decades been trying to ingratiate himself with the regime of Argyll, who would not touch him with a bargepole. Not much changed when the duke died in 1743 and Ilay succeeded him. Out of desperation Lovat entered into Jacobite plots, but even so he was nowhere to be seen when the prince landed. His intentions remained obscure, if suspicious. His son the Master of Lovat was said to be straining at the leash to join the rebels; this would be unlikely without the countenance of his father, a notorious domestic tyrant.

To stop the Frasers coming out, Forbes thought to use MacLeod. He, still professing eagerness to rebel, met Lovat and got him to agree it would be marvellous if their two clans marched south together. Nothing happened, however, and Lovat could only wait and remind MacLeod of his engagements. Meanwhile, Lovat's demeanour gave such grounds for distrust that in December the royal commander at Inverness, John Campbell, earl of Loudoun, arrested him. A provocative move looked foolish when Lovat escaped to his most inaccessible castle, Gorthleck, and called out his clan. MacLeod had no further reason to sail under false colours: he raised 400 men of his own and attacked the Jacobites of Aberdeenshire, to be repelled by them at Inverurie. He sat out the rest of the rebellion on Skye, until the result at Culloden prompted him to steal the cattle and burn the houses of his insurgent neighbours. So, of those earlier Scottish Jacobite leaders, the wicked young man betrayed the cause, while one wicked old man played safe and the other had nobody but himself to blame for conduct that took him to the scaffold in 1747.

None of this deterred Charles while he held glittering court that autumn at the Palace of Holyroodhouse. By October he felt ready to move on, and in December he had got as far as Derby. Then he turned back, much against his will, because his generals feared his army would be encircled and annihilated. It made a fighting retreat to the Highlands, where the prince hoped against hope to hold out until French help came. From 1 February 1746 he was in or about Inverness, a burgh less than ardently Jacobite. Until the last moment Forbes had stayed on at his nearby seat of Culloden working, not without success, to keep the district loyal. He made off just before the rebels arrived and, with Loudoun, led the garrison of Inverness to the north, where a pursuing force chased them round and round. Meanwhile Charles disposed more of his units to guard approaches to his Highland fastness. He had some reduce forts in the Great Glen. He had others seize Atholl, gateway to the high passes over the Cairngorm mountains. He left the easy road to Inverness, from Aberdeen 100 miles away, ill guarded, yet it was from there that Cumberland struck in April, against next to no opposition. The Jacobites were caught unawares, and had to make frantic efforts to concentrate their forces. Cumberland's 9000 redcoats reached Nairn, just 15 miles distant, by the time the rebels were ready to offer battle, and then with an army still under strength. While in theory they mustered 5000 men, it seems doubtful if that number fought at Culloden.

There, for the first time, the prince assumed personal military command of his forces, after the last of many volcanic rows with his best general, Lord

George Murray. Murray was a professional soldier and the prince an ama-
teur; Murray was also a shrewd judge of men and events, while the prince
was neither. So Murray often assumed the unpleasant but necessary duty
of telling the prince things he did not want to hear. It had made for
worsening relations between them. Now Murray told the prince he was
making a bad choice of battlefield on Drummossie Moor: there 'could
never be more improper ground for Highlanders'. Flat and boggy, it would
favour the enemy's superior cavalry and artillery. When Murray could not
get his way as commander of the army, he demoted himself to take charge
of the Atholl brigade.

Charles planned to fight on 15 April. He then drew up every available
soldier on the moor. But 15 April was also Cumberland's birthday. He gave
his redcoats a rest at Nairn, and paid out of his own pocket an issue of rum
to them. When Jacobite officers found out about this, they urged the
prince to surprise the duke and fall on his camp the next dawn, when his
troops would be asleep or still drunk. Although the capable Murray led the
Jacobites for the last time, their assault dissolved in confusion. Many were
fatigued after forced marches from other parts of the Highlands. They had
slept in the open the previous night. None had eaten more than a biscuit
handed out at noon, for by now supplies had more or less broken down.
The clansmen were too exhausted to march a dozen miles over rough
country in freezing darkness. Just before sunrise Murray realized that not
enough of them had kept up with him even to launch an attack, and he
called it off. The effort was still costly. Large numbers dropped out to sleep
by the wayside or set off for Inverness in desperate search of food, and were
to take no part in the real battle. So the Jacobites may have been four or
five regiments short on the field of Culloden, although other reinforcements arrived during the morning.

The remainder returned to Drummossie Moor by nine o'clock on 16
April. Charles summoned provisions from Inverness, under threat of burning the town. He meant to give his men food and sleep before fighting the
next day. But word came that Cumberland was on the march towards them
with his hungover troops. The Jacobites had no choice but to face him
dog-tired and starving. By mid-morning, cold and misty with rain and hail
coming on, the two armies were drawn up, their closest units 500 yards
apart. The royal army's left and the Jacobites' right each rested on a tall drystone dyke walling an enclosure of the estate belonging to Culloden
House. Cumberland marshalled his regiments in three lines, while Charles
marshalled his in two, with cavalry at the rear. The lines did not run in parallel. The Jacobite left was about 300 yards further from the enemy than

the right. The prince may have selected this set-piece array from his experience of wars on the Continent, but in their campaign under him the clansmen had never waited for the enemy to come to them, and never been asked to withstand a barrage of artillery.

Battle opened with an exchange of cannon fire soon after eleven o'clock. Jacobite artillery was always something of an embarrassment, and it soon fell silent. Cumberland had sixteen guns placed in between battalions of his first and second line. They blasted away to devastating effect. Packed together on a narrow field, the clansmen's ranks were shredded. A couple of cannon also aimed at Charles, mounted on a horse behind them, and forced him to move to a safer position. His soldiers grew furious as comrades fell in swathes around them, and they had again and again to reform their lines over dismembered corpses. As the bombardment went on, it seemed possible their army could be annihilated at long distance. The sole realistic option now was the Highland charge, but the prince held off from ordering it because he was trying to direct one regiment round to the rear of the royal army. He wanted to await its attack and exploit the confusion it would sow. Nothing came of this.

Cumberland read the situation better and anticipated the charge. He ordered his infantry to level their muskets. He instructed his artillery to switch from roundshot to grape. In his one attacking move of the engagement he sent his cavalry into the walled enclosure on the Jacobites' flank. These had not enough men to guard it, and dragoons soon penetrated along the entire length of their right. Riflemen took up position behind the drystone dyke. Under its cover the horse made for the rear of the Highland army and set about harrying it.

The clans were raising shouts of 'Claymore!', the old clamour for a charge. Colonels sent messages to the prince, who now had no overview of the field, asking him to give the order. When at last he did, delay still followed because every one of his couriers back to the colonels was killed. In the end a senior officer had to carry the order all round by himself.

But Jacobite discipline was collapsing. Out of desperation Mackintoshes in the centre had already rushed forward. When the prince's order came, they were followed by Frasers, Stewarts and Camerons, and by Murray's Atholl brigade on the right. On the left the MacDonalds, already practically mutinous because the Murrays had been stationed in their age-old place of honour in the line, found they had furthest to go; in the event they failed to reach the enemy. They still made an awesome spectacle. An English soldier, Alexander Taylor of the Royals, said 'they came running like troops of hungry wolves'. This was the Highland charge, which had swept all before it since the Wars of the Three Kingdoms, and for a century given the clansmen military superiority over any other force in the British Isles. At Culloden that superiority was about to be broken for ever.

The fire from Cumberland's army now grew so terrible that it forced oncoming clans in the centre to change direction. They veered to their right and squeezed the Atholl regiments against the dyke, under the guns of the riflemen posted there. Facing murderous volleys from both front and flank, Murray's soldiers performed a miracle to come to grips with the redcoats at all. They got to the first line and, hacking with their claymores, burst in among two regiments, yet these did not break. They bulged backwards, until the attackers came up against the second line. There the duke's troops used the tactic he had taught them, the decisive answer to the Highland charge. Each soldier, instead of thrusting his bayonet towards the clansman coming straight at him, was ordered instead to stab at the one to his right. That Highlander would be holding his sword arm aloft, claymore in hand, ready to strike down his enemy. Before he could do so, he would find a bayonet of the British army in his breast. The tactic required these regular soldiers to discipline themselves against their instinct, but they were well trained and it worked. The Atholl brigade was butchered, and lost half its officers and men. It had no choice but to fall back. Lord George Murray was among the last to leave the mêlée.

This was the climax of Culloden. The rest of the Highland charge petered out under the relentless barrage. In no man's land heaps of dead and wounded Jacobites mounted. Those still living had, in the tradition of the charge, thrown away their firearms for close combat with claymore and targe. Now, helpless and enraged, some just stood and hurled stones. Others made feints in desperate efforts to draw the redcoats forward. These, resisting all temptation to break rank, kept shooting. The moor became a killing field, and the Jacobites started to run.

The royal cavalry cut in on both flanks and almost surrounded the defeated Highlanders, slaughtering disarmed or wounded men without mercy. A few units held steady. At heavy cost Charles's cavalry and a couple of mercenary regiments from France, mostly of Irishmen, made heroic efforts to screen the fleeing clans. Two Jacobite commanders, Alexander MacDonald of Keppoch and Lord Strathallan, died in vain counter-attacks. A rout began, followed by butchery on the road to the west.

Cumberland, sword bare in his hand after the custom of victors, entered Inverness that afternoon. He took formal surrender of the French regiments and promised to treat them as prisoners of war. He received also the keys of the town and of the tolbooth, from which he released captive royal soldiers. With churches ringing their bells, he went to the home in Church Street of a beautiful and notorious Jacobite lady, Anne Mackintosh, who had won the nickname of Colonel Anne because she called out her clan for the prince. (Her husband was an officer in the Black Watch on the other side.) Cumberland meant to pass the night at her house, in a bed where Charles had been the last to sleep.

The prince spent that night at Gorthleck with Lovat, who could offer no aid or comfort and advised him to abandon Scotland. Next day he set off westwards by way of Fort Augustus and Invergarry to South Uist, where he waited for a French ship to take him off. Enforced seclusion after such tumult might have been idyllic, except that the ship did not turn up. Charles's pursuers would soon learn of his whereabouts and force him to move on, but for one reason and another all attempts to catch him failed.

Before leaving Gorthleck the prince received a letter from Lord George Murray, who had escaped Culloden and mustered a Jacobite remnant of about 1500 men at Ruthven, a fort on the upper reaches of the River Spey. He reproached Charles with all the errors that had led to the final disaster. Several chiefs remained even yet ready to fight on, but the prince's reply told every man to seek his own safety. The Jacobite rebellion was over.

Even if Charles had been taken, he would have suffered a less cruel fate than those he left behind. On Drummossie Moor a thousand corpses lay, beside many wounded clansmen, some of whom stayed there through three nights of bitter cold and rain. Cumberland ordered them to be sought out. He ended his message with: 'The officers and men will take notice that the public orders of the rebels was to give us no quarters.' Historians have verified that the paper purporting to give such orders was forged, but the troops understood what the duke meant. They acted as his execution-ers. On the moor stood several rough byres where the wounded found refuge. Redcoats surrounded three of them, secured the doors and set light to the thatch, with clansmen still inside. Mrs David Taylor of Inverness came across one while out searching for her brother-in-law, a Jacobite sol-dier. She said: 'I saw in the rubbish the bodies of several of those who had been scorched in a most miserable, mangled way.' Thomas Stewart, Forbes's secretary at Culloden House, testified that nineteen wounded Jacobite officers were shot against a wall of the park. The grieve, William Rose, said that from his house another twelve men were taken away on a promise of getting medical help, then killed near by.[4]

The treatment of these survivors from Culloden set a pattern for Cumberland's pacification of Highlanders no longer able to resist him. After giving his troops a rest he marched down the Great Glen to Fort

Augustus. On arrival there at the end of May he found the fort wrecked, thanks to Jacobites who had overwhelmed its Hanoverian garrison two months earlier. Parts of it were blown up, the rest burned. One gruesome discovery by the duke's soldiers as they poked around was a dozen bodies in a cistern, the decayed corpses of captured comrades who had been drowned in it. From Cumberland's point of view, however, such incidents put his army in the right frame of mind for its job here in the heart of enemy territory. He meant to show 'that it is as much in his Majesty's power to march his force into that country which they have hitherto boasted as inaccessible as into any other part of his dominions'. The isolation of the Highlands had to be broken too.[5]

Jacobite bands remained at large. Even from Fort Augustus they could be spotted roving the hills. It was time to put a stop to all this. In Inverness, Cumberland had listened to Forbes, who sought to preserve the rule of law and avoid punishing the innocent with the guilty. There were rules he wanted followed. Chiefs had to answer for their conduct, but clansmen, if they handed over their arms and could show they had played no leading part as rebels, were allowed to return home with a warrant of their innocence and immunity from punishment. 'Unnecessary severities create pity,' Forbes lectured Cumberland, 'and pity from unnecessary severities is the most dangerous nurse to disaffection, especially if continued for any time.' The duke found this guidance irksome. Behind his back he called the judge 'that old woman who talked to me of humanity'. One day he burst out to his face: 'The laws, my lord! I'll make a brigade give laws!' At Fort Augustus, Cumberland was rid of Forbes and had no moral leash to strain at. He would 'pursue and hunt out these vermin among their lurking holes': break the chiefs' power, waste their lands and seize or destroy all means of life on them.[6]

His campaign is legendary for its atrocities, and has earned him immortality as Butcher Cumberland. He had trapped rebels still in arms within two cordons, a military one down the Great Glen and a naval one in the Minches, patrolled by a royal flotilla. The mountains between were pierced by lesser glens leading into their fastnesses. Brigadier John Mordaunt started at the northern end of this zone by marching 900 volunteers from Inverness along the Beauly Firth, among the Frasers, 'to destroy all the rebels he finds there'. He burned everything. Inland lay Strathglass, full of Catholics and so to be harried with special zeal. The man with this job was a Lowlander, Major William Lockhart, a brute who, far from controlling his soldiers, set them the worst example. He let clansmen be murdered in cold blood, despite having warrants of immunity, and their women be raped. They all soon learned to run straight up the nearest brae if a platoon approached. In Glen Cannich a farmer's wife in panic left her baby in the house. Soldiers entered, and one came out with the infant spitted on his sword.[7]

On 28 May Lockhart led the first big raid out of Fort Augustus. With 180 volunteers he headed into Glenmoriston. The people were Grants, helpless to resist him because most of their able-bodied men had either died or been captured at Culloden. On the descent into the glen the soldiers met three clansmen, whom Lockhart had shot without further ado, before throwing their bodies over horses for a later purpose. The first township they reached was Dundreggan, where they began to corral the cattle to drive away. The tacksman came up with his warrant of immunity. 'If you were to show me a warrant from heaven,' said Lockhart, 'it would not hinder me.' While his troops set fire to the tacksman's house, Lockhart ordered him to be stripped and led to a tree, to be hanged high with the corpses of his three tenants, as a lesson to all. His wife was stripped, too, of everything but her rings, which the raiders wanted to steal as well. Unable to pull them from her, they drew their swords to sever her fingers, but she managed to get them off herself. The tacksman already had a noose around his neck, and was about to be strung up when one of Lockhart's officers, also of the name of Grant, felt the call of his blood. He stepped forward with a hand on the hilt of his sword, and told the major to halt or answer to him. Lockhart shrugged his shoulders, ordered his soldiers into column again and marched them on up the glen. The brief check to him might as well never have happened: they continued to burn, rape and kill.

South of Fort Augustus three long lochs ran west deep into the hills: Loch Garry, Loch Arkaig and Loch Eil. Lord George Sackville took a force along the first, Colonel Edward Cornwallis led another by the second and Captain Caroline Scott had to deal with the area round the third. They were to rendezvous, after finishing their work, on the Atlantic coast. Of these the most brutal was neither of the Englishmen but again the Lowlander, Scott. He had held Fort William against the rebels and took this chance to strike back. He led raids on the lands of two Jacobites: Alexander MacDonald of Keppoch, fallen at Culloden, and Charles Stewart of Ardshiel, a survivor of that field who left eight of his family dead there. Now Stewart skulked in a cave behind a waterfall on the hill at the back of his home by Loch Linnhe, so, unknown to Scott, he saw all that went on below.

Stewart's house was one of the loveliest in the west, a fine stone-built mansion amid budding orchards. Scott demanded the keys from Lady

Ardshiel, not just of the house but also the 'little keys', to open its charter-chest. When she handed them over, he took her to the door and told her to go, for now nothing here belonged to her or her husband. Then he had the place gutted. He had all the Scotch slates, mined up the road at Ballachulish, lifted from the roof. He had the timber taken from the frames, the nails pulled out and straightened. He had the walls levelled, setting aside the valuable moulded architraves and lugs. He had each tree felled. He had the stones of the house scattered, and everything else loaded on carts to be carried away and sold. The House of Ardshiel vanished.[8]

Scott went on to Keppoch. He began by hanging, with the ropes of a salmon-net, three unlucky fellows he happened to meet on their way to surrender their arms. When the raiders neared, clansmen opened fire and held them up long enough for Lady Keppoch to flee to the hills with her new-born baby. But as resistance it was a token: soon troops got through and left her house a smoking ruin. Not that submission would have helped. Scott headed another patrol up Glen Nevis, peopled by Camerons, a strongly Jacobite clan, but the tacksman here had stayed home in the rising, even though two of his brothers joined it: one now dead, the other a pris-oner. Still, to be on the safe side, he surrendered to General John Campbell of Mamore, commander of the duke of Argyll's militia, so his tenants felt they had nothing to fear when Scott came. The first the redcoats met did not even run. They were seized, bound and led to a tree. As the knots of the noose tightened beneath their ears they still did not understand what was to happen to them. That would do, they said, the joke had gone far enough. Not until they swung did they know this was their death. The rest of the people fled up the glen and hid in caves, leaving the troops to burn the houses, fire in the air and shout obscenities that echoed off the hills.[9]

While little Jacobites, or even non-Jacobites, stayed and suffered, most big Jacobites kept a jump ahead of their pursuers. Prince Charles himself was still at large: he had in June crossed back to Skye dressed as Betty Burke, maid to Flora MacDonald. A month later Flora was in custody and Charles again on the mainland somewhere, while John MacGinnis, the old boat-man who had carried him there, was caught and flogged; but MacGinnis would reveal – and probably knew – nothing. The one important catch of these weeks was Fraser of Lovat, taken prisoner on an islet in Loch Morar, remote but leaving him no escape when cornered.

Seaborne operations were carried out by a fierce, wiry little Aberdonian, John Fergusson, captain of HMS *Furnace* in the Hanoverian flotilla. Although he never did find the prince, he stopped at nothing in the attempt. He searched as far as St Kilda. At sight of his sails the wretched islanders took to caves in the cliffs, weeping and wailing. Once a few were enticed into the open, and their Gaelic could be translated, it turned out they knew nothing even of King George II, let alone of the prince who had tried to snatch his throne. So Fergusson was in an ugly mood when he sailed back to Eigg, where the people were of Clanranald, to look for a fugitive kinsman of their chief, John MacDonald. They had already surrendered some arms and got certificates for them, but as Fergusson searched he found more. He threatened to burn every house unless they satisfied him they were quite disarmed. MacDonald gave himself up, hoping to calm the captain down, but he was found to have on him a list of Eigg's active Jacobites. Fergusson shoved thirty-eight of them into his hold and kept them there for weeks, fed on pease-meal mixed with seawater or urine. His men went ashore, slaughtered cattle, pillaged crofts and, as usual, raped women. He meted out the same treatment on the islands of Barra, Mull, Rona and Raasay.[10]

With the navy at their backs, other forces swept inland. From Skye, where he had been on the day of Culloden, Loudoun returned towards Fort Augustus with orders to 'drive the cattle, burn the ploughs and destroy what you can belonging to all such as are or have been in the rebellion, and burning the houses of the chiefs'. His kinsman Campbell of Mamore marched on his flank by way of Sunart and Morvern. They still could not catch the prince, nor his closest followers. The clansmen's fidelity, when Charles had £30,000 on his head, was extraordinary. After surviving many perils he was eventually rescued in September by French ships from Loch nan Uamh, close to where he had first set foot on the mainland. But beyond a silent devotion to the prince the Gaels' resistance did not go. Otherwise, and strangely for such a warlike people, they submitted to their fate. Culloden had stunned them, and Cumberland made sure they would not recover quickly from the shock.

If officers such as Lockhart or Scott had been Gaels, someone would have taken revenge on them, as the clans' code demanded. But the sole Jacobite reprisal of 1746 struck a youth who was more or less a clansman himself, Alexander Grant of Knockando, commander of militia from his own loyal country in the Gaelic-speaking part of Moray. After burning out Camerons in Glen Spean he crossed Loch Lochy to Clunes, where he attacked the defenceless home of the fugitive tacksman, and stripped and robbed his wife and servants. Then he set off, in the footsteps of Colonel Cornwallis, on the drove-road running westwards by Loch Arkaig. Here at the Wood of Muich he met one MacOllonie, who offered to surrender arms lying at his feet. Grant asked why he had not done so before. He said that, when he had seen men killed whether they surrendered or not, he took his family to the hills. He may have thought it safe now to give himself up to a brother Gael, but no: he was tied to a tree and shot. Grant marched on to the rendezvous at the coast. His deed had, though, been witnessed by Camerons watching from the hillside, who saw it was ordered by an officer in a blue cloak on a white horse.

In Kintail, Grant met a friend, another young laird, George Munro of Culcairn. He, in a few days, marched back along Loch Arkaig with his men. The weather was foul, and he wore the blue cloak Grant had lent him; he was riding a white horse too. Where the road passed the scene of the murder, he saw a woman and boy standing in the rain, she with her plaid drawn over her head. Since neither ran, he halted to speak to them. A shot out of the wood killed him. In this terrain hot pursuit was impossible. The woman and boy, taken into custody, said they knew nothing. Troops searched for months. They heard that MacOllonie's father and brother, rebels both, had been skulking near by, but never caught them. Camerons in the glen did hand a man over: he had refused to join the rising, and in contempt for his cowardice they accused him of Grant's murder. It remained unsolved, however.[11]

One pity of the Highland disaster in 1746 was that, as Forbes feared, it overtook the innocent too. Clans had again hedged their bets. Until 1745 a rising star in the younger generation of chiefly families was Ewen Macpherson of Cluny, who grew rich on a racket purporting to protect neighbours from cattle raids. He would rather not have risked rebellion, and had actually accepted a commission from King George II when he was kidnapped by Camerons in August 1745: he felt it prudent to join up with the Jacobites. He did not arrive in time for Culloden, but later sheltered the fugitive Charles in the cave amid the mountains where he himself lived until he escaped to France.

Other families once more placed members on both sides. The almost comic case of Colonel Anne Mackintosh and her husband, Angus, with his commission in Loudoun's regiment, has already, been mentioned. Even Lord George Murray had a son on the other side. The earl of Airlie, out in the '15, lay low and put his clan under the command of his son the dashing David, Lord Ogilvy. The same course was followed by a chief in the wilder Highlands, MacDonald of Glengarry. And large areas took no part at all in this rebellion: Argyll and counties north of Inverness stayed loyal as always, and indeed raised militias for the government. Jacobitism was at the end more than ever confined to the central massif of Scotland, from landward Aberdeenshire to the western coast, split by the Great Glen. In that final fastness, too, some clans refused to rise. Chisholms of Strathglass, MacDonalds of Sleat, Mackenzies, Mackintoshes and Clan Chattan in general, MacLeods of Assynt and of Dunvegan had been all Jacobite once but were divided now. MacLeans of Ardgour and of Coll, MacNeills of Barra and MacRaes revolted in 1715 but not in 1745. Campbells of Glenorchy switched straight from Jacobite to Whig. Only Buchanans, Frasers of Lovat, MacLachlans, MacLeods of Raasay, MacNabs, and MacNeills of Gigha ventured support for Jacobitism where they had given none before and, of these, Frasers alone counted as an important clan.

Some contemporaries still thought they all deserved what they got, but the retribution meted out to them went beyond anything needed to control a defeated people. This is a matter of hot debate even today, and it is important to define what the victors' actions amounted to. Modern terms – ethnic cleansing and genocide – have been used by Professor Allan Macinnes of Aberdeen University.[12] If these terms are chosen to describe events rather than to rouse emotions, they must mean an intention to empty the Highlands of their people by extermination or expulsion. There was wild talk of extermination among cocky young officers of Cumberland's entourage, but the project looked more formidable in the cold light of morning than while the port was being passed. In reality, after the real fighting finished at Culloden, the numbers who died at the royal troops' hands ran into three figures but perhaps not into four. The population of the region ran into six figures, and three times over. The duke toyed with the idea of reducing those 300,000 by expulsion of whole clans to the colonies. The idea seems to have come from Forbes, possibly to guide Cumberland's mind along non-genocidal paths, yet surely in the knowledge that it was impracticable. When consulted by the government in London on what to do next, the duke did reply, without elaboration, 'that nothing but transplanting can succeed'.[13] A government, however, needs more than royal musings to make policy. It followed a clearer course: the Gaels were to stay but to be civilized, by force if necessary. Repression that could go the length of massacre was horrible. State terrorism, another of Macinnes's terms, is a fair enough way to portray policy in the summer of 1746, but it is still not the same as ethnic cleansing or genocide. Policies are seldom simple; nor was this one.

The initial ravages soon gave way to mere humiliations. A new Disarming Act passed at Westminster reinforced previous ones with stiffer penalties and stricter enforcement. Even so, it remained hard to disarm clansmen who did not want to be disarmed. The Disclothing Act, banning Highland dress, was an overreaction to the practice by Jacobites of fitting out their soldiers in tartan whatever their origin. These measures represented a contemporary form of political correctness which, like the modern counterpart, often left its enforcers looking ridiculous. The Scottish establishment scorned it, to judge from the fact that John Campbell, chief cashier of the Royal Bank of Scotland in Edinburgh, had a smug portrait of himself in Highland dress, complete with claymore and pistols, painted in 1749.

Beyond the ravages and humiliations a further price was paid, but in land rather than in blood. A political battle to set the price took place between the government and some of its most faithful servants in Scotland. Cumberland and other powerful Englishmen wanted to reduce Scotland to a conquered province, like Ireland, but this never happened. Forbes and his colleagues worked hard to make sure it did not. They at length persuaded the Hanoverian regime that good Scotsmen existed, and even good Highlanders with no wish to rebel. They succeeded because this happened to be the truth of the matter.

Scots still had to accept a price bigger than after the '15. Most of it was paid directly by Jacobites. They forfeited more property this time – forty-one estates in all – and the forfeitures met no defiance or subterfuge from the rest of the landed class. But a wider circle of Scots, loyal or disloyal, paid a price too. The British state concluded that certain legal forms sustaining power among the leaders of Scottish society could in the wrong hands become crucibles of rebellion. In the heritable jurisdictions, which made many Highland chieftains and some Lowland landowners at once lords and judges of their people, the British state had a point. All such Scots could at length be persuaded, for enough compensation, that heritable jurisdictions had to go. This was the most important result of the '45. Those affected made the best of it. They took the money and turned away to rejoice at the demise of Scottish feudalism as a mark of national progress.

It was assumed that the way then lay open to Highland improvement, although, in the sense of greater social stabilty and better pastoral agriculture, this had been going on since the Union and before. Whatever its immediate impact, the '45 did not alter the basic course of Scottish history. All the more pity, then, that the Highlanders suffered so much. They would actually have fared better if their fates had been shaped by impersonal economic forces, as in the Marxist theory beloved of Scottish historians. But their fates were shaped by Prince Charles, and by the compound in his character of heroism, humbug and harum-scarum. His intervention in Scotland proved purely destructive. He achieved nothing for himself or his dynasty; he wrought havoc in the society on which he descended; and he eliminated much of its leadership and ruined people's lives. Modernity had begun to touch the Highlands anyway. The question here, as in most European societies over the next century and more, was whether the changes forced by modernity would come with a greater or lesser degree of trauma. The Jacobites ensured it was a greater.

One widow of Culloden was Christiana Fergusson, whose husband, William Chisholm, served there as a standard-bearer. He killed sixteen enemies on the field and then, as calamity loomed, led his clan away, carrying aloft its banner adorned with a boar's head to guide the men as they sought refuge. They found a barn where, however, they were soon surrounded by redcoats. Chisholm guarded the door and held them off until some climbed on the roof and shot him in the back. Christiana wrote in his memory a fine song, *Mo Rùn Geal Òg* ('My Heart's Youthful Prize'), which begins:

> *Och a Theàrlaich òig Stiùbhart,*
> *Se do chùis rinn mo léireadh,*
> *Thug thu bhuam gach ni bh'agam*
> *Ann an cogadh 'nad adhbhar.*

> Oh young Charles Stewart,
> Your cause has destroyed me,
> You have taken all I possessed
> For fighting your war.[14]

7

Like so many infuriated demons
Highlanders in the empire, to 1776

'QUI VIVE? QUI vive? Qui vive? Qui vive?' Four times the French challenge rang out: 'Who goes there?' Each time the right response came
back out of the night: 'France, et vive le roi!' Quebec's sentries heaved a
sigh of relief and shouted to one another along the cliffs overlooking the
black waters of the St Lawrence river, 'Laissez-les passer, ils sont nos gens
avec les provisions' ('Let them pass, they're our people with the supplies').

These sentries were Canadian lads, sons of 80,000 Frenchmen who lived
by farming, by fishing or by harvesting the furs and timber of La Belle
Province. To the oldest of their families it had been home for 150 years,
so, during the global war now going on, they gladly joined up with the
militia to defend it, since the mother country could spare from its armies
only a small task force for Canada. Those regular troops, faintly effete in
their white uniforms, with pleasure resigned to scruffy locals the more
menial duties, such as night-watch. After this night, 13 September 1759,
they would rue it.[1]

There was already about the Canadian accent a drawling, rustic quality
that marked it out from the rat-a-tat of metropolitan French. Perhaps,
more to the point, there was also in it something not so different from the
Highland lilt. At any rate, the reassuring answer to the sentries' challenge
came not from one of their own but from Donald MacDonald, captain in
the 78th regiment of the British army, Fraser's Highlanders. He had been
a Jacobite and acquired his perfect French in exile after the Battle of
Culloden, before deciding it was time he reconciled himself to King
George II. MacDonald sat now in one of many boats, full of British soldiers, borne in silence along the St Lawrence, descending on doomed
Quebec. As it happened, that same night a French convoy of supplies was
awaited down from Montreal – a dangerous trip, for it meant slipping past
forty-nine British warships anchored in the river. This explained why the
Canadian sentries were so alert, but also why MacDonald was able to fool
them.

In the dark before dawn, right according to plan, the boats grated on gravel in what became known as Wolfe's Cove, after the commander of the operation, James Wolfe. Sitting near him was a young Scot, John Robison, one day to be professor of natural philosophy in the University of Edinburgh. He recorded how, as they nosed towards the shore, the melancholy general recited Grey's 'Elegy in a Country Churchyard', then said, 'Gentlemen, I would rather have written those lines than take Quebec'.[2]

It was the last moment for quiet thoughts. From now on it would be all action. Above the cove, the banks rose 200 feet. A first wave of 1800 troops landed with no opposition and scaled the slope. Not until they occupied the top did some Canadian sentries realize that there might be something amiss, something big.

These militiamen opened fire but were dispersed. They ran into Quebec to raise the alarm, giving Wolfe time to bring ashore the rest of his 4500 men. When the capital of New France awoke behind its walls, the red ranks of the British force were deployed a mile from its western gate, on the Plains of Abraham. Probably unknown to the Fraser's Highlanders, who now took their position in line of battle, the place owed its name to one of their nation: to its original owner, Abraham Martin, who, although born in France in 1589, bore the nickname of *l'Ecossais*, 'the Scot'.

Shocked and shamed by the turn of events, the French commander, the Marquis de Montcalm, rode out there in drizzling rain a couple of hours later, after a hasty reveille of his own forces. Until now he, they and the civilian colonists had felt confident and secure. For three months the British navy had blockaded the St Lawrence and even bombarded Quebec, but that made little difference when attempts at landing in strength could be repulsed. The French hoped to crouch behind their defences until another ferocious Canadian winter drove the enemy away.

The British could secure victory only by a full-scale enagagement, where the superiority of their regular soldiers would count. That was what Wolfe now succeeded in forcing on his opponent. Aiming his blow right at the heart of French Canada, he knocked its passive defences sideways. Outwitted and outgeneralled, Montcalm had no choice but to launch an immediate, desperate assault in the open field against a better army.

Even before Montcalm arrived, skirmishing broke out. The Canadian boys could not resist taking pot-shots at the British, who replied. Fire died down as Montcalm ranged his forces, similar in strength to Wolfe's, so as to incorporate a body of militia in every regular battalion. At about ten o'clock he ordered the advance. Ensigns unfurled the big silver colours of the fleur-de-lys; drums rolled out the charge; the soldiers cheered and started forward. It at once turned out that their general had made a grave error of judgment, for at a run their mixed formations, trained to different degrees, began to fall apart.

The British big guns tore the French with grapeshot, but the infantry-men stood impassive. Wolfe's orders were not to fire a shot until the enemy got within 40 yards of the point of their bayonets. Sergeants had put down white markers at that distance in front, and the disciplined soldiers awaited the word. When it came, they produced, according to legend, the most perfect volley ever fired on a battlefield, like a single cannon-shot. The enemy fell in a writhing, screaming mass. A second volley finished them off. Those still on their feet ran back towards the city; the moment had come for the Highlanders.

The men of the 78th, after the custom of the clans, now flung their mus-kets aside, drew their claymores and set off after the foe, 'like so many infu-riated demons'. The result was appalling to civilized people. Nothing like it had been seen in a clash of European armies since the Battle of Prestonpans in 1745, a shambles of cloven skulls and hewn limbs, mortal remains of soldiers who had no idea what hit them, while survivors were too shaken by the havoc to think of anything but safety. Fraser's shattered any French hopes of turning the tables. It was, in fact, here on the Plains of Abraham, rather than in Scotland, that the last victorious Highland charge took place. And symbolically it ensured some old ways of the clans, at least the martial values of use to the British state, would carry over into the new Highland era that had begun with the demise of Jacobitism.[3]

The 78th of 1759 was little different in character from any regiment that had gone south with Prince Charles in 1745. Its colonel, Simon Fraser of Lovat, was in fact a veteran of the last Jacobite rising, though he had been aged just nineteen at the time. He showed more sense than might be expected in one of such tender years and was by no means a creature of aristocratic reaction. Since people tend to become more conservative as they get older, it is notable that the final political act of his life was to vote in the City of Westminster for the great radical Charles James Fox at the general election of 1780.

Fraser had been propelled into rebellion by his appalling father, Lord Lovat. It was not that Lovat felt no love for his son, to whom he gave the affectionate nickname of The Brig (or Brigadier). It was just that the boy, like all other human beings, existed in Lovat's mind only to serve his own ambitions. He kept telling his heir he was 'absolutely under my command', and threatened to make him a cowherd on the estate if ever he disobeyed. Young Simon put up a brief show of defiance when it came home to him how much he was a mere pawn in his father's plots. As the rising took shape in Scotland, he tried to get away to Leiden in the Netherlands to study law. He was hauled back to be browbeaten into tearful submission. With that he seemed to resign himself to a role as scapegoat, raised the clan and set off to rendezvous with Prince Charles's army, by now in England. It is not certain if Fraser fought at Culloden, but he meant to. His regiment may have been one of those unable to concentrate there in time, or else his faithful clansmen later conspired to conceal the fact that he had been on the field.[4]

Fraser took to the heather but soon surrendered. At least Lovat's tyranny, which was widely known, saved his son's head. On release he resolved to be a good boy. He turned down the Pretender's offer of a regiment in the French service, having had enough of Jacobites. Instead he went to study law at Glasgow, and while there received a full pardon. After he qualified as an advocate in 1752, preferment came fast. That year he was taken on by the Crown in prosecution of the Appin murder. James Stewart of the Glens stood trial for killing Colin Campbell of Glenure, the government's factor on the forfeited estate of Ardshiel. Campbell had fallen to a sniper's bullet near the ferry at Ballachulish (the incident is used by Robert Louis Stevenson in *Kidnapped*). Against Stewart the evidence could only be circumstantial, but he must have sensed his doom as soon as he heard he would be tried on circuit at Inveraray, with the Lord Advocate leading for the pursuers, by three judges: Lords Elchies and Kilkerran and then Archibald, third duke of Argyll, in his capacity as Lord Justice General, usually an honorary office. It looked for all the world as if the Campbells' heritable jurisdiction had never been abolished, only disguised as Scottish justice. Stewart was hanged but, guilty or innocent, he had been the victim of a show trial.[5] Scotland as yet knew little of the random violence against authority by a disaffected peasantry that had emerged with the Houghers in Ireland, there destined to help in keeping nationalism alive. For now Scots Gaels had, if anything, more reason than Irish Gaels to resort to such a desperate but destructive tactic, which the authorities felt necessary to nip in the bud before it politicized the lower orders. When the arch-Whig MacChailein Mòr fitted the noose around the culprit's neck, the ex-Jacobite Fraser had to assist and show that men like him upheld the new Highland order.

With this feather in his cap Fraser presumed a little too much. He had done everything asked of him, and a less boisterous lad might have contented himself with rising in his profession. But – like father, like son – he was hard to deter from awkward ventures of his own. The government soon heard from him again when in 1753 he sought a parliamentary candidacy in Inverness-shire. He hoped to succeed the sitting MP, Norman MacLeod of MacLeod, who lived in Edinburgh because he had become too unpopular to visit his constituency and so was useless for any public purpose. MacLeod gave Fraser a hardly helpful blessing and wrote to the Secretary of State, the duke of Newcastle: 'I am most willing to yield in his favour, and really he has got it so much in his head that it will be a mean to make his fortune, that I shall be sorry if he's baulked.' But the alleged 'revival of Jacobite clanship' provoked horror at Westminster. Argyll, always on guard for his electoral control of Scotland, at once distanced himself. He wrote to the Prime Minister, Henry Pelham: 'I have lost no time in letting everybody know how much I abhor the measure, both for the sake of the young man and of the public; if he really intends to stand I think his head must be turned.' Argyll summoned Fraser to Inveraray to explain himself and found him eager to please:

> He then went on with the history of himself in such a manner as that I must have been void of common humanity not to be affected by it. I said what I could to comfort him but persisted in a positive negative to his standing, so that I take it for granted that affair is over.[6]

The government did not spurn Fraser's talents: it only wished him, for heaven's sake, to deploy them somewhere other than in politics. An alternative appeared when the Seven Years' War broke out in 1756. During the eighteenth century the British state grew into a gigantic war-making machine, its burgeoning commercial and imperial interests matched by a vast increase in military commitment and success overseas. Inside Britain this tightened the state's grip over civil society, giving rise to not altogether groundless protests against loss of liberty. It meant, too, that the war-making machine had to suck in unexploited resources from the periphery, without bothering much about their antecedents. At least for Scottish Highlanders the process was oratorically idealized by William Pitt the elder, who conducted the war and addressed the House of Commons after the peace:

> It is indifferent to me whether a man was rocked in his cradle on this side or that side of the Tweed. I looked for merit wherever it was to be found. It is my boast that I was the first Minister who looked for it, and I found it in the mountains of the North. I called it forth, and drew it into your service, a hardy and intrepid race of men.[7]

This fine speech marked a turning point in several respects. It set forth how all Britons could be united by a novel ideal of Empire. It pointed out to the English the advantage within that new dispensation of partnership with the Scots. And it began the rehabilitation of the Highlands. So far the policy of Scottish and British governments alike had been to transmute Gaelic society and culture from barbarity to civility, or, where that failed, as to some people it had clearly done by 1745, to destroy them. This now changed.

Some Highlanders, too, had been persuaded that the process of trans-mutation could work, notably the house of Argyll. Deep irony lay in the fact that the second duke, Red John of the Battles himself, attempted this transmutation in the military sphere. All he did was ruin the Campbells as the martial mainstay of Scots Whiggery, at a time when few other chiefs found it necessary or desirable to follow his lead. From 1710 in Kintyre and then from 1737 in the rest of his lands (on the advice of Duncan Forbes), MacChailein Mòr tore down the feudal structure that gave his clan its fighting force. He sought to sidestep the tacksmen, the chief tenants and gentry of Clan Campbell, who had always raised and led it in war. He did so by cutting them out of their intermediary economic role, which went together with the military one: a whole tier of the Highland hierarchy was to vanish.

In the old system the duke portioned out his territory to his kin, who, as tacksmen, rented it to tenants. In the new system these last would lease their farms directly from his factors, the managers and lawyers he employed. Argyll's main motive was no doubt financial. The service of his debts cost him more than the estate's entire rental, and now more of this would come straight to him. But his rents rose too high for poor peasants to pay, and the profit fell short of his hopes. Meanwhile, the military con-sequence was calamitous: Campbells had saved Calvinist Scotland in every conflict since the Reformation, yet in the '45 they did next to nothing, because their structure of command had been eliminated. The second duke was by then dead. The third duke, previously Lord Ilay, had already understood his brother's huge mistake and tried to reverse it. On succeed-ing to the title, he told his factors to select tenants according to their loy-alties rather than their pockets, but he was too late to rescue the Campbells' martial might in time for the last Jacobite rising.

Afterwards the duke of Argyll also decided in his own way – a different way from the duke of Cumberland's – that the old Highland society, if it could not be transmuted, had to be destroyed. This policy he devolved on his political manager, Andrew Fletcher, Lord Milton, nephew of Andrew Fletcher of Saltoun, the fiercest foe of the Union in the old Scots Parliament, who had won from his countrymen the fond epithet of The Patriot. Milton made his way in life, however, as handyman to the

Hanoverian duke. He now framed a plan to change Gaeldom for ever by radical social engineering. He meant to get rid not just of tacksmen but of chiefs too, thus dismantling the entire feudal hierarchy. He wanted most of the central Highlands to be taken into public ownership and administered by an official commission in Edinburgh (which he, of course, would run). This territory of the state would comprise not only forfeited lands but also any others in the rebellious region that the Crown might care to purchase.

Such an extension of public power at the expense of private property was startling to the mind of the eighteenth century even at its most auto-cratic. But Milton worked hard on Newcastle, who knew what sterling ser-vice he had given to the British government in clearing up the mess after the '45 and who proved not impervious to his lurid message. Milton said the chiefs, whose prosperity and security depended on the number of fighting men at their disposal, maintained control of the Gaels by keeping them in ignorance and poverty. This discouraged 'all attempts to introduce the knowledge of the Protestant religion and our happy constitution, and the true notions of husbandry, trade and manufacture'. Tacksmen had 'been successful instruments to keep the common people in slavery'; they also thought themselves 'of too high blood to stoop to trade and manu-facture'. The only freedom for the clansmen was, with the connivance of their chiefs, to indulge 'in thefts, rapines and all other villanies they can commit'. Not until the structure of Highland power had been recast could other measures, such as encouragement of industry, succeed. The key was the chiefs: 'so far as we can get rid of them, we ought'. Their lands 'should be purchased at the public expense, so far as they are not already forfeited, and vested in the Crown'. And if that seemed a little bold, Milton assured the duke, 'most of the proprietors would be not unwilling to sell them at a reasonable price, and the purchase money of these lands would be but a trifle in comparison of the sums that have, and probably must still be laid out to keep these parts of the Highlands in subjection'.[8]

In the stunned aftermath of rebellion this argument carried some weight, although it could not ultimately prevail amid the conditions of the age. Milton himself grew old, and the long wrangle between Edinburgh and London about what to do next in the Gàidhealtachd told against a simple but thoroughgoing solution. The eventual legislation on the forfeited estates, the Annexing Act of 1752, turned out a pale shadow of what he had wanted. But even their rejected policy brought out how far Argyll and Milton, two well-informed gentlemen charged with the practical conduct of affairs, thought clans and chieftains were still vital forces in the Highlands, which had to be deliberately done away with if the future was to turn out better than the past.

The Annexing Act applied to only thirteen of the original forty-one forfeited estates; most had meanwhile found buyers on the free market by whom their debts could be paid off. The remainder stretched from Stirling to Inverness, with outliers in the west and north. For more than three decades they were managed as a public enterprise, with a half-hearted purpose of making a profit out of them but a keener intention of instilling Hanoverian loyalty in their people. The unpaid commissioners who ran them were instructed to apply the rents to promoting 'the Protestant religion, good government, industry and manufactures, and the principles of duty and loyalty to His Majesty'.

Should a clinching argument be needed against the equation of Jacobitism with backwardness, it lies in the stagnation and decay of these estates under the Crown. They were meant to be models of development to the rest of the region, with their accumulated profits used for continuous development so that disaffection would be tackled at root. But their revenue never even covered the expenses of administration. A freeze on rents to foster loyalty removed one incentive for the natives to emulate hard-working, law-abiding, Lowland Presbyterians. After the Seven Years' War places such as Callander and Kinlochrannoch were seeded with settlements of old soldiers thought more promising, but they took on the habits of their neighbours, lolling about and tippling whisky; they also introduced venereal disease. The commissioners themselves seemed affected by Highland indolence. Their sluggish bureaucracy performed no better than any other absentees who let their lands run down and lose money. After a quarter of a century the mark of the annexed estates was their lack of agricultural improvement, let alone of industry and manufactures. Some good had been done by investment in roads and bridges, but the commissioner Lord Kames felt obliged to admit that the money spent in the Highlands was 'no better than water spilt on the ground'.[9]

If conventional wisdom about transmuting Highland society reached its limits on these estates, might there not be an alternative in accommodating and absorbing the values of the clans? This was surely the implication of Pitt's speech at the end of the war. Of course, his oratory clad a calculation. He thought recruitment of Gaels would serve two purposes, providing both a steady supply of soldiers for service overseas and a means to pacify a restive region by finding its young ruffians something useful to do. In other words, instead of demilitarizing the clans, as Red John of the Battles had tried with dire results, why not turn tribesmen into troopers for an imperial power?

To a limited extent it had already proved possible to employ the clans not for the rapine and pillage that marked their military service to their chiefs but for the public good. As far back as 1667 the earl of Atholl formed the first Highland independent company to police passes over the mountains. Other such companies appeared before the Union, then again afterwards, notably those formed by General George Wade to garrison the forts linked by the 260 miles of military roads he built in the 1720s. A decisive step came in 1739 with the reorganization and expansion of some older units into the Black Watch as a regiment of foot in the British army: the 43rd (later 42nd), known in Gaelic as Am Freiceadan Dubh after its tartan of the government's standard issue, a sombre pattern of blue, black and green, in contrast to the red coats of the Saighdearan Dearg, the regular infantry.[10]

This experiment had its troubles, most of them of the government's own making. The Black Watch, too, was formed for the specific purpose of policing the Highlands, as the soldiers' terms of enlistment told them. In 1743, with the sort of suave effrontery of which only the British establishment is capable, the 42nd was ordered to the West Indies. Before it even embarked, it mutinied. Of course, the mutiny was crushed, and three ringleaders died before a firing squad. Even their officers felt for them: a future colonel of the regiment, Lord John Murray, thirteenth son of the duke of Atholl and half-brother of several Jacobites, had portraits of the three hung in his home. Am Freiceadan Dubh went to Flanders, where it redeemed itself by its heroism at the Battle of Fontenoy in May 1745. When in October the Jacobite crisis prompted the recall of eleven regiments from Europe, the Black Watch was one of them. But, while the others headed north, it was kept in Kent to man the defences against any French invasion.

The 42nd afterwards went to be stationed in Ireland under an impeccable Whig, John Campbell of Mamore, commander in the Highlands after Culloden and later to become fourth duke of Argyll. When the Seven Years' War broke out, it was sent as part of a large expeditionary force to America. Before its embarcation came an interesting change in its colonelcy, signifying also a change in attitudes towards the clans. Mamore gave way to Francis Grant, whom the rank and file of the regiment wanted: they were ready to raise the money to buy the commission for him, had he not been given it anyway on merit. He was a brother of Ludovick Grant of Grant, chief of a clan dubious in allegiance during the '45: while he paltered, many of his clansmen joined the Jacobites. Now the Grants offered a commitment to the Crown previously withheld and, with the award of the colonelcy to their chiefly family, it was accepted.

Am Freiceadan Dubh also acquired, through the efforts of recruiting parties sent home from its Irish base to the Highlands, a second battalion. The commander was Lord Loudoun, another Campbell, but he had as his deputy a neighbour of Grant's: James Abercromby of Glasshaugh in Banffshire, MP for the county since 1734 and a friend of the philosopher David Hume. Abercromby assumed supreme command of British forces in North America after Loudoun's recall in 1758.

The pattern of Lowland Whigs joining Highland gentlemen to recruit Gaels repeated itself. Another regiment now raised was Montgomerie's Highlanders, under Archibald Montgomerie from Ayrshire, later earl of Eglinton. He had one sister married to Sir Alexander MacDonald of Sleat and a second to the laird of Abercairney, on the southern fringe of the Highlands. Through these the regiment drew its main strength from the north. It became a fine, strong corps, which in 1758 lost 104 dead and 220 wounded in a single American action, the capture of the French stronghold at the head of the River Ohio, Fort Duquesne, which was promptly renamed Pittsburgh.[11]

Shoulder to shoulder, then, Scots Whigs and Scots Jacobites, often related to one another, took the chance to raise troops and set a seal on the reconciliation of the Highlands with the Hanoverian dynasty. This was, after the '45, the equivalent of the legal defence of common interests mounted after the '15 by the Scottish landed class. Of course, they could not have undertaken it this time without the military prowess and renown of the Gaels. Nobody doubted they made valiant and steadfast soldiers, as their rebellions had shown. Not the least element in their martial temper was fealty to clans, led by those same landed gentlemen, which gave the soldiers a sense of unity and mutual trust of obvious utility on the battlefield. The government noted with relief that these fighting qualities had not after all been extinguished by Butcher Cumberland, but could now be exploited under the discipline of a regular army.

Some Highland gentlemen were understandably taken aback at the volte-face. To the heavy hint from a member of the Cabinet, Lord Hardwicke, that he should recruit a regiment, the third earl of Breadalbane replied: 'It is impossible for me to answer your Lordship's questions, what men I can raise and in what time, for I have for many years taken great pains in that part of the country where my interest lies to bring people's minds from the thought of arms to that of industry and improvement.'[12] But Scottish improvement could evidently be put on hold in the face of more pressing British priorities. Ten Highland regiments would be raised in the Seven Years' War, precursors of no fewer than thirty-seven Highland regiments raised by 1800, comprising perhaps 70,000 men in all.

Others played their parts, but Simon Fraser was in many ways the key to all this. Argyll now rewarded his earlier political complaisance by getting him an offer of the command over a Highland battalion, thus promising him another big step forward on the road to rehabilitation, which had somehow not come about with a full pardon. The newly commissioned colonel somewhat belied his reputation as a golden Apollo by resorting to traditional heavy-handed methods of recruitment on his estate, but he found 1500 soldiers in no time. Fraser's corps of officers also bore a marked Jacobite tinge. That Donald MacDonald with the perfect French accent did not belong to the lands of Lovat but to Clanranald, which had been the first to rally to Prince Charles's standard at Glenfinnan. Another captain was John Macpherson, whose elder brother Ewen Macpherson of Cluny had married Fraser's sister Janet; the couple tarried yet in their French exile. Two lieutenants, Roderick MacNeill of Barra and Alexander MacDonell of Barrisdale, were also of prominent Jacobite clans.

The truth, however, was that none of the regiment now hankered after the old days. The veteran Malcolm Macpherson of Phoiness, one of the most skilled and murderous swordsmen in Fraser's Highlanders, made no bones about his reason for still following the fortunes of war: to take personal revenge on the French for their false promises in 1745. There had once been the Auld Alliance between Scotland and France, protecting the Scots from English aggression and giving the French the chance to wage war on two fronts against their hereditary enemy. Traces of the alliance lingered on at Quebec in 1759. The commander of the citadel was Jean-Baptiste Roche de Ramezay, alias Ramsay: his branch of the family had emigrated from Scotland to France around 1600, before his own father moved from Burgundy to Canada in 1685. Montcalm's aide-de-camp was James Johnstone, another survivor of Culloden but one still in exile on the wrong side and nervous at the thought of falling prisoner to the British.

These old ties cut no ice with Highlanders on the Plains of Abraham. The strength of their switch in loyalties can be gauged by the fact that Fraser and his men there happily followed a general who had once fought against them. This was Wolfe, a veteran of Culloden on the other side. He had then spent several years in garrison, mainly enduring the tedium of building roads. He disliked Scotland, especially the weather, and even yet his attitude to Highlanders was grudging: 'They are hardy, intrepid, accustomed to a rough country, and no great mischief if they fall.' Their change of heart since the '45 was now sealed in blood. Just as Wolfe met his fate in the midst of the charge, victim of a sniper's bullet, and Montcalm too was hit while being swept along by the mob of fugitives, so Highlanders began to die, for the first time, for Britain and the Empire. From the ramparts of the city the Governor of New France, the Comte de Vaudreuil, had watched the battle aghast, and rushed out to organize some cover for the retreat. He rallied about a thousand Canadians, who kept up fire on the pursuers. Fraser's took the brunt of it; the colonel himself was wounded. Out of 658 British casualties, this one regiment suffered 168, including the deaths of the two gallant lieutenants, MacNeill of Barra and MacDonell of Barrisdale. While it mourned the fallen, it felt proud of its part in the victory. After the remainder of the regular French army retreated to Montreal, Ramezay hoisted the white flag over the citadel and the British took Quebec.

At the end of the campaign Fraser and his Highlanders came home as heroes. His friends in Inverness-shire revived the idea of making him their MP. Argyll again put in a veto, but he was at death's door and, once he passed through, voters of the county defied the political establishment and unanimously elected Fraser on the day after he arrived in London. Highland politics also attested the vitality of clannish sentiment. A Scots MP was often as much a representative of his family as of his constituency, and in the north the two could be hard to distinguish. No popular constituencies existed in Scotland, and every MP who had not won his seat by bribery took it on the strength of his family's interest. Since the Union, Ross had been contested by Clan Ross and Clan Mackenzie, with the latter gradually gaining the upper hand. Inverness-shire was contested by Frasers and Grants until they united their fortunes by intermarriage. No such manoeuvres disturbed the even tenor of electoral ways in Argyll – a county that never returned anyone but a Campbell – or in Sutherland, where the noble house of the same name reigned supreme.

Fraser's victory came at the general election of 1761, after the accession of King George III. He shortly appointed as Prime Minister his former tutor, John Stuart, earl of Bute, almost a Highlander himself. Although schooled at Eton, he had spent his youth on the isle of Bute pursuing his interests in agriculture, architecture and botany. But, as the first Scot to head a government since the Union, he faced virulent English prejudice, on account both of his nationality and of the royal favour shown him. From the opposition rose idle talk about British politics coming under the control of a sinister Highland phalanx riddled with Jacobitism. Against this background Fraser had to deal with the political embarrassment of being elected an MP without his own knowledge or consent. (He showed, however, no inclination to resign.) He wrote to Bute to explain his constituents' mood:

I do upon my honour assure your Lordship that I was totally ignorant when I arrived in London twelve days ago of everything they had done . . . I am persuaded their motives for choosing me were founded on no other attachment but personal friendship and the honour I have of commanding a regiment of the King's troops raised in that county . . . I have always avoided the least appearance of encouraging that attachment of clanship and for seven years avoided going to that part of the country till I had the sanction of Government for making use of that attachment to raise a thousand men for the King's service.[13]

Bute remained 'much offended', but a huff did not answer the question of what to do with a popular hero who was also a political embarrassment. The government could not contest the validity of his election, a common practice in the eighteenth century, as he had not even been opposed; he was to remain the unchallenged MP for Inverness-shire until he died in 1782. For now he had to be got out of the country, apparently. He was transferred to the army of Portugal, a satellite of Britain, on the understanding 'it would be considered British service'. He spent ten years there, becoming commander-in-chief for King Joseph and governor of a province. By the time he returned, he was wealthy enough to take a house in Downing Street, where he struck up a close friendship with the Prime Minister, Lord North. It was then but a short step to recovery of the forfeited lands of Lovat. On Fraser's behalf North wrote to the king, who supported a successful petition to Parliament in 1774. The new laird of Lovat was displeased to find that the estate's debts came back with it.[14]

This did not deter Fraser from going on and raising in 1775 another Highland regiment of two battalions, the 71st, to be sent to insurgent America. On 22 November he made his first recorded speech in a House of Commons he had entered fourteen years earlier, in order to explain his choice of officers. 'I think all the officers ought to be of North Britain', he said sweetly to members restive yet in Jacobite paranoia, though the Empire was collapsing round them; as usual, they wanted to fight the last war, or in this case the second last war. Edmund Burke and Charles James Fox, no less, rose to voice misgivings. An exasperated Lord North replied: 'I am sorry to acquaint the House, that the recruiting service is very far from being successful, and by the plan of operations already agreed on, it is necessary that the forces shall be ready for embarcation in the spring.' And that was that.[15]

To a House in one of its fatuous moods the Prime Minister had brought home a necessary evil, but among his ministers none more excelled in that – indeed he made a distinguished career out of it – than the Lord Advocate

The king who laid the foundations of a new Britain and set out to destroy the foundations of the old Highlands: James VI of Scotland (1567–1625), James I of England (from 1603), by John de Critz

From the Covenants to high culture: four chiefs of the Campbells, the greatest because the most ruthless Highland clan. Clockwise, they are the cast-eyed Archibald, eighth earl and first marquess of Argyll, Covenanting leader, executed in 1661 (portrait by David Scougall); Archibald, ninth earl, conqueror of the Inner Hebrides, executed for rebellion in 1685 (by L. Schuneman); John, second duke of Argyll, architect of the Union of 1707 (by William Aikman); Archibald, third duke, a leader of enlightened Scotland (by Allan Ramsay)

The marquess of Montrose, hero of Scottish royalists, rides calmly to be hanged, drawn and quartered in Edinburgh in this romantic Victorian interpretation by John Drummond. His arch-enemy Argyll skulks on the balcony to the right

A winner and a loser: the Jacobite John Graham, Viscount Claverhouse (by David Paton), killed in victory at the Battle of Killiecrankie in 1689, and his opponent in command of the defeated forces of William of Orange, Hugh Mackay of Scourie (by William Barnard), who escaped the subsequent slaughter in the pass

Two losers: the Old Pretender, James VIII *de jure* (by E. Gill) and the Young Pretender, Charles III *de jure*, Bonnie Prince Charlie (by Maurice Quentin de la Tour)

The original Fort William before it was turned into a goods yard by the West Highland Railway. It had been often repaired in the meantime, but this is much the view that would have greeted MacDonald of Glencoe, only covered in snow, when he approached to offer his submission to the government on 31 December 1692

Left: The heavy impression made on a fellow officer with an eye for caricature (George, Viscount Townshend) by William Augustus, duke of Cumberland, after he had advanced to crush the Highlanders at the Battle of Culloden in 1746

Below: A wistful Flora MacDonald calls to mind the flight of Bonnie Prince Charlie over the sea to Skye (by Richard Wilson)

Two great landlords of the nineteenth century: the first duke of Sutherland, condemned by posterity for the economic reorganization of his estates but here treated with unusual forbearance by the cartoonist James Gillray, son of a Highland soldier; and the eighth duke of Argyll (by George Frederic Watts), who resigned from the Liberal Cabinet of 1881 over its land reforms

George IV (by Sir David Wilkie) enters the palace of Holyroodhouse at the start of his visit to Edinburgh in 1822, the first by a reigning monarch for nearly 150 years. He is portrayed already in his tights but yet to don his kilt

of Scotland, Henry Dundas. He now began lobbying for general restoration of the annexed estates. Although he came of a long line of Lowland lawyers, he was half a Highlander himself, through his mother, Ann Gordon of Invergordon, daughter of a large landowner in Easter Ross. While his dedication to improvement of the region was beyond doubt, he found the regime bequeathed by the '45 a hindrance to him. Nobody knew what to do until the new course suggested by the fate of the lands of Lovat and their restoration to Fraser on grounds of his proven loyalty.

Dundas persuaded the Treasury that general restoration was the best way to be rid of an unwanted burden, and won agreement to it in principle from the governments he served.[16] In 1783 he himself became a commissioner for the estates, in effect with a brief to wind the old policy up. In 1784 he introduced a bill to disannex the estates from the Crown. Dispossessed families had been atoning for the crimes of their ancestors, 'and there is not one of those families in which some person has not since spilt his blood in his country's cause'. Dundas again stipulated that if the estates were to be restored, so too should the debts as they had stood when the government took over. Otherwise heirs would be getting them back in better condition, and a premium would have been placed on rebellion. The return to the Exchequer (£90,000 in the event) could be used for a variety of public works. By contrast the estates, though valued at £9000 a year, were producing £6700 gross and, after deducting for management and repairs, £4000 net. This 'is no extravagant boon that I ask for', Dundas remarked, but he promised it would please the inhabitants of the estates and discourage emigration.[17]

It was the first time Parliament had adopted a reform in the Highlands, as opposed to suppressing rebellion or raising revenue. By it, according to the most eminent Gael, Adam Ferguson, 'the affection of all Highlanders [was] gained to the state and the King'.[18] Actually the state retreated, or rather gave up pretence to a control it could not exert. This would never have happened had there been any risk of a return to anarchy in the region. Instead Dundas relied, after the state had achieved so little, on private landowners to rebuild a sound fabric for it. It would not destroy but reinforce the social order. The landowners agreed. Conservatives, they favoured – in contrast to their Liberal successors – keeping and increasing population on the land, in a hierarchy that would be a social and economic good for the nation.

So they also disliked emigration, as a loss of human resources and an affront to their benevolence. This was why Dundas stressed that restoration of estates would stop the flood of emigrants to America, which since the

end of the Seven Years' War had surpassed anything seen before. It especially worried a friend of his, Thomas Miller of Glenlee, Lord Justice
Clerk, who warned there was real danger of emptying the country. He
proposed that, as an initial control, a register of emigrants should be compiled. This was done from 1773 to 1776. It showed that during these years
4000 people left Scotland, most of them from Argyll, Inverness-shire,
Perthshire and Renfrewshire. Modern research has put the total Scottish
emigration for 1760–75 at 40,000, about 3 per cent of the whole population and one third of the general British emigration to the colonies.

Some special factors must, then, have been at work in Scotland. These
seemed plain: a move to commercial farming, with enclosures and higher
rents, made by landowners as they caught up with the fad for agricultural
improvement. The move was taking place in both Lowlands and
Highlands, but at this stage more quickly in the Highlands. Dundas wrote
in 1775 a thoughtful memorandum on the problem. He gave due weight
to the conventional explanation: 'The severity of some great proprietors
by a precipitate and injudicious rise of rents was the immediate cause of
emigration in some part of the country.' Yet this was not the whole story.
Dundas went on to note, like Milton before him, that the old Highland
chiefs had wanted as many people as possible on their lands to manifest
their power. Stripped of it by the repression after 1745, they could only
regard themselves as landlords, their dependants as mere tenants. There
had, of course, always been emigration from the overpopulated north,
attested by the many Highlanders in the Lowlands, 'more than half of our
day labourers, of our menial servants, our chairmen, porters, of our work-
men of every kind'. But it was by the final collapse of a social system that
they were 'induced to look for protection on the other side of the Atlantic,
or, to speak more properly, are induced to wander there for want of that
cherishment and protection that their fathers had felt in their old
habitation'.

The answer was to find a substitute for the traditional order. Dundas dismissed any idea that this would revive the Jacobite threat: 'It is to talk like
children to talk of any danger from disaffection in the north. There is no
such thing and it ought to be the object of every wise ruler in this country to cherish and make use of the Highlands of Scotland.' He doubted the
value, not to say legality, of banning emigration: 'In a small country, where
there are daily opportunities of getting away, such an idea is impracticable.'
Policy should instead find inducements for people to stay. There was often
still no real focus of loyalty for the Highlander other than his clan – to
Scotland perhaps but to Britain, as yet, hardly at all. This explained why

Dundas proposed as a first step to hand back the forfeited estates to formerly Jacobite families, to symbolize a new policy of repairing the social fabric.[19]

The outbreak of colonial rebellion in 1775 demanded a more immediate expedient, however. Every able-bodied emigrant could add to American and reduce British strength. Highland lairds, led by Sir James Grant of Grant, clamoured for Dundas to do something. In response he forbade the Scottish Board of Customs to clear from its ports, while hostilities lasted, any more ships carrying emigrants, and sheriffs instructed ministers to pass on the news to their flocks. In other words, a ban on emigration from the Highlands became, with the support of the landlords and at the somewhat reluctant behest of Dundas in the Scottish branch of government, the official policy of the British state.[20]

8

Love Scotland better than truth

Gaelic culture after 1745

O N 2 SEPTEMBER 1773 Samuel Johnson and James Boswell embarked for the isle of Skye from Glenelg, on the mainland. It was raining, as it would do for most of the month they passed on Skye, their furthest destination in a Highland journey that was to attain literary immortality with books about it by both of them. On landing at Armadale they were met by Sir Alexander MacDonald of Sleat, who over the next few days would disappoint them with his lack of 'feudal and patriarchal feelings'. Dr Johnson said to him: 'Were I in your place, Sir, in seven years I would make this an independent island. I would roast oxen whole, and hang out a flag as a signal to MacDonalds to come and get beef and whisky.' Boswell found Sleat 'bore with so polite a good nature our warm, and what some might call Gothick, expostulations, on this subject, that I should not forgive myself were I to record all that Dr Johnson's ardour led him to say'.[1]

Johnson and Boswell spent the night of 6 September at a tacksman's house, where lavish Highland hospitality greeted them. The 'numerous and cheerful company' held a ceilidh: 'They talked in their own ancient language, with fluent vivacity, and sung many Erse songs with such spirit, that, though Dr Johnson was treated with the greatest respect and attention, there were moments in which he seemed to be forgotten.' Unused to being a wallflower, he crept off to his bedroom and wrote a Latin ode:

> *Sit memor nostri, fideique merces,*
> *Stet fides constans, meritoque blandum*
> *Thraliae discant resonare nomen littora Skiae.*

> Mindful of each other, and of the reward of fidelity,
> Let that faith be constant, and let the shores of Skye
> Learn to resound with the gentle name of Mrs Thrale.[2]

Evidently Johnson had not yet quite got into the Hebridean swing of things. By his own account, he tasted whisky just once on the whole trip: 'It was strong, but not pungent, and was free from the empyreumatick taste or smell.' Matters improved, despite worsening weather, when on 8

September he and Boswell set off by boat for Raasay. The latter recalled: 'The wind had now risen pretty high, and was against us; but we had four stout rowers, particularly a MacLeod, a robust, black-haired fellow, half-naked and bare-headed, something between a wild Indian and an English tar. Dr Johnson sat high on the stern, like a magnificent Triton.' With them were Malcolm MacLeod of Raasay, rebel of the '45, and the Revd Donald MacQueen, erudite minister of Kilmuir in Trotternish, one of the northern peninsulas of Skye, recently commissioned by the General Assembly of the Church of Scotland to translate the Pentateuch into Gaelic. The voyage became somewhat alarming: 'After we were out of the shelter of Scalpay, and in the sound between it and Raasay, which extended about a league, the wind made the sea very rough. I did not like it', Boswell wrote. But Johnson responded: 'This now is the Atlantic. If I should tell at a tea-table in London, that I have crossed the Atlantic in an open boat, how they'd shudder, and what a fool they'd think me to expose myself to such danger!'[3]

Putting the danger out of their minds by means of learned debate, they soon got on to the subject that most interested Johnson, who asked MacQueen about Fingal.

> He said he could repeat some passages in the original; that he heard his grandfather had a copy of it; but that he could not affirm that Ossian composed all that poem as it is now published. This came pretty much to what Dr Johnson had maintained; though he goes farther and contends that it is no better than such an epic poem as he could make of the song of Robin Hood; that is to say, that, except a few passages, there is nothing truly ancient but the names and some vague traditions. Mr MacQueen alleged that Homer was made up of detached fragments. Dr Johnson denied this; observing, that it had been one work originally, and that you could not put a book of the Iliad out of its place; and he believed the same might be said of the Odyssey.[4]

Johnson and Boswell enjoyed themselves on Raasay before crossing back to Skye to visit another tacksman, Allan MacDonald of Kingsburgh, 'completely the figure of a gallant Highlander', and his wife, Flora, 'a little woman, of a genteel appearance, and uncommonly mild and well-bred'.[5] She was the Flora MacDonald who had helped Prince Charles Edward Stewart to escape his pursuers, and Johnson spent a night in the bed that the prince had slept in. The tour went on to Dunvegan, seat of MacLeod of MacLeod, whose mother had once met Johnson in London and received them now. They stayed more than a week:

His notion as to the poems published by Mr Macpherson, as the works of Ossian, was not shaken here. Mr MacQueen always evaded the point of authenticity, saying only that Mr Macpherson's pieces fell far short of those he knew in Erse, which were said to be Ossian's. – Johnson: 'I hope they do. I am not disputing that you may have poetry of great merit, but that Macpherson's is not a translation from ancient poetry. You do not believe it. I say before you, you do not believe it, though you are very willing that the world should believe it.' – Mr MacQueen made no answer to this. – Dr Johnson proceeded, 'I look upon Macpherson's Fingal to be as gross an imposition as ever the world was troubled with. Had it been really an ancient work, a true specimen how men thought at that time, it would have been a curiosity of the first rate. As a modern production, it is nothing.'

He later remarked of these exchanges: 'A Scotchman must be a very sturdy moralist, who does not love Scotland better than truth.'[6]

On Skye the visitors were hearing echoes of the greatest literary controversy of the age – in Scotland, Britain and all Europe – over James Macpherson's publication of several volumes purporting to be translations into English of poems originally written in Gaelic by the ancient poet Ossian. It caused such a sensation because it burst on a world of letters accustomed to mannered fiction, decorous poetry and high-minded history, all with heavy admixtures of moral philosophy. Beneath the polished literary surface there suddenly stood revealed abysses of raw instinct and emotion, of lust and bloodlust, and the reading public loved it all. From Lisbon to Riga young men (young women less often) went into fits of gloom, contemplated lovelorn suicide and so on. It marked the start of the Romantic movement. Yet the question remained whether Ossian was authentic.

Johnson had wanted to come into the heart of Gaeldom to look into matters for himself, though he hardly approached them with an open mind. Skye was one place where Macpherson had collected materials. He himself hailed from Badenoch, where he was known as Seumas Bàn, Fairhaired James. As a child he had witnessed the aftermath of the Battle of Culloden: since his clan was Jacobite, its territory suffered Butcher Cumberland's ravages. Gaelic was Macpherson's mother tongue, and he grew up with its culture, though as a tacksman's son he was schooled in English and went on to university at Aberdeen. His professor was Thomas Blackwell, who had a literary theory exalting the Sublime, to be found in such epics as the works of Homer. Macpherson could link this with his own tradition, which sometimes constructed new epics out of Classical ones, just as the Iliad had been put together by the recension of Pisistratus in ancient Athens: Johnson was wrong that it had been one work. Alastair mac Mhaighstir Alastair, the finest Gaelic poet of the age (who also taught the language of Eden to Prince Charles), followed the practice. Drawing on older examples, he resurrected the epic with his *Birlinn Chlann Raghnaill* ('The Ship of Clanranald'), the ship being a metaphor for a world where man has to struggle with nature. He still had originality to spare in both his matter, manfully martial or lyrically libidinous, and his manner, pushing Gaelic verse in various ways forward from exhausted conventions. Another bard entertained no doubt of mac Mhaighstir's achievement:

> *Gun tug thu bàrr air Hòmar*
> *Ge b'e ceòl-fhear mòr sa Ghreugais e.*

> You have surpassed even Homer
> Great musician though he was in Greek.[7]

Macpherson was to imitate mac Mhaighstir's method of collecting, copying, collating and concocting. So the affair of Ossian was not, as received wisdom has it, the tall story of a louche loner and his literary hoax. It was a more tangled tale in a complex cultural context linking Highlands and Lowlands, as represented in an eager young poet from the Gàidhealtachd and an intellectual coterie in Edinburgh. The link ran through Adam Ferguson, who belonged to both worlds. Born in 1723 in his father's manse at Logierait in Perthshire, Ferguson was on that side of humble stock; his grandfather had been a blacksmith. His mother's family were bonnet lairds, that is, feudal superiors of a modest patrimony, in western Aberdeenshire. Ferguson began his education at the parochial school. In order to study for the ministry he went to college at St Andrews, then Edinburgh. There he plunged into the rich intellectual and social life that set this apart from other Scottish universities.

Ferguson made lifelong friends of a group of fellow students of divinity, later to become ornaments of the nation. William Robertson, minister of Gladsmuir from 1744, rose to be principal of Edinburgh and historiographer royal of Scotland. John Home, minister of Athelstaneford from 1747, shocked strict Calvinists by writing and staging a play, *Douglas*, then later became private secretary to Lord Bute, the Prime Minister. Alexander 'Jupiter' Carlyle, minister of Inveresk from 1748, was known for his good looks, verve and wit. These three held parishes within a few miles of one another in East Lothian. In the capital itself, Hugh Blair was a minister of the Canongate, later of St Giles, a charge he occupied concurrently with the chair of rhetoric and *belles-lettres* at the university; he was famous for his sermons, which even Dr Johnson liked. Finally John Jardine, minister of the

Tron, provided a useful political connection as son-in-law to George Drummond, the evergreen Lord Provost. At Edinburgh, a municipal university, the town council elected the professors.

These youngsters formed a club to discuss literature and philosophy, which gathered in the house of the architect William Adam, in the Cowgate. They were a good-humoured bunch and long recalled this as the best time of their lives. Among its excitements was the approach in September 1745 of the Jacobite army, led by a Prince Charles the same age as themselves. They joined the volunteers raised to defend the capital, but these were disbanded without a fight as the Highlanders occupied it. If not, they might have been ordered out to the Battle of Prestonpans, to die alongside the redcoats; and much of what follows could never have been written.

Ferguson missed all this. That spring he had been the first of his friends to be whisked away from Edinburgh, as deputy chaplain to the Black Watch. He was just half-way through his studies, but the system of patronage in Scotland could ignore such trifles, often for good rather than ill. The patron of the 42nd was the duke of Atholl, also the patron of Ferguson senior's living. The duke's brother Lord John Murray, colonel of the regiment, wanted a better chaplain for it; the incumbent did not speak Gaelic and could pay a deputy £60 a year. The dowager duchess of Atholl recommended young Ferguson. Although a 'kindly relation' had long existed between his family and the ducal house, the dowager duchess was more intent on finding a chaplain to act as a 'kind of tutor or guardian' for her son, who needed help to 'keep in peace with his officers'; he was the one who had pitied the mutineers of 1743.[8]

Instead Murray had to look out for Ferguson. Am Freiceadan Dubh played a heroic part in the Battle of Fontenoy in May 1745, Britain's worst defeat during the War of the Austrian Succession. It is said that as the regiment advanced into the fray, Murray was astonished to see Ferguson leading the men, claymore in hand. When his colonel urged him to return to the rear with the surgeons, where he belonged, Ferguson ignored him. Murray then gave the chaplain an explicit order, saying his commission did not entitle him to fight in the front rank. 'Damn my commission!' roared the hot-tempered Ferguson, throwing his papers at the colonel as he charged on.[9]

The Black Watch returned as forces were concentrated to meet the Jacobite threat. It arrived in November, not to be sent north but to be kept south of the River Thames on guard against invasion from France. On 18 December, to the troops in cantonment at Camberwell, Ferguson preached a Gaelic sermon on the second book of Samuel 10:12, 'Be of good courage, and let us play the men for our people, and for the cities of our God'. He lambasted the Jacobites and French, recalled the men's blessings as British subjects and urged them to fight for the Protestant religion, the United Kingdom and King George II. Yet he was sensitive enough to note that many soldiers before him had family or friends on the other side: 'If you oppose your acquaintances, it is to prevent their ruin', he said; 'If you oppose your relations, it is to save them and their posterity from slavery for ever.'[10] The dowager duchess felt so impressed that she had the sermon translated into English and published.

Ferguson did not return to Scotland until 1751. On furlough he divided his time between Edinburgh and Logierait. He would now have preferred to leave the army and find a parish, but could not. He made it hard for himself because he sought to avoid being pigeonholed as a Highlander, and the Kirk had a policy that Gaelic-speaking ministers, who were in short supply, must serve in Gaelic-speaking parishes. Instead he applied in vain for parishes in the Lowlands for three years, before giving up and going on the grand tour as tutor to a young Gordon, probably Cosmo Gordon of Cluny. When Ferguson wrote to Adam Smith from Groningen, it was as a 'downright layman', presumably meaning he had lost hope of a clerical career.[11]

The alternative was more humble work shepherding rich kids around the Continent. In 1756 Lord Milton, political manager for the third duke of Argyll, sent Ferguson back to Groningen with his son John, who was to pursue his legal studies there. The lad suffered from depression, and his father hoped a change of scene would cure him. Ferguson could hardly cope with this. He told Milton his heir ought to be locked up, though later they became friends. For what it was worth, Ferguson advanced up the scale of tutorships: Bute engaged him for two of his sons, pupils at Harrow School. The nearest Ferguson came to a real job was as keeper of the Advocates' Library in Edinburgh, a post he took over from David Hume in 1757, probably at the latter's behest. It paid £40 a year – less than Ferguson had from his regiment – but it gave access to 30,000 volumes in one of the finest libraries in Europe. That Hume passed it up to Ferguson shows how worried friends felt about his situation. Still nominally chaplain to the Black Watch, he was probably having to pay for a deputy, as the regiment had gone to America. Robert Adam believed that getting Ferguson a parish would make a man of him: 'God knows, whilst he . . . continues a poor damned droning Presbyterian of the gospel according to Logierait, he might as well have made him a Highland cow.' With luck he could 'be of use to himself and his country'; otherwise he would have to settle for yet more grand tours with scions of noble houses, to 'have £400 from one, £500 from another settled on him for life so that he may bid old presbytery kiss his arse'.[12]

David Hume and John Home decided they had to do something for Ferguson, aged thirty-five and getting nowhere in life. An academic chair seemed to be the answer. They set about a trawl among professors liable to be displaced, either as incompetent, on leave of absence or at death's door. They came on John Stewart, in the chair of natural philosophy at Edinburgh, who obliged them by dying. Home asked Milton to support Ferguson as successor. Hume, from London, appealed for help to Robertson, now a best-selling author with his *History of Scotland*. There was a rival in Ferguson's cousin James Russel, a better-qualified candidate. Hume felt sorry that two men of such merit, 'whom we all love so much', should be competing. He hoped Russel would stand aside; if not, 'what a cruel and distressful situation does it leave poor Ferguson!' With Jardine as go-between, Lord Provost Drummond and Lord Milton persuaded the town council to elect the hapless Gael.[13]

Ferguson had meanwhile made the acquaintance of Macpherson and entertained him at Logierait. They discussed Gaelic poetry, and Ferguson gave Macpherson a letter of introduction to Home. These two then met in September 1759 at Moffat, a spa in Dumfriesshire; Home was there for some ailment, Macpherson as tutor to a laird's children. Home had never got over his encounter with the Gaels in 1745, when he was taken prisoner and held in Doune Castle – one of those cases where the captive learned to love his captors – so he felt fascinated by Macpherson too. They bumped into each other on a bowling green and then, retiring for a chat over the sulphurous waters, found they shared a Romantic sensibility, a penchant for heroism and patriotism – the blend that gave rise to Ossian. When he learned that Macpherson happened to have Gaelic poems about him, Home with some difficulty talked him into producing an English translation of one. 'The Death of Oscur' ran to just 700 words, but it contained most of the elements of the later Ossianic verse: valiant warriors, passionate lovers, human turmoil mirrored in stormy nature, refuge in melancholy with release in death and so on. Macpherson showed more specimens to a highly delighted Home, who took them to literary friends in Edinburgh and London, probably including Bute. They felt impressed too. Blair, in the middle of preparing his first public lectures on rhetoric, showed a special interest. He promised to get an anthology of the translations published, if Macpherson could produce enough of them to make a small book. Blair recalled that Macpherson was 'extremely reluctant and averse' despite 'much and repeated importunity', but in the end he agreed. The result came out as his *Fragments of Ancient Poetry Collected in the Highlands of Scotland*.[14]

To rave reviews the first edition of 1760 appeared with fifteen poems, said to be by Ossian and translated by Macpherson. In an introduction Blair surmised they were just a fraction of a vast fund of Ossianic poetry awaiting discovery in the Highlands. A Gael might have put it differently, but at bottom this was true. The folklore of the Fianna remained a living if decayed tradition, in verse and prose, dating back to the Middle Ages, when Scotland and Ireland had partaken of a common culture. The real question was how legitimately Macpherson represented it.

Blair mentioned that this corpus included an epic about an ancient Scottish king, Fingal. He and his friends now urged Macpherson to go and look for it. Again he showed extreme unwillingness: he had no money, for one thing. Blair passed round the hat to the literati so that Macpherson could end his irksome tutor's employment and make a Highland trip. He spent four months in Perthshire, Argyll and Inverness-shire, then on the islands of Skye, North and South Uist, Benbecula and Mull. He carried letters of introduction to chieftains and clergymen, people the literati knew but he did not. He recorded recitations and gathered manuscripts, including the Book of the Dean of Lismore, today one of the nation's literary treasures. He stopped off in Badenoch, where he enlisted help from members of his clan, such as Lachlan MacPherson of Strathmashie, a poet in his own right. They started work on texts that were somehow to blend the character of the genuine poems or stories of the Fianna familiar to them with the romance the literati were looking for.

This sojourn sowed the seeds of the later controversy. Whatever came of the convoluted editorial process, it would be aimed not at Gaels but at English-speakers, in particular the literati of Edinburgh. They had to be given what they wanted if the exercise was to succeed at all. So where Gaelic names seemed uncouth, they were rendered dulcet; where stories seemed terse or crude, they were turned tender. Strathspey's school of poets began to sew the fragments into a seamless whole with no rough edges. In January 1761 Macpherson got back to Edinburgh to finish the work. He showed manuscripts to Ferguson, who thought, from his imperfect knowledge of Gaelic orthography, they looked authentic. Blair would drop in – he lived upstairs from Macpherson in Blackfriar's Wynd – to keep an eye on progress. A publisher was sought in London. According to Jupiter Carlyle, Macpherson had amassed more lines of Ossianic poetry 'than all Homer, Virgil, Milton, Tasso and Ariosto put together'.[15]

The wistful prose-poem 'Fingal' appeared at the end of 1761, to a yet
more rapturous reception. Controversy began in earnest as critics vied in
praise or blame of the book. Since few knew Gaelic, and Macpherson
treated with contempt any questioning of his sources, a definite conclusion on their authenticity proved impossible. The poem was no mere
forgery, as his fiercest foes claimed. But if he could not exactly produce his
originals, this was because they did not exactly exist. He was by training a
student of Classical, not Gaelic, literature and had no special philological
skills. He had found some manuscripts in Old Irish (hard to read even for
trained scholars today) and some old men declaiming a classical Gaelic
different from his vernacular of Strathspey. A youth ambitious to get into
print could make little of all this. What he could do was concoct an epic
out of materials and ideas he had gathered, if couched in another language,
so as to tickle current literary taste. And why not? In Gaeldom plagiarism
had little meaning. Bards never claimed copyright or troubled themselves
whether others thought them original. Iain Lom and John MacCodrum,
among modern poets, used Ossianic material. Since Gaels were the ones
that produced the epic, they surely had some right to fix its character.
Macpherson did imitate, as best he could, a genuine tradition, if overlain
by a polite veneer for the intended audience. Yet it remains true that no
poem like 'Fingal' or the less authentic sequel of 1763, 'Temora', has ever
existed in the Highlands.

The controversy turned into a new war of the three kingdoms. In
Ireland men of letters protested that Macpherson had stolen their national
heroes. They did put their fingers on his attempt to anchor Ossianic legend
in Scotland, to detach it from its Irish origins or even deny them. Ever since
the Middle Ages Lowlanders had railed at Highlanders for being too
Hibernian, and Macpherson wished to counter this, to people the Gaelic
past with loyal heroes rather than racial cousins of papist traitors.[16] But the
Irish reaction was as nothing compared to the English one. Scepticism in
London soon descended into bigotry. At a popular level, newspapers seized
on the alleged swindle of Ossian as another stick with which to beat the
Prime Minister, the woebegone Bute. At a learned level there was no
friendlier reception. Dr Johnson launched himself at once into the fray,
calling Ossian a case of 'Scotch conspiracy in national falsehood'. He set a
tone for others, such as Horace Walpole, who lashed out against 'those
Scotch imposters and their cabal'. But these critics pontificated from total
ignorance of Celtic literature, which Johnson refused to believe existed.[17]

Nothing daunted, then, Edinburgh's literati continued to act as cheer-
leaders for Ossian, although Hume had his doubts. To that extent, Johnson

and Walpole were right about its being a collective rather than individual enterprise. Macpherson had all along been diffident – in showing his fragments to Home, in publishing them at Blair's behest and in going to recover the lost epic. 'The whole publication, you know, was in its first rise accidental', Blair later reminded Hume; 'Macpherson was entreated and dragged into it.' His diffidence may have arisen from fear of being exposed as a fraudster, or it may have confirmed his credibility, for which fraudster has to be cajoled into his fraud? Whatever the truth, the appearance of the Ossianic poetry required a meeting of minds, a conjunction of Macpherson and the literati. They needed his texts; he needed their interest and support, social and intellectual contacts, publishing and marketing skills. Blair was unwise enough to call it 'our epic'. In the foreword to 'Fingal' Macpherson thanked Home for his 'uncommon zeal' and others 'earnest in exhorting him to bring more [Gaelic poetry] to the light'.[18]

What was the motive behind the zeal and earnestness? In a word, patriotism. Hume had boasted how modern Scots were 'really the people most distinguished for literature in Europe', but Scots often deal with insecurity by boasting. While Hume was right at the time, it had yet to be proved that the recent burst of national genius was more than a flash in the pan. A country's culture will have more staying power if it has roots too. If it was to outdo a neighbouring country that could vaunt itself on William Shakespeare, those roots had to go deep. Yet they could not go deeper than Homer, because he was where European literature had begun: so a poet comparable to Homer would do nicely. Hence Ossian – bard of a Celtic community lost in the mists of time, whose epic power and passion transcended, yet somehow conformed to, the human sensibility and poetic discipline of a later, more rational, more polished age. Ossian would give Scotland her proper place in the history of Western culture.[19]

This tortuous train of thought entailed a further twist. The values of Ossianic poetry – heroism, honour, valour, virtue – were conducive to a martial spirit. For Blair, 'Fingal' pointed the moral that 'wisdom and bravery always triumph over brutal force'. The poem tells of proud, brave Scots defending their country against brutal Scandinavian aggressors. The medium is not as gruesome as in Homer, but the message is the same: that war has about it a terrible necessity which can make it worth the cost. The dauntless Fingal does his duty as warlord in a world of never-ending adversity, one thing after another. 'Fingal never flies', he proclaims; 'where danger threatens, I rejoice in the storm of spears.' Yet he and his followers fight only for good causes that console them for their sacrifices. So Ossian was an example also of the sort of heroism that marked out the

Scots in their perpetual battle to secure a nationhood in fact never to be secured.[20]

Ossian trumpets, then, both the poetic genius and the national nobility of Scotland. It brings together, too, her past and her present. It presents the values of a barbaric era clad in the elegance and decorum of a civilized one. It looks back to a golden age, as the poetry of Greece and Rome often did – though the Ossianic golden age is not free of strife but, rather, peopled by a race seeking in it the highest virtue. These men know nothing of contemporary corruptions. Unlike Homeric heroes, Ossianic heroes have no personal flaws or moral conflicts of any kind. To readers now this makes them boring; but readers then apparently preferred inspiring myths and ethical lessons to complex characters and dramatic tensions. At least, the literati of Edinburgh preferred those things. It was their answer to modern malaise, because they saw in it a healthy dose of elemental vitality. That was what made the Scottish Enlightenment, compared to the syphilitic salons of France or the arid academies of Prussia, an affair of good talk, good humour and good drink, still on a par intellectually with anywhere else. As this rough vigour coursed through the closes and tenements of old Edinburgh, it carried a heathery reek of the wild winds over the Firth of Forth which sweep down on the capital from the Highlands. The Scottish Enlightenment had brawn as well as brains because it was in part a Highland Enlightenment too.

It was so because of Ferguson. In 1764 he swapped the chair of natural philosophy at Edinburgh for that of moral philosophy, and in 1767 published *An Essay in the History of Civil Society*. This is often reckoned to have founded the modern discipline of sociology. It set out theories of the Scottish Enlightenment, that mankind progressed through historical stages marked by different forms of social and economic organization, and different cultures or moralities. Ferguson's tone is cool, yet he makes unmistakable reference to such sensitive matters as the Union. He says powerful and advanced societies can overcome weak and backward ones, 'but the happiness of men . . . consists in the blessings of a candid, an active and a strenuous mind [and] we need not enlarge our communities, in order to enjoy these advantages. We frequently obtain them in the most remarkable degree, where nations remain independent, and are of a small extent.'[21]

Ferguson defines two sorts of primitive society: the savage, merely hunting and fishing, and the barbarous, reliant on a pastoral economy with some idea of property. Both are warlike, the people going round in bands and fighting each other all the time, but with progress the warrior separates out from the citizen. Once war is devalued, 'the ambitious will naturally devolve the military service on those who are contented with a subordinate station . . . A discipline is invented to inure the soldiers to perform, from habit, and from the fear of punishment, those hazardous duties, which the love of the public, or a national spirit, no longer inspire.' Here, surely, can be heard the authentic voice of the chaplain to the Black Watch.[22]

Ferguson adds that this 'separation of arts and professions' is the key to progress. Like Adam Smith, he believes division of labour makes a people more productive and wealthy. Yet it charges a moral price. For example, it degrades the workers, whose jobs seldom demand any special skill: 'Manufactures prosper most, where the mind is least consulted.' They may no longer be slaves, as in the ancient world, but their values are more degenerate than savage ones. Ferguson denies that even education can help. The proletariat does not have to be lettered, just grovelling and selfish. It is unfit to take part in politics: democracy cannot work in a modern economy. But a moral price is paid at higher levels too. Soldiers and statesmen are no longer all-rounders. Their specialization amounts to 'an attempt to dismember the human character, and to destroy those very arts we mean to improve'. Worse, the rich indulge in conspicuous consumption. They may even see it as a foundation for public life, if they do not regard politics as beneath them. They must then become 'the refuse of that society of which they were once the ornament; and from being the most respectable, and the most happy of its members . . . become the most wretched and corrupt'. And once corruption takes hold, despotism stalks not far behind.[23]

Beneath Ferguson's philosophy lies Macpherson's poetry: the message is that, for all its progress, the modern world has flaws, not least the loss of virtues known to earlier stages of development, as among Highlanders. Macpherson did serve his own purposes too, different from those of the literati. They felt excited at their historical insights. They thought to see history happening before their eyes. 'This is the historical age and this the historical nation', Hume said. In a generation Scotland had gone from burning witches to building a machine for rational living in the New Town of Edinburgh. But Ferguson and Macpherson also found matter for mourning here. The passing of Ossian's world symbolized to them the end of a Gaelic way of life. They had crossed not only thresholds of time, like brother Scots, but also the Highland line. They saw the historical development underlying the present contrast of Lowlands and Highlands. Descrying the drawbacks of it too, they spoke up for the Highlands as no Lowlander would, yet couched the contrast in terms that Lowlanders would understand. Sir Walter Scott is usually credited with the reconciliation of the nation's two halves, yet its origins can be traced to Ossian half a century earlier. Macpherson knew the Highlands were being integrated into the rest of Britain, their culture falling victim to commercial values. He wanted to bear witness to a social order that had previously been uncorrupted for two thousand years. Something might be saved if he could at least give non-Gaels an inkling of it. While the age of Fingal was vanished, at least the memory of a nobler community could be carried down into the decadent eighteenth century. For Scotland, Macpherson succeeded.

If the history and outlook of the Gael could be rationalized in this way, perhaps his language might have been preserved as an enlightened enterprise as well. But hindrances were great. The main educational agency in the Highlands, the Society in Scotland for the Propagation of Christian Knowledge, avowed a naive faith in the civilizing capacity of English education:

> Nothing can be more effectual for reducing these countries to order and making them useful to the commonwealth, than teaching them their duty to God, king and country, and rooting out their Irish language, and this has been the care of the society so far as it could, for all the scholars are taught in English.[24]

Still, teachers in the society's charity schools needed Gaelic to talk to the children, at least to the wee ones. The type of man required was hard to come by. He had to be educated, sober and serious, with a thorough grasp of Calvinist theology. He had to be happy to live on a pittance, yet full of missionary fervour. On top of everything else, he had to speak Gaelic. In practice the society was obliged to breed up its own bilingual teachers. Clever little Gaels got a sweetener of 12 pence Scots (one English penny) every day they went to school. At the end of their third year they received a suit of clothes and a pair of shoes. They were now expected to carry some of the teaching load themselves, at 18 pence Scots a day. If they wished, they could then be employed as schoolmasters at the first suitable vacancy.

Yet the society still aimed to wipe out Gaelic. The teachers and their brightest pupils were meant to spread the English language and English values (also known as Christian knowledge) to the rest. Alexander Buchan, catechist on St Kilda, was told: 'Be diligent not only to teach them English but also to write, and lay in on such as profit by you to do all they can for the edification of others.'[25] He spent fourteen years in work that he finally judged a failure. This was because, in a place where no more than four or five adults had even a smattering of English, he was forbidden to instruct people in their mother tongue. He asked if he could teach Gaelic reading.

No, the society said. Otherwise the books he had at his disposal were quite unsuitable for teaching children to read, let alone read in a foreign language: the English Bible, Confessions of Faith and works of Calvinist theology, all of which he could only teach by rote. Although the society did publish, it chose nothing but English titles in order to promote a rapid anglicization of the Highlands, which would render all Gaelic writings redundant. Many requests came in for a supply of 'Irish' psalters and catechisms for the charity schools. No, the society always said. It sent to any teachers reported to have taught Gaelic reading and told them to stop.

Not only teachers but also ministers thought the rule silly, indeed damaging. The Revd James Robertson of Balquhidder in Perthshire wrote to Edinburgh helpfully pointing out that, if children could be taught to read the Gaelic psalms, 'this would be of good use in families who have nothing but Irish', because otherwise they must remain wholly ignorant of the Bible. No, said the society. James Murray, teacher at Blair Atholl, did coach his children in the Gaelic psalms 'for the good of their ignorant parents, who understand not the English tongue, that the children, when they go home at night, may be in case to read to them'. He requested eighteen psalters to be sent to him. No, said the society, and by the way he was not to teach Gaelic reading. When it found out he was still doing so, it asked his minister and presbytery to censure him. Instead the minister sprang to his defence, saying his method should be followed elsewhere for it 'would make religion to flourish more than it does in that country'. No, the society said. Three other ministers argued that the society's policy frustrated its own ends. Children taught to read the English language went home able indeed to read the Bible, but unable to grasp even the plainest historical parts of it, and soon forgot what little they learned. The three urged a policy not of instruction exclusively in English but of simultaneous translation between the one language and the other. By modern standards this was an advanced (and doubtless too demanding) technique, but at least it showed some sympathy for the dilemmas of teachers in the classroom under orders to use a medium unknown to the children. Even so, the society said no.[26]

Such was the chorus of dissent, though, that the society had to formulate some response to the problems its own policy raised. It suggested that, as soon as children began to read the English catechism, the teacher should make them translate each question into Gaelic and then back into English, until he was sure they grasped it: this, of course, without reading a Gaelic version. The society also ruled 'that all the scholars be exhorted to learn to speak English and told the advantages thereof, and that none who can speak any of it be allowed to speak Irish'. It proposed that a Gaelic–English vocabulary should be printed, 'and scholars obliged to learn so many words weekly'.[27] A commission was sent to the presbytery of Lorne, which took fourteen years to produce the volume because the reverend brethren selected the wrong man for it, politically if not linguistically.

Their chosen drudge was none other than the poet Alastair mac Mhaighstir Alastair, teacher at the charity school in Ardnamurchan. He spent too much time on his love life, then on putting its ecstasies into verse, to focus on a more tedious labour, although he supported the idea. By the time of the '45 he had already been dismissed by the society for the offence he gave to 'all sober and well-inclined persons, as he wanders through the country composing Gaelic songs stuffed with obscene language' – a not unfounded charge, it must be added. Meanwhile he did manage to finish the vocabulary, and so become the author of the earliest Gaelic school-book.[28] Later, in 1751, he was the first to publish a volume of original Gaelic verse, *Ais-eiridh na Sean Chanain Albanaich* ('The Resurrection of the Old Highland Language').

By then the society was trying to beat Gaelic out of Highland children. It laid down a new rule in 1750, requiring that 'thereafter the scholar attending the charity be discharged either in the schoolhouse or when playing about the doors thereof to speak Erse on pain of being chastised and that the schoolmasters appoint censors to note down and report to the schoolmaster such as transgress this rule'.[29] This draconian measure amounted to a confession of failure. All it did was produce a literate population unable to understand what it read.

In the end the society gave way, though on the evangelical rather than educational arguments for Gaelic literacy. It had found it could not in reality do much to control what language Highlanders spoke, but its overriding aim was, of course, to propagate Christian knowledge, and so it began to publish some Protestant literature in Gaelic. The turning point came with the commission for a fresh translation of the New Testament awarded to a staunch Calvinist, the Revd John Stewart of Killin. He finished in four years, although publication was delayed by a squabble over payment discreditable to the society. At last, in 1767, ten thousand Gaelic New Testaments rolled off the press.

It was a historic moment for the language of Eden. For two hundred years it had been at odds with reformed religion. At last Gaels were not to be denied the Scriptures because of political prejudice against their mother tongue. A strong argument for this change of heart had come from a man who yet affected to dismiss Gaelic as a barbarous dialect. Dr Johnson, no less, took a personal interest in translations of the Bible for the heathen, who to his mind included the Gaels. In 1766, seven years before his journey to the north, he had written to William Drummond, a bookseller in Edinburgh and director of the society, saying he was surprised there could be any question about giving people Christian instruction in their own language:

> If obedience to the will of God be necessary to happiness, and knowledge of his will be necessary to obedience, I know not how he that withholds this knowledge, or delays it, can be said to love his neighbour as himself . . . To omit for a year, or even for a day, the most efficacious method of advancing Christianity, in compliance with any purposes that terminate on this side of the grave, is a crime of which I know not the world has yet had an example, except in the practice of the planters of America, a race of men whom, I suppose, no other man wishes to resemble.[30]

At last the society said yes, cowed by this exalted intervention. It passed a new regulation providing for teachers in the charity schools to instruct their pupils in both Gaelic and English.

9

A nation no longer

Improvement and emigration, to 1776

IN THE DARKNESS before dawn on 27 February 1776 a force of 1500 Highland soldiers, wrapped in their plaids against a chilly night, straggled soaked and cursing over rock and bog through a trackless forest. Some were sons of men who had had much the same experience on the eve of the Battle of Culloden, but these were a world away from there.

It was in the backwoods of North Carolina that they had got lost while trying to launch a surprise attack. They remained 20 miles short of their ultimate objective, Wilmington, a port on the Cape Fear river and the colony's capital at the time. In the name of King George III they meant to recapture it from American rebels who had seized it and obliged the royal governor, Josiah Martin, to take refuge on a ship offshore.

The Highlanders were marching down from settlements inland established by immigrant clansmen in the 1730s and later expanded by refugees from the '45. They prospered from various crops in this fertile country – including tobacco, which, shipped back to Glasgow, aided the city's economic ascent. At first it was back-breaking work, for deep forests of pine had to be felled before the land could be tilled. In the strange, humid heat of the Carolinian days the toil could be too much for the wiriest Gael. Slaves were purchased to perform it and the labour on the plantations that followed. The settlers still used Gaelic among themselves, so the slaves learned it too. A woman arriving on a later shipment, under the fierce sun of summer, was dismayed to hear a couple of African stevedores speaking the language of Eden on the waterfront at Wilmington. '*A Dhé*,' she cried, '*tha mi an dòchas nach tionndaich sinn uile dubh mar sin*' ('My God, I hope we don't all turn black like that!'). Gaels themselves became American planters, 'a race of men whom, I suppose, no other man wishes to resemble', as Dr Johnson had put it.[1]

Also among the later arrivals in Carolina were the tacksman of Skye, Allan MacDonald of Kingsburgh, and his wife, Flora, the Jacobite heroine. Forsaking their native island, the couple led a group of their kith and kin to a place up the Cape Fear river called Cross Creek (now Fayetteville).

Allan and Flora had long ago fully switched allegiance from Stewarts to Hanoverians. In character and by conviction loyal people, they refused to join the American revolt which broke out in 1775. On the contrary, as it spread south from New England early the next year, Allan mustered forces to defend Carolina for the king. He did it in Highland fashion, by sending round the fiery cross. Out of their farmsteads hewn from the forests, 3500 men assembled under the royal standard in the market place of Cross Creek, where they were given an envoi in sonorous Gaelic by Flora herself, mounted on a white horse. In two regiments they set off for Wilmington.

By 27 February a single natural obstacle lay between them and their goal: the swampy Moore's Creek. A bridge traversed it, guarded by rebel sentries. MacDonald hoped to overcome them by stealth, and sent forward through the night a vanguard under Colonel Donald MacLeod. As its platoons blundered about, one came on the bridge quite by chance. The captain, Alexander MacLean, could make out figures at the other end. To their challenge he answered he was a friend. 'A friend to whom?' they asked. At his reply, 'To the king', they threw themselves to the ground and took cover. MacLean still thought they might be his own men, who had somehow got across. There was only one thing for it, to shout a Gaelic challenge: 'Co tha siud?' ('Who goes there?'). Silence met him, and MacLean knew he faced enemies. He ordered his troops to open fire.

Their shooting brought up Colonel MacLeod and the rest of the force. Officers examined the bridge, a crude structure of three tree trunks laid parallel from bank to bank with planks nailed between them. The Americans had removed half this flooring, and for good measure greased the trunks with soft soap and tallow. But with the stillness on the opposite side, there seemed no reason not to cross. MacLeod formed up his line, called for a drum roll and set his pipers to rend the air of the dawn with their rants. He led three cheers for George III, then ordered an advance, giving pride of place to Captain John Campbell's men with their claymores: just as well, because these, along with most of the force, had no rifles.

MacLeod himself was the first to step on to one of the treacherous trunks, Campbell on to the other. They found they could keep their balance if they thrust the point of their swords into the wood. In this ungainly fashion they waddled over, followed in single file by their troops.

They never knew what hit them on the further bank. Out of the rising sun came fire from cannons, quite unexpected, and a volley from rifles. They had run into an ambush. Campbell fell dead, MacLeod wounded.

Even so, MacLeod staggered to his feet and tried to lead a charge. It had hardly got going before a hail of bullets swept the bridge clean, with the Gaels being blasted into the water or jumping in to save themselves. MacLeod still rushed forward with a few men near him, towards the flashes in front. These came from earthworks the Americans had prepared. They wiped out the clansmen, although MacLeod kept going until he dropped just a few paces from the foe.

Highlanders who had not crossed the creek returned fire, but now they had no stomach for a fight and began to make away. Once the remaining officers gave up trying to rally them, a rout began. All ran back to where they had left their supplies. They unhitched horses from the wagons and, with as many as three men mounted on one animal, they fled. As they crashed among the trees they passed their base camp and rearguard, yet further back, where MacDonald slept in his tent, struck down by fever and unaware of the débâcle. Once he had roused himself, he called a council of war. The first report he got decided things: just two barrels of flour remained to feed the beaten army. He ordered everybody to return to Cross Creek, fortify it and hold out pending further instructions from Governor Martin.

For MacDonald, however, the War of American Independence was already over. Too weak to travel, this patriarchal figure stayed in his tent and awaited capture. He was taken before Colonel James Moore, defender of Wilmington, but retained enough military dignity to insist on formal surrender. He tendered his sword to the American, who returned it and promised he would be well treated. MacDonald was held for more than a year, before being released on parole by personal order of George Washington. He did not get back to Skye until 1783, to be reunited with Flora, who had been evacuated through Charleston: two of many Scots forced to abandon new homes they had just found in America.[2]

Before his departure from Skye in 1773 MacDonald had received the visit of Dr Johnson and James Boswell. Although he did not stint in hospitality to them, they could see he was 'embarrassed in his affairs'.[3] Indeed he had already decided to emigrate in, by his own account, a kind of old-fashioned disgust over conditions at home. He felt sickened at a moral breakdown accompanying a social breakdown. He wrote to his lawyers in Edinburgh: 'It is melancholy to see the state of this miserable place; the superior summoning the tenants to remove for not paying the great rent, etc. and the tenants the superior for oppression, for breaking the conditions of his tacks, and for violent profits.' With everyone on the make, there was 'no respect of persons, as the best are mostly gone, stealing of sheep

etc. constantly, and picking and thieving of corn, garden stuffs, and potatoes perpetually, lying, backbiting and slandering'. Honesty had fled,
MacDonald lamented, and in its place stood villainy and deceit, fed by
poverty.[4]

This disintegration of a patriarchal society was what most struck
MacDonald's visitors. On it they blamed the 'epidemic disease of wandering', the wave of emigration they saw going on. In anchorages around the
coast they came across – never without regret – ships laden with people
taking leave of their island. On the way off it Johnson and Boswell were
stranded by storms for several days at Armadale while they waited to sail to
Mull, and had to find amusements. Boswell recorded for 1 October:

> In the evening, the company danced as usual. We performed, with much
> activity, a dance which, I suppose, the emigration from Skye has occasioned.
> They call it America. Each of the couples, after the common involutions
> and evolutions, successively whirls round in a circle, till all are in motion;
> and the dance seems intended to show how emigration catches, till a whole
> neighbourhood is set afloat.[5]

The odd thing was that the Englishman, Dr Johnson, seemed the more
sombrely affected by the scenes of farewell, for to him a patriarchal society was a work of God. He felt sorry for emigrants soon to be destitute in
a spiritual as well as a material sense. They could not know what awaited
them on the other side of the ocean and never suspected they were about
to lose what lent meaning to their lives, a culture of which they and their
homeland would be alike bereft:

> A nation scattered in the boundless regions of America resembles rays
> diverging from a focus. All the rays remain, but the heat is gone. Their power
> consisted in their concentration: when they are dispersed, they have no
> effect. It may be thought that they are happier by the change; but they are
> not happy as a nation, for they are a nation no longer.[6]

As ever when troubled by something, Johnson talked non-stop about it
and Boswell, as ever, scribbled his sayings down. The resulting reflections
are quite on a par with modern academic analyses, and more elegantly
expressed. Basic causes of the problem could be easily identified: a rising
population on a limited quantity of land with a consequent general increase
in rents, all amid a loosening of social ties in 'clans . . . newly disunited
from their chiefs, and exasperated by unprecedented exactions'. When
Johnson probed further, he learned that the people of Skye had long been
wanderers but that their behaviour had recently changed. Emigrants had
formerly been those surplus to local requirements of manpower, or else

people with no property, who transported just themselves. Now, however, Johnson was seeing 'families, and almost whole communities, go away together', selling their stock to raise the necessary money. 'Once none went away but the useless and poor; in some parts there is now reason to fear, that none will stay but those who are too poor to remove themselves, and too useless to be removed at the cost of others.'[7]

Like other pundits of the time, Johnson tended to blame agents going round and enticing away potential emigrants at the behest of speculators who had bought up American lands. Highlanders heard not that these virgin territories were a wilderness, from which no living could be eked but by endless toil; on the contrary, they were supposed to be 'happy regions, where every man may have land of his own, and eat the product of his labour without a superior'. While the first emigrants could doubt-less be spared, this was no longer true when 'whole neighbourhoods formed parties for removal'. Johnson thought they were deluding them-selves, but could imagine how 'he that goes thus accompanied, carries with him all that makes life pleasant. He sits down in a better climate, sur-rounded by his kindred and his friends; they carry with them their lan-guage, their opinions, their popular songs, and hereditary merriment; they change nothing but the place of their abode.' And it was striking how often richer men led the people away: 'Nor are they only the lowest and most indigent; many men of considerable wealth have taken with them their train of labourers and dependants; and if they continue the feudal scheme of polity, may establish new clans in the other hemisphere.'[8]

Johnson meant by this the MacDonalds and others like them, the tacks-men, gentlemen of the clan or *daoine uaisle*, the median group in the old Highland social structure, in between peasants working the communal holdings and chiefs holding sway over their whole territory. Tacksmen had been officers of the clan in time of war. In peace they formed a middle management for the system of communal agriculture known as runrig. This, with minute divisions of good and bad ground for tenants of each township, demanded organizational skills even while it preserved indigence and inefficiency. The tacksmen, usually younger sons, brothers or cousins of the chief, helped to maintain a myth that the clan was of one blood. For the sake of his own authority, the chief found it prudent to act on a con-sensus of these gentlemen. Yet sometimes he might harbour suspicions of the cadet branches of his family as they grew away from the parent stem and, every couple of generations or so, weed out from the tacksmen's ranks his more remote connections to replace them with closer ones.

If not, there was no telling what might rear its ugly head, as the fifth

duke of Argyll discovered on inheriting his estate in 1770 and embarking
on its development. MacChailein Mòr was warned to expect trouble from
the islanders of Mull and Tiree: 'In this disposition it's thought that long
leases might render them too much independent . . . and encourage the
people to that sort of insolence and outrage to which they are naturally
prone, and much incited by their chieftains of the MacLean gentry.' The
duke's forebears had conquered these islands a hundred years earlier yet had
only ever exerted a distant authority over the native MacLeans, without
putting in Campbells above them as tacksmen. Now a double price had to
be paid: in persistence of the hereditary enmity and in the obstacle it put
up to progress, because the long leases judged impolitic would have let the
MacLeans make improvements on their holdings. The duke took the bad
news in good part. For Tiree he returned the instruction, on its rising population, that 'as I have no inclination to subject them to any sort of distress
I will give them encouragement to settle in a fishing village which I mean
to establish in a convenient situation on the island'. As for Mull: 'You must
get the tacksmen of farms to accommodate poor people upon their
different farms with cott-houses and yards free of rent where that is necessary, and send me a list of the number in that situation with their characters.' It cannot be claimed the duke felt no responsibility for his people,
whatever they thought of him.[9]

As Argyll's instructions show, old political pressures were now reinforced
by new economic ones. Tacksmen of the clan, like all its members, had to
be provided for out of the total produce or rental of the estate, which typically would grow some crops but count its wealth rather in the cattle it
carried. A tacksman was a man who held a tack, or lease. By custom he
got one from his chief at a peppercorn rent for a set term of years or the
duration of one or two lives. The low cost was a sign of the chief's esteem
for his close kin, knowing they would never leave him without the means
for his conspicuous consumption; these were not, after all, calculating,
commercial relationships. The tacksmen could then exact a larger rent
from the clansmen and live on the difference between the two. Some tacksmen farmed on their own account, but most, like the chiefs, relied on
rental. Compared to the low productivity of the land, it was heavy – equivalent to perhaps one third of output – and in this primitive husbandry
another third of the crop had to be kept back for seed. Most tenants in fact
survived from their livestock, keeping sheep and goats for their own use
and cattle to pay the rent. Because wealth was measured and rent paid in
cattle, the pasture tended to be overstocked with weak beasts: in spring they
often had to be lifted by the farmhands from byre to field. In any event, no

clansmen could count on more than a small margin of subsistence between the rock and the hard place.[10]

By contrast with them the tacksmen stood high in social status, basking in their chief's reflected glory. This status did not always find an exact economic reflection, for there were greater, richer clans and lesser, poorer clans, or relatively fertile, fruitful parts of the Highlands and desolate, barren parts. In Argyll no cadet of Clan Campbell would have made so bold as to compete with the splendour of MacChailein Mòr's Inveraray, but some put up beautiful little Palladian mansions – the houses of Airds, Ardmaddy, Appin, Islay, Limecraigs, Lochnell and so on – with Venetian windows staring out not at the terra firma of the Most Serene Republic but at Caledonia stern and wild. On the other hand Edmund Burt, an English officer building Highland roads under General George Wade in the 1720s, stood open-mouthed, as if he had just stumbled on a clearing in some tropical jungle, at the down-at-heel but dignified greeting from a tacksman at the lower end of the scale:

> He met me at some distance from his dwelling with his Arcadian offering of milk and cream, as usual, carried before him by his servants. He afterwards invited me to his hut, which was built like the others, only very long; but without any partition; where the family was at one end and some cattle at the other . . . He was without shoes, stockings, or breeches, in a short coat, with a shirt not much longer, which hung between his thighs and just hid his nakedness from two daughters about seventeen or eighteen years who sat over against him.[11]

The word 'plaid' seems unknown to Burt or his correspondent – a reminder that while, even before the calamity of 1745, this society and culture had been affected by external pressures, they yet retained, for all their poverty, an exotic complexity and richness of their own. Now the social intricacy was to be simplified and the cultural plenty depleted. Even as Burt wrote, the class of tacksmen was shrinking and losing power because of, for example, the second duke of Argyll's policy of having the rental of his lands pass to him without mediation. There was little point in the mediation of tacksmen except in the paramilitary society of the clan, which was just what he sought to dismantle. Although the third duke felt forced to reverse the policy, the slow spread of law and order at length ratified it. Yet for several generations to come Highland landowners often thought the number of men on their estates more important than the levels of rent, despite the huge debts that still encumbered most of them. The third duke of Atholl wrote to Sir James Grant of Grant in 1772 that they should never forget they owed all they had to the loyalty of their clans: 'We ought to live and let live – by squeezing the very vitals of the poor I believe I could squeeze £600 or £700 a year more out of them than I have at present but neither the blessing of providence nor the approbation of my own heart would attend it, so I am better as I am.'[12]

Such sentiment softened economic relationships among the different strata of Gaelic society, hindered any agricultural revolution and, above all, fostered the division of holdings to house as many clansmen as possible. A rapid rise in Highland population followed, from 337,000 in Dr Alexander Webster's census of 1755 to 382,000 at the first official census of the United Kingdom in 1801.[13] The old social structure could not hold such numbers. Somewhere along the line a breaking point had to come, although development remained sluggish and no acute crisis occurred for the time being.

The pressure found release through two safety valves. One was a change from communal to individual tenure, which allowed for improvement and higher productivity. The other was a market for this novel type of holding. Landlords began to advertise farms or even estates where the lease was expiring, and to sell the renewed lease by *roup* ('auction'): fine for landlords, hateful to tenants. Tenants had to bid against their neighbours, and could not stop strangers coming in to outbid them. Rents went up too, although the aim of raising rents was not to clear the land of people but to find people to pay them: an element of choice remained, and so did a rising population.

What happened overall was the spontaneous emergence of a new agrarian order through the devolved actions of many economic agents unknown to one another. The resulting market emerged at different times in different places, but emerge it did and had to do because of the change in the conditions of supply and demand, a fixed extent of land and ever more people on it. Beholding this, most Scottish historians abandon their habitual sub-Marxist determinism and ascribe everything to the malice of landlords. But they would do better to stick with determinism: the economics is elementary, and landowners were no more able to resist the motions of the invisible hand than anybody else. Even dukes as benign as Argyll and Atholl could not in the end sit back and watch their neighbours' rentals rocket. For the tacksman, too, the day was bound to come when he had to pay an economic rent for his land or lose it. That day had arrived by the time Johnson and Boswell got to Skye.

Johnson presents a picture of the tacksmen faced by social as well as economic crisis. With the old order in dissolution, they face downward mobility so drastic that they prefer to desert their homes, while they yet have the means to go elsewhere and the authority to take their people with them. Although discouraged by feudal superiors and political authorities alike, the tacksmen are not to be stopped when they see the alternative in America of unlimited freehold land. Crossing in a body with their followers, they hope to recreate the life they leave behind in a more hospitable setting for it, preserving their leadership of a community and adding economic independence to it.

The sadness shining through Johnson's account came from the tacksmen who fixed their sights on a Scotland of the past, not an America of the future. Some went in a conservative, not a progressive, frame of mind, to preserve a piece of the Old World, not take part in building a New World. This was why they refused to support the American Revolution. In reality, their efforts to create little Scotlands beyond the seas were doomed, not least by that revolution and the ideology of the nation it created, which undid all feudalizing schemes of settlement from the Highlands. MacDonald of Kingsburgh, 'a large stately man, with a steady sensible countenance', was a failure in the last venture of his life. He returned to Skye defeated in every way.[14]

But then, he was not alone in setting off for America with high expectations. An English traveller, William Gilpin, passed by Killin in Perthshire one day in 1775 to find, preparing to emigrate, a group of thirty families, or 300 people. These were prosperous families, then, in parties that included servants as well as immediate relations; some, on his inquiry, said they were taking £200 or £300 with them, and none seemed to have less than £30 or £40. He later recalled:

Early the next morning the whole company was called together by the sound of bagpipes, and the order of their march was settled. Men, women and children had all their proper stations assigned. They were all dressed in their best attire, and the men armed in the Highland fashion

– in other words, illegally. 'They were a jocund crew; and set out, not like people flying from the face of poverty; but like men, who were about to carry their health, their strength, their little property, to a better market.'[15]

Of course, high expectations could not universally be fulfilled. A notorious emigrant voyage in these years was that of the *Hector*, which sailed in July 1773 from Loch Broom, near present-day Ullapool, to Pictou on the northern shore of Nova Scotia. The 189 passengers have gone down in Highland myth as among the earliest victims of clearance, yet they had not in fact been cleared. They left of their own free will, in reply to advertisements in Scottish newspapers placed by a couple of speculators in

American land: John Pagan, head of a merchant house in Glasgow, and the Revd John Witherspoon, former minister of Paisley and now principal of the College of New Jersey (today Princeton), who three years later would be a signatory of the American Declaration of Independence. The episode showed a less savoury side of Witherspoon in his eagerness to profit from the land he had acquired with his partner. It is not going too far to say that he and Pagan conned the people who answered their advertisements, in pitiable naïvety, about the prospects in Nova Scotia. Still, that does not make it a story of involuntary departure. Many of the emigrants came from the annexed estates, so had been living under the most amiable, if ineffective, regime in the Highlands, and they found the money to pay the passage themselves.

There is no denying their misfortune, all the same. In mid-Atlantic they ran into a hurricane. They were thrown in heaps about the hold, awash in a soup of vomit, urine, liquid excrement and bilge-water, sick and covered in sores. This went on for a fortnight. Life does not get much worse, and they prayed for death. They landed, starving and exhausted, in September to discover not the smiling landscape of fields and farmsteads they awaited but a kind of wilderness never seen in Scotland, with forests growing down to the water's edge. When they asked after their designated plots, they were told to go and look three miles inland, amid dense stands of pine. It had turned too late in the season to plant crops even if arable soil could have been found. Some set off carrying their possessions to walk two days and nights across trackless waste to the nearest existing settlement. Others opted to stay put, without an inkling of the ferocious Canadian winter about to hit them. They had to survive in flimsy huts, learning the hard way to fish through ice and hunt through snow, although survive they did.

It is pleasant to relate how their frustration and hardship at last brought a happier result. In time they turned their land, along valleys radiating from the harbour at Pictou, into rich farms, where they could live out their lives on holdings of their own creation – the best of them around the harbour itself, on a tract still known as Loch Broom. One of their ministers, James MacGregor, wrote back to his brethren in Scotland in 1791 that, although he had been 'in as disadvantageous circumstances, I suppose, as any whom the synod ever sent to this continent; and though indeed I have been in it, in weakness, in fear, in trembling, yet I account it the happiest thing that ever befell me, that I was sent to America'. In Canada these emigrants have entered into the foundation myths of the nation: 'We venture to say that there is no one element in the population of these Lower Provinces, upon which their social, moral and religious condition has depended more than upon its Scottish immigrants, and of these that band in the *Hector* were the pioneers and vanguard.'[16] But in Scottish myth they have become displaced; so far as they suffered oppression rather than misfortune, it was the oppression not of the chieftains and other superiors in Scotland but of the speculating businessmen (in particular, one of the Founding Fathers of the United States) who lured them across the ocean.

Many of the tacksmen did well to escape from between the upper and nether millstones grinding them into ruin at home. Occasionally they achieved success on their own terms, in the transfer of a familiar social structure from one hemisphere to the other with just a necessary but acceptable degree of change. In this way Glengarry County, at the eastern extremity of the present-day Ontario, turned into a Highland preserve and remained Gaelic-speaking until the twentieth century. Whole emigrant townships settled there on generous plots of land surveyed and allocated by the tacksmen, who also liaised with the colonial authorities, so that all had a stake in making the settlement work. A decisive influence came also from the county's Catholic priests: the name of Father Alexander MacDonnell, who himself led a party across the ocean, is revered there to this day. The community cohered around the social hierarchy and conservative values it brought with it, yielding economic dividends no longer available at home. Similarly, after careful planning and budgeting for the settlers' voyage and immediate needs on landing, the tacksman Captain John MacDonald of Glenaladale sent a party from the lands of Clanranald to Prince Edward Island in 1772. He later wrote:

> These have been truly fortunate, rescued from indigence and hunger, that persecutes all that remain, there are not half a dozen dead of the two hundred and odd souls that left the Highlands; they have property and plenty, a secure footing in the world, a provision for their children.[17]

Not everyone was as luckless as the MacDonalds of Kingsburgh.

More often success came because the emigrants adapted at once to local conditions. A good many tacksmen of Clan Chattan ended up in America – men of the names of McGillivray, MacIntosh, MacPhail and MacTavish, from the north-eastern side of Loch Ness. Some left against their will, as Jacobite prisoners and transportees, others as free agents seduced by glowing reports of the New World from exiled kinsmen. They did not make the mistake of trying to create little Scotlands beyond the seas. On the contrary, they took things as they found them.

In the Carolinas, for example, trade inland had collapsed after two disastrous Indian wars early in the eighteenth century. Unlike English colonists, intrepid Highlanders felt not in the least afraid of fierce tribes up country. On the contrary, they found much in common with them: martial values, oral culture, a social structure of clans. These Gaels rebuilt the trade. They bought the abundant produce of American nature, especially deerskins, which could be turned into beautiful leather. In return they brought what Indians coveted, above all rum and gunpowder. From this traffic Archibald McGillivray became the richest trader in the southern colonies. He returned to Scotland in 1745 and purchased the estate of Daviot in Inverness-shire for £10,000. His cousin Lachlan did better still: fleeing Savannah in Georgia during the American Revolution, he abandoned a plantation worth £100,000 yet still carried away enough to acquire and restore the old seat of the chiefs of McGillivray at Dunmaglass. He had wed a princess of the Creek nation, of which in 1783 their son Alexander was elected paramount chief. He for ten years repelled American encroachments on its territory. He seemed to have secured its lands and rights when he signed a treaty with President George Washington in 1790, but future governments of the United States broke the solemn word given to McGillivray and his nation.[18]

Other members of these extended families had made their way to Albany in upper New York, an emporium of the colonial fur trade, where the Gaels' ability to get on with the Indians again served them well. At the revolution they withdrew to Canada and re-established themselves in Montreal, now in co-operation with former foes the French *voyageurs* and in competition, strange to say, with an English outfit, the Hudson's Bay Company. Simon McTavish, known as 'the Marquis', a lover of fine wines, fat oysters and pretty girls, united his brother Scots in the rival North West Company, one of the first big businesses in the New World, trading to Britain, Europe and Asia. Its agents, the Nor' Westers, were mostly drawn from the ranks of Highland tacksmen, educated men of good family, a cut above the seedy traders of other nations. Alexander Mackenzie, who would become the first man to cross North America overland, started his career with his brother Roderick running a depot on Lake Athabaska, right up at the edge of the Arctic. It was dubbed the Athens of the North, because in that howling wilderness they founded a library. They were just as Scottish in their tenacity, bravado and readiness to seize what pleasure they could from lives of hardship and danger. They thought little of walking 600 miles on snow-shoes to pass Hogmanay with a friend, dining on roast beaver and boiled suet pudding, washed down with their favourite 'eggnog', rum laced with caviare. The following is the account of a dinner laid on by Alexander Mackenzie and William McGillivray, McTavish's nephew:

We dined at four o'clock, and after taking a satisfactory quantity of wine, perhaps a bottle each, the married men . . . retired, leaving about a dozen to drink their health. We now began in earnest and in true highland style, and by four o'clock in the morning the whole of us had reached such a state of perfection that we could all give the war whoop as well as Mackenzie and McGillivray, we could all sing admirably, we could all drink like fishes, and we all thought we could dance on the table without disturbing a single decanter, glass or plate by which it was profusely covered.

The party ended like this:

Mackenzie now proposed to drink a toast to our memory and then give the war whoop over us fallen foes or friends all nevertheless on the floor, and on . . . attempting to push the bottle to McGillivray at the opposite end of the table he slid off his chair and could not recover his seat, while McGillivray in extending himself over the table in the hope of seizing the bottle fell hopelessly to the floor.[19]

The Scots' taste for devilment could turn ugly too. Contest between the North West Company and Hudson's Bay Company grew over time so violent it could no longer be tolerated. With much arm-twisting from the Canadian and imperial authorities, the two companies merged. Highland gentlemen continued to provide senior personnel to the combined business: George Simpson, who ran it through the mid-nineteenth century, was descended from Duncan Forbes of Culloden. Nor was the Canadian Arctic the sole distant quarter of the globe where tacksmen left their mark. Another wilderness, the Australian outback, was to be opened up to pastoral agriculture by emigrants named Erskine of Mar, MacDonnell of Glengarry, Mackenzie of Flowerdale, MacLeod of Talisker and MacNeill of Barra. The steady stream of these talented Gaels leaving the Highlands between 1750 and 1850 suggests that, far from being harried and oppressed, they had enough optimism and resolve to surmount both the difficulties they faced and the obstacles put in their way.[20]

That still could not make the sight of an old society breaking up any prettier. Dr Johnson's is interesting testimony, gathered at first hand by an outside observer who, through his bearish growls, showed much sympathy for the old society. It is confirmed by testimony from within. MacDonald of Sleat, who first welcomed Johnson and Boswell to Skye, headed the sole chiefly family that at this stage visibly repudiated its historic obligations to its people. One had tried to sell surplus members of the clan to America in the 1730s; in the 1770s his successor was still taking out his troubles on his tacksmen. That such an attitude remained exceptional is shown by the astonishment at it of Sleat's neighbours, the MacLeods of MacLeod, not always popular chiefs themselves. Their factor, Alexander MacLeod of Glendale, told in 1771 how Sleat had done so much damage to relations with his tacksmen that they 'won't stay under such a tyrant' even if he should offer them land on the former terms: 'They propose to go all in a body to North Carolina and settle near each other, ten of the most substantial gentlemen have already signed a covenant of this nature.' They were now 'inviting other gentlemen to join them and giving encouragement to the country tenants to follow them'; a hundred families had at once agreed.[21]

It is, then, no surprise to find the bard of Sleat, John MacCodrum, wishing well to the emigrants:

> *Triallaibh nis, fhearaibh,*
> *Gu dùthaich gun ghasinne.*
> *Cuiribh cùl ris an fhearann*
> > *Chaidh thairis am màl oirbh*
> *Gu dùthaich a'bhainne,*
> *Gu dùthaich na meala,*
> *Gu dùthaich an ceannaich sibh*
> > *Fearann gu'r n-àilgheas*
> *Gu dùthaich gun aineis*
> *Gun chrionadh gun stanard,*
> *Far an cnuasaich sibh barrachd*
> > *'S a mhaireas ri'r làithean . . .*

> Go now, men,
> To a country without want,
> Turn your back on the land
> Whose rent is too high for you,
> For a country of milk,
> For a country of honey.
> For a country where you can buy
> As much land as you want,
> For a land without poverty,
> Without blight or shortage,
> Where you will gather more
> Than can last all your days.

There is sympathy for the emigrants' plight here, and not the faintest of praise for the landlord. Still, MacCodrum's witness has to be suspect because he was employed by MacDonald of Sleat, and in the elation he conveys at the idea of leaving Skye he may have an ulterior motive. He, at

any rate, stayed behind; yet the tone is no less positive in the poetry of the
emigrants themselves, as in this by Rory Roy Mackenzie:

> *Siud an imrich tha feumail*
> *Dhol 'nar leum as an tir s'*
> *Dho dh'America chraobhach,*
> *'S am bi saors' agus sìth.*

> *Faigh an nall dhuinn am botul,*
> *Thoir dhuinn deoch as mu'n cuairt;*
> *'s mise a'fear a tha deònach*
> *A'dhol a sheòladh a'chuain . . .*

> We have to emigrate,
> To leave this land at one bound,
> For forested America
> Where there will be freedom and peace.

> Get us a bottle over here;
> Pass round a drink to us;
> I'm a man very keen
> To sail the seas . . .

Mackenzie ignores the horrors of an oceanic voyage under sail, although
of course those horrors awaited emigrants of whatever origin or nationality. He gives no hint that they may have a terrible time on landing either,
but again many immigrants have had that, whether Gaels in Nova Scotia
or Sicilians in New York or Chinese in San Francisco. It is a moving record
of sacrifice, by Scots among myriads of others, for a greater good, but it
cannot be regarded as uniquely Scottish, or uniquely Highland. If modern
Scots have cast a retrospective pall of gloom over these events, emigrants
writing at the time found their sadness at leaving home overborne by
excitement at fresh prospects and, after arrival, by a sense of satisfaction at
a hazardous transition successfully accomplished. Michael MacDonald
wrote from Prince Edward Island in 1772:

> *A, 's àlainn an t-àite*
> *Th'agam 'n cois na tràghad*
> *Nuair thug e gu bhith 'g àiteach ann*
> *Leis a'chrann, leis a'chrann, O.*

> *Ni mi 'n t-aran leis na gearrain*
> *'S an crodh-bainne chuir mu'n bhaile;*
> *'S cha bhi annas oirnn 's an earrach,*
> *Chuirinn geall, chuirinn geall, O.*

> Ah, beautiful is the place
> I have right on the shore,
> When the time comes for tilling it
> With the plough, with the plough, Oh.
>
> I'll produce bread with the horses
> And I'll put the cows on my field;
> We won't be short in the spring,
> I bet that's so, bet that's so, oh.

MacDonald's reference to the want of a Highland spring – which for infants and old folk often meant starving to death – is oblique, like a distant bad memory. His prime interest lies in a promised land where people cast off their woes. And this is the way America was usually depicted, rather than as an abode of exile and misery, in the conventions of Gaelic poetry.[22]

The most talented Gaels were leaving, people who in the Highland hierarchy came closest to a middle class. At home they had the standing to talk to their chiefs man to man, yet they mixed on intimate terms with their clansmen too. In their houses they formed libraries of classical and modern books, enough to keep Johnson and Boswell engrossed on rainy days, yet they knew the Gaelic songs and conversed with the people in the language of Eden. No doubt it was precisely because they possessed information, intelligence and motivation enough that they could weigh up the prospects of staying or going, and decide to go. Some even agreed that their chiefs' demands for higher rents were fair, as the old rents had been unrealistic. How such rents could be paid out of the unimproved agriculture of ever more people was a problem that had to be left to others. So ancient loyalties loosened: with the decline of the clan, the tacksmen lost their place in the natural order of things.

Nearly everyone saw this loss as a misfortune. Chiefs sought to discourage the emigration, and the British government to stop it – especially as tacksmen often led away with them the more venturesome tenants and their capital (from cattle they sold), leaving just the subtenants and the poor behind. Highland society became more polarized between chiefs and peasants, an ill omen for the future. The loss of a middle class proved deep and durable in another way, for the Gàidhealtachd was afterwards seldom able to generate native enterpreneurs and suffered accordingly from a vicious circle of poverty and decline. At this stage the emigration was almost entirely voluntary, undertaken by valuable members of society in defiance of the landowners and the state. For most it would prove beyond doubt better – better, that is, for themselves – to go than to stay.

10

Seats of oppression

Eviction and development, to 1800

SCOTS LIKE FIGHTS, although in fact most Scottish fights never take place because they are called off beforehand at some stage during the ritual preliminaries dictated by custom. Still there can also be miscalculations, and one occurred on a day in June 1792 at the farm of Kildermorie in Strathrusdale, Easter Ross, an area known locally as the Struie, rolling country that rises to high moors. The farm belonged to Captain Allan Cameron and his brother Alexander, who had arrived the year before from their native Lochaber to rear sheep – an agricultural innovation, or improvement, round here. They got a tack of the land from Sir Hector Munro of Novar, MP for the Inverness Burghs, a son of this soil who had made a fortune from an Indian military career. Little is known of Allan Cameron except that he was an old soldier, and he may have served under his landlord while Sir Hector was colonel of the 89th regiment of foot, a corps raised by the duke of Gordon, who owned a good bit of Lochaber.

The Camerons had had trouble with the locals. They got rid of thirty-seven families from their land yet did not evict all the small tenants; it might have been better if they had, because then no trouble could have followed. Instead, they set aside some corners of the strath where those they kept on could graze cattle. Endless niggles about demarcation arose. Sheep readily live on moor and mountain, so people no doubt resented good pasture being given over to them while their cows had to make do with unwanted ground. When from time to time the Camerons found cattle in fields reserved to themselves, they poinded the beasts. They demanded money for releasing them and promises that the trespass would not happen again.

Trouble rumbled on for months before suddenly coming to a head. One day all the cattle from Strathrusdale somehow got into the sheep farm at Kildermorie, where the Camerons' shepherds rounded them up. The locals, angered at frequent poindings, resolved to pay no more fines. Instead they set out to free their animals by force. They sent for help from their neighbours on the estate of Ardross, who were cutting peat at the time but at once downed tools and marched over to Kildermorie. At their head

144

came Alexander Wallace, the tallest and toughest fighter of the Struie, known as Alasdair Mòr or Big Wallace. By the time he arrived he had fifty men behind him.

Cameron's shepherds vanished at this, but he was gamely intent on defending himself with the help of his consumptive brother, three servants and a woman. He grabbed a shotgun and a dirk 12 inches long. He told the oncoming mob 'he would shoot them like birds and send the rest of them to Botany Bay'. When it came to the point, though, he had to face their champion man to man. As the pair grappled, the scornful Big Wallace seized Cameron's shotgun and twisted the barrels 'like a widdie' – as if they were of rope. He took the dirk and tossed it behind him to one of his family, who would keep it as a souvenir. Then he turned away in contempt, leaving his followers to beat up Cameron and those with him. When the men of Strathrusdale had finished, they freed their cattle and went home.

The mortified Cameron wanted to prosecute his assailants. Witnesses received a summons to give precognitions on 25 July at Alness, down on the Cromarty Firth, but their neighbours stopped them going. The law was mocked and the locals laughed. On 27 July a wedding took place in Strathrusdale where guests made merry not just over the happy couple but also over the Camerons' discomfiture. The merrier people got, the more extravagant the plans they dreamed up for pressing home their advantage. They wondered if they might gather a flock of all the sheep in the counties of Ross and Sutherland and drive them south until they crossed the Beauly river, the boundary of Inverness-shire. Big Wallace was there, loud-mouthed from his whisky. He bayed that they would scotch like vermin the sheep and their shepherds.

Such drink-fuelled blethers ought to have died down the morning after, yet the excitement spread. When people went to church the next Sunday, men appeared to read a 'proclamation' at the doors. It said that any who wished to take part in a great drove of sheep should muster in Strathoykel, near the head of the Dornoch Firth, on 31 July. About 200 turned up there, and smaller numbers at other places, some armed. It was reported that they again intimidated farmers where they went to collect the sheep, as far away as Lairg, 5 miles into Sutherland. They brought flocks from four parishes together until they had several thousand animals. Then they started the drove. By 4 August they had reached Kildermorie and added the Camerons' flock to the monstrous multitude.[1]

The lairds of Easter Ross took alarm. They knew that there was revolution in France, and that its ripples had even reached Scotland. Every 4 June, the birthday of George III, Scots went out to get drunk in the king's honour, but in 1792 the festivity in Edinburgh had turned ugly. A mob gathered in George Square in front of the town house of the country's political boss, Henry Dundas, also Home Secretary in London, and burned him in effigy before breaking all his windows. In a country where next to no political disturbance had occurred for four decades, it was a sensation.[2] Up in Easter Ross the gentry resolved not to stand for anything of the kind. They met at Dingwall with the sheriff depute of the county, Donald Macleod of Geanies, and discussed how to foil the drove. They organized their own men and asked for three companies of the Black Watch from Fort George at Inverness. In the small hours of 5 August at Boath, just north of the Cromarty Firth, this force pounced on the men keeping watch over the flock, fifty or sixty of them for 6000 sheep. Most fled in time, but eight were taken prisoner and others captured later. Soldiers saw the sheep back to where they had come from, and an uneasy peace settled over Easter Ross once more.[3]

That was the end of the protest that, in the Gaels' oral tradition, came to be remembered as *Bliadhna nan Caorach* ('the year of the sheep'). While they had always bred sheep, this episode locked itself into their consciousness because it represented something new and threatening, something that was indeed to transform their way of life for ever. The old Highland sheep had been small, skinny and shaggy, almost like puppies, yielding little meat or wool. But by now meat and wool were needed in wider Scottish and British society, as cities grew with industrial workers who could no longer provide food and clothing for themselves but bought them from markets. The markets were supplied by agricultural workers in the countryside. On this division of labour, meat and wool turned into commodities to be produced as efficiently as possible. This created a demand for better breeds of sheep – in Scotland first the Blackface, then the Cheviot. And it required more intense use of factors of production, above all land, with its withdrawal if necessary from less efficient uses. The new sheep-farming steadily spread until by the late eighteenth century it hit the Highlands. According to the myths, it was here a monopoly of Lowlanders or even Englishmen, yet this is untrue. The spirit of enterprise that carried some Gaels to America took others into improving agriculture. Sheep farms flourished especially around the southern end of the Great Glen, whence wool could easily be transported by sea to textile mills. That was where the Camerons of Kildermorie had come from. Now in Ross they aimed to emulate men of their name who prospered from sheep in their own Lochaber – Allan Cameron of Invercaddle or John Cameron of Corrychoillie, not to mention Donald MacDonald of Tulloch or Alexander MacDonald of Glencoe, all Gaels but capitalist farmers too on a novel pattern. Highland sheep entered into competition with Highland cattle. They also entered into competition with Highland people.[4]

Although minor in themselves, the events in Ross have assumed larger historical dimensions because they marked the first popular resistance to that fundamental economic change. On the king's birthday of 1792 Henry Dundas had been absent from Edinburgh, but his nephew Robert was there in George Square. This charming but fussy little hypochondriac held the office of Lord Advocate, in charge of law and order in Scotland. Now he was watching like a hawk for any further signs of activity by political radicals. It cannot have been wholly uncongenial to him to receive a letter from Sir Hector Munro saying his constituents were 'at present so completely under the heel of the populace that should they come to burn our houses, or destroy our property in any way their caprice may lead them to, we are incapable of resistance', for all the world like French aristos faced with *sans-culottes*. The Lord Advocate passed the letter to his uncle, with what other information he had culled on 'the alarming outrages in Ross-shire'. Henry Dundas did not hesitate to sanction 'the most vigorous and effectual methods . . . for bringing these daring offenders to punishment'. The lower classes had to be shown 'that they will not be suffered to continue such acts of violence with impunity'.[5]

The round-up of the drovers was a matter of satisfaction, then, to the rulers of Scotland. In September the captives went on trial at Inverness before Lord Stonefield and a jury. First to appear were eight men of Strathrusdale alleged to have attacked Cameron, but they were acquitted by a majority of riot, assault and battery. The defence brought out that Cameron, without giving due legal notice of his intentions, had met them with arms and threatened them with violence. The jury accepted that they acted in self-defence. Next, some of the drovers entered the dock. They were found guilty. Stonefield sentenced two to be transported for seven years, two more to be banished from Scotland for life, one to be imprisoned for three months, and the last to be fined £50 sterling and imprisoned for one month, or until the fine was paid. There was an operatic sequel. On the night of 24 October the pair sentenced to transportation escaped from the tolbooth of Inverness, perhaps with help from outside or even inside. A public notice named them as Hugh Breck Mackenzie, aged forty (Breck from the Gaelic word for 'scarred by small-pox') and John Aird, aged forty-five, 'straight and well-made'. A reward of £5 was offered for their recapture, but nobody claimed it. The fugitives were supposed to have gone to ground somewhere along the Moray

Firth, hidden by local people. The authorities judged it best not to search too hard for them.

This act of oblivion may seem surprising after the blood-curdling sentiments with which the Dundases had greeted news of the nuisance in the north. But the one thing not to do when trying to sway the mind of Henry Dundas was to disturb public order. He took pride in being the first Scot since the Union – leaving aside the wretched Lord Bute – to have risen high in the counsels of the United Kingdom. And he knew this eminence, whence huge benefits could and did flow to Scotland, depended on his keeping the country quiet, so his colleagues in London would not have bad old memories stirred. On any hint of disaffection among Scots, therefore, he always came down like a ton of bricks.

Yet beneath his aggressive public posture Dundas had his doubts about the condition of the Highlands: his own mother, after all, came from Easter Ross. The prime focus of his career was the British Empire. This eminently practical politician turned in his way into a visionary, reflecting on how the far-flung imperial possessions might be brought into some measure of economic integration with one another, in a process that could affect and profit every part of the mother country, including Scotland and including the Highlands. He loved to kick ideas about with original thinkers as well as with acknowledged experts, especially if they happened to be Scots. It was no accident that one canny compatriot whose brains he picked, John Knox, published a survey with the title *View of the British Empire, more especially Scotland, with some proposals for the improvement of that country, the extension of its fisheries and the relief of its people.* Actually it was about the Highlands. It shows the broad perspective of Dundas's circle. Knox did not mince his words: 'The situation of these people, inhabitants of Britain! is such as no language can describe, or fancy conceive . . . Upon the whole, the Highlands of Scotland, some few estates excepted, are the seats of oppression, poverty, famines, anguish and wild despair.' As things stood, in other words, the Highlands could make no contribution to the Empire.[6]

Knox's work came out under the aegis of the Highland Society. Its founding in 1784 coincided with Dundas's restoration of the forfeited estates to old Jacobite families. The two moves went in tandem. The British state was withdrawing from the Highlands but still needed some agency to pay heed to the needs of the region as a whole, a private or voluntary body with public, philanthropic purposes. The society fitted the bill. Under the affable fifth duke of Argyll as president, its membership consisted of landowners and literati. It had economic aims: it published essays on improvement and enclosure, management of livestock, new crops and so on, with gold medals for their authors. It also had cultural aims: it investigated the authenticity of Ossian and in the process collected many Gaelic manuscripts which were deposited in the Advocates' Library in Edinburgh. It brought out a vocabulary of Gaelic in 1794, an Old Testament in 1803 and a full dictionary in 1828.

With these the society set off quite a flood of Gaelic publishing now that, as the language of Eden had been taught in the charity schools for a generation, a readership was there. Leaving aside some short-lived period-icals, the market wanted sacred literature: Bibles and catechisms, but also Dugald Buchanan's poetry. No original work in Gaelic has been reprinted more often than Buchanan's *Spiritual Songs*, which went through twenty editions from 1767 to 1844: clearly a commercial proposition.[7] Their appeal lay in not only their religious but also their aesthetic and psycho-logical power. In vigorous images Buchanan works through Highland complexes still recognizable, with an innate wildness mired in a terrible conviction of sin. The reason for his making metaphors of sheep may be intriguing, but he writes of fellow Gaels as of lambs gone astray:

> *Ri meilich chruaidh ta'd ruith gach nì*
> *An dùil gum faigh an inntinn clos;*
> *Ach dhaibh ta 'n saoghal gun iochd no truas*
> *Mar mhuime choimhich fhuair gun tlus.*

> Bleating hard they chase everything
> Thinking they'll get peace of mind;
> But the world's as merciless to them
> As a cold unloving alien nurse.[8]

The Highland Society encouraged non-literary activities such as piping as well: all a stark contrast to, not to say complete reversal of, the previous official suppression of Gaelic culture. The governors of Scotland now viewed linguistic renewal with goodwill. For their part the Dundases, while in charge of the nation's public affairs from 1775 to 1830, made it a rule, for instance, always to appoint Gaelic-speaking sheriffs to Gaelic-speaking counties. Henry Dundas's son, another Robert, insisted on this even in the face of entreaties by people as powerful as the countess of Sutherland.[9]

The linguistic renewal showed how economic and cultural improve-ment might interact to benefit the people, so long as the Highlands pre-served the peace and good order attained only within living memory. Henry Dundas was not so naïve as to think peace and good order came of themselves; they had to be fostered, even imposed on a region still in the throes of profound long-term transformation. Yet this should not turn into counter-productive tyranny. On the crucial point at issue in 1792 the Lord Advocate voiced the dilemmas. In reporting the unrest in Ross to Henry Dundas, he explained how the spread of sheep-farming was 'a measure very unpopular in those Highland districts where sheep are not yet introduced, as it tends to remove the inhabitants on those estates from their small possessions and dwelling houses'. This, given his public position, his prissy lawyer's caution and his desire always to please his uncle, amounted to an expression of sympathy for the motives of those who resisted the sheep – if not, of course, for their conduct.[10]

The underlying sympathy in official circles is revealed at greater length in a report written in August the same year, in between the arrests in Easter Ross and the trials in Inverness, by Lord Adam Gordon, commander-in-chief, Scotland. Gordon occupied a special place in Henry Dundas's affections. He, in raising his nation's status inside the United Kingdom, had reclaimed for Scots certain high positions tacitly withheld from them by the wary English after the Union. One such position was commander-in-chief, Scotland. At Dundas's behest Gordon became the first Scot to be appointed to it since 1707. Dundas liked the Gordons, staunch political allies and convivial social companions, and he liked old soldiers who had seen plenty of active service, as Lord Adam had done in Europe and America. The commander-in-chief sent his report from Fort George to the Lord Advocate, and it is safe to assume it went straight to Henry Dundas.

Gordon, who was on a tour of inspection of Highland fortifications, found the region settling down and needing no more military intervention. It had had an unpleasant experience yet, 'if I was to hazard an opinion upon the matter . . . it is a decided one that no *disloyalty* or hint of *rebellion* or dislike of His Majesty's . . . *government* is in the least degree in these tumults'. Their origin lay rather in fear that landowners 'were about to let their estates to sheep farmers, by which means all the former tenantry would be ousted and turned adrift and of course obliged to emigrate unless they could be elsewhere received, any probability of which they could not discover'. Gordon shared the dismay. Like the rest of the Scottish ruling class, he believed that 'the strength of the nation depends on the number of people'. In the lands of proprietors who respected this idea, 'there had been no disturbance . . . nor has the Duke of Gordon or Mackenzie of Seaforth lost one man on their wide extended Highland estates'. Of course, 'everybody knows the wonderful attachment a Highlander has to his *native spot* be it ever so bare and ever so *mountainous.*'

Such sturdy sentiment would be lost for ever 'if these calculating gentle-men shall by any means or from *avarice* once dispeople their estates and fill them with sheep': they should not think they could come running to gov-ernment in case of trouble then. Even so, Gordon did not dispute their absolute right to do what they wanted with their property, work though that might against the public interest. Disorder remained far worse, and ringleaders of 'the late daring mobs . . . disgraceful to any civilized coun-try' had to be brought to justice. 'Thank God as yet no blood has been spilt,' wrote Gordon, 'but the law will take its course.'[11]

Such was the unease among the rulers of Scotland at this first popular resistance to economic change in the Highlands. One level down, the reac-tion of a Gael, Sheriff Macleod, seems just as interesting. Macleod had not hesitated to enforce the law against the drovers, even though they tried to play on the understanding they felt he must have for their plight. He stood out as a political opponent of the Dundases: it was due to his electoral ener-gies that the parliamentary constituency of Ross remained in the hands of the dwindling band of Scots Whigs. He was besides respected in the county as a model improver, one who took account of the people's interests as well as his own. On his estate, some miles to the east on the Moray Firth, he had mounted an ambitious programme to convert moor into arable land by 'inclosing, mixing the different soils by trenching, and laying on lime', which also gave employment to locals. As a result, during the last Highland famine, of 1783, the starving had come down here from the mountains to be fed: 'But for those supplies, disorder and rapine would have prevailed, and the poor, rendered desperate by famine like so many hungry wolves, would have broken loose and laid hands on whatever they could find.' What a contrast from the previous famine! Then, in 1741, many were 'found dead on the highways and in the fields; and others, though long fasting, expired as soon as they tasted food'.[12]

Sheriff Macleod deserved well of the people of Ross, then, and in July 1792 the drovers let him know they would exempt him from their action and leave his sheep alone. Yet they got him wrong. He refused to support them in any way against lawful authority. He later wrote: 'The spirit of vio-lence was carried so far as to set the civil power at defiance; the laws were trampled upon; there appeared no safety for property; and the gentlemen of the country seemed to be subjected to the power and control of an unruly and ungovernable mob.' He insisted that, contrary to some modish opinion, sheep-farming benefited everyone. Although it had been intro-duced to Ross fifteen years earlier, there was 'not as yet one single family been obliged to emigrate on account of sheep'. To be sure, 'some families have been obliged to change their situations, and move from one farm to another'. They might dislike being shifted around, but they could hardly claim a right to live for ever in one place, and their reaction was not 'a good reason why a proprietor should preclude himself from letting to a more enterprising and active occupant'. Highland lairds ought to 'have the same liberty of improving or managing their properties as seems to them the most conducive to their interest' – even if depopulation followed, which Macleod anyway thought unlikely. He assured the people of Ross that 'introducing a source of wealth and a staple of manufacture hitherto unknown amongst them [would] increase their numbers and their happiness'.[13]

Here were the thoughts of a humane, liberal, progressive landlord optimistic about prospects both for improvement and for the people affected, because confident that an expanding economy could absorb the displaced population. He represents the type of those leading Scotland towards a better future. After the chiefs, the most influential Highlanders were gentlemen with an enlightened education, as Macleod had had in studying law at Edinburgh. There he belonged to the circle of the Adams of Blairadam, which a generation earlier had welcomed another Gael, Adam Ferguson. Macleod in his turn imbibed the values of improving Lowlanders. Application of their values had brought spectacular results and made their region's economy one of the most dynamic in Europe. That, too, had involved displacement of the population.

Scottish historians have begun to take note of the Lowland clearances, which carried huge numbers off the land at the behest of its owners. For example, in the Dundases' parish of Temple, Midlothian, the population fell by one third in the late eighteenth century.[14] Yet neither here nor elsewhere in the Lowlands was there any unrest to speak of. The economy absorbed people into new activities without much pain. It could not have been unreasonable of Sheriff Macleod to suppose that, given similar vigour and purpose, spectacular results might be achieved in the Highlands too. Of course, the terrain and climate made this harder: a new rural economy here would, for example, still have more stock than grain, in contrast to the Lowlands. But the policies could be adjusted and the commitments of men such as Macleod, rooted in this soil, might win the same popular assent to a process of benefit to all in the end.

So Macleod saw no good reason for resistance. Individual occupancy had, after all, never been assured in the old Highlands either. Clansmen might have believed in a hereditary right to occupy some holding or other on their chiefs' territory, but that could not have amounted to a right to a specific plot because no such guarantee had been feasible in an unstable society. Clans often lost territory to their foes, through blunder, delusion or misdeed: broken men and exiled chiefs had been living proof of it. Mobility was nothing new in the Gàidhealtachd. What Macleod and his like might hope was to make it a force for good rather than ill. Then Highland and Lowland lairds would be espousing identical aims, public-spirited and indeed patriotic.

A possible consequence of the work by Macleod and his like might have been for the social structure in the Highlands to move closer to that in the rural Lowlands. Out of a new agriculture, driven by markets, a class of independent farmers could have arisen alongside a class of labourers without land who lived by working for them. In much of the Highlands to the east of the Great Glen, together with the Black Isle, this is more or less what did happen, although farms remained smaller and farmers poorer than in the Lowlands. In the north and west things were different. There individual plots survived, but constantly diminishing in size as larger and larger numbers of tenants squeezed on to them. In such a conservative society, to be landless was in effect to drop out of it. So people divided their parcels of land over and over again, often to let their children stay, marry and have a family of their own. The old peasantry in communal settlements had not evaporated. It just turned into a new peasantry on smallholdings, or rather groups of such holdings, with a residual element of common grazings on the hills behind. This is the definition of crofts, as they came to be known. While one class, the tacksmen, vanished from the Gàidhealtachd, another emerged, much more numerous and much more precarious. The intricacy of the old Highland society polarized into uniformity on two tiers, landlords and crofters, with greater risk of a straight conflict of interest.

In the end the novel structure did not make its members better off on either tier: for once, Scots improvers failed to improve. There followed instead something like what happened in Ireland or other peripheral parts of Europe where the penalties of a rapid rise in population could never be offset by rewards from development. The Highland population did not, to be sure, rise as fast as the Lowland population, because part of the natural increase continued to be creamed off by migration. People living on the fringes of the region drifted into the booming economy of central Scotland, to find seasonal or permanent employment as described by Dundas in his thoughtful paper on Highland problems of 1775. So the population grew fastest in the furthest parts. According to Dr Webster in 1755, the Inner and Outer Hebrides contained 19,000 people. By the census of

1801 they contained 30,000 people – an increase not of a mere 13 per cent, the average for the whole region over the period, but of 60 per cent.

No doubt there were many reasons for the growing Highland population, but a couple stand out. One was the early spread of vaccination against smallpox, a scourge especially of little children. Infant mortality in the Gàidhealtachd must have been frightful. Adam Smith wrote in *The Wealth of Nations*: 'A half-starved Highland woman frequently bears more than twenty children. It is not uncommon . . . for a mother who has borne twenty children not to have two alive.'[15] Edmund Burt, again sounding like a traveller to Africa today, felt shocked to find so many filthy, ragged, barefoot, verminous, scabby, pot-bellied waifs in the north: 'I have often seen them come out of the huts early in a cold morning and squat themselves down (if I may decently use the comparison) like dogs on a dunghill.' They were 'strangely neglected till they are six or seven years old'; it could not have been worth wasting affection on them before they proved they were going to survive infancy.[16] Highlanders did, however, benefit in one way from living through the winter under the same roof as their cattle. They knew a bout of the cowpox protected them against the lethal smallpox. So the principle of vaccination struck them as natural, while Lowlanders often shunned it as contrary to God's will. Of ministers reporting regular practice of vaccination in their parishes in the *Old Statistical Account*, half came from the Highlands and islands.[17] The fall in infant mortality set the rise in population rolling.

Another reason was the introduction of the potato. It is first mentioned in Martin Martin's account of the Hebrides in 1695. The main Highland crops then were still oats or bere (an inferior variety of barley), although the staples of the human diet came from cattle: butter and cheese as long as they lasted and, in spells of want, congealed blood drawn from the beasts' veins. This did little for the cattle, and for humans the nourishment caused dysentery. Gaels remained conservative in their eating as in their other habits, however, and not until the famine of 1741 did a big switch to the potato follow: it withstood Scotland's weather at its worst like no other crop. After it was planted on South Uist in 1743, the cultivation of it spread within a decade to the rest of the Hebrides and reached the mainland. By the famine of 1782–3, when once more the early onset of an arctic winter caused the harvest to fail, many were dependent on the potato: 'Nothing alarmed the people so much as the risk which the potatoes ran', wrote John Ramsay of Ochtertyre of the crisis in Perthshire.[18] They were nutritious, resilient and fecund, offering high yields from marginal land. They could be grown in places where nothing else could – on any spare spot around the crofts, even on moor and mountain. Gaels learned the technique of going up there, marking out a patch of ground, fertilizing it with seaweed or excrement and planting potatoes in it. These so-called 'lazy beds' were the wonder of visitors.

Highland lairds tolerated or even encouraged the congestion as giving them a pool of labour for various useful purposes, including improvement: they saw people as part of the wealth of the country, such as it was. They kept a wary eye on emigration, although when the American War ended in 1783 the renewed movement outwards was more subdued than might have been expected from the great surge before 1776. Loyal Scots could hardly look for a warm welcome in the United States. As for Canada, the country had problems enough in absorbing refugees from the Thirteen Colonies and in settling demobilized soldiers promised a grant of North American land, both of which groups contained many Scots: the last thing wanted was shiploads of haggard Highlanders too. More war from 1793, now with revolutionary France, again halted emigrant traffic. When pent-up demand found release after the Peace of Amiens in 1801, the Scottish authorities soon stepped in. The Passenger Act of 1803 set regulations for health and safety at sea which, while justified in themselves, had a side-effect of pushing the cost of a transatlantic passage beyond the means of most Gaels. The law was piloted through Parliament by the Lord Advocate, Charles Hope, Dundas's brother-in-law.[19]

In time of war the British state, too, had obvious reasons for wanting to retain the Highland population: it gave an endless stream of recruits to army and navy. The interest of Union and Empire concurred with that of the chiefs. Since 1745 these had learned the value of recruitment for sustaining their shaky prestige, living down their Jacobite pasts or retrieving their forfeited estates. They were the ones that drove the recruitment on. By 1800 no fewer than thirty-seven Highland regiments had been embodied, of perhaps 70,000 men in all. Several won immortal fame in the field: Cameron Highlanders, Gordon Highlanders, Ross-shire Buffs, Seaforth Highlanders, Sutherland Highlanders. It was here the traditions of the clan most clearly survived. Recruitment came first through the call of the clan, with officers appointed from the chief's kith and kin, then bringing in contingents of their tenantry. In 1778, when the Seaforth Highlanders were raised, half the soldiers hailed from the earl's estate in Ross, the rest from estates of other Mackenzies. Raising a regiment was not a step to be taken lightly: it could cost £15,000 to go through the motions of embodiment, with extras to follow. When the duke of Gordon raised his in 1793, he allowed for 66 gallons of whisky to be shared out among the men; each also got a shilling and a kiss from the duchess. The heavy expenditure was offset by qualifying chiefs for patronage from the British state or by placing veteran officers and men on its payroll.[20]

Dundas always happily killed two birds with one stone. He had, in part, martial motives for another exercise in Highland philanthropy, the British Fisheries Society. The best recruits for the navy – three times larger than the army – came from jobs giving relevant experience, in the merchant marine or in fishing. The latter remained undeveloped in Scotland. Dundas set out to remedy this through the foundation of the society in 1786, again with Argyll as governor and himself as a director. It was financed from private subscriptions matched by grants from the government. The money went to buy land and build villages with everything needed for the fisheries. Three villages were soon founded, at Tobermory on Mull, Lochbay on Skye and Ullapool in Wester Ross; a fourth would be sited at Pulteneytown, next to Wick. Lochbay failed, but the rest survived. In the nineteenth century Wick grew into one of Europe's greatest fishing harbours, and in the twentieth century Ullapool still offered a haven for factory ships from the Communist bloc, with Russian heard alongside Gaelic in the streets. Dundas had also, to aid navigation round the rugged Scottish coasts, had the first Commissioners for Northern Lighthouses appointed in 1786. Now fishing offered a livelihood to Highlanders. In 1787, 5000 barrels of herring were landed in Scottish ports; by 1796 the number had risen to 131,000. Some recent writers see even in this a fiendish plot against the Gael, dwelling on the hardships of a fisherman's life, which are undoubted; but throwing excrement over a patch of moorland and planting potatoes in it was not much fun either. The point holds that if a growing population had to live on a given extent of land, fresh sources of income became vital.[21]

Some of those sources seem today improbable. Britain was industrializing with such vigour that the expansion reached out to the far north. Scottish coal, although it had been exploited since the Middle Ages, was not yet being produced on an industrial scale, and Highland timber offered a substitute. An Fhùirneis is a place-name in several parts of the region, marking where in the eighteenth century furnaces were constructed, that is, charcoal-burning kilns for smelting iron. One of these is now an open-air museum at Bonawe, near the mouth of the River Awe on Loch Etive, in the heart of Clan Campbell's country, although the place was run by an English investor, who also built workers' housing. This Highland industry did not, however, survive the discovery of coal seams and iron ore close together in Lanarkshire.

One of little longer duration, though of greater importance at the time, was kelp. This is both a collective name for a variety of seaweeds and a word to designate their calcined ashes, containing an inferior alkali that nevertheless had value for the early manufacture of soap and glass. Britain could get alkali by importing barilla from the Mediterranean region or wood-ash from America and the Baltic countries, but wars often cut off supply. Then, with prices soaring, Highland kelp came into its own, especially in the quarter-century to 1815, when Britain was almost continuously fighting France. In the Western Isles, above all, it soon provided the main source of income, overtaking crofts. Again, people employed in kelping did not lead pleasant lives, as they waded waist-deep into the ocean and stood for hours cutting seaweed with saw-toothed sickles. And, once peace came, they suffered the abrupt loss of a livelihood to which they had grown accustomed over a generation. Such swings in an economic cycle have at some scholarly hands become another stick with which to beat the landlords: they are accused of having irresponsibly ignored the volatile nature of the kelp market and its human cost.[22]

It should not be thought that Gaels were incapable of enterprise of their own. Today, when the regiments stand under recurrent threat and the fishing has been ruined by European policy, the one industry that flourishes after three centuries – and that has spread Scotland's fame round the world – is one that the people created in defiance of the authorities. Whisky has been distilled and drunk in the Highlands since the Middle Ages, if not earlier. The British state always imposed punitive taxation on it. A single exception was made for Duncan Forbes of Culloden, in view of his sterling services to the state. He retained a right to distil and sell duty-free whisky from barley grown at his estate of Ferintosh in Easter Ross, a privilege not abolished until 1785. Robert Burns, no less, mourned it:

> O Whisky! soul o plays and pranks!
> Accept a Bardie's grateful thanks!
> When wanting thee, what tuneless cranks
>   Are my poor verses!
> Thou comes, they rattle i'their ranks,
>   At ither's arses![23]

What the state sought to do with its regulation was to concentrate output in large distilleries easier to control – such as the one at Bowmore, built by the Campbells of Islay in 1779, whence flows forth to this day a robust, complex, peaty whisky with a nose-warming, astringent aroma. What the state actually did was turn distillation into a cottage industry and create a black market. In 1782 HM Excise seized over a thousand illicit stills in the Highlands. This did not dam the deluge of spirituous liquor for a moment. A couple of decades later Thomas Guthrie, future hero of the Free Church, was growing up at Brechin in Angus, on the Highland line. As a boy he saw a procession of thirty impudent smugglers ride through the town after selling their bootleg, beating time with cudgels on empty casks slung over their shaggy horses, to 'the great amusement of the public and mortification of the excise men, who had nothing for it but to bite their nails and stand, as best they could, the raillery of the smugglers and the laughter of the people'.[24] The problem could not be solved until in 1823 an act of Parliament in effect legalized the stills and laid the foundation for the modern industry.

In all, there was real hope by the turn of the nineteenth century that Highlanders would no longer have to eke out a bare subsistence under the awful handicaps of climate and terrain. While landlords shifted peasants about their estates, where possible they also set up model villages too, in which better ways of life might be learned. The dukes of Argyll had built not only a splendid capital for Clan Campbell at Inveraray but also lesser settlements at Oban, at Southend in Kintyre, at Bunessan on Mull, at Scarinish on Tiree. Ardersier was created by Campbell of Cawdor; Grant of Grant named the new Grantown after himself; the duke of Gordon founded Kingussie; the Mackenzies of Applecross built Lochcarron, and the Mackenzies of Seaforth followed suit at Dornie and Plockton, while redeveloping Stornoway; the MacLeans of Coll established Dervaig; the Sinclairs of Ulbster added a New Town to Thurso. Some of these survive as important places, while others remain in obscurity and a few have more or less vanished, but all were planned by landlords in the prevailing spirit of economic optimism. It hardly suggests they were hell-bent on expelling the Gaels from their homeland.

Certain historians have taken to labelling the late eighteenth century in the Highlands as the 'first phase of clearance', in uneasy awareness of its scant resemblance to what happened in the nineteenth century. The question arises whether it can be called 'clearance' at all. The term was never used at the time, so it is impossible to say what contemporaries might have meant by it. Nowadays it is bandied about so sloppily that some blameless souls take it as a synonym of genocide. It is important, therefore, to establish a more exact meaning. If 'clearance' is taken to mean the disappearance of a population from its habitat – such as the disappearance of Albanians from Kosovo in the Serbs' ethnic cleansing of 1998 or, to go further back, of the Jews from Berlin after these were transported to the camps by the Nazis – then in the Highlands of 1800 there was not a single county, not a single island, not a single parish, not a single estate that was cleared in this way. On the contrary, the population continued its rapid increase. Amid the pressure on resources a good many Highlanders were bound to 'change their situations', in Sheriff Macleod's apt phrase. Landlords, deploying ample legal powers, did often direct the movement. Their main resort to coercion, however, came in seeking to stop emigrants, and not without success. Absence of depopulation, together with use of coercion rather to promote the opposite result, vindicates a denial that in this era any Highland clearances took place.

II

The rage of improvements

Eviction and development, to 1830

A T DAWN ON 13 June 1814 parties of men under Patrick Sellar swept along Strathnaver, which runs down from moor and mountain to the middle of the northernmost coast of Scotland. On the authority of Elizabeth Gordon, countess of Sutherland, they were there to turn this part of her estate over to sheep. After taking a lease of it, Sellar had served notices of eviction on people living in the townships of the strath. He told them to leave by Whitsunday, early in May. He took care to give them notice well in advance, so they could reflect on what must come, pack their possessions and prepare their minds. Often, to stress the moral as well as legal rectitude of the proceeding, a minister would go round when the notices were read out in English to threaten the people with hellfire in Gaelic, if they showed any disobedience. Yet they were not just being thrown out: a few miles away new homes stood ready for them. Here in Strathnaver, however, many stayed on to the last moment in inertia or anxiety at what awaited them where they were to be resettled by the sea, in a planned village at the mouth of the River Naver named, after the countess, Bettyhill. Now their time was up.[1]

Sellar's men moved against people defenceless in law and in fact. From each house they ordered the family out in tones that brooked no argument. Any slow to gather their goods could find the roof going up in flames above them, for nothing was to be left here that might permit continued human habitation. Sellar felt keen to deal with one William Chisholm, 'a tinker who had taken possession of an extremely wild piece of ground in a morass among the mountains, and was accused by the tenantry of bigamy, theft and riotous conduct, and was put down in my instructions as a person to be expelled from the estate'. Sellar later claimed the people supported his chastisement of this unsavoury character, helping to unroof his home and demolish it; Chisholm, although he was paid for the burned timbers, later stole new ones and built himself a second hideout. At any rate, when the evictors arrived at his first one they found nobody but his woman's bedridden mother, Margaret Mackay, almost 100 years of age. Her daughter came up and protested to Sellar that she was too ill to be moved. By one report, he replied: 'Damn her, the old witch. She has lived too long. Let her burn!'[2]

Sellar laid faggots against the timbers of the house himself. As flames took hold, the old lady was pulled out just in time, her blanket already smouldering. 'God receive my soul! What fire is this about me?' she cried, perhaps imagining that it was the moment of her passing and that she had been damned. Neighbours carried her to a shed, and barely managed to stop this being burned too. She died within five days.

There was yet less excuse for the treatment of Donald MacBeth, on his death-bed, stricken with cancer in a house near by. His son Hugh had had to go off to another relation's funeral, and appealed for his father to be left in peace for the few days until his return. When young MacBeth got back he found just the stones of his home with the sick man lying among them; he too died soon afterwards. Every other native of Strathnaver had vanished, and it remains more or less empty to this day – of all but sheep. The process was to be repeated over most of Sutherland.

It was the most emotive episode in modern Highland history, indeed in the whole of modern Scottish history, and the controversies it caused continue yet. The attempt at full-scale improvement of such a vast stretch of country, one twentieth of the surface of Scotland, could not have been undertaken without the fortune of the countess's English husband, the marquess of Stafford, who in 1833 was granted the dukedom of Sutherland in his own right in recognition of his standing as the richest British subject of his day. 'For that he was dull I think there can be little doubt', wrote a relation, but his possessions earned him a notable nickname, the Leviathan of Wealth. He had an annual income of up to £300,000, much of it paid by tenants in the fertile Midlands of England. This revenue was swelled by his inheritance from a bachelor uncle, the duke of Bridgewater, renowned as a builder of canals and collector of Old Masters, many of which are now on show in the National Gallery of Scotland.[3]

Stafford was more of an English businessman than a Highland landlord. Yet in the controversies his nationality has never been much of an issue, for he was aided and abetted by Scots. He was a stranger to Scotland until he married the daughter of the seventeenth earl of Sutherland. She had been orphaned as a baby, and a long dispute followed as to whether a female could succeed to the ancient feudal dignity with its windswept patrimony of a million acres. She made a good match for Stafford rather in her beauty and vivacity: they were celebrities in London. It still came as a surprise when, in 1790, the marquess, aged thirty-two, was appointed ambassador to a Paris racked by revolution: a sensitive posting for a man with no diplomatic experience. He and his wife did not hide their sympathies. The countess befriended Marie Antoinette, and her son played with the Dauphin; she sent them clothes after they were imprisoned. The embassy had to be withdrawn in a hurry as war between Britain and France loomed. The marquess and countess returned to a round of pleasures, until in 1803 he came into his title and properties. Their revenue from the county of Sutherland contributed a tiny fraction of their income: would not everyone benefit if this estate was made more productive? Now they had the capital to invest in it.[4]

Lowland improvers hastening to advise Stafford believed that, a century after the Union and half a century after the last Jacobite rebellion, Highlanders remained as primitive as ever. The Lowlands had seen spectacular progress and now boasted one of the world's most advanced economies. Amid the upheavals there had been, and still was, much individual suffering, yet nobody doubted the net benefit to society. With hindsight it is easy to see the errors in applying Lowland analysis to Highland problems, yet Lowland improvement had started from a point hardly more auspicious: the Lowlands are, after all, not so very much flatter, warmer or drier than the Highlands. Here improvement might surely follow the same lines, if rather behindhand. Still, while the Lowlanders' good intentions paved a road to hell, it is as well to recall that they could not agree themselves about the way forward for Highlanders – only that they should take one.

But Highlanders had been following on in a patchy fashion. The amiable but businesslike fifth duke of Argyll never drew up a masterplan for his estates, but over the thirty-six years he ruled them the copious instructions he issued to his factors amounted to much the same thing. A visit just to the Inveraray of today will confirm their extent and ambition. The castle's policies alone contained steadings and cottages, gardens and hothouses, coach-houses and stables, dairy courts, hay barns and cowshed rings, not to speak of a textile mill, spinning factory, weaving house, fulling mill, combing shop and dye-house. The duke elsewhere sprinkled his lands with fishing villages and harbours, furnaces and quarries, mines for lead or coal, inns, schools and custom-houses, all linked by roads where there had been none before. His greatest monument was the Crinan Canal, built between 1793 and 1801 for coastal trade between the Sound of Jura and Loch Fyne, or rather, between the wild Atlantic Ocean and sheltered waters leading into the Firth of Clyde, a highway and crossroads of commerce. The project meant, for example, that with a safe passage and settlements to house them, merchants could come from Glasgow to buy fish, instead of fishermen having to sail, imperilled by rocks and storms, right round Kintyre to reach their nearest big market. So the needs of the city as well as its hinterland would be served, and a vision of economic integration consummated. In benevolent yet emphatic fashion Argyll showed his people what improvement could do for them.[5]

In their articles for Sir John Sinclair, editor of the *Old Statistical Account*, many ministers of the duke's domains sing the praises of his work and its effect on the people. 'The change is greatly in their favour', says the Revd Dugal MacDougal of Lochgoilhead: 'The partiality in favour of former times, and the attachment to the place of their nativity, which is natural to old people together with the indolence in which they indulged themselves in this country, mislead them in drawing a comparison between their past, and their present situations.' The kindly Argyll is still generous to these dodos: 'The principal proprietor of this country has happily discovered all along a marked aversion to remove his people, and often refused the higher offers of the few, for possessions held at inferior rents by the many', reports the Revd John Smith of Campbeltown. Others are not so sure. The Revd Lachlan McLachlan of Craignish says: 'In this, as in most Highland parishes, the people follow the old system of agriculture with little or no variation. They have neither skill or encouragement to attempt any material change.' The Revd Alexander McFarlane of Kilfinan finds 'tenants in this parish are so much attached to the ancient mode of cultivation, that modern improvements can scarcely be said to have found their way to our latitude . . . Few of the tenants, indeed, understand farming as to do justice to their grounds.'[6]

So what is wrong? For Dunoon, a vacant charge, Sinclair penned the entry himself. He hints at an answer:

> Tacksmen still continue to retain some subtenants, who, having a cow's grass, some ground to raise potatoes, and a little grain, for the sake of the straw, as fodder during the winter, with the opportunity of fishing, etc, find themselves easier and better off than when they occupied a larger possession.

The Revd Patrick Campbell of Kilninver concurs: 'The largest hill or glen planted with black cattle required only one herd to tend them, as well as the sheep do; so that both these methods of management, with stocking with black cattle or with sheep, thus far make no alteration in the population.' What the duke tried would turn out an impossible balancing act, for relative values of different products change over time. He introduced sheep-farming on top of runrig and cattle, thinking they could co-exist in a stable manner. It seemed for now tolerable that this did not stop people leaving the land in response to underlying change for places 'where they found sufficient employment, and where many of their children, by the advantages of education (which they could not enjoy in their own country), have raised themselves to independence, become useful members of the community, and a support and comfort to their parents in their old age', as the Revd Hugh Mactavish of Inverchaolain observed. In the 1790s, when these pieces were written, optimism about Argyll's brand of improvement remained unbounded, even if it was not really working.[7]

None of the duke's projects has survived, and they were already being abandoned in his time. His improvements at Inveraray are now mere tourist attractions. The harbours, furnaces, quarries and mines stand deserted; the Crinan Canal is open, but mostly used by yachtsmen. The county of Argyll houses today fewer people than when the duke fought on Butcher Cumberland's side at Culloden. Highland investment turned out again to be 'no better than water spilt on the ground', to quote Lord Kames on the annexed estates. This life's work anyway came crashing down in ruins with the succession in 1806 of the sixth duke. A crony of the Prince Regent, he saw his inheritance as a means of bankrolling his pleasures and paying his debts. The rents were not enough, so he followed the time-honoured chiefly custom of borrowing on the security of his lands, until he could borrow no more. Then they were put under trust, and partly sold. In his rake's progress this duke ran through £2 million. He was no advertisement for a hereditary aristocracy, and it would take all the efforts of later dukes of Argyll to repair, with a renewed sense of social obligation, the damage he did.

The fifth duke, at least, had represented the aspirations of his class at their best. His friend Henry Dundas, half a Highlander himself, yearned to see the region prosper. Governing Scotland for three decades, he had a vision of the north as productive country, its green glens stocked with lusty clansmen, comely womenfolk and bonny bairns. But, ever the realist, he came to see that his vision bore little relation to what his exertions had delivered. Out of office in 1802, he asked for a report from a crony of his own, Henry Mackenzie, born in Edinburgh to Highland migrants, the sentimental novelist who doubled as collector of Scottish taxes and a sort of spin doctor to the Dundases, if by today's standards a genteel and elderly one.

The report showed how far opinion among the rulers of Scotland lay from the commercialism threatening to run riot over the Highlands.

Mackenzie recalled the decline of the clans and the historic social system, now being replaced by an impersonal cash nexus. Worse, despite emigration, the population had grown beyond the capacity of the country to feed it. Some 'general political effects', Mackenzie found, could be expected from the situation:

> It tends evidently to dissolve all connection between the great landed proprietors and the body of the people, it turns the domains of the latter into a mere chattel, productive only of so much money to the proprietor without influence or attachment even from the few inhabitants who occupy them.

This increased 'the propensity to a mere trading and manufacturing community'.[8] Mackenzie proposed public intervention, a U-turn on the state's withdrawal from the region two decades earlier. Now action was to be economic rather than political. With a grant from the government Thomas Telford began to build the Caledonian Canal, to foster trade by a safe passage from western waters to the North Sea: it was, with Neptune's Staircase, a masterwork of construction, yet a financial failure. Further grants came for roads and bridges, to give the Highlands the basis of their modern network of communications. Money would be found for religious and educational provision. Stricter regulation discouraged emigrants. In sum, what may be called the Tory policy for the Highlands had the aim of making the people thrive while keeping them where they were. Still, old Mackenzie comes over as pretty clueless. He had no brilliant ideas to make more of this official policy than any before (or after). The Dundases, with little to show for their own efforts, were not in a position to stop more drastic changes being imposed on hapless Gaels by confident reformers of a Liberal persuasion.

Perhaps the origins of this more systematic thinking lie in the Highland Society, the very body whose efforts the Dundases judged by implication to be producing the wrong results. Yet the inquiries the society commissioned added up to quite an elaborate analysis of the region's problems, sturdily empirical rather than aridly theoretical. In fact, if members looked up their Adam Smith to see what the father of economics had to say, they could find little but a passage on the Gentle Lochiel as arcadian patriarch against the bucolic backdrop of Lochaber. The deafening silence of *The Wealth of Nations* on the economy of the Highlands may be a sign of its author's essential sagacity.

Instead the society sought well-informed advice from men of the world and repaid it with gold medals. The conclusion was that resources existed for the region to flourish, but that these had to be consciously exploited. They lay untapped, for example, in the fecund population: just the idea behind bans on emigration. The counterpart was provision of employment on the spot. This, though, meant revolution in an economy where every community had fended for itself. Gaels would now have to specialize, to buy and sell from one another and trade with distant regions. They should be brought together in settlements where they would find a division of labour not only desirable but also necessary. The society applied, in other words, the nostrums of the age, but up to a point further than Smith might have cared to do. If always an acute critic of historical evidence, he preferred, rather than venture forecasts, to take refuge in his scepticism about human nature. He never advised treating the Gàidhealtachd as a laboratory for the Scottish Enlightenment's general theories of development, with a painless passage to the commercial stage to be induced so that primitive, undifferentiated labour gave way to sophisticated specialization. Yet this is what Highland panjandrums of a later generation decided to do.

These figures followed intellectual fashion, but this was shifting away from the sceptical tolerance, with its disinterested benevolence, that had marked public life in enlightened Scotland at its best. A silver age succeeded the golden one. Elder, sager heads gave way to younger, cockier ones. A sign of the times was the appearance in 1802 of the *Edinburgh Review*, the first of the many reviews that became a hallmark of Victorian culture, forums where the nineteenth century worked over its worries, not only literary but also scientific, social, political and economic. The *Edinburgh Review*, with a circulation huge for its time in Britain, Europe and America, was the trendiest organ of the new age, an ancestor of modern quality journalism, clever, irreverent and probing. It laughed at Scots Tories. It campaigned for political economy, or free markets as they are called today. Its economic commentator was John Ramsay McCulloch, who felt embarrassed about his Highland-sounding name (which came from Galloway). The distance he moved from the Dundases may be gauged by the fact that in 1826 Robert Dundas, Henry's son, rejected endowment of a chair of political economy at the University of Edinburgh because it was bound to be awarded to McCulloch, who flounced off to London instead. The distance lay in this: Adam Smith knew nothing of modern capitalism and did not foresee the industrial revolution, something recognized only in the nineteenth century as marking an epoch. Before it the Highlands had been, for all the differences, enough like the Lowlands for intelligent men to believe they might develop similarly. After it they never could be the same.[9]

Yet intelligent men, too, peer through a glass darkly, and experience alone could teach them this lesson. The founders of the *Edinburgh Review* had not yet learned it. Francis Jeffrey, its editor for thirty years, Francis Horner, who died young, and Henry Brougham, who rose to be Lord Chancellor of England, had all been students under Dugald Stewart, professor of moral philosophy at Edinburgh, who himself had been a pupil of Adam Smith. Stewart's lectures on political economy would remain unpublished for half a century; in the mean time this treasure trove was preserved only in notes his students had taken and circulated as cribs among themselves. The youngsters at the *Edinburgh Review* were conscious they had a monopoly of knowledge that they could take out and wave in the face of every problem a new century confronted. It was one of the main reasons for their heady success.

A successful magazine gathers, then as now, eager freelances about it. The *Edinburgh Review* paid well and lured bright young things needing the money. Among them was James Loch, scion of merchants in the capital who had risen in the world. He took a step up by going to the Bar, where, however, nothing is to be earned at the outset. So he got work from Jeffrey, a fellow advocate who knew what it was like. In his articles Loch, all his friends agreed, acquitted himself splendidly. He could write with apparent authority on subjects he knew little about, always an asset in a journalist. Among those to which he turned his hand was the land of Scotland – how to exploit it, how to improve it, how to reform the law and practices governing its use. Land reform, an obsession with Scots for the next two centuries, can be said to have started with Loch. As a devotee of political economy he did not, of course, think the land any business of the state: the land, too, had its proper place in commercial society 'whose arrangement is only to be preserved by allowing free scope to the master principle of individual interest'.[10] What he had to say might rather be of interest to an aristocratic family with a lot of land, wondering what to do with it.

Here was where the marquess of Stafford and the countess of Sutherland came in. Her estate was an 'object of curiosity' to her, 'quite a wild corner inhabited by an infinite multitude roaming at large in the old way, despising all barriers and all regulations, and firmly believing in witchcraft so much so that the porters durst not send away two old women who were plaguing us one day, believing them to be witches'. Only eighty years had passed since the burning of Janet Horne, whose family still lived in the parish of Loth, shunned by neighbours. When the countess joined her husband in 1807, she found even him aroused from his habitual torpor: 'We travelled in wind and snow through the Highlands and met Lord Stafford

highly pleased with his journey and the improvements he saw in every part
of Scotland, for he is seized as much as I am with the rage of improvements.' He was to spend £250,000 on her lands, £100 million at today's
prices: a straight transfer from England and a hefty dose of regional aid by
any standards. The noble couple first went on in the enthusiastic but direc-
tionless fashion of their friend the old duke of Argyll. The virtue for them
of Loch, whom the marquess met at a dinner party, was that he could rationalize the process, tell them what they were up to and where they were
heading: they would have to go a bit further than MacChailein Mòr,
although this might make all the difference.[11]

Loch first co-operated with lesser men already employed by the estate.
They included Sellar, who, if never invited to write for a review or dine
with a marquess, was still doing well as procurator-fiscal for Moray,
appointed on the strength of a reference praising his 'conduct of business
and character for humanity'. In Sutherland he joined a kinsman, William
Young, who had made a name as an improver. They were sharp fellows, a
credit to any society with careers open to talents, but they never showed,
because they were unable to show, the intellectual certainty Loch brought
from enlightened Edinburgh. Soon they ceased working together, and
Loch carried on alone. A social difference comes out in a letter of Loch's
patronizing Sellar as

a clever keen Scotch writer [solicitor] with more than their usual share of
active exertions . . . often called for to enforce very disagreeable but necessary acts of vigour, added to which he has a quick sneering biting way of
saying good things in the execution of his duty which I do not think has
made him popular with anybody.[12]

He was not a nice man, then, and the countess harboured her own
doubts: 'The more I hear and see of Sellar the more I am convinced he is
not fit to be trusted further than he is at present. He is so exceedingly
greedy and harsh with the people, there are very heavy complaints against
him from Strathnaver.' When hostile reports appeared in the press, she sent
out to her peers a woebegone apology probably drawn up by Loch:

We have lately been much attacked in the newspapers by a few malicious
writers who have long assailed us on every occasion. What it states is most
perfectly unjust and unfounded, as I am convinced from the facts I am
acquainted with, and I venture to trouble you with the enclosed . . . If you
meet with discussions on the subject in society, I shall be glad if you will
show this statement to anyone who may interest him or herself on the subject.

She did not fail to find a response. The gallant Brougham of the *Edinburgh Review*, now a scourge of Tories in Parliament, wrote to Loch offering to pronounce there a public vindication of the estate's policy: 'You know I would not even for your sake do any such thing if I had my doubts – but I really think Lord and Lady Stafford *have* been ill-treated.'[13] Even Sellar admitted his faults: 'I fear I have been bred to too much precision, and possess too much keenness of temper to be so useful in my office as I ought and as I sincerely wish to be. A man less anxious might better suit the situation and the nature of the people.'[14] The countess agreed: in 1816 she sacked him. In fact, he had been quite a minor character in this unfolding drama. If he bears the weight of history's censure, he remained a small cog inside the wheels of Loch's strategy, the dash for improvement by the noble couple and the general challenge to the Highlands by modernity. It is often at the level of the dour, overzealous subaltern, lacking a broad view, that cogs jam and wheels break.

A broad view was what the noble couple sought of Loch when they made him their commissioner, a plenipotentiary to turn words into deeds. Sutherland is a rugged but varied county. It runs from smiling farmlands on the Dornoch Firth in the south-east to the forbidding wilderness round Cape Wrath in the north-west; there the visitor will feel himself at the end of the earth. The tract in between is penetrated by long glens, where the populace spread in times preceding the age of improvement to practise the traditional agriculture. Loch's plan was for art to be imposed on this nature. The interior would be turned over to sheep, on farms big enough to form an economic unit under a single tenant: the most rational use for that land in a modern Britain with an efficient division of labour. The people would be moved to new coastal villages, where opportunities awaited them in industries and fisheries. In a nutshell, it was Scotland's first big experiment in social engineering, and Loch stands at the head of a line of social engineers stretching down to the present. They still promise breakthroughs, which was what Loch meant to bring to the Highlands by executing his plan on a grand enough scale.

Yet the greatest monument to Loch now is in words, in the controversies he caused. They often start with a refusal to concede any substance to his plan. On this view, the old Sutherland was a rustic idyll. The bard of the country, Rob Donn, is prayed in aid. He, according to the Gaelic scholar Ronald Black, 'represents a golden age which was brought abruptly to a close by the brutal Sutherland clearances of the early nineteenth century'.[15] Donn, who died in 1778, had come not from the countess's estate but from the adjacent lands of Lord Reay, chief of Clan MacKay, covering a third of the county, including the fastness about Cape Wrath. The Reays had long forsaken their precipices for the Netherlands and would at length sell up to the countess, but they left behind men such as Rob Donn, in no obvious distress. On the contrary, he lived to the full a life of droving and hunting, had thirteen children and gave the people a lot of laughs with songs and poems cast in their dialect, rich with local reference, making fun of their foibles and showing no shyness about their sex lives. He turned his fearless honesty also on social problems of his time. Reay's factor, a man hard on tenants, once had a suit made but would not wear it until some occasion when Rob Donn could be present to make up an impromptu verse in its praise. The result ran:

> 'S math a tha i air do chùlaibh,
> 'S tha i nas roh ùrraichd air t'uchd;
> Bu chaomh leam i bhith leathann trom
> Mur dèanadh i call no lochd –
> Ach chan eil putan innt' no toll
> Nach do chost bonn do dhuine bochd.

> It is excellent behind you
> And even finer on your chest;
> I'd like it to be broad and heavy
> If it caused no loss or harm –
> But there's not a button or hole in it
> That did not cost a poor man a coin.

A romantic image of the old Sutherland was to be deepened by another revered, if more disturbing figure: Hugh Miller. He intervened three decades after Sellar appeared in Strathnaver; in fact, it was Miller that did most to give currency to the term 'clearance', in place of the less emotive 'removal' or 'eviction' used before. He was a stonemason from Cromarty who pulled himself up by his bootstraps to become one of the Victorian era's authorities on geology, a paradigm of the achieving Scot. The inner turmoil his scientific discoveries caused him, to his Evangelical religion and his youthful belief in the literal truth of Genesis, may have led him to commit suicide in 1856. In his later years Miller lived off journalism, often recycled into books. He reviled Highland (not to speak of Lowland) land-lords, together with the political economy that motivated them.[16] So powerful were these writings that it is not claiming too much for Miller to see in him the author of that standard modern view of Highland history where clearance stands as the central fact.

Basic to it is a tract Miller published in 1843, *Sutherland as It Was and Is, or how a country may be ruined.* He denounces the countess, by then dead, and the policies continued by her son the second duke. Miller starts from an idealized picture of the former Sutherland: 'We are old enough to remember the country in its original state, when it was one of the happiest and one of the most exemplary districts in Scotland.' It had 'snug farms'; people lived 'in very comfortable circumstances' and in a 'state of trustful security'; shortages occurred in the less 'genial' parts, but crofters' stocks or savings tided them over these little crises. Indeed, 'the country never heard of dearth in Sutherland'. Altogether, 'never were there a happier or more contented people, or a people more strongly attached to the soil . . . nor one who does not look back on this period of comfort and enjoyment with sad and hopeless regret'.[17]

Then came clearance. In popularizing the term, Miller makes it fuzzy: 'The county has not been depopulated, its population has merely been rearranged after a new fashion.' What enrages him is not the movement but the end of a way of life. Now people squat by the sea 'in the selvage of discontent and poverty'. They 'fell down upon the coast of the country . . . on moss-covered moors or bare exposed promontories, little suited to the labours of the agriculturist, [and] commenced a sort of amphibious life as crofters and fishermen'. This followed from the infatuation with political economy of the countess, her husband and factors. They ran 'an interesting experiment . . . as if they had resolved on dissecting a dog alive for the benefit of science'.[18]

This gruesome image recalls that Miller was what would today be called a columnist rather than a reporter, concerned with comment more than fact. Yet the people of Sutherland had not been so 'strongly attached to their soil' as to remain immune to surges of Highland emigration. From Dunrobin at one end of the county to Assynt at the other, and from Strathnaver in the middle, they had joined the first big surge, in the years before 1776.[19] In the *Old Statistical Account* the Revd William Keith of Golspie echoes Sheriff Macleod of Ross in calling on landlords to introduce sheep for the very reason that, as the most profitable products of this soil, they would deter the emigrations he had witnessed.

Other ministers offer a check on Miller. The word 'clearance' and its synonyms are unknown to them, for nothing of the kind has yet taken place. So they have no axes to grind, no reason to depict the people's condition as better or worse than it is. The Revd William Mackenzie of Assynt recalls failed harvests in 1766, 1772, 1782 and 1793; 'in short, by observation, the narrator can truly say, that every ninth or tenth year turned out distressing, either by loss of crop, loss of cattle, perhaps both'. Why? 'Very little progress in improvement has been made', answers the Revd Walter Ross of Clyne. The Revd John Bethune of Dornoch sets out how 'the arable ground is, for the greater part, in constant tillage. It is therefore no wonder, that it yields poor crops, in return for much labour and expense. Nowhere can the poor be on a worse footing than here.' He recollects the sarcasm of an Englishman who found 'a herd of meagre cattle here, gleaning a scanty subsistence on a naked spot', while every hut was built of turf and thatch. 'Though Sutherland was not destitute of stone and grass,' the visitor said, 'the people chose to build their houses of the latter, and leave their cattle to feed on the former.' The Revd Alex Falconer of Edderachillis thinks that, 'considering their toil in cultivation [they] would surely find their account in abstaining from agriculture totally'. The Revd Aeneas McLeod of Rogart reports: 'As in all the neighbouring parishes, the poor beg from house to house, and from parish to parish, and very frequently from county to county.' The Revd James Dingwall of Farr, whose charge included Strathnaver, adds:

> Very little of the parish is cultivated, compared with what is lying waste and commons. It is, therefore, by no means surprising, that it does not supply the inhabitants with provisions . . . The situation of the people, in 1783, was deplorable. They killed the few cattle they had, and ate their flesh without bread or salt. Many left the parish, and went to other places for employment.

The picture is not of 'comfort and enjoyment' but of desperate poverty and insecurity. The way to remedy matters while keeping the people in the county was to find them jobs on the side, of just the kind Miller thought so deplorable.[20]

Loch meant thus to remedy matters by a single upheaval. It cannot be said his plan failed in the way Argyll's piecemeal projects failed. Loch left Sutherland as it is now, a strip of civilization along the eastern shore with a brooding hinterland. His fishing villages are there yet, at Golspie, Helmsdale and Portgower and over on the Atlantic coast at Lochinver. The head burgh of Dornoch is still a handsome stone-built place, rather than the miserable cluster of huts Loch found. Brora almost had the makings of an industrial town, with a coal-mine, brickworks, tileworks, lime-kiln, saltpans, harbour, not to speak of a horse-drawn railway and a distillery at nearby Clynelish: this, at least, produces even now a fine malt whisky. Today the county looks empty, or rather desolate. Yet Loch never meant to empty it, just to move its people over the 500 miles of road and 134 bridges he built, and by no more than about 20 miles in the worst cases, to make them productive rather than unproductive. In fact, he did not empty the county: its population continued to rise, if at a modest rate, to a peak of 25,000 in 1861.

It is half that now, after 150 years of net emigration. Yet this formed no part of Loch's plan. He was against it: 'The idle and lazy alone think of emigration.'[21] For all his radicalism and rationality he shared the general view of the Scottish ruling class that the people formed part of the wealth of the country. The English vicar the Revd Thomas Malthus had just published his *Essay on the Principle of Population*, showing how the hunger of humanity would always outrun the food it could grow. When the countess of Sutherland read this, she felt only half-convinced: 'He longs to drown children but proves that population, do what you will, will take care of itself.'[22]

All this belonged to a ferment in the world of letters where the people of Sutherland did not speak the language, in any sense. The smart alecks of the *Edinburgh Review*, champions of every modish cause, were not on their side. The Tory authorities in Edinburgh, if disapproving, had no power to stop aristocrats doing what they wanted on their own land. But people who could not raise their voices beyond their glens, or find someone to speak for them, might at least vote with their feet. The first systematic emigration from Sutherland in the new century was organized in opposition to Loch's plan, not as part of it.

Across a hill from Strathnaver lies Kildonan, a parish drained by the River Helmsdale on its course to the North Sea. Much of it was also turned over to sheep in 1813, under the compulsion of a military force called up by the Sheriff of Sutherland, George Cranstoun, a Whig from Edinburgh who had come north to deal in person with this delicate affair. Quelled, the indignant people yet sent an appeal to the Prince Regent, but the government regretted it could not intervene. One man was ready to listen, however: Thomas Douglas, fifth earl of Selkirk.

If Loch regarded himself as an advanced thinker, he met his match in Selkirk. While the former was a radical the latter came close, in Scottish terms, to being a revolutionary; he had gone to Paris in 1791 to sip at the bloody wellspring of the French Revolution. This is not the place to speculate on the psychology of aristocrats who seek to overthrow the social order, but meanwhile Selkirk, ever preferring simplicity to complexity, had reduced his principles to one: that those suffering economic displacement should leave for a land of the free. So he urged emigration on principle, after a manner alien to the Scottish élite. When he put his ideas to the countess of Sutherland in 1813, she turned them down flat as 'totally inadvisable'.[23] Selkirk had already planted two colonies of Highlanders in Canada, in the face of official displeasure. The rulers of Scotland were furious at him – with a war against France and recruitment a constant necessity, the last thing they wanted was glens emptied or Gaels upset. Thought was given to suppression of his tracts, but in those days an earl could not easily be shut up.

In 1805 Selkirk had published his *Observations on the Present State of the Highlands of Scotland*. He argued that emigration was the answer to all their problems. He, too, valued words only as a prelude to deeds, and again he outdid Loch. From the Hudson's Bay Company the earl purchased 116,000 square miles on the Red River in what is now Manitoba. This was why, when petitioners for the people of Sutherland came to see him, he was pleased to respond to their plaints. He said he could emancipate them by sending them to the Wild West. More than 700 applied to go, of whom he selected 100. They had just reached their goal after a terrible journey, and founded a settlement they called Kildonan, when many were massacred by the hostile fur traders of the country, men of mixed Scots, Indian and French blood, at the Battle of Seven Oaks in June 1816. For fifty years after this there was no more Highland emigration to the Wild West.[24]

Wherever they turned, the people of Sutherland seemed trapped and cheated by fate. At least, though, Scotland had the rule of law. After Sellar finished with Strathnaver in 1814, the dispossessed sent a petition to the countess complaining of his cruelty. It confirmed her own unease. She consulted her husband, and at length the matter came before Robert MacKid, Cranstoun's sheriff-substitute, a lawyer in Tain, who was himself a tenant of the noble couple at Golspie. Perhaps MacKid was all the keener on this case because he may have had no place in their plans either, so he was possibly waiting for a chance to have a go at Sellar. Now he got it. He went to Strathnaver and set with enthusiasm about his inquiries. The people were all too ready to talk. On the evidence gathered, he decided Sellar had broken the law. He clapped him in the tolbooth at Dornoch, where the last witch had lolled. While Sellar awaited trial, his friends had to move heaven and earth to get him out on bail.

In April 1816 Sellar came up at Inverness before Lord Pitmilly, charged with culpable homicide, fire-raising, oppression and real injury. The charge of homicide referred to Margaret Mackay and Donald MacBeth. Scottish trials were marathons which, once started, went on without a break until they finished. Sellar's lasted from ten o'clock on the morning of the first day until one o'clock on the morning of the next. MacKid could not make his charges stick without proof of a direct link between Sellar's actions and the deaths. After the fifteen hours the jury acquitted him in fifteen minutes. He burst into tears.[25]

The affair was still not over. Wrangles continued between MacKid and Sellar, in which Sellar came off the better. Life was good to him. In Strathnaver he made a fortune as a sheep farmer and lived at ease to a ripe old age. By contrast, the countess and marquess threw their money away. People unable to subsist under their plan ended up emigrating. Once the Whigs took over the government of Scotland in 1830 they encouraged this, and other parts of the Highlands were cleared. Among the new intake to Parliament after their Reform Act was James Loch, who served twenty years as Liberal MP for the Wick Burghs. Stafford got the dukedom he craved. Tories had shunned him since his bad press as an improver, but now a progressive British state gave his work this seal of approval.

It had been an improvement too far. Yet the bitterness and frustration in which it issued did not stop Scotland essaying more of the same, down to the present. The forlorn settlements for the dispossessed on the coast of Sutherland were premature versions of the peripheral housing schemes around Glasgow and Edinburgh; the distance modern Glaswegians had to be moved for their own sake from, say, Townhead to Castlemilk is not so far short of that from Strathnaver to Bettyhill. Each stands for the failure of grandiose but flawed social experiments, master plans drawn up by enlightened and progressive lovers of humanity in the abstract. Today in Scotland these master plans are still visible, often linked to land reform. It all sounds terribly familiar.

12

Very vulgar and gaudy

The revival of Highland culture

IN THE EARLY afternoon of 15 August 1822 the royal yacht was tugged by steamboats into shallow waters off Leith, the port of Edinburgh. Under the dismal weather common in the Lothians at this season, with drenching rain and a heavy swell on the Firth of Forth, the vessel moored 2 miles out. It carried King George IV, the first reigning monarch to visit Scotland in 171 years. The downpour did not deter the capital's citizens, who streamed down Leith Walk to see him land. Scores of small boats thronged the harbour eager to accompany him from ship to shore.

But nothing could happen until an official delegation went out to greet the king. It was led by Robert Dundas, Viscount Melville, First Lord of the Admiralty and political manager of Scotland, and by Sir Walter Scott, into whose eager hands the arrangements for the visit had been entrusted. George IV learned that the Great Unknown, the as yet unacknowledged author of *Waverley*, the most successful novel of the age, had arrived alongside. The king exclaimed: 'What! Sir Walter Scott! The man in Scotland I most want to see! Let him come up!'

Scott was glad of the chance to speak to his sovereign because he wished at all costs to avoid a damp start to the historic visit and the lavish programme he had organized for it. In the royal presence he began: 'Impatient, Sire, as your loyal subjects are to see you plant your foot upon their soil, they hope you will consent to postpone your entry until tomorrow . . .'

Scott then made one of his famous witty speeches, knelt and kissed hands. King George graciously agreed to his suggestion and sent to Leith to announce there would be no disembarcation that day. Meanwhile he called for cherry brandy to celebrate his coming. After the toasts some of those present requested the privilege of keeping their glasses. Scott, spotting a chance to add to his collection of historical knick-knacks at Abbotsford House, asked for the king's own glass. He handed it over and Scott tucked it into the tail-pocket of his coat. He protected it all day, in the rocking boat and the rumbling carriage that took him home hours later. When he got to Castle Street, he flopped down in relief to tell his wife all that had happened – and jumped up with a yelp. Too late: the glass was crushed.[1]

The next morning dawned bright for the royal entry into the capital. The landing took some time for, at the age of sixty, the king was frightfully fat. After formal greetings he heaved himself into his carriage and headed the procession that marched up into the city, under triumphal arches adorned with flowers, amid the most enormous crowds ever seen in Scotland. He continued to the Palace of Holyroodhouse, to cheers from the multitude and salutes from the guns. So far, so good. George IV was not a beloved king in England. He had had a rakish youth and gone through a messy divorce with Queen Caroline, who died soon afterwards. From Scotland, however, no breath of disloyalty had come or was to come during the whole fortnight of his visit.

Yet Scott wanted more than to help in restoring the repute of the monarchy, in eclipse ever since the long, final madness of old King George III, dead just a couple of years. Nobody was more aware than Scott of his nation's troubled history, the loss it had suffered when its sovereigns moved south or the pain it felt in the sacrifice of its independence. He sought to stress, though, how all that was over: Scotland had become a happy, prosperous country reconciled to its place in the world. Still missing was a clear expression of this dignity and security, a visible healing of wounds. What better than to bring King George to Scotland, to impress on him the richness and antiquity of her heritage and to win from him recognition of her worth?

Scott succeeded. The monarch now resides in Scotland for part of every year, yet no royal visit is better remembered than that one in 1822. It defined the unionist Scotland, which only then came to life and has only recently reached its end, as a place of loyalty and tradition playing a full part in the greater entities of Union and Empire. Yet the fact that Scott's compatriots had still to adjust to his vision is underlined by their bemused reaction to events he staged in the guise of rituals hallowed by the ages. Actually he made them up.

Once George IV arrived at Holyrood, he went to the Presence Chamber and sat on the throne to receive the Honours of Scotland. Scott himself had found them in a battered kist at Edinburgh Castle, where they had been consigned to oblivion in 1707. He had to do some fresh detective work to make the presentation look authentic. He wanted it performed by officers of the royal household, who in Scotland, unlike in England, were of old hereditary. As none had needed to perform their functions for over a century, nobody remembered who they were or ought to be. The one directing the ceremony, the Knight Marischal, was Sir Alexander Keith of Ravelston, from a family that had blotted its escutcheon by joining the Jacobites. Keith was probably in truth not its head, but Scott dragged him out of obscurity and put him in charge. Now Keith beckoned forward esquires bearing the Honours of Scotland. He lifted each piece from its cushion and passed it to the right hand of its hereditary bearer, who received it kneeling. The bored duke of Hamilton took the crown as premier peer. Dashing young Lord Francis Leveson-Gower took the sceptre in the name of his mother, the countess of Sutherland (who had stayed behind in London to nurse her sick husband). The nervous earl of Erroll took the sword of state. Then, after addresses from sundry dignitaries, the king must have felt relieved to be off again. (He never slept in shabby Holyrood, but stayed in comfort with the duke of Buccleuch outside town at Dalkeith House.) George's first duty had been brief, but sufficient to find a lasting place in national pageantry. It is now accepted custom for a new monarch to receive the Honours of Scotland, as Queen Elizabeth did at St Giles in 1953.

Other events in the Edinburgh of 1822 might as well have taken place in London for all their significance or for any difference they made. Two at Holyrood, the Levee and Drawing Room, were much the same, except in the first the king got kisses from men while in the second he gave kisses to ladies. At the Drawing Room he brushed 457 female cheeks – or meant to, because at high speed he sometimes missed. At the Levee worthy chaps queued to kneel, kiss his hand and walk out, satisfied by the thought that for ever after they could say they had done it. About 1200 passed before him in 75 minutes, so spending an average of four seconds in his exalted presence. In London this was normal protocol, but in Scotland it was unfamiliar. One old laird shot through without stopping, unable to see in the gloomy room. Erroll hissed at him, 'Kiss hands, kiss hands!' He turned and retired backwards, planting kisses on his own hand and blowing them at the king.[2]

Now it was that George IV made the greatest impression by appearing in Highland dress, brilliant with jewelled brooches and burnished weaponry, his feathered bonnet cocked as Chief of Chiefs. Scott had sound historical reasons for making the king dress up like this. The cleft between Highlands and Lowlands, often dwelt on in his novels, was one of the wounds he wanted to heal. He had besides asked the chiefs to bring troops of their clansmen to parade amid the austere classicism of the capital, where once their presence would have been greeted with horror. Melville, while he did not discourage 'celtification', grew nervous at hundreds of men wandering around Edinburgh armed to the teeth. He wrote to the duke of Atholl advising him to leave his private army at home: 'I think we have had fully as many of the Gael, real or fictional, as is prudent or necessary.'[3]

What does a Scotsman wear under his kilt? George IV found his own answer to the eternal question. His was a mini-kilt, no protection against a Scottish August, so he had beneath it a pair of tights, 'buff-coloured trousers like *flesh* to *imitate* his *Royal knees*, and little bits of tartan stocking like other Highlanders halfway up his legs', as described by an amazed spectator. The outfit did please his female admirers. Lady Hamilton Dalrymple denied it was immodest: 'Since he is to be among us for so short a time, the more we see of him the better.' Males felt less impressed. Lowland gentlemen still disliked Highlanders, of which the present generation seemed as idle, scruffy and drunken as ever. Even chiefs, welcome guests, preferred to stress they had put the bad old days behind them.[4]

Nobody then thought that kilts and tartans represented a real Scotland or, if they did, that it would be worth showing off. Another spectator summed up these sore feelings in his impression of the levee: 'The King did not seem to move a muscle and we all asked ourselves when we came away, what had made us take so much trouble. He was dressed in tartan. Sir Walter had ridiculously made us appear a nation of Highlanders.'[5]

It was, indeed, all Scott's fault, yet he turned out right and his critics wrong. He had a sixth sense that tartan pageantry was bound to be magnificent, while the alternative of Presbyterian sobriety would look drab. So magnificent was the pageantry that it set off a tartan frenzy far into the future. Scots eagerly inquired into the lore of tartan, got themselves togged up in kilts and picked furious quarrels about who should wear what and how. The craze received a secondary boost from the spurious *Vestiarium Scoticum*, sumptuously published by the Sobieksi Stuart brothers in 1842, purporting to show a tartan for each clan, based on a manuscript of the sixteenth century. Discredited by scholars, it made fortunes for weavers or tailors and was good enough for Scots at large, who to this day wear many patterns first depicted in the book. Crusty old Sir John Graham Dalyell wrote in 1849: 'Thirty or forty years ago no reputable gentleman would have appeared in a kilt on the streets of Edinburgh.' He recollected 'some expressions denoting surprise, not unmixed with disapprobation from ladies, that a young Highlander, though a person of family distinction, should appear in one at an evening party where I was present'. Dalyell puts it in a nutshell: the kilt was for lithe, handsome, devil-may-care youths, not for aged curmudgeons with paunch and arthritis. The tartan frenzy rose or fell according to fashion, but in a sense it is still not over. The

Edinburgh of 1822 forever fixed a certain image of the Scotsman, to himself and to the world.[6]

Nobody could have guessed that this favourite image would turn out to be a Highland one. In arranging the iconic side of the visit Scott called on a trusted crony, David Stewart of Garth, an old soldier and a veteran of the Napoleonic Wars, hero of the Battle of Alexandria in 1801, when he had persisted in leading his company of the Black Watch despite severe wounds. Stewart was also a Highland laird, with an estate near the head of Loch Tay in Perthshire. More to the point, he had made himself, before it became so fashionable, Scotland's greatest expert on tartan.

Tartanry was still an infant science, in fact altogether chaotic. Stewart had sought to bring some order and system to it, to define which clans should be entitled to which pattern. The task did not prove easy. One way of tackling it was just to write and ask chiefs about their tartans. Colonel Alexander Robertson of Struan replied that he had himself, years before, tried to find out, 'and applied to different old men of the clan for information, most of whom pretended to know what the pattern was, but as no two of the descriptions I received were exactly similar, and as they were all very vulgar and *gaudy*, I did not think proper to adopt any of them'. Some of Stewart's correspondents, such as the McNab and Lord Ogilvie, could give precise details. Others had no idea but promised to dig up the facts and forward samples of their tartans; this often meant copying designs from old portraits of the family. Yet others denied their clans had ever had a tartan, and several claimed the same tartan, the one now known as Black Watch – a dark pattern of blue, black and green, the government's standard issue to the regiment since its formation in 1739. Struan summed things up:

> It does not appear to be ascertained, either by tradition or authentic history, that the different clans in the Highlands of Scotland, wore any distinctive pattern or tartan. It is well known that they all had particular colours, or standards, emblematical of some of their most honourable attachments, but as far as I have been able to discover, *they wore no uniform garb.*[7]

Nothing daunted, Stewart wrote up the results of his researches in a book, *Sketches of the Highlanders*, which became almost as popular as Scott's novels and was published just in time for the royal visit. This delightful salmagundi contains, among many other things, a map showing the territory held by different clans, making it the ancestor of all the maps still sold to tourists. And it entitled its author to be the one in attendance on George IV as, in an ante-room at Holyrood, he squeezed into his Highland dress. Stewart adjusted the tartans, the weapons, the jewels – and made sure the seams at the back of the pink tights were straight.

Yet for all his diligence Stewart had not quite teased out the history of tartan, which remains somewhat obscure. The word itself may be of Old French origin. Only English uses it. The Gaelic is *breacan*, from the adjective *breac*, meaning multicoloured but also, by extension, checked or striped or even spotted, as in the face of someone who has survived smallpox. In his epic *Birlinn Chlann Raghnaill*, Alastair mac Mhaighstir thus described the heavens at the onset of the storm buffeting his metaphorical ship: '*Chinn gach dath bhiodh ann am breacan air an iarmailt*' ('All the colours in a tartan plaid were gathered in the sky').[8]

From the start, then, 'tartan' represented the paradox of a word current only in the Lowlands for something authentic only in the Highlands, if there. Whatever it was, it had soon crossed the Highland line. The accounts of the Court of King James V for 1538 contain an entry on the purchase of three ells of 'heland tertane to be hois to the Kings grace'. George Buchanan remarked in his *History of Scotland* (1582) on the Gaels' liking for material he called 'marled' (a Scots word with the same meaning as *breac*, even to the spots on the face: *mirls* is the native name for measles). 'They delight in marled clothes, especially that have long stripes of sundry colours; they love chiefly purple and blue', says Buchanan. In earlier times, he went on, they had worn

> mantles or plaids of diverse colours sundry ways divided; and amongst some, the same custom is observed to this day; but for the most part now they are browns, most near to the colour of the heather; to the effect, when they lie amongst the heather, the bright colour of their plaids shall not betray them.[9]

Buchanan typifies early writers on the subject in being maddeningly inexact. 'Diverse colours sundry ways divided' may or may not mean tartan like today's – cloth woven in stripes of various colours crossing at right angles and arranged in the same sequence in both directions, warp and weft. Nor does Buchanan specify whether each clan has its own tartan; but, while this is a matter over which men once might have drawn blood, acceptance now prevails that the idea is modern rather than ancient. Nor does he reveal how far Scottish national dress of the present, kilt and accoutrements, resembles anything worn by Gaels of yore.

Just as mysterious is Buchanan's remark that tartan was fading away in his time. Clansmen he knew from his home in Stirlingshire probably did don plaids with a brown or yellow ground, the colour of the wool or natural dyes, to their simple checks. This was the sort of garment peasants wore all over Europe. Yet Highland dress was the dress of the whole community, not in itself peasant dress. Alexander Mudie conceded in 1711 that the plaid might seem 'uncouth, because not used elsewhere; yet it must be owned, that as they are used by those of the better sort in the Highlands, they make a manly as well as a decent habit'. Gentlemen of the clan no doubt had finer cloth with fancier checks and in brighter colours, from imported dyes. But availability probably did most to dictate what was woven and what worn. Surviving pieces of fabric, as well as early portraits, show that not every pattern was regular and symmetrical in the modern manner. The portraits, naturally all of chiefs or tacksmen, reveal besides that some wore different tartans at once.[10]

Despite this original individualism, a trend to uniformity set in. Sir Robert Gordon, tutor of Sutherland, pulled a tacksman up for presumption in 1618, 'requesting him to furl his pennon when the Earl of Sutherland's banner was displayed and to remove the red and white lines from the plaids of his men so as to bring their dress into harmony with that of the other septs'. An epic poem in praise of Bluidy Claverhouse, the *Grameid*, by James Philp of Almericlose, describes the rallying of the Jacobite clans in 1689, when not all came clad in tartan: there were leather tunics for Raasay's men, fur bonnets for Stewart of Appin's, red stripes for MacDonald of Glengarry's plaids, yellow for MacLean of Duart's, yellow and blue for men of Glen Roy. Martin Martin, in his Highland survey of 1695, first wrote how the pattern might show where a man hailed from: 'Every isle differs from each other in their fancy of making plaids as to the stripes in breadth and colours. This humour is different through the mainland of the Highlands, in so far that they who have seen those places are able at first view of a man's plaid to guess the place of his residence.' Perhaps the earliest to insist on uniformity, at least for social or ceremonial purposes, was the chief of Grant, who in 1703 led a hunt and 'ordered 600 of his men in arms, in good order, with tartan coats all of one colour and fashion'. They were 'to have ready tartan short coats, trews and short hose of red and green set dice all broad springed'.[11]

Recruitment of clansmen for regular armies after 1707 curbed personal whim too. Whether or not Jacobites of the '45 counted as a regular force, their prince ordered them all into tartan, Highlanders and Lowlanders (or indeed English and French) alike. They looked not so smart by the time they got to Derby, where an observer found them 'a crew of shabby, lousy, pitiful-looked fellows; mixed up with old men and boys; dressed in dirty plaids, and as dirty shoes, without breeches; [they] wore their stockings, made of plaid, not much above half-way up their legs, some without shoes, or next to none, and with their plaids thrown over their shoulders'. But for their weapons, he added, 'they appeared more like a parcel of chimney sweepers than soldiers'.[12]

Military requirements also caused the kilt to replace the original article of dress, the belted plaid. A belt held this long piece of cloth hanging down and draped about the body or wrapping it like a cloak. Edmund Burt said the plaid was 'set in folds and girt round the waist, to make of it a short petticoat that reaches half way down the thigh, and the rest is brought over the shoulders, and then fastened before', so that Highlanders 'make pretty nearly the appearance of the poor women of London when they bring their gowns over their heads to shelter them from the rain'. There are prints of soldiers wearing the plaid in such cumbersome ways. It seems clear why the freedom of the kilt was preferable for any man who had to go into battle. The word 'kilt' was not recorded in the English language until 1730; it originated in Old Norse, not Gaelic. Thomas Rawlinson, English manager of a foundry in Glengarry, is said to have employed a tailor to make the first, as more convenient than a belted plaid. Ian MacDonald of Glengarry liked it and had a chiefly one made for himself. At any rate, since the kilt was a garment banned by law after the '45, people must have been wearing it by then.[13]

In the period of proscription, no others than regular troops could legally wear tartan. Already loyal units raised in the Highlands, the Independent Companies and Black Watch, had been put into their sombre uniform; General Wade said in orders to companies recruited in 1725 that their tartan must be as 'near as they can of the same sort and colour'. That of the Black Watch was to be taken over with modifications by the 78th or Seaforth Highlanders, raised in 1778, by the 92nd or Gordon Highlanders in 1794 and by the 93rd regiment or Sutherland (later Argyll and Sutherland) Highlanders in 1800. Gordons added to the pattern a yellow stripe, Seaforths a red and a white stripe, Argylls a yellow and a white stripe, the grounds of the latter two also having more blue in them. These three regimental tartans were then appropriated by Clans Campbell, Gordon and Mackenzie respectively. One regimental tartan with a separate origin, of the 79th, the Cameron Highlanders, raised in 1793, was just invented by the mother of Alan Cameron of Erracht, its first colonel. Again, the family adopted it.[14]

The trend, then, was for regiments to define formal Highland dress and its stylized patterns. They added dirks, sporrans (invented about 1770), powder-horns, the *sgian dubh*, Glengarries, feathered bonnets, shoulder plaids (ornamental rather than functional), decorative basket-hilts for swords, silver brooches with crests or jewels, and what not. Civilians took all this over once the ban on tartan was lifted in 1782. While never enforced on the upper echelons of society anyway, the ban lent a *frisson* to their new liking for tartan. At a lower level some Gaels resumed the old costume, although it would never again be universal. A visitor to Strathtay in 1800, Thomas Garnett, saw people in 'a short jacket of tartan or woollen cloth, woven in squares of the most vivid colours' but also thought it 'fast wearing out in the Highlands', as 'many dress in the English manner'. Elizabeth Spence in 1816 found Highland dress rare in Inverness, though in Glen Urquhart people appeared 'in bright showy tartan'. The judge Lord Cockburn, a lover of picturesque detail, was surprised on the Highland circuit to come across no kilts.[15] In Skye people wore homespun garments, but had forgotten the kilt and claimed it never was an article of dress there. They would soon be won back to it by its worldwide fame. The German sage Johann Wolfgang von Goethe thought revolutionary French troops weedy, but '*die Bergschotten des Herzogs von Wellington mögen freilich andere Helden gewesen sein!*' ('the Duke of Wellington's Highlanders must have been altogether different heroes!'). He found eager assent from his secretary, a witness in Paris when, victorious over Napoleon, the Scots marched in:

> *Das waren in der Tat schöne Leute! Alle stark, frisch und behende, wie aus der ersten Hand Gottes. Sie trugen alle den Kopf so frei und froh und schritten mit ihren kräftigen nackten Schenkeln so leicht einher, als gebe es für sie keine Erbsünde und keine Gebrechen der Väter.*

> What fine men they were indeed! All so strong, keen and smart, as if God had just made them. They were so carefree the way they carried their heads, and they marched along so lightly with their strong, naked thighs, as if they had never heard of original sin or the primal curse.[16]

Yet the Lowlands put up some resistance to tartan frenzy. There the regiments did not assume Highland dress until 1881, and then they felt none too happy about it. Even when ordered to wear tartan they would not go into kilts, but preferred trews. Yet tartan and the Scottish martial tradition from now on became synonymous. This happened in the first place under royal patronage, but equally because landowners raising volunteers liked to invent for them a striking uniform. The frenzy took on a life of its own, little related to the Highlands. It was a British, unionist, imperialist enthusiasm. Not every Scot subscribed to it.

Tartan was Tory – worn above all by those connected to the army, pillar of a conservative social order, next by the upper class and only then by anyone else taking a fancy to it. Many Scots saw it as an affectation. Other leaders of society on the whole did not wear it – not judges, professors or moderators of the General Assembly of the Church of Scotland. Their main contact with tartan came from the overpowering wallpaper and carpets at Balmoral, where Queen Victoria invited them in the summer. These pillars of the establishment rose from the firm plinth of Lowland, Presbyterian, enlightened Scotland, which, despite a dearth of colour, remained confident in its own solid worth. Victorians engaged in changing and renewing this sort of Scotland – Thomas Chalmers or Thomas Carlyle or Lord Kelvin or William Robertson Smith – saw no need to do so in a kilt. The one man in that milieu who did wear it, John Stuart Blackie, professor of Greek at Edinburgh, counted for what he was, an amiable eccentric.

In the twentieth century the poet Hugh MacDiarmid counselled against tartan. He was a Communist and nationalist, at one with the proletariat in viewing the cult of the kilt with contempt, as buffoonery, at best something for tourists to gawp at, but to good Scots typical of all they did not want to be. The Marxist sage Professor Tom Nairn of Melbourne dubs the cult the 'Tartan Monster'. Conceding the huge role of Scotland and of Scott in European Romanticism, he is 'also conscious of the importance in Scotland itself of a kind of pervasive, second-rate, sentimental slop associated with tartan, nostalgia, Bonnie Prince Charlie, Dr Finlay, and so on'. He sets out on a po-faced analysis but finally cannot restrain himself: 'How intolerably vulgar! What unbearable, crass, mindless philistinism! One knows that kitsch is a large constituent of mass popular culture in every land: but this is ridiculous!'[17] So it is rash of the latest contributor to the debate, Professor Tom Devine of Aberdeen, to have declared in a newspaper, under the headline 'Historian's Shock Claim on Birth of Tartanry', how modern Scottish identity, no less, was 'from the national dress to the imagery of Highland landscapes . . . created by a rich élite to ensure the country reaped the profits generated by the British Empire'. That the identity cannot anyway be reduced to one thing but is, as Scott wished, a blend of different elements seems obvious. The shock Devine wished to deal had, however, long been defused by Nairn: 'This is a popular sub-romanticism, and not the vital national culture.'[18]

Yet in the twenty-first century it is back with a vengeance: scarcely a wedding or dinner takes place that is not graced by kilts. In the 'Tartan Army', which followed the Scottish national football team in its run of qualifying for the World Cup from the 1970s, the people made it their own; with the same hopeless fidelity as the old Jacobites they have in kilts followed the squad right through its later, more dismal fortunes. While the fashion had before hardly trickled from the top down, it now spread from the bottom up. If the proletariat bared its knees when bent on devilment, why should the bourgeoisie balk? The rise of nationalism also prompted Scots to look, not just be, Scottish. All this, too, can ultimately be traced to the visit of George IV, although Scots seem more given to colour in dress or behaviour the more insipid, in football or politics, they have become.

The gap between image and reality did not go unremarked even at the time of the royal visit in 1822, for example, by Stewart of Garth himself, incensed that Gaels celebrated in Edinburgh were at the same time being driven from the Highlands. He saw this as a matter of more than local significance. One of many engaging views he argued in the *Sketches* was that virtue increased with altitude: 'It may not be irrelevant to state, that, notwithstanding the recent depopulation of the higher glens, their inhabitants have always been more athletic, better limbed, and more independent in their minds, than the inhabitants of the lower glens.' So it was a duty of landowners to manage their estates in such a way that a numerous tenantry could live as high up as possible: purity would cope with poverty.[19]

Stewart berated landowners neglecting that duty. The duke of Atholl was 'running the same race of avaricious oppression and ignorant infatuation which is so quickly driving so many land holders to their ruin . . . who in their hunting for profit and increased incomes showed no pity for the suffering of others, nor cared what became of them'. Alasdair MacDonell of Glengarry, founder of a Society of True Highlanders, evicted 1500 people, 'yet Glengarry with a consistency only to be equalled by the rest of his character goes about the country attending public meetings and making speeches in his own praise as a true friend to the Highlanders'. As for the countess of Sutherland, 'I care not for her opinion, nor wish to have any opinion or principle in common with a person who has caused such undeserved and general misery among so many thousands of virtuous unoffending human beings.' But later, after Stewart took the trouble to go to her county, he changed his mind, indeed expressed 'high satisfaction and admiration at the liberality' she had shown to her people.[20]

Stewart's championship of Gaels arose from his own generous paternalism. This still did not enable him to avoid the crisis faced by all landowners after the end of the Napoleonic Wars, a period of great tension in Lowland Scotland too and, indeed, in Britain as a whole. The inflation of wartime ended, while the real domestic prices of many products plummeted as foreign trade returned to normal. For the Highlands this meant drastic falls in returns from sheep, cattle and, above all, kelp, an industry that collapsed. Meanwhile thousands of demobilized soldiers returned to the glens to seek work no longer to be found. Decades of improvement were suddenly seen to have been of little net benefit. The optimism of the turn of the century evaporated.

All at once it struck Scots that the whole social order was changing. In the eighteenth century it had seemed immutable, hallowed alike by religion and philosophy. Even the wars had not disturbed it. But once the nation's tremendous martial exertions came shuddering to a halt in 1815, economic differences and problems once taken for granted suddenly appeared intolerable. In Glasgow in 1820 a workers' insurrection was just forestalled, though it never became clear how far it might have been the work of *agents provocateurs* anyway. Some landlords tried to tar Highland discontent with the same brush, but the analogy was strained. Men such as Scott and Stewart may have underrated the true problems, yet they did make a more positive response: the task of leaders lay in looking to the character of the people and to mutual obligations within society. This was how to deal with revolutionaries, radicals and Whigs. For example, after Britain's triumph in the wars when Scottish, more especially Highland, soldiers had played a never less than glorious part, everyone could take pride in the values of military service and in values also of morality and order, of religion and patriotism. In Scotland the nation could be rebuilt around these. In such sentiments the Gaelic voices of Adam Ferguson and James Macpherson echoed yet. Scott and Stewart hearkened and acted.

Yet Scott the Lowlander went bust, dragged down into a financial maelstrom not of his making, and so did Stewart the Highlander, by following the advice he gave the nation. He inherited his estate late in life, in 1821, when it carried debts of £30,000 on a rental of £1000 a year. He was in effect bankrupt from his outset as proprietor. Yet he had written that in the old Highlands 'insolvency was considered disgraceful and *prima facie* a crime'.[21] The one way he now saw of saving the estate was to subsidize it from West Indian plantations also owned by his family. While as a youth he had thought the slave trade an 'atrocious and inhuman traffic', slavery no longer seemed so bad as his own financial fate closed in. Yet the plantations, too, were in a mess and never yielded him an income.

In 1829 Stewart went to be Governor of St Lucia, whence he busily sent back dispatches. He found the slaves in general happy and well fed, thanks to the fertility of the soil. They had their own allotments, from which they could sell produce and at length buy their freedom if they wished. They appeared not to be overworked, even if some planters did make them toil by night as well as day; they could also take time off in lieu, although Stewart resolved that the governor ought to regulate working hours. Still, he could not see why female slaves should be subject only to light punishments 'while women were sent to the treadmill and whipped in England'. On the other hand, St Lucia had hospitals for old and sick slaves. It would be good for active ones to get some education, as much in morals as in 'the mechanical art of reading'; after all, some 'would sell their own father or child for a cask of rum'. This catalogue of bland prejudice and wishful thinking Stewart solemnly set down just four years before the emancipation of slaves in the British Empire and the collapse of the entire economy of plantations. He did not live long enough to find out how flimsy a basis it was for the way of life in the West Indies, let alone the Highlands. It is tempting to ask whether, in seeking to sustain the one from the other, he did not sacrifice the moral value of his paternalism.[22]

Not long after his death in harness in 1830, Stewart's estate went the way of so many others. A crowd of creditors received 10 shillings in the pound, this despite his having followed willy-nilly policies of improvement that he condemned in his fellows. He had urged his own tenants to emigrate – in other words, to clear themselves off the land so that he could raise rents. He wrote: 'I have wished to encourage voluntary emigration, and that thinning of the population which is absolutely necessary – but I am decidedly hostile to the desolating system of turning out and extirpating a whole race.'[23]

Previous butts of Stewart's censure thought it a distinction without a difference. One of Atholl's factors, James Findlater, wrote in 1824 how Stewart 'after his song of praise upon his selected few for their continued consideration to their highland tenantry now begins to play up the other tune. On the estate of Kynachan he is said to have warned his tenantry there (who seem to have no leases) to pay additional rents or remove at the first term.' Findlater had spoken to a tenant who, with his rent rising from £50 to £80, recalled how his landlord 'had so often repeated that no offer of a higher rent or other inducement should ever affect him that . . . he is no man at all, that could say so much and act so contrary'. From the north Patrick Sellar chipped in to gloat over 'a selfish petty Highland laird who sees no further than the limits of the little sovereignty where Donald approaches him with fear and trembling – hunger in his face – a tattered philibeg of Stewart on his other end'.[24] This is the voice of systematic improvement at its most acridly self-righteous. But where was the morality in all this? In a traditional way of life to be paid for out of black slavery (and if not this, what else)? Or in a new way of life that, by the actions of independent economic agents, paid for itself?

The questions turn yet more pointed bearing in mind that there were indeed Highland lairds unencumbered by morality, concerned with profit and nothing more. One could be found not in Sutherland but in adjacent Easter Ross, at Culrain. It was the property of young Hugh Munro of Novar, heir to the old general who had been the first round there to lease land for sheep in the 1790s. And it was here in Strathoykel that the men of Ross had gathered in *Bliadhna nan Caorach*, the Year of the Sheep, to set out on the great drove – a place for long Highland memories and fierce Highland emotions.

Early in 1820 Munro gave notice to 500 tenants at Culrain. He offered no resettlement: they would just have to go, he did not care where. Yet it was not as if the estate had been straitened. The rental was rising; the tenants had never fallen into arrears. When they received the notices, they offered to pay more. The sad fact was, though, that Munro could earn three times as much from a single sheep farmer as from all of them. His law agent arrived with the statutory witnesses to serve writs of removal, warning the people to quit by Whitsunday. A hostile mob saw off him and the other harbingers of their doom.

At this point higher authority had to intervene. The sheriff of Ross was still Donald Macleod of Geanies, now aged seventy-six, 'that fine old country gentlemen of olden times' who had dealt with the trouble in the Year of the Sheep. He reacted now as he had reacted then. He asked military support of the Lord Advocate (who, fearing revolution in Glasgow, did not respond), and he convened the local landowners. As its colonel, he called out the county's militia. In the spring, riding in his carriage, he led a force of a hundred north from Dingwall to Culrain. There the way was blocked by a noisy crowd, apparently of more women than men, although he claimed most were men wearing women's clothes. As he got down from his carriage with the writs, they pressed in on him and his escort. An altercation broke out, then a riot. A woman struck the first blow with a stick, and soon both sides were thrashing at each other. The militia fired one blank volley but could not still the maddened mob. Sheriff Macleod's force ran, carrying him with them and abandoning his carriage, which was wrecked. They did not stop running for 4 miles, until they reached Ardgay on the Dornoch Firth. Here they barricaded themselves in an inn. The people threw stones at the windows, shouted insults and at last went home in jubilation.

Macleod stayed put at Ardgay for a week, unwilling to return to Dingwall but wary of venturing back to Strathoykel. He feared the locals might storm the inn. In fact, their resistance was over and soon they gave in, accepted the writs and prepared to leave. John Prebble attributes this to Highlanders' old weaknesses, 'their lack of leadership, their childish faith in the laird . . . and, most insidious of all, their melancholy belief that they had been a doomed race since Culloden'. There is one trouble with his tear-jerking litany. The men of Easter Ross, northern Whigs to a man, had rallied to the British government in the '45; Munro's regiment had stood in Butcher Cumberland's second line, eager to doom members of their race who were Jacobites.[25]

The riot at Culrain still had an effect. James Loch wrote to his staff: 'In these times, depend upon it every motion is watched and if you do anything at all which will occasion public observation it will be brought before the House of Commons.' For the remaining removals from the interior of Sutherland he gave an instruction to 'avoid using fire in any way whatever'. Whether or not that soothed their pain, they met no resistance. It may be surprising that the trouble did not spill over from Easter Ross, yet, however unhappy the people of the countess's estate were to leave their homes, they still had an assurance of somewhere else to go, and not too far away. It is worth asking then whether Sutherland presents us with the lineaments of a clearance in the full sense of the term, the sense of coercive depopulation proposed in a previous chapter.

What Munro of Novar carried out at Culrain was indeed clearance in that full sense: he threw all the people out, with nowhere else to go. Then his estate stood empty, whereas in Sutherland 25,000 people still earned a living, or at least had encouragements to do so. 'For twenty years after Strathnaver and Culrain there were no more great clearances', writes Prebble[26] – on that point, at least, the bloodhound of lairdly misdemeanour may be trusted. Of course the Highlands still lost part of the natural increase in their population, as they had done for centuries. Of course the remaining population was mobile, more mobile than before, as under economic pressure Highlanders 'changed their situations', in Sheriff Macleod's apt phrase, or were 'rearranged after a new fashion', in Hugh Miller's equally apt one. But, except on a small and local scale, as at Culrain, no clearance, no coercive depopulation took place. If it had, the numbers of Highlanders could not have continued to rise.

In fact clearance, in the manner depicted by modern Scottish myths, remained as yet morally impossible for most Highland landlords. It could expose them to the opprobrium of their peers. It could add to the revolutionary potential of a Britain in crisis. And it appeared repulsive in itself: it was done, if at all, shamefacedly, on the quiet, without spectacular evictions, without the use of force, but little by little, through opportunistic changes in rents and leases, as was happening all over Britain and would later happen in much of Europe. It happened this way because most Highland landlords still accepted some moral responsibility for their people, even if they might take opposite views of what that actually involved. This sense of moral responsibility came out in their actions, whether in trying to maintain the traditional way of life intact, in the case of Stewart of Garth, or else in trying to create a novel, viable way of life, in the case of the countess of Sutherland. In truth, both worked in vain. They only put off the evil day.

13

'I'm proud of my country'
The Disruption of 1843

ONE CONGREGATION TOOK to 'sitting in a hole', in the words of the Revd Thomas Guthrie, doctor of the Free Church of Scotland. Its members at Ballater in western Aberdeenshire were, when their flock first formed in 1843, forbidden to meet anywhere in the village. The area around belonged to an estate under trust, that of Farquharson of Monaltrie, and the trustees would not hear of providing a plot for religious dissenters to erect a place of worship. They gathered in the open air until a friendly tenant farmer offered them use of a sheep-cote, 9 feet square, with walls 5 feet high. When they asked leave to raise the roof at their own expense, the estate again refused. Still, there was nothing to stop them lowering the floor. They dug out the earth until they had enough clearance to stand beneath the rafters. But when it was raining the water ran down round their feet, which, with leaks from the roof, made worship a drenched experience.[1]

Another congregation, of the parish of Duthil in Strathspey, met in a wood of fir trees above Carrbridge, 700 feet high. There they built a rude pulpit set about with benches, from which they sometimes had to clear the snow before they began the service. During a blizzard in the winter of 1844 their presbytery wrote to the laird, the earl of Seafield: 'We cannot believe that it is your Lordship's wish to oblige them to continue meeting in the open air at the risk of health and even of life, in such weather as the present.' But it would remain his lordship's wish for some time to come, until they could find a better arrangement.[2]

A third congregation, at the township of Paible on North Uist, revolved about the pulpit according to the way the wind blew. Their minister preached under a 'peculiar jutting rock', placing himself so that the weather was behind him. If the wind veered, he and the congregation would shift round to preserve some shelter for themselves from the stormy blast, without missing a word of the sermon.[3]

A fourth congregation, in the parish of Torosay on Mull, met in a gravel pit near the shore. At high tide it was liable to flood, and then they would have to scramble up the sides. They erected a tent which could hold only a certain number of worshippers. If more came to the service, the minister stood at the entrance looking out towards those who had to sit on the rocks or the heather and bracken beyond. The tide once rose faster than expected during the solemnities of a communion. Rather than interrupt it, they stayed ankle-deep in the water until it finished.[4]

A fifth congregation floated rather than sank. Strontian lay on the estate of Ardnamurchan, which covered the whole of the westernmost peninsula of the mainland of Scotland, 40 miles long and all the property of Sir James Riddell. He, too, refused the Free Church a site for a place of worship. Rather than meet in the open air, the members decided to buy a ship. They raised £1400 and sent an order to a sympathetic builder on the River Clyde. They found an anchorage in Loch Sunart, and moored the vessel 150 yards offshore. On a Sunday they could either row to it in their own boats or be ferried out by volunteers.[5]

A longer voyage was demanded of the minister for Eigg, the Revd John Swanson. He could not obtain a manse there and lived instead at Isleornsay on Skye, a good 10 miles across the Sound of Sleat. To visit his parishioners he procured a small vessel, the *Betsy*, 12 tons in burthen and 30 feet long. He had to spend so much time on her that she came to be known as the floating manse. When the first General Assembly of the Free Church took place in Glasgow in the autumn of 1843, Swanson sailed all the way to the Clyde in her. He arrived to acclaim, but his welcome from the rough Scottish waters was not always so warm.[6]

It has to be said, though, that a good many in the Free Church seem to have secretly relished such worldly adversity. It recalled the Covenanters of old, gathering at their armed conventicles amid the hills and glens, ever ready to break off prayers or psalms and fight the royalist soldiers of Bluidy Claverhouse hunting them down. It let the Free Church feel persecuted. It presented the ministers as heroes. It made the members believe they were martyrs. This was true Scotch religion, with a vengeance. Better still, the landowers' refusal of sites for places of worship caused outrage well beyond the Free Church. In its pioneering years it set out with stupendous energy to replicate, across every one of over a thousand parishes in the country, the local structures of the established Kirk whence it had seceded. This meant in the first instance a place of worship, without which nothing more could be organized, the schools and the missions to the poor that the Free Church meant to follow later. In fact, these supplementary arrangements tended to falter, for they all needed money and the pockets of its members were not bottomless. Even so, the spectacle of dauntless self-help invited admiration, whatever had brought it about. At length the Parliament at Westminster mounted an inquiry into the refusal of sites, and its moral pressure forced the lairds to give way.

Hugh Miller was to the fore in the campaign for sites, not least in his tract *Sutherland as It Was and as It Is*, otherwise concerned with the alleged clearances. Here in Sutherland, too, dwelt a devout population, 'wonderfully clean and decent', which had almost wholly seceded from the established Kirk. The people gave evidence of virtue and piety both in their fortitude against hardship at home and in the valour of sons they sent to fight for Britain abroad. According to Miller's report of their sentiments, the refusal of sites completed their degradation: 'We were ruined and reduced to beggary before . . . and now the gospel is taken from us.' The first duke of Sutherland had removed them from their homes and here was the second duke denying them their one consolation, 'deepening and rendering more signal the ruin accomplished by his predecessor'. Although they respectfully petitioned him, he forced them to worship in all weathers 'on the unsheltered hillside' while threatening with eviction anyone who harboured a minister of the Free Church. In Miller's purple prose this 'ground into powder what had previously been broken into fragments – to degrade the poor inhabitants to a still lower level than that in which they had been so cruelly precipitated'. When the duke passed through Helmsdale, the men stared stonily at him or turned their backs and went indoors, while the women baaed like sheep. The refusal of sites set a final, fatal seal on the alienation of lord and people: if to contemporaries any single thing marked an end of traditional society, it was this. The Highlanders endured, says Miller, 'atrocities unexampled in Britain for at least a century'.[7]

Such, among ordinary folk, were the consequences of the greatest domestic event in Victorian Scotland, the Disruption of the Kirk on 18 May 1843. The General Assembly had that day been due to open at St Andrew's Church in George Street, Edinburgh. As a crowd of thousands waited outside, the retiring moderator, the Revd Dr David Welsh, professor of ecclesiastical history at the capital's university, led a prayer to open proceedings. At this point the normal thing would have been for the roll of new commissioners to be called. Instead Welsh rose and, to a breathless hush, said: 'There has been an infringement on the constitution of the Church, an infringement so great that we cannot constitute its General Assembly.' He went on to read a long protest against attacks on the Kirk mounted over ten years by the British Parliament. Redress had been sought in vain, so he and all who believed in the spiritual independence of the established Kirk now had no choice but to leave it.[8]

The moderator laid his protest on the table, turned and bowed to the royal commissioner, stepped down from the chair and walked to the door. As he went, other ministers and elders got up to follow, row after row. Outside, when they emerged, the crowd first cheered but then fell into a solemn silence. Many more who had pledged to leave the Kirk were wait-ing in George Street. Although no plan for a procession had been made, the crush grew so great that they were all forced to walk in column, three or four abreast. They marched a couple of miles to a prepared meeting place. There they constituted themselves the Free Protesting Church of Scotland. More than 450 ministers signed a deed of demission, by which they gave up their charges, their manses and their incomes. Nearly 40 per cent of the clergy and perhaps half the laity of the Kirk seceded.

'Well, what do you think of it?' someone asked the Whig judge and former editor of the *Edinburgh Review* Francis Jeffrey, who was spending the afternoon at his home in Moray Place. He replied, 'I'm proud of my country. There is not another country on earth where such a deed could have been done.'[9]

The issues behind this caesura in national life are so remote from today's concerns as to be scarcely explicable to modern Scots, let alone anybody else. The conflict of Church and state in Scotland had mounted during a series of disputes about the appointment of ministers to particular parishes. By pure Presbyterian doctrine they ought to have been called by the con-gregations. But there was an act of Parliament of 1712, the Patronage Act, a spiteful infringement of the Treaty of Union, which said ministers had to be chosen by lay patrons, the heritors or landowners of the parish, just as they often were in England. Presbyterianism had never been loved at Westminster, and this act put it in its place. For over a century the Kirk submitted because there was nothing else to be done.

The ruling party in the General Assembly, the so-called Moderates, even made a virtue of acquiescence where it could be turned to advantage in relations with the state. They salved their consciences by passing on the nod an annual protest against the Patronage Act, but as a mere gesture. For some of their reverend brethren this was too much: they left the Kirk to form dissenting sects, the Relief Church and the Original Secession Church. Others resolved to carry on an Evangelical struggle from within, and developed a strong agenda of reviving Calvinist orthodoxy, biblical instruction and fiery sermons, while working out a fresh version of Christian social ethics. The agenda came into its own after the Reform Act of 1832, which for the first time created a popular parliamentary electorate in Scotland. The voters soon decided they wanted to elect their ministers in the same way as they now elected their MPs, and at the same time pay off a grudge. The General Assembly, where the Moderates lost their majority, passed acts to ease this, but the old and the new systems clashed. The will of the Church and the will of the state were incompatible. Those penalized went to law, eventually to the House of Lords. There the Kirk lost: the supremacy of Parliament was confirmed. After fruitless attempts at compromise the Disruption followed.

It turned out, however, to be about much more than legal technicality or indeed the relations of Church and state. Ever since the Reformation of 1560 a continuum had in most respects been maintained in Scottish life, to which even the Union of 1707 made little difference. The state looked after temporal concerns and the Church looked after spiritual ones, widely interpreted to include education, care of the poor and curbs on the Scots' sins of drunkenness and fornication. There had been collisions as the state repeatedly interfered in the government of the Church, but gradually the two came to terms and in the eighteenth century reached an equilibrium.

The Disruption smashed that equilibrium. On one side of the scales established religion simply dropped away, unable any longer to perform its appointed tasks in society since so many Presbyterians had seceded into the Free Church. The balance then fell down heavily on the opposite side, the side of the British state, the only other entity equal to those tasks in the modern era; its influence proved to be an anglicizing one. A vital element of Scottish identity vanished, for the Kirk had been, along with the law and the universities, one of the national institutions guaranteed under the Union. Scotland was forced to adjust to a much less autonomous position inside the United Kingdom. She began to feel more like a province than a nation. It is possible to read into the Disruption a presage of later Scottish nationalism, in its rejection of the absolute sovereignty of the Crown in Parliament. But the ancestry is indirect, and leaders of the Disruption took care to keep its nationalist undercurrent well submerged. Rather, it was the development of a more British Scotland, which few Scots really wanted but all found inevitable, that sowed the seeds of later political dissension.[10]

In the Highlands the impact of the Disruption proved both distinct and deeper than in the rest of Scotland. Here, too, the clergy led it. The Kirk was organized in four Highland synods. In the synod of Argyll, only 19 of 52 ministers came out into the Free Church, to use the contemporary term, and in the synod of Glenelg only 17 of 40. But in the synod of Sutherland and Caithness 22 of 29 came out, and in the synod of Ross 23 of 29. In the four synods together 81 of 150 came out. A good many of them were young ministers, called to their parishes in the ten years preceding the Disruption, when the people won the freedom to make known their preferences, to which patrons often deferred. In the synod of Argyll 9 out of the 19 had been appointed in that decade; of Glenelg 6 out of the 17; of Sutherland and Caithness 6 out of the 22; of Ross 9 out of the 23. When the people had a choice, they tended to prefer Evangelicals.[11]

This goes to show how, while the clergy led the Disruption in the Highlands, it was the people that made it. In remoter regions it won over the vast majority of them: in Sutherland, in Ross and Cromarty, in Lewis and Harris, and in much of mainland Inverness-shire. These areas saw almost everyone secede except landowners, their families and servants, with a few lawyers and the like – 'all who are not the creatures of the proprietor, and have not stifled their convictions for a piece of bread', as Miller put it.[12] No Christian Church since the Reformation had suffered such a catastrophe. In Sutherland the Auld Kirk, as it was soon known, held on to just 200 members out of a population of 25,000; in Lewis it retained 500 out of 17,000. In the presbytery of Latheron in Caithness, with six parishes and 8000 inhabitants, a single man stayed with the Auld Kirk, and in the parish of Lochs on Lewis again a single man remained. This parish was named after its many lochs, and the man happened to live on the opposite side of one of them to the minister of the Auld Kirk and his church. They arranged that if on a Sunday the man waited at the edge of the loch, then the minister would row over and get him. This continued until urchins dressed up a scarecrow and stood it there on a Sunday when the man did not wish to worship.[13]

The numbers are impressive, but as ever the numbers do not answer the bigger questions. The biggest of all is why the Disruption struck such a deep chord in Highlanders as to commit a poor people in effect to the voluntary organization of religion, and all that then went with it, in a manner that profoundly marked their way of life and continues to mark it down to the present day. Up to 1843 the general assumption was that the Highlands would be saved from their past and present by becoming more like the Lowlands. On the face of it, the Disruption took another step in that direction. Yet in the end it made the Highlands less like the Lowlands.

In previous chapters something has been said about the early evolution of an intense Highland spirituality. The rise of Evangelical popular religion was common to much of Britain in the eighteenth century and reached its peak in the nineteenth century. Because of the different national culture it took a different form in Scotland, and more especially in the Highlands because of the different regional culture. It was suggested above that this came about through the weakness of established religion, that is to say of the Church of Scotland, by reason of its huge parishes and dearth of Gaelic-speaking ministers. All the same, it did its utmost to convert the people to orthodox Calvinism and at least largely excluded rival doctrines. But the effort was long blighted by the official hostility to Gaelic, and the conversion never really took place until the people had the scriptures in their own language. Once they did, after 1767, the effect was electric. The good news of the Gospel burst on the Gaels as it once had done, in the days of St Paul, on the Ephesians and the Thessalonians.

This was still not quite what a polite age regarded as established religion. It often made ministers uneasy. John Calvin may have preached the priesthood of all believers, but Scottish Presbyterianism liked, and likes, everything orderly and respectable. Religion ought not to be a matter of do-it-yourself, in other words. Yet that it was what it became over much of the Highlands. The minister was often a distant figure, perhaps only able to speak English anyway. In thirty of the vaster parishes he became less distant as in the 1820s a grant from the government provided for building so-called parliamentary churches, additional places of worship, although this also caused some social segregation of the faithful. In any event, the coverage remained inadequate. The unofficial arm of orthodox Presbyterianism, the Society in Scotland for Propagating Christian Knowledge, had still not filled all the gaps either. Most of its charity schools clustered along the Highland line, the frontier of Gaeldom, and in practice equipped their pupils to move across it to lives in the Lowlands. The society's work on the ground might also sometimes be captured by the less than orthodox, by literate members of the tenantry who offered themselves as catechists and schoolmasters because they wanted the income, not from any desire to instruct the people. One was accused in 1792 of occult practices, of 'recourse to certain herbs and an iron key which were thrown into another's milk in order to restore the fruit of it'.[14] The society could not by itself even eradicate the last heathen traces, let alone complete the work of conversion.

For Christianity the people turned instead to enthusiastic laymen. There were itinerant preachers, active in both Highlands and Lowlands. There were also, blossoming as if by a miracle from this thin, sour soil, *Na Daoine*, the Men, holding no official clerical office but sustaining a virtual clerical authority by dint of holiness and zeal. Without this penumbra of lay evangelists, organized religion in Gaeldom would scarcely have been possible. They, rather than the ministers, shaped it. They were also the first leadership of any sort to emerge from among the Highland people.

The people would flock, sometimes in thousands, to hear an itinerant preacher as news of his coming spread by word of mouth for miles around. They would put up a tent to protect him from the weather, listen to a long sermon, of hours rather than minutes, and sing the Gaelic psalms in wind, rain or snow. Perhaps most preachers were Gaels, but a few were Lowlanders or even Englishmen. Sheriff Robert Brown of Inverness felt anxious when some of these arrived to evangelize camps of labourers digging the Caledonian Canal. They 'addressed the people by interpreters, and distributed numerous pamphlets, calculated, as they said, to excite a serious soul concern'. The effect did not wear off after they went on elsewhere but, quite the reverse, 'men who could not read began to preach, and to inflame the people against their lawful pastors, whom they had never suspected of misleading them. They next adopted a notion that all who were superior to them in wealth and rank were oppressors whom they would enjoy the consolation of seeing damned.' To Sheriff Brown, at least, this seemed the real reason for other problems in the Highlands:

> Many of them took into their heads that all labour not necessary for the support of existence was sinful. When the fumes of discontent had thus been prepared, through the medium of fanaticism, to which, it is known, the Highlanders are strongly attached; at last those levelling principles which had been fermenting in the south made their way among them, and excited an ardent desire of going to a country where they supposed all men were equal, and fondly flattered themselves they might live without labour.[15]

So the preachers fomented both sedition and emigration: the authorities could not view this with indifference.

Yet the government of Scotland remained so limited that the preachers were not really to be stopped. Just as it possessed no power to shut up the earl of Selkirk when he advocated emigration, so it had just to look on as other, pious landowners did their bit to foul the nest of paternalist Scotland with do-it-yourself evangelism. James and Robert Haldane of Airthrey (an estate now occupied by the University of Stirling) had applied to Henry Dundas, who ruled India as well as Scotland, to go out and witness to the heathen of Bengal. He turned them down flat, on the grounds that the British Empire had no business disturbing its subjects in their religions. It turned out that he could actually control India better than he could Scotland, for the two brothers promptly set up in 1798 a Society for the Promotion of the Gospel at Home. Such committed Christians were the Haldanes that they sold off some of their own land in order to finance the foundation of schools or Sunday schools and the distribution of the scriptures in the north. To these ends they sent out forty preachers.[16]

The Evangelicals did not have to work wholly outside the Presbyterian discipline of the Kirk but remained present inside it too; in fact, studious management proved necessary to keep them under restraint at the General Assembly. There they could never have come as ministers or elders unless Evangelical congregations had sent them. While enormous gaps remained in the Church of Scotland's organization of the Highlands right down to the nineteenth century, in patches it had done better. Areas such as Easter Ross or the adjacent stretch of country round Inverness boasted a strong and early reformed tradition which had equipped them with a continuous line of ministers dating from the first years after the Reformation of 1560. Their names can be traced in the *Fasti Ecclesiae Scoticanae*. The typical Presbyterian boxes in which they preached, humble rustic kirks of the seventeenth or eighteenth centuries, to this day stand witness to the vigour of the tradition at Alness, Contin, Cromarty or Cullicudden, at Dunlichity, Kiltarlity, Moy or Old Urquhart. The tradition included sabbatarianism, a simple, general, easily understood test of allegiance in a region often violently contested. So while the rise there of Evangelical religion did owe much to impulses from outside, it also drew strength from within.

There is no better evidence of this than the emergence of *Na Daoine*, the Men. The Scottish Reformation was in essence something for the laity: the minister preached to the people in their own good Scots tongue from high in a pulpit where all could see and hear him, instead of standing with his back to them at an altar and mumbling in Latin. If he then had to read aloud to them from a Bible in English, it made no real difference because, this being Scotland, the people began to answer back, to join in disputation with a God they assumed to be as tendentious as themselves. By the late seventeenth century there was a minister, Thomas Hog of Kiltearn on the Cromarty Firth, who urged them on. He had been a student at Aberdeen in the time of the Covenants and a member there of praying societies which encouraged all who came along to take a spontaneous part in the devotions. Hog was deposed from his parish at the Restoration of King Charles II and only returned to it after the Presbyterian settlement of 1690. But during those two ministries, and probably in between, he emboldened laymen to seek their own role in religious life, to lead the prayers or to speak of spiritual experience, for the sake of their souls and as an example to the rest.[17]

All this took a further turn when it crossed the linguistic frontier into the Gàidhealtachd. Lowlanders had made reformed worship public and communal, but this was something less possible for Highlanders, always so ill served in religion. Their communal needs had to be satisfied in an originally profane way by the ceilidh. Yet since communal needs could be spiritual as well as material, the ceilidh might also assume a religious tinge and be given over to discussions of scripture as well as to entertainment. From there it was but a short step to the *Latha na Ceiste*, renewal of the discussions on the Friday before a communion, led in the absence of the ministers by the Men. Most ministers offered communion just a couple of times a year, but they still did not like these fellowship meetings, as they called them. The Presbyterian victory of 1690 had been hard won, and the equilibrium of Church and state during the eighteenth century was never less than precarious. It depended on the exercise of internal discipline in the Kirk and on a hierarchy, with ministers answerable to local presbyteries, these in turn to provincial synods and the whole structure to the General Assembly, which deliberated in annual session on more or less the entire domestic affairs of the nation. As an establishment the Church of Scotland could not do just what it wanted, then, but had a responsibility for public order, which included licensing ministers with the sole authority, civil and divine, to preach the Gospel in their parishes. The itinerant preachers and the Men came across as a challenge at once to spiritual office and to public order.

This was why in 1737 the synod of Sutherland and Caithness went so far as to ban fellowship meetings from its jurisdiction. The practice was 'irregular and disorderly and tends to propagate the animosities of the people in these bounds against their ministers'. In fact, it could get much worse than that. At Halmadary in Strathnaver there occurred a couple of years later a case where a fellowship meeting proposed to offer a human sacrifice. A huge raven had perched on the roof of the house where the meeting was held, cawing and cackling in its sinister fashion. The people believed it to be an evil spirit whose spell could only be broken if they lifted the roof and cut a child's throat. They did lift the roof, but luckily someone had the sense to protect the child. The religious intensity of the Highlands often was, and still is, hard for outsiders to understand, in part because it has a history of its own. Here it seems to have bypassed a thousand years of formal Christianity in Scotland to move straight from bloodstained paganism to Evangelical enthusiasm.[18]

In the Presbyterian hierarchy, where most of the work is done by sluggish committees, it took until 1758 for the General Assembly to consider objections entered to the ban on fellowship meetings by the synod of Caithness and Sutherland. In a sensible move it set the ban aside. What could then follow was the coaxing of the meetings and the Men back into the fold of the Kirk. These might accept that the minister would with greater propriety conduct the prayer, praise and readings of *Latha na Ceiste*. It could no longer get out of hand if he sat in the chair seeing to good behaviour and sound doctrine. In return, he might order the proceedings with deference enough to the Men and what they had to say. All this came together in time, and fellowship meetings were confirmed as accepted practice in the Highland Church.

The Men, no longer suspected of usurping spiritual office, set themselves apart in other ways, in conduct that was even at that time eccentric. They grew hair and beards to an apostolic length, wandered about wrapped in cloaks with piratical coloured kerchiefs bound round their heads, and spoke in tongues, in oracles and allegories. But the people revered them in their contempt for the world. And the people, too, began to 'see visions, dream dreams, revel in the wildest hallucinations' or to be 'seized with spasms, convulsions, fits and screaming aloud'.[19] The difference in demeanour of the Men did not make them uncongenial at least to Evangelical ministers of the Kirk. The Revd John Kennedy of Dingwall commended them as Hog might have done two centuries earlier: 'When a godly Highland minister discerned a promise of usefulness in a man who seemed to have been truly converted unto God, he brought him forward into a more public position by calling him first to pray and then to speak to the question at the ordinary congregational meetings.'[20]

The tensions tugging at Highland religion were yet not stilled. This being Scotland, some people still rejected reasonable accommodation and resorted to schism if they found the slightest deviance in the established ministers' doctrine or practice. Such people were labelled separatists, a fair enough description. It drew a distinction between them and the first groups of seceders in the eighteenth century, who, in the Relief Church and the Original Secession Church, at least tidily replicated Presbyterian hierarchy. These dissenting Churches also sent missionaries north, who achieved their greatest success in Orkney and Shetland. Some converts there were crofters and fishermen, with a way of life like that on the nearby mainland, but more were townsfolk, artisans in Kirkwall, Stromness and Lerwick – towns with modernizing economies (from fishing and ships' chandlery) and in that respect outposts of the Lowlands, or at least with a character reassuring to Lowlanders.

Separatists were different and disturbing figures. They remained confined within the Gàidhealtachd. They had no hierarchy, only individual congregations. Since they would not trust backsliding ministers, they readily resorted to laymen for the cure of souls. These might stand before the parochial church on a Sunday morning and call on the faithful as they arrived to stay outside and worship with them in the open air rather than go inside to be corrupted by established religion. They were clearly men of confidence and eloquence, not hopelessly downtrodden but a sort of alienated élite, perhaps a counterpart in the spiritual sphere to the tacksmen in the material sphere who had washed their hands of the condition of the Highlands and departed for something better.

Among the separatists was Norman Macleod, master of a charity school at Ullapool, who probably never took clerical orders but just accepted a request to lead a congregation in Assynt. He retorted in kind to attacks on him from established ministers. He abused one – who had formerly been a friend of his while they were students at Aberdeen – for his 'false conversion, scraps of philosophy, fragments of divinity, painted parlour, dainty table, sable surtout, curled cravat, ponderous purse, big belly, poised pulpit, soft and silly spouse'. No doubt he sounded even better in the language of Eden. With an acid tongue and an overbearing manner he exerted a magnetic influence on his flock, which, in flight from famine, he was to lead around the world by way of Canada and Australia to New Zealand. There, at the other end of the earth, they at last discovered a promised land for the elect of God and lived together in a settlement that survives to this day.[21]

Yet in some happier time and place Macleod might have fulfilled himself in a regular ministry: his type was not, before long, altogether uncommon. For now he could find no home in the Church of Scotland, or any Church. To him the Kirk was defiled. The Moderates compromised it at every turn, not only with the state but also in pandering to their parishioners, whom they should have been berating for their sins. Another Evangelical told with disgust how neglect of duty might include toleration of 'superstitions and superstitious observances which had been handed down through the dark age of popery from the still darker age of druidical idolatry'. Kennedy of Dingwall accused the Moderate minister of being 'the great cattle dealer at the market, the leading dancer at the wedding, the toast master at the farmer's dinner and if the last to slide off his chair at the drinking bout, it was because he was more seasoned than the rest'.[22] But such ministers needed to be farmers of their glebes because of their pitiful stipends. To follow this way of life in other particulars at least helped to keep them in touch with their flocks: they were only human, after all. But no, said the separatists, their business was to spurn the world.

In social background the two opposing groups of pastors seem to have been much the same, and it stretched a point for separatists to paint themselves by contrast as champions of the crofting population under an economic juggernaut. Yet they cultivated a sense of oppression, of deprived rights and privileges, crucial to their new identity and new mythology, with a focus in religion. In retrospect it is hard to take seriously the extremity of their strictures on the Kirk. The tendency to vilify and demonize deviants from Highland rectitude had, though, already set in.

Together the Evangelicals – some inside and some outside the religious establishment, some irenic and some divisive, some sober and some wild – brought about a fresh configuration of Highland society. They emerged as a new group to give it leadership, not from any high social position, still less from any great material possession, but in the sense of moral and intellectual leadership. The degeneration of the old way of life fostered this. Down to the present, and far from the Scottish Highlands, people have continued to seek in fervent religion a refuge from the change and decay all around them, a means of coping with the ravages of a modernity not desired or understood and a rationale for rejecting its economic demands above all. The Gaels, demoralized and leaderless, found their ayatollahs in turning to Evangelicals for guidance, unity and consolation. These told them their baffling fate was no mystery but a divine judgement, an occasion not for recalcitrance, let alone resistance, but for resignation, renunciation, repentance and renewal of faith in a kingdom not of this world. One of the Men, Alexander Gair, said: 'I see in Scripture that the manner of the Lord's dealing with His people is that He brings them to a wilderness to prove them, and to let them see what is in their hearts.'[23] Gair worked in Sutherland, where the people in all their afflictions seem to have taken him at his word.

At any rate, a century of labours by the motley band of Evangelicals created a people for whom puritan Presbyterianism was, in the words of a resolution that would be adopted by the inaugural General Assembly of the Free Church, 'riveted in their souls'.[24] This gives some idea of why the Disruption made an impact on the Highlands that was unmatched elsewhere in the nation. Evangelical religion had taken firmer root there, through men and means over which the Kirk exerted little control, especially at the lay level. This religion was a matter of do-it-yourself, livelier than any to be found in most regular places of worship, especially when done in Gaelic rather than English. A tendency to defy religious or secular authority resulted, even issuing in schism if not contained. It then came as no surprise to find much of the Highland population moving almost as a body over to the Free Church in 1843. While the Disruption was led from the Lowlands, everything in the Highlands stood waiting for it: fertile ground well prepared, yielding a prodigious harvest.

Once the Disruption happened, it set a seal on all the other changes under way. Highland leadership passed from landowners to Evangelical ministers. The landowners, whatever else they did, made fatal religious errors. If their refusal of sites arose in part from loyalty to the residual Kirk, they later looked to the south and to England for the social identity conferred by the Episcopal Church, at best genteel, at worst snooty, above all alien. In the conversion of the Highlands to Presbyterianism the main influence had come from the Lowlands, carried by missionaries steeped in Covenanting history. In English-speaking areas – in Easter Ross, Caithness or the Northern Isles – there remained after the Disruption little difference between Highland religion and Lowland religion. But the Gàidhealtachd retreated into a spiritual laager. Free in 1843 to take over Presbyterianism on their own ground, the Gaels turned it into the redoubt of an oppressed, introverted culture estranged from the Lowlands.

Yet it was not a static culture, and it gave proof of its resilience by development out of its own internal impulses. Even while the Victorian ruling class and its capitalist ideology continued to transform the Highlands, the culture repudiated their influence. All the same, evangelical Presbyterianism, in its relation to modernity, looked as much forwards as backwards. It offered spiritual nourishment answering a need not of the old, feudal society but of the new, commercial one. It came to terms not with chiefs but with landlords. It did so in values that hardly questioned the social order as such but, on the contrary, conformed to the novel religious and economic individualism of the age. In lives of hard work and self-reliance the itinerant preachers and the Men, the separatists and the seceders, were after their own fashion meeting demands that improvement had always made of Gaels. At any rate they rejected the historic Highland values.

At least the Gaelic language survived; indeed for a spell it was strengthened through a fusion of its literary tradition with evangelical Presbyterianism. The result was to encourage many new voices, in a chorus that swelled into the twentieth century. There was a poetic school of ministers: the Revds Kenneth Macleod, Neil Ross, Angus MacKinnon and Angus Finlayson. Women expressed their devotional spirit in verse. In 1908 Catherine Macfadyen of Tiree, a charming matron of eighty-nine, was among the first generation to receive an old-age pension. She felt pleased rather than impressed:

> Fhuair mise crùn airgid
> A tha dearbhte bhon Rìgh dhomh,
> Ach cha dèan e bonn stàth dhomh
> Nuair bheir mo chàirdean don chill mi:

An Tì a dh' fhuilinh 'nam àite,
Mur dèan mi tàir air an Fhìrinn,
Bheir E crùn a bhios buan dhomh
'S oighreachd shuas ann an Sìon.

Crown of silver's been given to me
Confirmed by the King,
But no good will it do me
When buried by my kin:
He who suffered in my place,
If I scorn not the Scriptures,
Will give me crown that's eternal
And inheritance in Zion.[25]

Since Evangelical religion had struck such deep root in the people, it was easy for ministers to turn a sanctimonious gaze on the last traces of the clans' customs, the superstitions, the songs and dances, and especially the profane poetry, which had shown little inhibition about sex, for example. All were condemned and, if possible, suppressed. Highland religion took on a gloomy air, although there were enough sinners in enough ceilidhs to keep the familiar entertainments of the people alive.

Given that the culture maintained some internal dynamic, even the Disruption proved to be only a stage in its development. In fact, the Free Church yoked together in growing discomfort two different cultures, the emancipated but closed culture of the people in the Highlands and the emancipated but open culture of the Lowland bourgeoisie – emancipated alike, that is, from the Tories' *ancien régime* before the Reform Act of 1832. Until then Scotland had been ruled by the landed gentry; now she was ruled by the professional and capitalist middle class, flexing its muscles after it had broken its bonds to reinvent Scottish civil society. For historical reasons, but also because the Free Church was a vehicle of emancipation, this remained a society more interested in religion than in politics, or at least more innovative in religion than in politics. Compared to the political scene, dominated by a gentlemanly, cautious, unionist and anglicizing Liberal party, the intellectual scene in Scotland was lively and independent, with successors to the Enlightenment not unworthy of its glories.

The Free Church, for its part, produced theological progress not out of any connection with England, where such a thing was unknown, but out of wide European contacts, in biblical criticism and in a new science of comparative religion. At the forefront of this progress stood William Robertson Smith, professor of Hebrew at the Free Church College in Aberdeen. With his scientific spirit and demand for the autonomy of criticism from revelation he shocked fundamentalists. In 1881 he suffered, after a trial for heresy at the behest of a 'Highland clique', deposition from his chair. It gave a fatal signal that the Free Church could not hold two cultures together. The result before long was the formation of, in essence, Highland Churches: the Free Presbyterian Church in 1893 and a new Free Church, resulting from a fresh schism in 1900. After two centuries of endeavour to bind the whole nation to a single vision of orthodox Calvinism, Lowlanders abandoned it and left Highlanders as the last guardians (in Gaelic) of Scotland's Covenants with God.[26]

14

One prolonged note of desolation
Eviction and development, 1830–1885

ONE OF THE most moving accounts of the Victorian Highlands comes
from the pen of Sir Archibald Geikie. He had been born and educated in Edinburgh, where he inaugurated the chair of geology at the university in 1871. As director-general of the Geological Survey of Great
Britain he set out the country's remote volcanic history in works that are
still standard. He ended up laden with honours as President of the Royal
Society from 1908 to 1912. Although he had entered the inner sanctum of
the British academic establishment, Geikie remained at heart a Scots
Liberal of a rather radical sort: early on he befriended Hugh Miller, com-
rade in science and scourge of lairds, and later Patrick Geddes, pioneer of
town planning as answer to all the world's problems. He was a man of wide
sympathies, then. They extended to the Gaels.

Geikie got to know their way of life on expeditions to their mountains,
starting as a boy. He was nineteen when, in 1854, he went to Skye, even
today a kind of adventure playground for geologists, full of complex, fas-
cinating evidence for them. Years later he evoke the scenes of his youth in
Scottish Reminiscences (1906). His was a winning, humorous personality, and
he had fine literary gifts which show up the rebarbative sub-Marxist jargon
of many Highland polemics composed since. Geikie knows his readers will
be confronted to greater effect by the brute facts of human existence if he
has first seduced them with charm. His memory of what he saw one day
on Skye comes across in so stunning a fashion because beneath it is a sense
of tranquillity such as had lain on the scene for ever until the tragedy he
witnessed there and flowed back once it was over. The passage has often
been quoted, but no apology is made for reproducing it here:

> One afternoon, as I was returning from my ramble, a strange wailing sound
> reached my ears at intervals on the breeze from the west. On gaining the top
> of one of the hills on the south side of the valley, I could see a long and
> motley procession winding along the road that led north from Suishnish. It
> halted at the point of the road opposite Kilbride, and there the lamentation
> became long and loud. As I drew nearer I could see that the minister with

208

his wife and daughters had come out to meet the people and bid them all farewell. It was a miscellaneous gathering of at least three generations of crofters. There were old men and women, too feeble to walk, who were placed in carts; the younger members of the community on foot were carrying their bundles of clothes and household effects, while the children, with looks of alarm, walked alongside. There was a pause in the notes of woe as the last words were exchanged with the family of Kilbride. Everyone was in tears; each wished to clasp the hands that had so often befriended them, and it seemed as if they could not tear themselves away. When they set forth once more, a cry of grief went up to heaven, the long plaintive wail, like a funeral coronach, was resumed, and after the last of the emigrants had disappeared round the hill, the sound seemed to re-echo through the whole wide valley of Strath in one prolonged note of desolation. The people were on their way to be shipped to Canada. I have often wandered since then over the solitary ground of Suishnish. Not a soul is to be seen there now, but the greener patches of field and the crumbling walls mark where an active and happy community once lived.[1]

The language is so fine as to divert attention from a couple of obvious gaps in the depiction. Even sober modern scholars of the Highlands who make use of Geikie, such as Professor Eric Richards of Adelaide, tend to dwell on his pathos rather than fill in the background. For instance, Geikie assigns to the minister, whom he knew well, a helplessly commiserating role. The Revd John Mackinnon served Strath from 1825 to 1856. He was indeed a beloved pastor, who kept his flock loyal with him to the Church of Scotland at the Disruption in 1843. He had written the article on the parish in the *New Statistical Account*, reporting a sharp rise in population between 1831 and 1837 from 3000 to 3500, 'without any means for their support, or any prospect of comfort'. A resulting rapid subdivision of the land 'has been, and will continue to be productive of the worst effects here, as well as over a great part of the Highlands. And unless some method be devised to provide for the superfluous population, and to check its increase in future, the most disastrous consequences may be anticipated.' These had already begun to appear with two failed harvests in 1836–7: 'The recurrence of similar calamities can only be prevented by striking the evil at the root, by the establishment of a systematic emigration conducted upon proper principles, and holding out such inducements as will overcome the *amor patriae* so strongly implanted in the breast of every Highlander.' Mackinnon took a hand himself by urging 200 people to go to Australia, 'and so satisfied is the writer . . . of the prosperity of that colony, that he has done all in his power to persuade his poor countrymen to emigrate to that country'. What was more, 'to convince them of his good intentions, as well as to prove the sincerity of his advice, he has himself sent thither three of his sons within the last two years, and, if spared, for a few months longer, he proposes to send a fourth.'[2]

On the strength of this it seems likely that Mackinnon, whatever else he said to the people by the roadside at Kilbride, congratulated them on the brighter prospects they faced in Canada. He was a typical Moderate minister, on good terms with the laird, who had presented him to the parish in place of his own father and would present his own son in place of him. The mutual devotion of pastor and people at Strath is one of the details casting doubt on the lurid Evangelical abuse of Highland Moderates. Members of the two parties did not, besides, always hold different views on the social situation in Gaeldom. The Revd Robert Finlayson of Lochs on Lewis was among the ministers who came out into the Free Church, with his whole congregation but for one man. He, too, paints in the *New Statistical Account* a gloomy picture: 'There are no lands . . . that can properly be called arable. The plough is not used at all. The people rear their crops on small detached plots ['lazy beds'] and cultivate the ground with spades.' So, given a fall in income from cattle and fish, he cannot fault those who abandon their homes on hearing of better conditions in Canada from family and friends already there – news that 'seems to have inspired them with the spirit of emigration; and nothing but reluctance to part with their scanty stocks of cattle, at the present very low prices, seems to retard the emigration of a great many people of the Lochs this year, to British North America'.[3]

By now, a quarter-century after the defeat of France, it had grown clear that the problems of adjustment to peacetime in the Highlands were no mere blip in the march of progress. On the contrary, Gaels faced a pitiless reality which decades of optimistic but unprofitable improvement, sustained meanwhile by the demands of an economy at war, had contrived to conceal. The region was hardly more productive than before, yet its population continued to soar: by the census of 1841 it passed 400,000, more than at any time before or since. The Highlands appeared to be the one part of Great Britain where the people had grown poorer since 1815. Landlords liking to see them as part of the wealth of their estates found them to be more and more of a burden. Many Highlanders did not have even minimal legal status as tenants but, without rights or security, squatted on the land of others who did, and made some informal arrangement to pay in kind for the privilege. The oppression was then often not of tenant by landlord but of one Gael by another. The Revd Finlay McPherson of Kilbrandon told how Lord Breadalbane had to step in: 'This is a complete check to that thraldom to which cottars are subjected, when left to the uncontrolled will of the merciless tenants, who would extract from their labour during the greater part of the year, giving them nothing more than a small piece of potato ground in addition to the house and garden.' Here in Argyll any who had their fill of nasty neighbours could escape to Lowland industries, but there was no such handy refuge in remoter regions. The Revd Alexander Nicolson of Barra gave figures for his island: 278 families with tenancies and 93 families, one-quarter of the total, 'who hold no lands whatever'. On North Uist the Revd Finlay MacRae wrote: 'There are no less than 390 families not paying rents, but living chiefly on the produce of small spots of potato ground given them by some of their neighbours and relatives.' Even so, he went on, 'to force the people away, has been entirely repugnant to the human feelings of the noble proprietor and his managers'.[4]

So, far from resorting to clearance, many landlords drifted towards their own doom, of bankruptcy and exile. Ranald MacDonald, eighteenth chief of Clanranald, already laboured under debts of £100,000 when he ruined himself for good by seeing his people through the dearths of the 1830s. He had begun selling land in 1813 and by 1838 let go the last of his inheritance in the Small Isles and adjacent mainland together with South Uist in the Outer Hebrides – except for a single antique pile where he continued, now landless, to reside. MacLeod of MacLeod, who also bore debts of £100,000, found hungry hordes waiting for him every day outside Dunvegan Castle, from neighbouring estates as well as his own, and did what he could to feed them. He was obliged at length to sell his mainland territory and the unentailed parts of his property on Skye, such as Glendale, where only MacLeod's Tables, a cluster of extinct volcanoes, stand as a reminder of who had held these mountains time out of mind. Nor could he stay at Dunvegan: 'I was myself utterly ruined,' he said, 'and forced to get work in London, and to live there.'[5]

Others were left with nothing whatever. The MacLeods of Harris ran right through an Indian fortune they had invested in fisheries since 1778. By 1841 the population of the estate almost doubled, and when the fisheries failed the MacLeods were forced to sell up too. General Roderick MacNeil of Barra, fortieth of his line since the ancient Irish hero Niall of the Nine Hostages, had been among the proudest of all chiefs. He claimed a hereditary right to sit down to dinner before every prince of the earth, as announced by his bard each evening from the ramparts of Kisimul Castle. His father had hated to see emigrants leave his overcrowded island, 'but if it is for their good, I should regret it less . . . at the same time, those that remain will in time be much better; this reflection always offers us something consolatory when one reflects he has seen for the last time those he has been accustomed to from early infancy'. The son complained on inheriting of being 'literally tied to the stake' of his huge debts. He went bankrupt as well. In 1840 the estate was sold by trustees, who said two-thirds of the population ought to leave.[6]

It was not the first era in which land had changed hands, by fair means or foul, across the region. The dynamic of its whole early modern history arose from the Campbells' self-aggrandizement at the expense of MacDonalds or MacLeods. The house of Sutherland remained expansionist in the nineteenth century, keeping its own estate and acquiring that of Lord Reay, chief of Clan MacKay (to a welcome from its downtrodden tenants).[7] Otherwise the ancient Highland aristocracy had largely reached the end of its appointed time. In 1800 most chiefs still held on to their patrimonies; by 1850 many had left for places that had given and were giving refuge to their people, in the Lowlands, England, the Empire and the United States. Chiefs shared the fate of clansmen, in other words.

Chiefs now yielded not to one another but to strangers. Bankrupt estates went on the market as never before, usually to be snapped up by outsiders. The whole Outer Hebrides and most of the Inner Hebrides, with perhaps half the estates in mainland parts of the Highland counties – more than a million acres in all – came into fresh hands. This was a social revolution.

The reasons are not far to seek. Many chiefly houses entered the Victorian era with overwhelming burdens of debt, in some cases stretching back two centuries. The time came when there was just no prospect of their debts ever being paid off or even reduced, given the slump after the end of the Napoleonic Wars. The debts tended, if anything, to rise as their improving projects sputtered to a halt, with no return on the investment and all the money lost. Karl Marx, from the distance of London, used the term 'landlord capitalism' to describe what was going on. But most Highland lairds had no capital, just debts raised on the collateral of their estates. It was capitalists that had capital. And it was capitalists, or their agents in law and finance, that now took over in the Highlands.[8]

Geikie's account touches but lightly on this, and the omission distorts it. The parish of Strath lay on the lands of Lord MacDonald of Sleat, great-grandson of the Sir Alexander MacDonald visited by Johnson and Boswell; he received a peerage in 1776. Efforts to set his estate on a firmer footing, often reprobated by his fellows, never really worked. As elsewhere, he just bequeathed the problems to future generations. Successive Lords MacDonald kept their heads above the deep waters of their debts by selling off land. For the fourth one the crunch came when in 1846 he owed £140,000. That he was also due great sums did not help. Elites of the clans had been used to lending money among themselves, to build up an edifice of debt saved from toppling over so long as they did not foreclose on one another, something in general unthinkable. But by now MacDonald, at the pinnacle of the edifice, was obliged to deal with money-grubbers unmoved by such chivalry. It was good for Scotland that she had developed a flourishing financial industry, if in the end bad for MacDonald when he turned to it from his down-at-heel kin. He borrowed £38,000 of trust funds and £20,000 of banks and insurance companies. By 1846 he was unable to service the debt. He had inherited £84,000 of the £140,000 he owed. True, he himself incurred debts of £56,000 on such trifles as Armadale Castle but also on allowances to poor relations built into the edifice. His income was £11,000 a year, a tidy sum for the time, although just £3000 remained once he paid fixed charges and interest.[9]

MacDonald's estate was put under trust. He remained the owner, but control passed to trustees charged with cutting costs and raising income until creditors were satisfied and let him resume his patrimony. The trustees' responsibility lay to the creditors alone; by law they could take nothing else into account. This may seem harsh, but the creditors were by no means all super-rich, and they had their rights too. Even financial institutions were only looking after others' money, often people of a sort who in Scotland were just starting to get by on what they had scraped together, widows or ministers or sea captains. The country would not long have kept many financial institutions if these had tolerated bad debt. Trusteeship was kinder than the shame and collapse of actual bankruptcy, when everything had to be disposed of pell-mell. Without safeguards for rights of property national development would have ground to a halt, and many more than the people of Strath would have suffered. To be sure they 'formed a very secondary consideration' amid all this, in Geikie's words. Time and again, MacDonald pleaded for his own misfortune not to be visited on his tenantry. But the trustees had to earn what they could, and decided the people must make way for sheep. The rest is recorded by the eminent geologist.[10]

This was, then, a coercive depopulation, or clearance. It did not always go on in as smooth a manner as the law-abiding people in Geikie's poignant account consented it should. MacDonald also owned North Uist, where in 1849 the wailing, hysterical tenants of Sollas resisted police who arrived to pull down the homes of those who would not leave.[11] For their part in the tumult three men came to trial before the aged Whig judge Lord Cockburn at Inverness. During his instruction to the jury he left room for no doubt that the evictions had been lawful and the conduct of the accused unlawful. Yet the jury 'unanimously recommended the prisoners to the utmost leniency and mercy of the court in consideration of the cruel, though it may be legal, proceedings adopted in ejecting the whole people of Sollas from their houses and crops'. Cockburn, who handed down sentences of a mere four months' imprisonment, felt relief: 'The popular feeling was so strong against these (as I think necessary, but) odious operations, that I was afraid of an acquittal.' He did acquit MacDonald of any responsibility: 'He was in the hands of his creditors, and they have their doer, a Mr Cooper, their factor. But his lordship will get all the blame.'[12]

Cockburn was right. Distress here did not come about in the fashion assumed by modern Scottish myths, through the landlord's greed.[13] If MacDonald had got his way, the people would have stayed on the land or, at worst, been conveyed to new homes with his aid and blessing, according to the consistent policy on his estate. On Skye he and his forebears conceived philanthropic projects in the same spirit as other Highland lairds who counted the people in with their wealth but wanted to find better uses for it and them. There was to have been a planned village at Kyleakin, though it came to nothing until the West Highland railway reached Kyle of Lochalsh in 1897, and a ferry between the two places created the main crossing to the island. But the existence of Portree as its metropolis, today booming as never before, is owed to the Lords MacDonald, who equipped it with a harbour built by Thomas Telford, superior houses and public buildings. They hired fishermen from the east to teach skills to Skyemen: these showed, however, little interest. They hired miners to demonstrate how to work seams of coal found down the coast from Portree to the Braes, with the same result. Nemesis at length overtook the estate, but it was hardly for want of efforts to erect on it a viable community. Sad sequels followed not from improvement but from defeat of improvement under that old Tory policy for the Highlands of making the people thrive while keeping them where they were. The finances of the fourth Lord MacDonald may be faulted, but not his good intentions.[14]

If the MacDonalds of Sleat just hung on to their patrimony, their more irresponsible peers could not. Alasdair Ranaldson MacDonell, fifteenth chief of Glengarry, had strutted about as a leader of the tartan cult in the time of Sir Walter Scott, although also doing good work as a patron of Gaelic scholarship. In *Waverley* he appears in the guise of Fergus McIvor, a paragon of rude nobility. But he needed no literary prompt to make himself a living caricature of a chieftain trailing round the country with retinue of bard, piper and what not, while decrying all improvement. A rival champion of Highlanders, David Stewart of Garth, saw through him and called him a mere hypocrite for clearing his own tenants. Yet before long the two men came to be squeezed by identical pressures as they sought to maintain or restore a way of life no longer viable, with the same ruinous results. Glengarry was the more extravagant: at his untimely death in an accident in 1828 he left to the sixteenth chief, his ten-year-old son Aeneas, little more than vast debts. This 'respectable young man', as Cockburn saw him, grew up and emigrated to Australia, where Scots were opening the outback to pastoral agriculture. This could never be less than a risky venture, however, and it did not work for him. He returned broken in 1842 to die at home.[15]

The estate was already under trust, and in 1849 was sold but for Knoydart. As the seventeenth chief was a minor too, his mother, Mrs Josephine MacDonell, took over a residual domain teetering towards bankruptcy. The rental was just £250, of which she had anyway relieved the 600 tenants while famine threatened. She could not even lease the place so long as it carried them. She agonized, overwhelmed by her situation: what was to be done with a property yielding no income, and its trustees pressing for the debts to be discharged? She felt touched that the tenants, sprung of a fierce tribe of papist bandits, were reduced to begging leave to stay. When she decided to remove them in 1853, she tried to ease their pain. She offered them free passage overseas with complete forgiveness of arrears and a guarantee that none of their goods would be confiscated; even their priest saw 'no other prospect of escape for them'. This cost £1700, which she did not have and was obliged to borrow. About 400 people accepted and left for Canada. A report came back: 'They are a fine, healthy body of emigrants . . . and owing to the increasing demand for labourers of all descriptions throughout the province, they cannot fail to do well.'[16]

Yet it all went wrong in the end. A remnant of seventy souls could or would not travel with the rest. They had missed their chance and now found nowhere else to go. New legal summonses against them were executed. When sheriff officers demolished their houses, they took refuge in abandoned cottages or as a last resort under temporary shelters of blankets. Mrs MacDonell tried again. She offered these destitutes free travel anywhere in Scotland, free lodgings through the coming winter and free compensation for their crops if they would only leave without further ado: few other landlords of the time would have shown such solicitude. It still did not work, and she was vilified in the press for her pains. She had made her choices, though, and prepared the estate for sale. It went to James Baird, the great ironmaster of Coatbridge in Lanarkshire, leader of the Scottish industrial revolution in its second stage of coal, steel and shipbuilding, benefactor of the Church of Scotland and high priest of the cult of Robert Burns. Baird was on his way to accumulating Highland territories worth £1 million. He put sheep on the hills of Knoydart, now empty of human beings but for the handful of natives who hung on in their helplessness: the rest vanished from history.

The final disintegration of Gaelic society went on apace in the Western Isles too. The Lords Seaforth, chiefs of Clan Mackenzie, had maintained their seat for two centuries on Lewis after migrating from Wester Ross, much of which they also still held. The estate was drowning in debts of £150,000 until a good Lowland marriage in 1817 brought in £75,000. The windfall was invested in every conceivable improvement – distilling, fisheries, kelp – but it all vanished into the abyss. Such a price had been paid, said Seaforth, that whatever might happen, 'there is little prospect of ourselves ever enjoying again the influence, or adding to the happiness of its population by residing in the Lewis'. When his heir showed no interest in struggling on, the family decided in 1844 to sell the estate.[17]

The greatest magnates, the dukes of Gordon or of Argyll, were not spared. Gordon, with his seat in Banffshire, gave up western lands in Badenoch and Lochaber accumulated by his house over centuries. The sixth duke of Argyll ended a rake's progress discarding Mull and Morvern. Morvern went to John Sinclair of Lochaline. Again the tenants preferred his regime to the former one. He bantered with them in the language of Eden and came out into the Free Church in 1843. He lived to a sturdy old age, and at ninety-three could still 'crack nuts with his teeth'.[18] Improvement did not interest him. If he acted the old-fashioned autocrat, he was also popular, the sole proprietor to be a Highlander himself in a period when every other estate of the district changed hands. Meanwhile the seventh duke of Argyll, a better man than his father, wept over Tiree: 'These people wish to remain, they are undoubtedly attached to that island, and I cannot think of removing them; they are my fencible men, and I love them.'[19] On Islay cadets of the Campbells rained a fortune from Glasgow on the local economy and culture. Walter Frederick Campbell laid down a special educational regime for his son, who as soon as he was released from his nursemaids came into the care of a piper, John Francis Campbell, 'and from him I learned a good many useful arts. I learned to be hardy and healthy and I learned Gaelic . . . I worked with the carpenters; I played shinty with the boys about the farm; and so I got to know a good deal about the ways of Highlanders by growing up a Highlander myself.'[20] But the family went bankrupt in 1848, fled to France and lived on charity from friends.

By then recurrent local emergencies had brought about a general caesura in Highland life. Of potatoes, now the staple of the diet, a working man might eat eight or ten pounds a day, the monotony relieved only by adding milk or meal to the mash. His wife and weans would get by with less, but if for some reason they had no potatoes – as often happened before the new crop was harvested in the summer – they might be reduced to boiling up a gruel of shellfish or roots or anything edible to hand. Should the new crop fail, they faced disaster. When this happened over much of the Highlands in 1836 and 1837, committees organized in the Lowlands came to the rescue and sent food to the poor.

Far more serious was the threat in 1846 from the same blight as caused famine in Ireland, where a million people or more died of starvation. In Scotland it wiped out the whole crop along the Atlantic seaboard and put 150,000 at risk. To Scots it came as no surprise that they handled a crisis better than the Irish. Landlords dug into their own pockets, while the English official appointed to direct relief, Sir Edward Pine Coffin, overbore laggards with his lugubrious name and imperious missives. Charities stepped in again and the government filled in any gaps, more competently than in Ireland, distributing food and seedcorn from naval ships. Scottish deaths from hunger were few, and even deaths from diseases induced by hunger, such as typhus, showed little increase. An estate already modernized, such as that of the duke of Sutherland, escaped crisis because the strain was less acute there; in his county only a single parish, and one not belonging to him, needed to take measures against famine. The population of Sutherland reached a peak of nearly 26,000 in 1851, and even by 1881 only fell to 23,000. Donald Mackenzie, minister of Farr, said:

> No man can charge me with being in favour of the evictions. They were cruelly and harshly done, but I have lived to learn, and my opinions now are very much changed on that subject. Before the potato famine came on, I was of opinion that the evictions were a gross mistake and a cruel evil to the people, but since then I have changed my mind, and I know that had something not been done with the population of Strathnaver at that time they would have died of starvation worse than in Ireland.[21]

It is odd that this insight escaped Hugh Miller, hound of the ducal house, although in the *New Statistical Account* he had noted with approval the improvement of his native Black Isle, with a change from tiny plots to bigger holdings, so that 'the people of Cromarty in general eat and dress rather better in the present day ... Their employments, too, though affected by occasional depressions, are in the main less interrupted.' They escaped the crisis in 1846 too.[22]

Where the land did now empty it was not left littered, as in Ireland, with corpses and graves. The non-famine worked its effect by showing beyond doubt how ceaseless and perilous the pressure on Highland resources had grown. This was the last crisis of subsistence in the region, not because the crises found a definitive solution but because the conditions causing them, or aggravating them, were now to be removed. The main cause had been the population. The numbers living in the seven crofting counties, as they would come to be known, levelled off for half a century or so at or around 400,000 – still 40 per cent higher than in 1755. All hands were turned to halting growth above this and to making emigration a rational resort rather than a counsel of despair. Boards formed in Glasgow and Edinburgh for the relief of destitution could mutate, with much the same personnel, into societies for financing emigration. One was set up for Skye in 1851, then another for the whole Highlands and islands in 1852, this under the patronage of Prince Albert; among its first tasks it took on the rescue of the tenants of Knoydart.

What has been called above the Tory philosophy of improvement, of making the people prosper while keeping them where they were, played itself out. There was a simple reason: it had failed. As now grew clear, techniques of improvement brought up from the Lowlands could not be transferred without further ado across the Highland line, let alone show there the same spectacular success. Chiefs relying on this result were bankrupted not just in their financial resources but in their whole improving outlook. Few had anyway been able to make a plausible jump from fathers of their people to commercial landlords, managing population along with other resources of a hostile region. Donald, son and successor of the Revd John Mackinnon of Strath, recalled how 'landlords, recognizing the evils of subdivision, attempted to put a stop to it; but it was looked on by the people as oppression, and created such discontent that though the rule was in existence, it was abandoned to a great extent in practice'.[23] If the chief gave way that easily to old Highland sentiment, he could only look on while his teeming tenants then sank deeper into destitution. But more and more Gaels, instead of sitting round waiting for someone to come to their rescue, moved themselves or had themselves moved. A small yet piquant example came on St Kilda, where a third of the people opted for assisted emigration to Australia in 1852–3. They left their laird, Sir John MacLeod of Harris, in tears on the quay in Glasgow imploring them to return.[24]

New men coming in to replace old chiefs had fewer illusions to soften their anyway more niggardly sense of social obligation. Already some were English or Anglo-Scots, such as James Baillie, a merchant from Bristol who acquired Glenelg and Glenshiel, or James Morrison, London's greatest draper, whose descendants still hold the estate he bought on Islay. Cockburn wrote: 'We shall see what the English purses and the English comfort of the southern supplanters of our banished, beggarly, but proud lairds, will do.'[25] He disliked 'base but wealthy Saxons', yet he, along with local myth-makers, overrated their impact. They might know little and care less about Highland traditions, seeing their estates as investments or playgrounds, trophies of worldly success. But *noblesse oblige* was an English principle too, less hag-ridden than in Scotland. Glengarry's lands, except Knoydart, went to Lord Ward, interested only in the shooting, but in 1860 he sold them to Edward Ellice, Liberal MP for the St Andrews Burghs and scion of an English family settled in Scotland with money from the Hudson's Bay Company and from speculation in American land. He led a lavish life in his fastness, receiving more than a thousand guests a year, yet 'did all in his power to improve the dwellings of the tenantry, and by plantations, fencing and roadmaking did much for their comfort'. His tenants, every one of whom he knew, welcomed the change from the fickle, profligate MacDonells.[26]

In reality English incomers were outnumbered by Scots, and their role was sometimes to make the transition to the new Highlands messier than it need have been. The strains emerged, for example, in one case where a single man straddled the transition, finally with the most melancholy results of all. John Gordon of Cluny, on his death in 1858 probably the richest commoner in Scotland, had paid £160,000 for Barra, Benbecula and South Uist. His family, with ancestral lands in Aberdeenshire and Nairnshire, rose through service to the dukes of Gordon and only ceased to be Highlanders themselves by the retreat of the Gàidhealtachd from the Grampian massif. On his inherited estate Cluny was a faithful and reliable landlord in the old style, firm rather than severe: 'A feature in his management of his estate [was] that he liked to have about him the old tenantry, seldom parting with any who had occupied his land for any considerable time and were willing to remain on it.' He first hoped his islands, poor as they looked, could also be improved without expelling the islanders. An observer said he wished 'to keep them all [and] in doing so he acts judiciously for his own interest, as well as most humanely with a view to the real interests of the people'. Yet the money he spent went for nothing. He tried to sell the islands on but when he could not, and famine loomed, he resorted to wholesale clearance.[27]

Shocking as this sounds, it did not so strike every contemporary. Sir John McNeill, chairman of the Board of Supervision, which ran a new Scottish Poor Law, went to report on Barra. He quoted the opinion of its tacksmen 'that the eleemosynary relief afforded to the people has had a prejudicial effect upon their character and habits; that it has induced many of them to misrepresent their circumstances with a view to participate in it; [and] that it has taught the people generally to rely more upon others, and less upon themselves'.[28] One tacksman later recalled, with approval, 'the emigration promoted by Colonel Gordon which relieved the property very well. The people of South Uist and Barra petitioned in a body to be helped away. He sent a vessel to South Uist and a vessel to Barra to take them. He also sent clothing for scores of families.'[29] This did not soften the baleful impression made on Lowland cities when Hebridean waifs appeared there on their way to the emigrant ships. A party from North Uist was stranded in Glasgow in 1848. Another arrived in Edinburgh in 1850 in a 'state of absolute starvation', raising in the capital the appalling prospect that they would become burdens on its poor rates. The outcry greeting these spectres, however, never deterred Cluny, who redoubled efforts to make them go, by coercion if necessary. He managed to lay the blame for their hardship not on the threatened famine but on himself.

Still, this new class of landowners had little choice but to seek means of limiting the level of population if they were to escape repeating mistakes of the past and ruining themselves into the bargain. Differences among them amounted to a matter of style rather than substance or effectiveness rather than outlook. The differences could appear stark, all the same. The judge Lord Cranstoun, the former sheriff-depute of Sutherland who had sent troops into Kildonan in 1813, was another Lowland Whig who made himself a Highland laird, at the estate of Arisaig on the Atlantic coast. It was in his time that, according to Eneas Macdonell of Morar, 'the first clearances commenced in this country, and I was then a young boy almost but I shall never forget the feelings of awe and fear that came over the people of the country when the last occurred'. When dearth arrived, the largest tenant and the local Catholic priest had to organize all relief, because Cranstoun would do nothing.[30]

Yet if Cluny and others were condemned, the Mathesons were praised. They typified one kind of successor to the old chiefs, as Highlanders who had gone out into the world to earn a fortune and now brought it back to the land of their fathers. James Matheson, Liberal MP for Ross and Cromarty in 1847–62, made millions smuggling opium into China. His nephew Alexander succeeded him as taipan of the great oriental trading house Jardine

Matheson, but resigned after a couple of years over his moral qualms about the traffic in drugs. On their respective returns, James bought Lewis and Alexander bought Lochalsh, original territory of the Mathesons.[31]

Benjamin Disraeli had Matheson appear in disguise in his novel *Sybil* (1845): 'Oh, a dreadful man. A Scotchman richer than Croesus, one Mr Macdrug, fresh from Canton, with a million in opium in each pocket, denouncing corruption and bellowing free trade.' His Lewis suffered some of the worst Highland problems, with a population growing by nearly 2 per cent a year. But in the disastrous harvests of the 1840s Matheson, unlike Seaforth, found means to cope. He imported meal on his own account and sold it to the people at a quarter of the cost. He could afford the £100,000 he spent on public works to create jobs for them. He never forced them out, but moved only those wishing to exchange bad land for better, or else gave free passage in his own boat to any seeking work on the mainland. In 1851 Queen Victoria made him a baronet for his philanthropy.

Yet experience of crisis also taught Sir James Matheson that numbers on Lewis had to be restrained somehow. He allowed no more subdivision but offered generous terms for assisted emigration, with a free passage and supplies for any family unable to pay its own way. He began with those whose rents were furthest in arrears, yet if they turned him down he made clear he would refuse more help and reserve his legal right to evict them for unpaid rent. His factors toured the townships setting out his terms, harping on the bright prospects in North America by contrast with the desperate outlook at home. Some tenants still balked, but from 1851 to 1855 over 2000 left for Canada 'without the intervention of a single soldier or policeman, with no civil disobedience of any sort'. Here we see an improving landlord in his autocratic vigour, not sparing himself either. Up to his death in 1878 he spent £384,000 on Lewis. Even John Prebble called him a 'benevolent proprietor'.[32]

As for Alexander Matheson of Lochalsh, who succeeded his uncle as Liberal MP for Ross and Cromarty, in 1884 he looked back over three decades in the Highlands since his retiral from the Orient: 'When I bought this property it was not for the value of profit or making money by it; it was entirely from the love I had to the country of my birth, and to the country which formerly belonged to my ancestors.' He wanted 'to have tenants of all descriptions upon the estate', none too big but every one resident:

I am very much in favour of small tenants paying £50 to £100 a year, and I encourage them as much as I can . . . but I don't think it desirable to have . . . crofts where the people can only subsist, and there is not sufficient labour for them to make a living by . . . I won't make a single small croft in addition to what is here; at the same time, I won't evict a single tenant so long as they pay their rents.[33]

The Mathesons set an example of a rational policy which they also made to work, for a good while anyway. Theirs was not so different from Cluny's, at least not in its aim of creating a viable estate. But where he was curt and choleric, they were cool and consistent. The question of their altruism or tyranny is little to the point: elements of both went into a quest for stability through higher income, lower costs and sound management. What followed was a matter not so much of morality as of practical response to adverse conditions. In the end even the Mathesons would be defeated on Lewis, though in Lochalsh they did succeed in preserving a smiling, populated countryside.

In the Highlands as a whole the population stabilized from mid-century, although on a pattern by no means uniform. On Skye, mostly still administered by trustees of MacLeods and MacDonalds, there were 23,000 people in 1841 but fewer than 18,000 by 1881. The small isle of Tiree, however cherished by the duke of Argyll, housed 4500 in 1831 yet no more than 3000 by 1881. Two islands stood out against the general trend. One was Cluny's Barra, where the population regenerated and by 1881 had risen above the level of 1831. The other was Matheson's Lewis, where it climbed from 17,000 in 1841 to more than 25,000 by 1881.

Clearance is the portmanteau term often employed to define the experience of the region in the mid-nineteenth century. It is convenient shorthand, but misleading if taken to mean a general, coercive depopulation. In fact, various trends brought a demographic crisis under control, so as to keep overall numbers at 40 per cent above the level of the mid-eighteenth century. If the old Highland economy could barely sustain that, it could not have sustained more without deeper poverty and actual, rather than threatened, famine. The old economy had been unable to adapt to a changing world, despite every effort by distracted chiefs. Their day was done when the way of life broke down, and they departed with their clansmen: a symptom, not a cause, of the breakdown. It would now be not the size of population that determined uses of the land, but uses of the land that determined the size of population. This equation no doubt had to be worked out under new masters free of history's burden. Into it went evictions, but more to the point a huge increase in the numbers of voluntary emigrants seeking, and finding, a better life elsewhere, leaving a more tolerable share of meagre resources to those who stayed behind.

15

Don't live starving where you are
Contested culture, 1850–1885

THE SUTHERLAND HIGHLANDERS, the 93rd regiment, played a big part in suppressing the Indian Mutiny of 1857. In their finest feat of arms they relieved Lucknow, where the white community was besieged in the compound of the British resident by rebellious sepoys. Colin Campbell, the Glaswegian commander coming to the rescue, had to start by taking the Secunderabagh, an enclosed garden with strong walls held by the mutineers as an improvised bastion outside the city. He told his Highlanders:

> When we make an attack you must come to close quarters as quickly as pos-sible. Keep well together and use the bayonet. Remember that the cowardly sepoys, who are eager to murder women and children, cannot look a European soldier in the face when it is accompanied by cold steel. 93rd! You are my own lads. I rely on you to do the work.

The struggle for the Secunderabagh began with cannonades to batter a hole in its rampart. The first soldiers to enter, from the Punjab Rifles, were shot down. Campbell turned to John Ewart, colonel of the 93rd, and cried: 'Bring on the tartan!'

With superb skill the Highlanders infiltrated the breach. One by one they forced a way in, each holding the defenders at bay while he let the next one through. When enough had done it, they set about the grim task assigned them by their commander. In four hours, for a loss of 76 officers and men, they killed 2000 mutineers, in a slaughter to yells of 'Cawnpore!' – a reference to the massacre of British wives and children in that city some weeks before. A silent, well-read Highlander known to his mates as 'Quaker' Wallace bayoneted twenty sepoys, reciting verses of the 116th psalm as he drove his blade into their bodies. The Scots were astonished to come up against female black slaves who 'fought like wild cats', but these they cut down with the rest. Ewart emerged from the carnage, covered in blood and powder, to report to his commander: 'I have killed the last two of the enemy with my own hands, and here is one of their colours.'

'Damn your colours, sir,' snarled Campbell. 'It is not your place to be taking colours. Go back to your regiment this instant!' But when it was over and they surveyed the corpses piled five feet high, on which dogs and vultures now made feast, they felt hugely proud of themselves. 'We had done *something* to avenge Cawnpore!' wrote one trooper, William Alexander. They struck up 'The Campbells are Coming' on the bagpipes to hearten the defenders of the residency just a couple of miles away.

The Sutherland Highlanders had made their presence felt in India as soon as they landed, straight from the Crimean War, some months before. According to another trooper, William Munro, they caused 'quite a sensation in the city of palaces [Calcutta], for a kilted soldier had never been seen there before. The natives gazed in silent awe at the peculiar dress and the stalwart figures of the new sahibs, or gagra wallahs (petticoat men) as they called them.' The corps was, of course, a bastion of the Free Church. Once, stationed in Canada, it had refused orders to parade on a Sunday when the service was to be conducted by a chaplain of the Church of Scotland. The men did not share the usual Evangelical views on temperance, however. Complaining that the Indian climate made them 'gey an' drouthy', they let the many Scots in Calcutta ply them with beer. Lady Canning, wife of the Governor-General, noted with dismay the troops' drunkenness and observed, 'the Highlanders have been by far the worst'.[1]

A streak of barbarism coloured the Highland image even into this era of the Gaels' rehabilitation. That process had gone on ever since, in the Seven Years' War of 1756–63, sons of the glens first showed what brave, steadfast soldiers they made fighting as well for the Crown as they ever did for their chiefs. Their horizons widened with imperialism. For prowess in battle Gaels and Sikhs, the great martial race of India, seemed two sides of the same coin: and Sikhs are famed as drinkers too. The British won the first Sikh War in 1846, but the fight put up by the hardy warriors of the Punjab aroused their deep respect. Wishing to treat the vanquished leniently, they at first preserved a puppet state under the boy maharajah, Duleep Singh. Many Sikhs would not admit defeat, however, and in 1848 they rose in revolt. In retribution their sovereignty was quashed and its symbol, the Koh-i-Noor, sent to Queen Victoria. Duleep Singh went into Scottish exile, to be installed at Castle Menzies in Perthshire and learn the ways of a Highland gentleman: the local lairds held the Black Prince, as they called him, in high regard.[2]

A good many of the Sutherland Highlanders who rescued British imperialism at Lucknow hailed from round the head of the Dornoch Firth. There, meanwhile, their kith and kin on the estate at Greenyards, or

Gruinard, had been evicted by the landlord, himself an old soldier, Charles Robertson of Kindeace. This estate, on the border of arable and grazing land, lay in country that had been troubled ever since improvement had begun there. It gave rise to rituals familiar by now: tenants of Greenyards met the man delivering the notice of eviction, stopped him, searched him and burned it before his eyes, although without molesting him in any other way. That was code for escalation of the dispute. The sheriff would next have to be called in with the police. When they arrived one morning in March 1854, they carried 'large baskets full of alcoholic liquors, of which they drank copiously before they made their savage onslaught'. On a track up into the hills waited a crowd of women, a dozen men and a lot of children looking on. The sheriff ordered them all away, although he did not read the Riot Act. They ignored him, so he instructed the police to move them on, something done 'with full force of their batons on the skulls of the women'. About twenty were knocked down and beaten where they lay: 'Such indeed was the scene of havoc made on these females on the banks of the Carron . . . that pools of blood were on the ground – that the grass and earth were dyed red with it – that the dogs of the district came and licked up the blood.' Four women were carted off to gaol at Tain, while the police returned to a tacksman's house to drink yet more whisky. A year later the estate had been cleared.[3]

The sepoys of the Secunderabagh and the Gaels of Greenyards shared fates in some measure; indeed, the incident in Sutherland became known, luridly, as the Slaughter of Greenyards. The analogy might be extended. Many Scots, thirty years earlier, had still wanted to preserve the old Scotland but been swept aside in the national quest for progress. In India, equally, there had been Scots who fell in love with an ancient civilization, only to be overborne by others eager to apply their scientific knowledge and technical skills to drive the country – for its own good, of course – along the road their own compatriots had traversed. Then Indian culture could be rehabilitated, just as Highland culture could be, once cured of its backwardness.

A new age wrought havoc on both, but the destruction had a creative side. As Scotland industrialized early in Europe, so did India in Asia. Modern liberty exacted more than economic change of traditional society. In India one result, unexpected to the British, was the nationalist movement. Scotland went off at a different tangent. Symbols of Highland culture were adopted for the whole country by Sir Walter Scott or even more by Queen Victoria, once she chose Balmoral as her favourite retreat: 'We were always in the habit of conversing with the Highlanders – with whom one comes so much in contact in the Highlands. The Prince highly appreciated the good breeding, simplicity and intelligence which makes it so pleasant, and even instructive, to talk to them.'[4] After Albert's death she sought companionship from her gillie, John Brown (and from her munshi or Indian secretary, Abdel Kader). If Lowland Scots remained sceptical of Highland sentiment, a counter came in the awakening interest of the English, who might still find Edinburgh, or rather Glasgow, a bit alarming but would pass on gratefully to the north. Such was William Wordsworth, writing of a Highland lass in his 'The Solitary Reaper':

> A voice so thrilling ne'er was heard
> In springtime from the cuckoo-bird,
> Breaking the silence of the seas
> Among the farthest Hebrides.
>
> Will no-one tells me what she sings?
> Perhaps the plaintive numbers flow
> For old, unhappy, far-off things,
> And battles long ago.[5]

Sometimes tourism might bring the visitor face to face with sights never suggested by the vaunted Highland romance and mystique. If ever he contrived to pass from castle to clachan, he would have found an outlook different from that suggested by winsome tales of rustic life. The Gaels had suffered collective blows that left them rootless and leaderless, and marked their mentality with guilt and foreboding. Yet they, like the Indians, managed to salvage something from the wreckage of their culture.

This state of the Highland mind is obscure to recent writers, who would prefer Gaels to have resisted their fate more fiercely than they did. Some chiefs had to the end of their era found themselves accommodating ever more people on their land, with a tolerance not lacking in sympathy, until the crisis of subsistence after the potato blight put a stop to it. For their part, the people felt reluctant to blame the chiefs: if these could enjoy their own again, the refrain ran, modernity might be held back. As community of interest crumbled away, no need remained for nicety between the remainder of the people and the new, hard-faced proprietors buying out the old, soft-hearted ones. The aliens were interested in efficiency, in creating sheep farms and sporting estates void of human habitation. This often negated a healthier demographic balance. With less land even for the stabilized population, crofters continued to squeeze on to it by subdividing holdings, already small enough, into fragments smaller still.

Yet, after the crux in the late 1840s, peace settled on the region again.

All reputable writers agree here. John Prebble ends his story with the painful episodes at Greenyards, Knoydart and Sollas, finding no more grist to his mill. The level-headed Professor Eric Richards of Adelaide analyses the 'decline of clearance'. He says the rancour at that same climax showed landlords the unwisdom of wholesale eviction. The Victorian conscience was potent, and expulsions by the strong arm of the law came to seem too crass. They also grew less necessary with better economic conditions and organized emigration. Now at any given time or place a few families departed, rather than whole communities.[6]

The behaviour of these Gaels, after generations under siege, might be read as an abandonment of peasant mentality, a retreat from peasant solidarity. They could take their fate in their own hands by new means for doing so. Just as Highland communities no longer had to be so self-sufficient, individual Highlanders might choose to be more self-sufficient. And just as strangers could get into the region for scenery and sport, Gaels could get out more easily than before. Railways now reached the north. By 1861 two lines ran to Inverness, with extensions to Wick and Thurso in 1870–4 and to Kyle of Lochalsh in 1897. Men might readily go to work for a season on Clydeside. From there shipping lines developed regular runs by steam across the oceans, with a vast improvement in speed and comfort from the horrors of the holds under sail. Men might readily go to work for a season in Montreal or New York too. If they prospered, they could send for their families. If not, they could come home. The net result was depopulation. The Highlands differed in this not a whit from similar regions of Europe, and Highlanders not a whit from similar peasantries of Europe, whether in Wales or Wallachia, in the Spanish or the Polish Galicia. Within the Highlands the towns grew as well, on the drift out of the glens: the population in settlements of over 5000 people more than doubled between 1851 and 1881.[7]

If some Gaels were still squeezed out, more and more made movement a matter of choice, a change of popular mentality not always welcome to those who witnessed it. A crofters' spokesman on Skye, Alexander Mackenzie, spoke in 1883 of earlier emigrants' experience: 'At that time a great many of them went away in communities, and they felt, when they were all going away together, that they would at least have some of the associations of their own country and see some of their friends, but according to the present system there is no chance of doing that.'[8] In a new age of global communications contact with family and friends need not be lost, though, and might indeed quicken the movement. George Patterson of Montreal wrote in 1877 how a general emigration had started with the original Highland settlers sailing on the *Hector* to Nova Scotia: 'It was by the representations of those on board to their friends, that others followed, and to the stream deepened and widened in succeeding years.'[9] The personal motives of these anonymous masses usually remain hidden to history, but a few letters have sometimes been preserved. Donald Campbell wrote to his family on Lewis in September 1851: 'Oh! young men of Ness, I want you to come here, and be not afraid. Leave the poor fishing at Ness . . . Oh! my brothers and sisters, and all of you, be sure and come here, and don't live starving where you are.' William Macpherson sent to his brother in June 1883 saying how sorry he felt that others had not gone with him to the Canadian West: 'If you, and Donald and Morag had come, we would have got three homesteads . . . It makes my heart sore to think the way you two are working at home, and having so little thanks and comfort for it, when we might have been here well and happy if you had come.'[10]

John Ramsay of Kildalton on Islay figured among the landlords who forbade subdivision of holdings and financed emigration for those who feared their families might then have to break up. He was unusual in taking a trip a few years later to see how they had got on in Canada. One of his old tenants, James McMillan, 'expressed himself as being highly pleased with Canada, and thinks he could never have attained the same independent position if he had remained at home'. Another, James Jamieson, 'spoke in very strong terms of the advantages which working men have in Canada, as compared with Islay, in bettering their position and acquiring independence, and especially of those who have a family being able to get the whole employed at good wages or settled on the land in their own neighbourhood'. Two more, Neil Gilchrist and William Black, 'felt that, if the welfare of their family was to be considered, there were many advantages in having come to Canada, especially in the fact that they were able to settle within reach, and that thus the parents have the pleasure of having them all around them, which they believed they could not have had at home'. Some still murmured against landlords, but Ramsay consoled himself with a thought that 'we so readily ignore the sufferings and hardships of days that are gone, and dwell only on the difficulties and annoyances of the present hour'.[11]

A paradox of modern mourning about clearance is that it all comes from descendants of those who stayed behind. Descendants of those who left see things differently. To Canada the Scottish critic David Craig set off, as he relates in *On the Crofters' Trail* (1990), with the hoary myths in his baggage. He felt puzzled when the emigrants' posterity would not confirm them: 'The people we met were proud to have been part of the migration rather than troubled that it had ever been necessary.' It was odd of them to insist their forefathers had not been cleared, but come of their own free will and made the most of things: 'I now began to work out a theory of why clearance material was more elusive than that of more voluntary emigration . . . From that point on we suspected that the hardest thing to find in Canada would be memoirs of veritable eviction.' Indeed: likening Highlanders to Jews in the Holocaust, Craig was reduced to fulmination to support his thesis that willing migrants had been cleared. 'Apologists for clearance sometimes emphasize that hundreds on Barra and South Uist "petitioned" to leave. So why the brutal compulsions at the last minute? Conditions as well as estate heavies (and the occasional minister) were *driving* them out.' No wonder their ambition and mobility escaped him: 'I had not expected that the Scottish settlers would move on, most of them, so soon, having used Cape Breton as a stepping stone to the American Middle West, the Canadian prairies, British Columbia.'[12]

During the later nineteenth century the net effect of emigration from the Highlands was a fall in the region's population no greater than in comparable areas of the Lowlands, and certainly not huge. The decline of 9 per cent contrasts with one of 28 per cent in Ireland over the same period (this without including the deaths of a million people in the Irish famine before the census of 1851, compared with few or none from the failure of the potato in the Highlands). Such facts bring into question the lazy usage of the term 'clearance' as a general determinant of the level of Highland population in the late Victorian era. Up to the crisis of mid-century the population was rising steeply. Then it levelled off. Clearance, such as it was, followed the same trajectory: it stopped just as the heaviest depopulation began. Historians have passed over an obvious inference that some new constellation of forces, different from those before 1850, might have come into play here. It was not an increase in clearance. What changed, surely, was that the Highlanders had learned for themselves, the hard way, how their mode of life could not support the existing, let alone an increasing, population. Better opportunities for voluntary migration, into the booming Lowlands or into the expanding Empire (there with some assisted passages), offered an obvious answer.

The trend was not uniform, however. Improvers' hopes had been to some extent fulfilled to the east and south of the Great Glen, in the Grampian Mountains, in eastern Inverness-shire, in Perthshire and in Argyll. Here Highlanders reacted to changes in life on the land after a fashion not markedly different from Lowlanders. The area had started on an evolution towards what it is today, one of big stock-rearing farms, of ranches almost. It was an evolution seen, on a far greater scale, in other parts of the world similarly endowed, not infertile yet unsuitable for crops, such as the American West and the Australian outback, regions that emigrant Gaels helped to develop. But the other half of the Highlands, with its inverted Gaelic culture, was not so open to or interested in the outside world. In the Hebrides and along the north-western coast of the mainland the people still saw their main chance in life as lying in a familiar plot of ground, even if of ever smaller extent. They remained alien to the hard-headed, go-getting ethos of Lowland Scotland. After the crunch came in the 1840s, they were clearly just not going to join in the headlong progress of the rest of the nation.

Scotland has always been a union of opposites, but the institutions preserved after 1707 to hold her together found their grip on the Highlands loosed too. Scots law enforced principles of private property that Gaels could not see as just. The Kirk sundered at the Disruption, and lost most of what loyalty it had ever won from them. Crisis arose for the national system of education, weak and patchy as it was in the north. Conflict at the foundations of Scottish society, with the Gaels everywhere on the defensive, might have resulted in destruction of their culture. Yet this was not so in every respect.

One reaction to modernity right across Scotland was the rise of Evangelicalism, of Christian fundamentalism, often issuing in denominational dissent and religious revival. In the Highlands it could take extravagant forms. On Lewis, 1822 was long remembered as *Bliadhna an Aomaidh* ('the year of the swooning'), because so much of that went on at meetings organized by a Gaelic teacher, John Macleod, who brought revival from Skye. There in 1843, the year of the Disruption, a minister found 'the cries of the people were such that his voice was drowned and he had to stop speaking . . . Hundreds fell down as if they were dead. This usually commences with violent shaking and crying out, with clapping of hands.'[13] Yet no revival arose from the surely more harrowing experience of dearth soon afterwards. James Hunter interprets this resignation to a divine decree as the 'chiliasm of despair'.[14] According to his materialist interpretation, fundamentalism is a reactionary force, sapping the spirit of the poor by blasting any seeds of political action in them. Disputes of Moderates and Evangelicals become class conflict, and the Disruption a revolt against landlords. Yet a link between privation and revival is hard to sustain. Revival often burst out from no obvious economic impulse. Besides, over time it did restore some self-confidence to the demoralized poor and teach them organizing skills that stood them in good stead later.

Gaels were caught up in this religious intensity once they had the Gospel in their own tongue. Worldly tribulation made prophecies of apocalypse and redemption work with power on the minds of such a passionate and visionary people. Knowledge of the Bible enriched their oral tradition in the spiritual poetry of Dugald Buchanan and his successors. But on the social crisis the Gaelic muse did not sing out loud; rather, she grew cautious and muted, hidebound by social and literary convention. Yet if Gaelic literature faltered, at least a literature of the Highlands written in English made its presence felt. It was a literature of lament. Donald Macleod had brought out his *Gloomy Memories of the Highlands of Scotland* in 1841, after being evicted from Strathnaver; he left for Canada, but saw the book republished in Greenock and Toronto in 1856–7. Donald Ross's *Glengarry Evictions, or Scenes at Knoydart* (1853) cast the distracted Mrs Josephine MacDonell as a she-devil. Alexander Mackenzie wrote histories of clans which, for a limited genre, are not without scholarly value, and preserved in print a record of Patrick Sellar's conduct in Sutherland.[15]

To landlords these must have seemed mere tokens of resistance. But they did worry about the effect on their reputation. In any straight contest with the people they would always win, of course, being ultimately able to call on the forces of order in Victorian Scotland. Yet this was not quite a straight contest, for other formations than the police, or indeed the army and navy, would enlist on the crofters' side. Landlords' bluster about rights of property cut no ice with radical and romantic champions of the Gaels such as John Murdoch, editor of a newspaper called *The Highlander*, or John Stuart Blackie, professor of classics at the universities of Aberdeen and Edinburgh. Both chose to mark themselves out from sober Lowland reality by going around in kilts. If ribaldry greeted them, they sensed they were countering the forces of the market with the call of a culture. They identified the fortunes of the crofters with a view of civilization different from that of hard-hearted Lowlanders, and in time they won a response from soft-hearted Lowlanders too. When at last crofters started reclaiming lost lands ('raiding', in the term of the time), they found outside support on a scale never to be looked for until then.

Murdoch, born in Nairnshire and bred on Islay, was long employed as an exciseman in Dublin, where he got to know the Irish nationalists Charles Parnell and Michael Davitt. In 1873 he returned to set up his newspaper in Inverness. Its main purpose was to vilify landlords. Murdoch said the condition of the Highlands would be but a 'gross question' should it become confined to economics: 'If our people had been educated in the spirit of the race instead of being made to drink at school into an alien spirit, they would not have been so slack in allowing one hold of their soil after another to slip out of their fingers.' He sought to connect the cultural problem with the economic: 'It is in the Gaelic language that we have, as in some of the songs of Iain Lom . . . in traditions, and in proverbs – a distinct recognition of the fact that the lands in the Highlands belonged to the clans as such, and not to the chiefs.' He took up the cry of *tir is teanga* ('land and language'). He wanted Highlanders to be taught to love family, home, literature and country. Then they would wish to stay in their mountains and cultivate their glens.[16]

Blackie was an Aberdonian, moved by devotion to the Highlands and pity for Highlanders as he pondered the solitude around Braemar, where he spent holidays. Later he ranged about the north to meet the natural gentlemen of the clachans. He decided 'ownership in land exists for the people; not the people for the sake of ownership': a tenet of the Scottish left ever since. He rejected Scots Liberals' facile faith in Britishness as a vehicle of progress. He hated imperialism, at home and abroad, for 'obliterating local types and establishing a uniform monotony of superficial polish'. He got close to denouncing the very Union, something almost unheard of, for 'superficiality, mechanism and monotony', compared to the Scots' 'heritage of a distinct nationality, nobly and manfully acquired'. He lived long enough to be inaugural chairman in 1886 of the Scottish Home Rule Association, the ancestor of the Scottish National Party.[17]

It was easy to dismiss Blackie and Murdoch as eccentrics. Distinguished scholarship on Celtic civilization could not be so easily pooh-poohed. The best came from William Forbes Skene, native of what had once been a Jacobite hotbed, not yet quite lost to the Gàidhealtachd: landward Aberdeenshire. As a youth, Skene was a protégé of Sir Walter Scott; as an adult he was an advocate in Edinburgh at a time when advocates still often counted as intellectuals too. In 1876–80 he published the three volumes of his *Celtic Scotland*, which made him the greatest Scottish historian of the century. They reconstructed the Dark Ages with such erudition and insight that much of their account still stands today. One argument that has not worn so well is that Scots Gaels and Irish Gaels were different peoples: the opposite is accepted now. A masked motive for Skene's insistence on this may have been that in his own day the Irish looked more anarchic than the Scots, the former being the bad boys and the latter the good boys of Empire. Modern Highlanders were unsavoury enough, lazing in the bosom of 'two graceless sisters, sluggishness and ignorance', but at least they had Lowlanders to put them right. And Scots at large felt uncomfortable about being lumped together with the Irish under the label of

Celts. This had not been much on their minds since 1707 – not after the Jacobite risings anyway. But Victorian antiquarianism dug it up from the collective memory, and then a streak of misrule in the Scots appeared all too easy to detect.[18]

So wild Highlanders had to find, or be found, a place on the side of the angels, if one different from that of even-tempered Lowlanders. Skene's picture of archaic society stressed its communal aspects, alien to modern individualism. He believed the Celtic peoples had formed for themselves a special conception of the land, or an organic identification with it. This could be detected yet, remained as valid as any current conception and ought not to be scorned just because it was ancient: thus did a Tory retort to the Whig view of history, that the past is only of interest in so far as it led to the present. Skene's interpretation implied that a breach in the iron laws of political economy might be justified on historical grounds in places preserving such survivals, to which peasants clung in defiance of those judging them backward, if not barbarous. The Scottish Enlightenment had laid all societies on the rack of a common analytical framework. In the real world, Skene suggested, different origins allowed different outcomes. Now, where things were going wrong, they might point to different remedies.

Scotland was gradually growing into a more pluralist nation; a lifting of prejudice against Gaelic gave one sign of it. This did not necessarily help Skene's argument for, whatever he might think, there was an audible linguistic continuum on either side of the North Channel. Gaels of Islay and of Donegal could understand one another. Anyway, Scotland and Ireland shared the literary language of Common Classical Gaelic, with its corpus of poetry stretching back into the distant past. The Church of Scotland, or voluntary agencies under its wing, had ceased to regard this treasury of the language as a war chest of popery and sedition. Now it was fine for young Gaels to be schooled in their mother tongue, at least until they mastered English. Many Highland schools used Gaelic as a language of instruction, and primers were printed in it. When the children grew up, they could buy books and newspapers in the language of Eden.

The situation was fast changing, however, under the impact of fresh and potent forces from beyond the Gàidhealtachd, the political reform and religious schism which had swept away the old Scotland between 1832 and 1843. The Free Church, carrying a majority of Highlanders into the Disruption, started by promoting Gaelic on evangelical grounds: so long as it was preached from the pulpit, schools ought to instil literacy in it. The Free Church did this in its own schools and taught the language to candidates for the ministry at its theological colleges in Edinburgh, Glasgow and Aberdeen. Yet its bitter rivalry with the Auld Kirk in every possible sphere also imposed a contrary policy. It mounted one challenge to the Church of Scotland in offering children an English education like that available in parochial schools. It mounted another in competing for support from a British state that found the sectarianism of the Scots baffling at best, and regarded claims on behalf of the Gaels as an irritating diversion from bigger business. All this worked its effect as schools and universities passed in a devious, painful process from control by the Kirk to control by the state.[19]

Light on this linguistic situation is cast by the report, published in 1867, of the royal commission on Scottish education under the eighth duke of Argyll. It sought answers to the range of problems besetting a system once national but now being fragmented. The commission paid special heed to Gaelic, delegating this part of its work to Sheriff Alexander Nicolson, a Skyeman who had exchanged a humdrum career at the Bar in Edinburgh for the mountains and poetry of the Gàidhealtachd; the highest peak of the Cuillins, Sgurr Alasdair, is named after him, and he published a huge collection of Gaelic proverbs.

Nicolson found only two out of ten Highlanders could easily read an English newspaper, while five could read a Gaelic one. The rate of illiteracy had halved over the previous thirty years, but this produced more readers literate in Gaelic alone than readers literate in both languages. Nicolson covered 1980 people who read either English alone or Gaelic and English, but 4464 who read Gaelic alone. The position had reversed from an earlier period, especially among women. Not all was well, however. Nicolson judged that if Gaelic education had reached a peak of utility, it was also passing that peak. In 1838, of schools run by the Society in Scotland for Propagating Christian Knowledge, 82 per cent had taught Gaelic. Now the figure was down to 50 per cent. True, the number of Gaelic speakers had meanwhile declined, although not so fast as to explain such a dramatic drop. The problem seemed to be that neither parents nor teachers valued Gaelic education except as a preparation for English education. For himself, Nicolson thought the system might turn bilingual; then Gaelic and English would no longer be so identified respectively with backwardness and progress. The commission concluded, more pallidly, that while it was useful for children to learn Gaelic reading, it would be a burden to the poor if their schooling did not acquaint them with English.[20]

Yet the Education Act of 1872, which followed Argyll's report and set up Scotland's modern system of schools, made no provision for Gaelic in the classroom. This was ever after held up by Gaels as proof positive –

beyond all tartan flummery – of the indifference, if not hostility, to them in the rest of Scotland that had been manifest ever since the Statutes of Iona in 1609. The argument is not without force, although a kinder explanation can be conceived. In 1871 the Gaelic Society of London asked the Liberal Lord Advocate, George Young, for the forthcoming act to give the language a statutory place in Highland education. He did not refuse, but replied that this might be better done by administrative than by legislative means. In other words, the linguistic question ought to be left to the future Scotch Education Department, rather than to a Parliament at Westminster, which might not prove so sympathetic – a fair point. Whether Young was being disingenuous is less clear. He figured among the most extreme of Liberal anglicizers in Scotland: he wanted rid of Scots law, so he could hardly have been expected to support Scottish education, least of all in Gaelic guise.[21]

In lurid terms the act banned the language of the people from Highland classrooms. Or rather, it handed everyday control of education to school boards filled with respectable citizens looking down their noses at a dialect of peasants and servants. So the new system of public instruction did not build on the foundations of Gaelic literacy laid earlier. As the Gaelic Society of Inverness protested: 'Children who knew no word of English were to be put through an educational drill for children who knew no word of Gaelic.' A system that might have won for Highland culture a due place in Scottish society turned out to be a catastrophe for it. Only with much time and effort could a few contrary concessions be wrung from the Liberal politicians running Victorian Scotland. Not until the Education Act of 1918, the enlightened measure of a Unionist Scottish Secretary, was generally permissive provision made to teach Gaelic in schools. But it is hard to imagine how the reactionary law of 1872, which made a mockery of the word 'liberal', could have been possible just a decade later. By then Nationalism was stirring right round the Celtic fringe. In Ireland and Wales, Celtic politics linked up with Celtic culture, but not in Scotland. Unlike Irish and Welsh, the Gaelic language, confined to a backward region, never became fused with nationalism. Because most Scots were Lowlanders in language and culture, Gaelic could not be raised as a banner of ethnic defiance or a bar to the surge of anglicizing uniformity.

At least Blackie strove to link the language with wider concerns: 'The moment the Gaelic language dies, the Highland people die with it and with the Highland people dies all the glory of Celtic chivalry and all the wealth of Celtic story.' He aimed to put Gaelic on the linguistic map so as to redefine Scotland's place in the world. In a grand philological sweep he bridged the gaps among turbulent Celts, noble Teutons and civilized Greeks or Romans: they were not separate races but one race, at different stages or in different environments. He had been a student in the Germany of the 1830s, an intellectual powerhouse despite political backwardness, envied by Scots conscious that the great days of their Enlightenment were over. He could harden up vague Scottish hankering after German achievement into firmer ideas for emulation, starting from philology and humanism at the roots of culture, passing up to romantic philosophy in its many branches, before blossoming in an idealistic nationalism. The average Scotsman cared not a hoot, but Blackie set off to revive Scotland's 'living connexion with the pulse of Celtic life, which still beats strongly in Wales, in Ireland and even in America'.[22]

Blackie did resort to racial or national stereotypes beloved of Victorians but hardly taken seriously today, if not damned as politically incorrect. During his time scientific racism gained currency as a legitimate field of study. Before the crimes of the twentieth century could so much as be conceived of, nothing yet arose to discredit it. Scots might even claim this new science as another of their gifts to the world, on the strength of speculation about human difference by the philosopher David Hume and the phrenologist George Combe. Early on, it had started for some reason to elevate the Germans, or Teutons, as a racial ideal. It took by contrast a dim view of the Celts for anarchic traits in their character. Yet the disparagement had a more positive side, in leading to a surmise that among far-flung Celtic cultures, the last in Europe to be touched by modernity, founts of culture still flowed pure and undefiled.

Historical linguistics was a related science to which Scots also made a great contribution: Kuno Meyer, the German Celticist who became a professor at the University of Liverpool, said that in Scotland philology vied in popularity with golf.[23] A huge advance in knowledge came about with definition of the extent of the Indo-European family of languages, from Ceylon to the Outer Hebrides. It was an exciting discovery which led to further speculations, not all of them sound. Investigators of folk-tales and folk-songs over that vast terrain discerned in them many similar themes. This seemed significant, for at the deep levels of European heritage might also be glimpsed the beginnings of religion and philosophy.

Here was a third new science, anthropology, also pioneered by Victorian Scots, by Andrew Lang in particular. From the Gàidhealtachd aspects of his work had been anticipated by John Frederick Campbell of Islay. In his *Popular Tales of the West Highlands* (1860–2) Campbell noted how stories in different regions of the world exhibited the same motifs, 'and they are used in striving to trace out the origins of races, as philologists use words to trace language, as geologists class rocks by shells and bones which they contain, and as natural philosphers use fairy-eggs in tracing the Gulf Stream'.[24] The exertion to push back the frontiers of the study of man was international. Materials from Celtic anthropology proved to be of use also to the Breton writer Ernest Renan, professor of Hebrew at the Collège de France. Renan got to know Scotland when he visited in order to pursue his interest in her philosophers. He wrote in *L'Ame Bretonne* (1896): 'Jamais famille humaine n'a vécu plus isolée du monde et plus pure de tout mélange étranger . . . Ainsi la race celtique s'est usée à résister au temps et à défendre les causes désespérées' ('Never has a human family lived more cut off from the world and more pure of any foreign mixture . . . So the Celtic race wore itself out resisting time and defending lost causes').[25] Matthew Arnold, professor of poetry at the University of Oxford, filled out this broader background with a whimsical resort to the Celtic literary device of triads. He identified in Victorian Britain a Germanic genius (in the English people), with 'steadiness as its main basis, with commonness and humdrum for its defect, fidelity to nature for its excellence'; a Norman genius (in the ruling class), 'with talent for affairs as its main basis, with strenuousness and clear rapidity for its excellence, hardness and insolence for its defect'; and a Celtic genius, with 'sentiment as its main basis, with love of beauty, charm and spirituality for its excellence, ineffectualness and self-will for its defect'. Arnold was intent on holding back the tide of philistinism in Britain. He thought one barrier to it could come from erecting chairs of Celtic.[26]

This was Blackie's goal too. He knew a chair at Edinburgh had been talked of since the turn of the century. Once he took the matter in hand he proved to be, among his other virtues, a fantastic fund-raiser. His great coup was to get a subscription from Queen Victoria herself. By the time the campaign bore fruit in the foundation of the chair in 1882, it was the best-endowed in the university. The first professor, Donald Mackinnon, gave his inaugural address on the Gael 'as the child of music and song' who, for all his faults and handicaps, 'has attempted, not unsuccessfully, to live not the day and the hour alone, but, in a true sense, to live the life of the spirit!' The sympathy awakened by Mackinnon and others prompted a notable era of Gaelic scholarship, in works already mentioned and in others: Alexander Cameron's *Reliquiae Celticae* (1892–4), Alexander Carmichael's *Carmina Gadelica* (1900) and William Sharp's *Lyra Celtica* (1896). In his introduction Sharp insisted that:

the apparition of this passing race is no more than the fulfilment of a glorious resurrection before our very eyes. For the genius of the Celtic race stands
out now with averted torch, and the light of it is a glory before the eyes, and
the flame of it is blown into the hearts of the mightier conquering people.
The Celt falls, but his spirit rises in the heart and the brain of the Anglo-
Celtic peoples, with whom are the destinies of the generations to come.[27]

It was the best repentant Victorians could do.

16

The great grievance
The Crofters Act, 1886

ON 5 OCTOBER 1886 a gunboat of the royal navy, HMS *Humber*, with a berth of 1640 tons and a crew of 85, carrying a complement of 75 marines besides, nosed its way into a remote harbour nestling among stern mountains and looking out to a wild seascape of craggy islands and spindrift. The expedition met no resistance. Surly natives emerged from squalid hovels to stare as the Queen–Empress's sailors hopped ashore with hooks and hawsers, moored the ship and let land the officers and men, all bright as buttons. But from up-country came signs of trouble. Around hilltops sounded the eerie blair of horns blown to warn villages near by that a distant government in London had sent its armed might to enforce its authority.

The scene took place not in a remote corner of the Empire but at Portree on Skye. It was neither the first nor the last time the Empire intervened in the Highlands with a gunboat. The task on this occasion was not to hunt rebels, as in days of old, but to help police to serve summonses for arrears of rent and rates. Nowadays a force of marines would seem heavy-handed for such a job, and so it seemed then. Behind it lay politics.

This represented the first effort by a new department of state, the Scotch Office as it was named when established in 1885, to flex its muscles. It had got off to a shaky start. It remained after its inaugural year a half-baked outfit, in charge of quangos and public appointments but still lacking greater powers that would later be taken for granted, as over law and order. One problem lay in the lack of a guiding hand, for there were four Secretaries for Scotland during those early months, three of them nonentities. First came the duke of Richmond and Gordon, a Tory peer who quipped of being qualified by two peerages and the best salmon river in Scotland for a job he still found 'quite unnecessary'. In January 1886 followed Sir George Trevelyan, an Englishman but MP for the Border Burghs, who resigned after two months because he disagreed with William Gladstone's plans for home rule in Ireland. Then came the earl of Dalhousie, whose tenure was terminated that summer when the Irish

Home Rule Bill fell, forcing an early general election which brought the
Conservatives back again. Now at last the Scotch Office found a worthy
chief in Arthur James Balfour, a scion of the Lowland gentry who would
one day be Prime Minister. He also owned the estate of Strathconan in
Easter Ross.[1]

Strathconan had come into the family's hands in 1830, when James
Balfour, a younger son with a fortune from India, set out to make a mark
with it in Scotland. He bought back ancestral lands in Fife, then his own
main estate, Whittingehame in East Lothian, and finally a Highland retreat.
On his death in 1845 he left a fortune of £1 million to his son James, father
of the future Prime Minister. Strathconan, like most similar estates, sheltered many squatters beside its regular tenants. Balfour wanted to restore a
sensible balance between the land and the people, so that they could stay
there all year round instead of migrating southwards for seasonal jobs. The
way would then lie open to other help for them: to improved agriculture,
better housing and facilities such as a school, with a teacher nominated by
the Free Church, of course. 'In a few years, by temporarily forgoing rents,
by expenditure of money on improvements to benefit the remaining tenants, but above all by making arrangements for large-scale emigration the
situation of the people was transformed', writes the family's historian. The
Prime Minister would say of the Highlanders he had known since his
youth:

> I have lived among them, and I defy anyone to live among them and not
> love them. They have to contend with inclement skies, with stormy seas and
> with barren soil; and their worst enemies are those who would hinder their
> superfluous population from seeking in other climes a happier home.[2]

Apart from his Scottish credentials, A.J. Balfour was a nephew of Lord
Salisbury, who preceded him as Prime Minister. It was his uncle that gave
the young man his first chance in the Cabinet. Balfour used the spring-
board of Scotland well, if not much to the Gaels' good. Rather, he made
a mark by showing he must have better means of dealing with them.
Whitehall's mandarins had agreed with Gladstone in not wanting the
Scotch Office. One untidy result of their ill will was that the Home Office
kept control of law and order in Scotland, or thought it did. Balfour put it
right. He protested that, with trouble in the north, his hands were tied
behind his back. He got his uncle to transfer the powers to himself.[3]

In September 1886 Balfour received disturbing reports from Skye and
went up to Inverness in person to see the sheriff. He felt appalled at the
shambles he found there. Crofters were refusing to pay rents while

landlords were refusing to pay rates, on the excuse that they could not do so while getting no rents. Balfour wanted to know what a Crofters Act had just been passed for, if not to solve such problems. With support from all sides in Parliament, including five radical Crofter MPs just returned by Highland consituencies, the legislation had given their voters much of what they wanted: security of tenure, fair rents and compensation for improvements, the whole to be supervised by a Crofters Commission.[4]

Even so, the Scotch Office seemed to have messed things up. The crofters and their MPs soon realized that the breadth of support for them had come about because the act evaded one big issue. Although the growth in Highland population had long levelled off, the crofting counties remained congested. The result was civil disobedience, refusal to pay rents and resistance to police who came to enforce collection. If anything, the act made things worse. The Crofters Commission promised as its first job to investigate grievances, especially over arrears of rent, some of which stretched back years. Crofters believed the arrears would be cancelled. If they were going in the end to be let off their debts, why cough up meanwhile?

When police knocked at their doors, the crofters laughed at them for landlords' lackeys, who were not even going to get wages for their pains, because these must come out of the unpaid rates. Such impudence in the face of authority was what made Balfour lose his temper in Inverness. So he called out the marines. On 15 September 1886 the Secretary to the Admiralty had a letter from a man he might never have heard of, the permanent under-secretary at the Scotch Office, with an unexpected message: 'I am directed by the Secretary for Scotland to request that you will inform the Lords Commissioners of the Admiralty that it is proposed to send a military force to Skye, to support the civil authorities in the administration of law in the island.'[5]

Two days later HMS *Humber* began ferrying police and marines from Portree to trouble spots around the coast. Defiant tenants were served with summary warrants for arrears of rents. They had to pay or see their goods poinded. This all went off in peace.

The second phase of the operation took place a fortnight later, to arrest people who had not complied with the warrants. Trouble was expected this time, and it came. At Bornaskitaig, near the north-eastern tip of the island, horns again sounded in warning as two dozen police and marines approached. They headed for a particular house, around which women of the township locked arms in a cordon, their husbands and sons standing by. Under the circumstances the sheriff seemed to think the men the softer target. He ordered some of them to be seized, and fighting broke out. Women weighed in, chucking muck from the middens at the sheriff and injuring him. The civil power having failed, he sent the marines into action and they arrested six men. At nearby Herbusta another mob was waiting. A messenger-at-arms went forward from the platoon of police to reason with the crofters, but they tossed turds at him too. He retired out of range and awaited the arrival of the marines, who were sheltering from a squall at the kirk. Tardy concentration seemed to sap their morale, however, and they all left without further ado. The planned arrests at Herbusta were to take weeks, with police making raids on the crofts by night and day. After intervention from a local minister most offenders gave themselves up.

A third phase followed a fortnight later, to remove poinded stock and goods. No local man would help the sheriff, who had to send to Inverness for horses and carts. On 18 November occurred the poinding of Mrs MacRae's baby. The messenger-at-arms entered her house at Peiness and wrote up an inventory: 'Dresser and crockery 1/6; wooden seats 2/-; spinning wheel 1/-; 2 beds and blankets £1; chair 1/-; graip 2/-; churn and top 1/-; quantity of corn £1; puppy dog 1/-; cradle and child 6d.' The incident has gone down in song and story on Skye. A revival of the island's Gaelic poetry, after a long descent into mediocrity, was one result of this crisis. It gave inspiration to Mary Macpherson, Màiri Mhòr nan Oran, ('Big Mary of the Songs': she weighed 17 stone). Her colourful, strident verses so stirred the people that they are still sung today. She was a lovably illogical lady, however. Some of her pieces, *Brosnachadh nan Gàidheal* ('The Rousing of the Gaels') or *Oran Beinn-Lì* ('The Song of Ben Lee'), praise Skyemen for their defiance and incite them to more of it. In *Clò na Cùbaid* ('The Cloth of the Pulpit') she even denounces clergymen, and of the Free Church too:

> *Tha luchd teasgaisg cho beag cùraim,*
> *Faicinn càradh mo luchd dùthcha.*

> Preachers care so little
> Seeing the condition of my countrymen.

Yet Màiri Mhòr found it hard to attack the old élites on Skye, or indeed elsewhere; her *Oran an Diùc Chataich* ('Song for the Duke of Sutherland') is a string of compliments to him, rejoicing

> *. . . gu bheil Cataibh air a riaghladh*
> *Le uachdaran ciallach, càirdeil,*
> *Aig a bheil suim da chuid daoine,*
> *'S chan ida caoraich mhaola bhàna.*

> . . . that Sutherland is now ruled
> By a sensible and friendly proprietor,
> Who cares for his people
> And not hornless white sheep.[6]

Here, as in other times and places, Scottish defiance left songs behind, but the question was again whether anything more useful would result. The might of the Empire could not be withstood for ever, even by Skyemen. Order was restored and several crofters went to prison, while Balfour left to hone his skills amid greater turbulence as Chief Secretary for Ireland.

Yet the episode on Skye does present a new pattern of power in the Highlands after a transition so fast that a decade earlier it could hardly have been imagined. The axis of landowners and peasants gave way to one of government and people. It was not, in essence, different from that in any other modern Western democracy, though here as everywhere modified by local factors. Whether the British government would forge a relationship with the Highlanders better than the chiefs had of old enjoyed with the clansmen was a different matter. At any rate, from now on the state would define the social dispensation in the region, first to maintain law and order, then to regulate relationships of tenant and landlord, with the landlord being ever more marginalized. Laws enacted from the 1880s onwards bound his hands to an extent unthinkable not long before. Control was just taken away from him by a state that, in any case, had learned it had little to gain from supporting him. This first wholesale retreat from the prevailing Victorian philosophy of individualism would make the state the main force in Highland history.

This was what emerged out of the fresh wave of unrest, even open lawlessness, which overtook the Highlands after a quarter-century of calm and relative prosperity since the crisis around 1850. Sheep farmers had meanwhile fared well, crofters perhaps better. The harvests, with a few local exceptions, turned out generous. The price of cattle remained buoyant. Rents rose little, at least for smallholdings, and they lagged behind the growth in incomes, which were boosted besides by seasonal migration to the booming Lowlands. Anyone still dissatisfied could emigrate, sometimes with a subsidy, always to a warm welcome overseas. So the pressure of population eased.

It came as all the more of a shock when the early 1880s brought back dearth, a succession of poor harvests and a general depression in agriculture. The winter of 1882–3 was the bleakest for thirty years. The potatoes failed, and other crops were lost in autumnal storms, which also sank or smashed fishing boats. Again crofters were in crisis. Meanwhile the Lowland economy went into recession as well, and so offered migrants no more jobs. Landowners, however, continued to collect rent as before. If there was default, they ordered eviction. This met with resistance, for local agents of the law proved far too weak to enforce it.

A change in Highland mentality may be marked by the fact that now crofters made, as it were, a positive refusal to pay rents, rather than simply being unable to afford them. They turned poverty to a purpose, to claim restoration of old rights. Among those on Skye, which the people said they had lost only seventeen years earlier, was a right to graze stock on land held by sheep farmers of Lord Macdonald. He answered refusals of rent with summonses of eviction. They were met in customary fashion. On 7 April 1882 crofters intercepted the sheriff officer on a track running down the eastern coast of the island and burned his papers before his eyes. The next stage of the rituals proceeded. Ten days later the law returned with sixty police from Glasgow. They faced a mob: 'men, women and children rushed forward in all stages of attire, most of the females with their hair streaming lovely in the breeze'. In this Battle of the Braes the police did succeed, before they beat a retreat, in subduing the mob and taking some prisoners. These were tried at Inverness and convicted, but sympathizers paid their fines. It could be reckoned a moral victory for the people. Trouble spread around Skye, then to other islands. In 1883 a gunboat and marines were sent to the Minches. The agitation worsened in 1884 and 1885. Thousands refused to pay rents and occupied sheep farms. On Skye order could only be restored by stationing there a garrison of 300.[7]

A climax came on Lewis in the winter of 1887–8. Crofters again refused rents and seized land: 'a reign of terror prevailed.' The number of police had to be doubled, and the navy landed 500 marines to guard the property of the Mathesons. These had in a sense created a crisis by their very success in managing the local economy so as to support greater numbers than ever before. People again squeezed into the available area of cultivation by subdividing crofts. Trouble really started after the Mathesons refused to hand back land that had been put under sheep and deer by the earls of Seaforth back in 1844. When crofters petitioned for access to it, the idea seemed grotesque to the factors, coming from people who had never been cleared. Yet to these that reaction seemed appalling: they were poor, they paid their rents and they obeyed orders, but land was a communal resource in shortage. Its possession gave meaning to life and the owner had no right, faced by manifest need, to refuse them what their forefathers had enjoyed.[8]

The people's moral outrage provoked them to a novel tactic: a raid or unauthorized occupation. Park, a cleared district south of Stornoway just turned by Lady Matheson from a sheep farm into a sporting estate, was invaded by a hundred armed men. They shot deer and had a picnic of venison. Yet they did not otherwise behave like revolutionaries: 'When supper was ready, an old patriarch from Marvig rose to say Grace in which he beseeched Almighty God for a blessing on the food which He had so graciously provided, and also on those gathered round him. He hoped the day would come when a church would stand on the spot where they now stood.' Some were arrested and sent for trial to Edinburgh, but the jury would not convict them. Heartened, a thousand people mounted the next raid with pipes playing and flags flying. They headed for the sheep farm of Aiginish and killed some stock, only to be beaten back by soldiers and marines. The ringleaders spent fifteen months in gaol. Lady Matheson fled the island after threats to her life.[9]

The crofters' new spirit of defiance also took a more conventional form, in pamphlets, protests, political campaigns and so on. The fruit of such activities could not have been so abundant without the direct action at the grassroots. But the advantage of more sophisticated methods lay in their capacity to win friends beyond the Highland line. While the Liberal establishment, a coterie of landowners, had man for man cleared more people from their estates than any other group, a radical fringe of the party deplored this. The region found spokesmen among them and among its many exiles. They had formed societies, even in London, for the revival of Gaelic culture and other good causes. Through them links were forged to Irish Nationalists. The Reform Act of 1884 opened up more piquant prospects. Crofters now had the vote and with it the ability to end the landlords' monopoly of Highland representation in Parliament. At the general election of 1885 candidates with local links, if Lowland intellectuals really, presented themselves as tribunes of the people. Five were elected: in Argyll, Caithness, Inverness-shire, Ross and Cromarty and the Wick Burghs. They became known as the Crofters' party.[10]

In parallel a Highland Land Law Reform Association had been set up in London in 1883. The next year saw the formation of the radical Scottish Land Restoration League, whose inaugural meeting in Glasgow was chaired by John Murdoch. 'Restoration' meant taking land away from the rich and giving it to the poor, an idea first inspired by Irish Nationalists and within a few years to be absorbed into the founding principles of the Scottish Labour Party. But it had greater appeal in the Gorbals than in the glens. There the more moderate association was the one that succeeded in forming local branches and recruiting crofter members. A group on Skye, 'hearing of the good news from Ireland, said they had a mind to turn rebels themselves'.[11] Yet to respectable tenants such as James Urquhart of Conan and Alexander MacLeod of Scuddaburgh this prospect seemed alarming, as far as they could express themselves in uncertain English:

> So much has been done for the Irish in consequence of the agitation there, that on its being pointed out by the agitators to people in Skye that they had only to agitate and make disaffected statements to get what they might want, that surely . . . it is no wonder if a certain number of the disaffected jump at the bait.[12]

The Scottish and Irish agitations were not in fact identical, although both grew out of rural conditions that had actually been improving for a couple of decades. For some time neither nation had seen evictions of defenceless tenants by alien, absentee, rack-renting landlords. Distant Whitehall made a facile association of ideas: that the aim of policy should be to stop the Highlands turning into another Ireland. A deeper motive was no doubt wariness of nationalism, already the main political force in Ireland and just starting to stir in Scotland. Yet Scottish nationalism, such as it was at this stage, had little to do with the Highlands. It was either a movement of antiquarian patriotism, so of high Tories even, or of abstract idealism, so more often of wild Radicals. Gladstone disliked both and felt wary of 'exceptional expedients', or random interventions by the state in answer to special pleading. Yet he did think something had to be done for the crofters, although he was vague on what. He supposed them to be exceptional on account not of their hardship but of their history.[13]

In his Cabinet, Gladstone had originally had the eighth duke of Argyll, chief of Clan Campbell and, unusually for a nobleman, an intellectual. MacChailein Mòr argued in his own writings that there had never been communal ownership in the Highlands: 'The idea is wholly unfounded. It is the reverse of the truth.' Any such development had been impossible in the old days because the clans were forever at war, and 'intertribal wars are the worst of all kinds of war – the most chronic, the most devastating, the most savage'. Members of a clan had owed what little security they enjoyed to their chiefs. So Highland laws of property were not in principle different from those elsewhere in Britain or Europe. In his own charters at Inveraray he found 'all the well known powers and obligations of ownership in land'. This meant crofters had not owned land in any sense, and their claims to the contrary were a fiction. Now the duke warned of 'a Land League on the model of the Irish, the leaders of which are working with Parnellites more or less' and 'have got hold of all the Hebridean islands'.[14]

But Gladstone would not listen to Argyll, either over Ireland (which had caused the duke to resign from the Cabinet in 1881) or over Scotland. On the contrary, the Prime Minister decided that landlords had in the last two centuries stolen crofters' rights, leaving them with a genuine grievance which it was the duty of Parliament to redress. He wrote to his Home Secretary, Sir William Harcourt: 'The crofters' title to demand legislation rested on the "historical fact" that they had enjoyed rights of which they had been surreptitiously deprived to the injury of the community.' Gladstone believed they had suffered a terrible wrong by 'the withdrawal of the common grazings to convert them into sheep farms', and felt moved to right 'the great grievance'. He at length set up the royal commission on the Highlands of Lord Napier and Ettrick in 1883–4. Gladstone had not, as a matter of fact, been keen to take this way forward. If observers expected the commission to be his poodle, it turned out to have a mind of its own, just as he feared.[15]

Napier, a laird from the Borders, was 'a benevolent looking old gentle-man with a dreamy pair of eyes and a slight burr in his speech', a good chairman who took pains to win the crofters' confidence. He was not long retired from an imperial career that culminated in the governorship of Madras. In that office he took his place among a sequence of Scots striv-ing to reform indigenous land law (the *ryotwari* system), which ideally made the peasant a proprietor with fixed and secure tenure. Also on the com-mission was Sir Kenneth Mackenzie of Gairloch, 'a half-sailor looking man of dark complexion speaking with the slightest possible suspicion of an aristocratic lisp', but also holder of a German doctorate in agricultural chemistry from the University of Giessen, where he had imbibed progres-sive ideas during the revolutionary year of 1848. At the general election of 1880 he stood as the Liberal in Inverness-shire but lost to a man now his fellow commissioner, Donald Cameron of Lochiel; he, as mediator at the Braes, had shown a Tory sympathy for sturdy peasants and wrung a com-promise from the stony Lord Macdonald. A second MP on the commis-sion, Charles Fraser Mackintosh, sat for the Inverness Burghs and was a champion of Gaelic education who helped to form the Federation of Celtic Societies in 1878. Sheriff Alexander Nicolson was now working on a new edition of the Gaelic Bible with the sixth member, Donald Mackinnon, just appointed professor of Celtic at the University of Edinburgh, 'a stout, good-humoured, smiling gentleman with a strong Highland accent, suggesting the keeper of a mountain hotel'.[16]

Napier wrote how the kind of witness they wished to call would find himself 'in the presence of six gentlemen, all but one of his own race, some speaking his own language, some bearing names known to every Highlander, all earnestly desirous to place themselves in contact with his inner thoughts and actual condition'.[17] The commission began its tour at the Braes in May 1883 and concluded at Tarbert on Loch Fyne in December. Its evidence and report ran to 5000 pages. It makes up the greatest single document on the Victorian Highlands, a remarkable work of collective oral testimony – and still a good read, not least because the members displayed in it an ample humanity, for good or ill. On Skye, Fraser Mackintosh complained to a witness, Alexander Macdonald of Treaslane, about a notice stuck up in the hotel at Sligachan threatening to prosecute trespassers on the surrounding estate (there was no law of trespass in Scotland). Macdonald wriggled: 'I do not believe it is intended to be carried out in its full sense. I am sure that, if you choose to go up to the hills, we will not object to it.'

Fraser Mackintosh came back in fury: 'I beg your pardon. I and two friends were subjected to the indignity of being assailed by a gillie on those hills.'

'I am sorry to hear it.'

'And what is worse we were called Glasgow tailors in a letter addressed by the lessee of those shootings, Mr Wolstenholme, to Mr Butters the landlord, complaining of the intolerable trespass upon our native hills.'

'But he was a Sassenach and did not know better.'[18]

The evidence goes into such detail that it is no wonder some of it has escaped historians' attention. For example, witnesses questioned on the Highland standard of living usually said it had been rising. 'Men who contented themselves with home produce at first must now have tea and all those extravagant outside luxuries or foreign ingredients,' said John Stewart of Ensay, 'and the young people going south get into these habits and accustom us to these things at home, so that we have all got more extravagant.' Kenneth Macdonald of Scaristavore remarked of his neighbours: 'So far as I can say conscientiously, they are getting better physically, morally and in every sense of the word. They are better clad, and they are better fed than when I remember them first.' Charles Robertson, a surgeon at Achtercairn, thought the people were fitter and stronger than in the past. 'You don't think the prevalence of luxuries . . . has had any bad effect on their health?' No, said Dr Robertson.[19]

The commission also knew, as its record shows, that it was being shadowed by Murdoch to prime witnesses about to appear before it. This accounted for a suspicious uniformity in certain other sequences of evidence insisting that, on the contrary, Highland conditions had got worse. One man probed by Nicolson about the source of his views was evasive: 'If you are kind enough to let me know the gentleman you refer to, I shall answer the question but not till then.' At last he admitted: 'I was told there was a very celebrated man speechifying on the pier at Tarbert, about ten days ago, the editor of *The Highlander*, and that is the only man who I ever heard came to Harris at all.' William Mackenzie of Clashnessie confessed that Murdoch had helped him to compose the statement he had just read.[20]

Murdoch, when he appeared in person, turned out less than impressive. He sought to put across a conspiracy theory, of an attempt 'carried out with the public money, to distort and debase the minds of the people, and have the schoolmaster as the co-labourer with the factor and the ground-officer in destroying all chance of the people ever raising their heads in their own country'. Calling for landlords to be bought out by the state, he was asked where the money would come from: 'Well, I don't know how that would be, I am not very fond of getting national funds. There will be a method found when we are intelligent enough for it. I am not very definite on that subject.'

'You don't know where the purchase money is to be found?'

'I am not very definite on that subject, but I have no doubt it could be found.'[21]

The final report, drafted by Napier in person, gave a meticulous account of Highland problems. It identified basic causes of poverty and discontent: in the crofting areas high rents, small holdings, insecurity of tenure, lack of compensation for improvements; and in the region as a whole the congested population, poor communications and failure to diversify. Conflict of landlord and crofter coloured everything:

> The opinion was often expressed before us that the small tenantry of the Highlands have inherited an inalienable right to security of tenure in their possesions while rent and service are duly rendered . . . an impression indigenous to the country though it has never been sanctioned by legal recognition, and has long been repudiated by the actions of the proprietors.[22]

One view to take was that crofter and croft, along with 'the handloom of the cottage, the sailing craft along the shore, the yeoman's freehold', faced doom in a new age. Yet for Napier a rescue need not, in the great scale of things, be a vain attempt to put brakes on progress. It might amount to no more than a complex system of interference on behalf of a class in the community which is not numerous, which does not contribute a preponderant share to the aggregate sum of national wealth, and which does, after all that has been said, possess, in ordinary times, conditions of welfare and happiness unknown to some orders of the people, for instance, the poorer sort of rural day labourers in England, or to those who depend on casual employment in the cities.

In particular, it would be useful to maintain a population of fishermen living on crofts as a reserve for the navy (an argument cribbed from Adam Smith). Workers on the land ought to have some sort of stake in it. There would always be a risk of famine. It was better to avoid 'collisions between proprietary rights and popular demands', and so on and so forth. But Napier's main reason for adopting his point of view lay in this: 'To suffer the crofting class to be obliterated, or to leave them in their present depressed circumstances, if by any justifiable continuance their condition can be improved, would be to cast away the agencies and opportunities for a social experiment connected with the land of no uncommon interest.'[23]

What on earth did his lordship mean? Land reform, then as now, was a great white hope of Scottish idealists. In their Victorian incarnation they expected it would, through creation of smallholdings, erode the power of wicked landlords, create a free peasantry and offer a better life to townies unable to stand overcrowding or unemployment. Land reform was supposed to be the answer to all sorts of problems, urban and social as well as agricultural. The reformers' American guru, Henry George, pointed up in his scriptural text of 1880, *Progress and Poverty*, an explicit link between the fates of populations on opposite sides of the Eurasian land mass:

> When the potato blight came, they died by thousands. But was it the inability of the soil to support so large a population that compelled so many to live in this miserable way, and exposed them to starvation on the failure of a single root crop? On the contrary, it was the same remorseless rapacity that robbed the Indian ryot of the fruits of his toil and left him to starve where nature offered plenty.

The culprits in either case had been 'a horde of landlords, among whom the soil had been divided as their absolute possession, regardless of any rights of those who lived on it'. Napier sympathized with the happy band of land reformers, to judge from what he did in India and wrote in Scotland.[24]

For the Highlands, Napier interpreted this as an advocacy of the traditional Celtic township – or rather, of its revival at the communal core of crofting in order to conserve a way of life always precarious and now threatened with extinction. Enough has been said in these pages to show that his appeal to history was wrong: crofting had emerged only about the turn of the nineteenth century. What Napier sought would anyway hardly have been recognizable to contemporaries as Highland. He aimed to create a kind of peasant commune run by elected officials. It would own the arable ground and pasture. It might dragoon labour for general purposes. There was to be collective responsibility for rents and for rates fixed by independent assessors. Improvements would require unanimous consent but be compensated individually. Owner-occupation was preferable to tenancy, which must compromise the commune's independence. If the land of a township should prove inadequate, it ought to have a right of compulsory purchase from surrounding private estates. This would all certainly have brought about a revolution in Highland life.

But Napier's bright ideas pleased nobody. They displeased two members of his own commission for a start, despite his best efforts to achieve unanimity. Cameron and Mackenzie, lairds who would face the practical consequences of any reform, had all along shared a suspicion of Napier's motives and cast doubt on evidence from crofters. In the end they signed the report but appended dissents, some fundamental. Cameron rued that those least affected by the proposals would be the alien, unpopular landlords, 'who have managed their estates on strictly economical principles, without any regard to the wishes of the inhabitants'; in other words, 'those who many years ago cleared the lands and converted them into sheepwalks'. Now 'they will get off scot free. Their people have already gone. There are no townships to enlarge, no population by which to form new townships.' Mackenzie, too, wondered if the commission needed to commit itself to a crofting system, in view of 'the narrow margin which, in ordinary seasons, separates the people from want' in certain districts. 'These are the districts where the crofting system is in fullest operation – a system which, however valuable as affording a home with pleasant surroundings to the labourer in those parts of the country where wage-paid labour is required, is elsewhere a general source of poverty.'[25]

Nor did the report please Gladstone, who found in it a curious, tenuous relationship to what he was after. Even more given than Napier to high-minded waffle, he often obscured within his clouds of rhetoric a sharp, by no means timid, sense of practicalities. He saw the report was not a practicality. Yet he had to do something about Highland unrest. What he did was ignore Napier and import to Scotland the Irish Land Act of 1881, with the three Fs: fixity of tenure, fair rents, freedom to inherit a holding.

Gladstone's was a superficial judgement because, if the troubles in the north of Scotland recalled those in the west of Ireland, they lacked the racial and religious overtones that had at times brought the latter to such a pitch of savagery.

Even so, the Crofters Act of 1886 borrowed its main features from Ireland and transferred them to the different, Highland context. The nod to Scottish conditions came in limiting its application by legal definition of the hitherto loose terms 'croft' and 'crofter'. The crofter was the tenant of a croft, registered and paying rent, initially of between £6 and £30 a year, in the counties of Argyll, Inverness, Ross and Cromarty, Sutherland, Caithness, Orkney and Shetland, or rather in parts of them (by no means the whole) where townships with common grazings already existed. The townships became inviolate, as no sale of them could affect their crofters' rights. These had security of tenure so long as they paid rent, and might leave their holdings to their heirs. They could turn to a Crofters Commission for judgement if their rents, including arrears, were fair. With minor reservations this amounted to absolute security of tenure. The commission in its inaugural form lasted until 1912, and in those twenty-six years heard 22,000 applications for fair rents. Its judgements reduced rents of £90,000 to £67,000 and cancelled arrears of £125,000. Mere figures understate the effect because landlords, rather than await a visitation, began to reduce rents even before the commission came along. Provision for compulsory enlargement of holdings brought a transfer of 73,000 acres from landlords to crofters, although the benefit proved small because of agricultural depression meanwhile.[26]

Yet today the act is oftener judged by its failings than by its successes. It did transform relations between landlords and tenants to the latter's benefit. An official apparatus displaced rights of property as then understood. Landlords, tacitly judged guilty of past abuses, were stripped of authority and control to be left with little more than paltry rents and sporting rights. Squeezed between these low rents and their high rates, most landlords were worse off than ever. So, with no resources for improvement, they had to let old methods of subsistence run down further. Unable to sell estates, even to the government, they recoiled in their social role. Just as on the crofters' side deference and loyalty crumbled, so on the landlords' side the traditional obligations of property were silently rejected. Nobody could any longer pretend that Highland society rested on foundations different from those in the rest of Britain. This qualitative change, elusive and hard to chart, expressed itself in small ways.

For instance, the third duke of Sutherland praised by Màiri Mhòr nan

A crofter cutting peats for his croft on Skye. By the time this picture was taken, in the late nineteenth century, the crofter had become the inheritor of the Highlands

A clachan, or crofting settlement, of black houses on North Uist, of a type prevalent in the Highlands during the eighteenth and nineteenth centuries. This one lies on an inlet of the sea and is protected by a strong wall against storms blowing off the Atlantic. The carts are bringing seaweed to fertilize fields behind the houses

A close-up of a croft on Skye. The picture is taken from the shoreline, as shown by the row of boulders and seaweed in front, with rowing boat and anchor behind. The croft shelters both humans and animals, the former in the windowed longer section on the left, the latter on the right. The roof is held down against the weather by ropes and rocks. A barrel beneath catches rainwater for washing; drinking water would have come from a spring

Crofters planting potatoes on Skye. The men turn the soil with a *caschrom*, or foot plough, the only implement that could be used on rocky ground, while women bear loads of seaweed to fertilize the soil

New ways come to the Highlands in the nineteenth century. After the Disruption of 1843 this anonymous photograph shows a congregation of the Free Church still lacking a place of worship as it prepares under umbrellas for communion in the open air at Ferintosh in Easter Ross

On a remote coastline of the isle of Mull, smoke from the burning of kelp for industrial potash adds to the atmosphere of gloomy desolation in this engraving by William Daniell

Modern means of transport opened the Highlands to the outside world. Neptune's Staircase, a miracle of contemporary engineering by Thomas Telford, raises the Caledonian Canal from sea-level near Fort William for its northward passage through Loch Ness to Inverness

The West Highland railway arrived at Kyle of Lochalsh in 1897. The station is filled with wagons for fish and sheep. The line has never carried many human passengers. Today the Skye Bridge spans the narrow strait to the snowy mountains beyond

An apparent scene of timeless serenity conceals a hive of industry at Castlebay, carefully hidden by the photographer behind Kisimul Castle, abandoned seat of the MacNeills on the isle of Barra. The village became a major fishing station, attracting workers from the Lowlands and buyers from abroad

The image and the reality of the Victorian Highlands. Above, remarkably clean and tidy crofters pass the time on an extraordinarily sanitized croft. The boy's bare feet are the only concession to honest poverty, but somehow the family can afford a kilt and Glengarry bonnet for him. Below, a hurried snapshot of an eviction on South Uist, about 1895, well after the Crofters Act

Culture comes to the modern Highlands in the form of a van from the Gaelic Books Council, visiting a scruffy croft somewhere in the isles

Highlanders and Lowlanders mix in the Poets' Pub, Milne's Bar in Rose Street, Edinburgh. The artist, Sandy Moffat, depicts Hugh MacDiarmid (in the centre, with pipe) talking to Sidney Goodsir Smith. Behind him, with pint and cigarette, is George Mackay Brown; behind him is Iain Crichton Smith and behind him Sorley MacLean. To their left is Norman MacCaig. To their right are Edwin Morgan and Robert Garioch. In front, in the hat, is Alan Bold, biographer of MacDiarmid. The prostitutes and revellers are fanciful

Oran was not just an improver but a benefactor. To his credit he had the railway north from Inverness and vast works of reclamation on his moors. He supported the Liberals like his forebears, and went the length of being a radical: when Giuseppe Garibaldi came to Britain to an ecstatic popular reception, it was the duke that paid all expenses, delighted to find besides that the Italian revolutionary liberator was, like himself, a furious smoker. But, on his estate in 1889, he ceased responding as he always had done to tenants' requests for building materials to improve their houses. The reply from a factor, noting that the state had now intervened, said its legislation 'has so greatly altered the legal relations between landlord and tenant bestowing fixity of tenure, and by means of the Commission, greatly lowering rents, it has been found more difficult to continue the system of help which prevailed in the selection of cases – the poorest of course having preference'.[27]

By contrast, crofters won privileges unheard of. Radicals among them still complained that the act fell 'far short of what Highland people were entitled to expect', as it brought no 'restoration of the land of the Highlands'.[28] But while crofters did not own their land, the act treated them as if they did. They were themselves averse from legal ownership, one reason why no general expansion of crofting followed and why great Highland estates survived. The surrogate for ownership, security of tenure, froze development of the crofting counties, suppressing what growth from internal resources might have been possible. The free market spreads its bounty unevenly, to be sure, and crofters had seen more than enough of its niggardly face. Now their security denied them its kinder aspect. A communal system suppressed initiative and leadership in the townships. Active, efficient crofters would be frustrated in any wish to expand their holdings by taking over those of lazier, sloppier neighbours and creating a more viable unit which might, in time, have been equipped to exploit modern technology and markets. On small, rigid plots they had little chance to accumulate capital. If wider opportunities appeared, these were seized from outside the crofting community, by farmers and merchants, often non-Gaels. A static structure emerged with not even the virtue of relieving congestion or the poverty that went with it.

That reply from Sutherland's factor, touching on the grim outlook for cottars and squatters, pointed up one division in Highland society that the act ignored, and if anything would make worse. It did nothing for the landless. They were excluded from the terms of the act because it covered only holdings worth between £6 and £30 a year, and cottars' plots were smaller. This realized an unspoken aim of Napier's: to leave the landless as exposed as before to eviction, which would offer the sole relief from congestion now that people in the stratum above them were to enjoy security of tenure. According to the analysis in his report, as many as 10,000 families subsisted 'without land, and without regular access to local wages, most of them, it may be assumed, scattered among the poorest sort of occupiers, to whom they are a heavy burden'. He ignored them, except in wishing their emigration. The result was to leave them in the same extremity as before. Many did emigrate, but enough remained to make a mockery of the act's good intentions.[29]

This rigid, stagnant system was to frustrate every attempt at a remedy for more general Highland backwardness through the twentieth century. In a new dispensation of, in effect, perpetual tenancies crofters won just a little more land. The legislation bound them to it, with scant scope for growth or modernization. A communal arrangement, while winning the people's loyalty, could move only at the pace of the slowest. The result was general incapacity for change, a society cemented in immobility. The act fossilized the crofting landscape as it happened to appear in 1886. While the Lowlands grew more prosperous, the Highlands hung back in a society static both materially and mentally, polarized between large estates and small crofts. This did not improve living standards and did not stem the Highland exodus. So conflict continued between landlord and crofter, fuelled by futility on the one hand and grievance on the other. Some conflicts are productive, but this one was sterile: the Highlands remained a rural slum far into a new century.

17

Fancy dreams

The crofting system, 1900–1945

TWO HOURS AFTER midnight on 1 January 1920 HMY *Iolaire*, making across the Minch from Kyle of Lochalsh, neared Stornoway on Lewis. In blustery but not stormy weather she carried 283 soldiers and sailors back at last from the First World War. Hogmanay, the most festive night of the Scottish year, was above all so in the Western Isles, where Presbyterians ignored Christmas. Although it was later denied that men on the ship had been drunk, the claim strains credulity. They, apparently the safe and sound survivors, were after all on the last leg of their journey home after a conflict from which thousands of Gaels never returned. Lewis had been the most fertile recruiting ground in the entire British Empire. Out of a population of 29,500, no fewer than 6700 men joined up, most of them in the Seaforth Highlanders, who fought in France, Flanders, Macedonia, Palestine and Mesopotamia. Of these Lewismen, 1151 died: one in six, culled from the ranks of able-bodied males already thinned by emigration. Now, buoyed by promises of land for the people, those that did return could look forward to better times.

It was a pity the officers of the *Iolaire* had posted no watchman to look forward. In the narrowing passage from the open Minch to the harbour of Stornoway she ran on to the Beasts of Holm. After settling off these rocks, she broke up in heavy seas. There were not enough lifebelts. Lifeboats got smashed as soon as they were launched. In the pitch darkness few could see how the Beasts were connected to dry land (although some on board knew just where they were and managed to struggle to a nearby croft to raise the alarm). If anybody had taken charge, or been capable of doing so, an attempt might have been made to get all the men ashore. As it was, they tried in confusion to save themselves and most were swept away to drown. Altogether, 205 died.[1]

They formed a tiny fraction of the 128,000 Scots killed in the First World War, in proportion the highest death toll of any Allied nation. Survivors came back to a homeland bled of its Victorian vigour. Lewis Grassic Gibbon's novel *Sunset Song* (1932) is set in the Mearns, the county of Kincardine in the lee of the Grampian mountains, crofting land in practice although not legally so; in any event, the work conveys the numbed despair of that era in that sort of country. At the end the minister, dedicating their memorial, says of the hour of the death of the men fallen in France: 'It was the old Scotland that perished then, and we may believe that never again will the old speech and the old songs, the old curses and the old benedictions, rise but with alien effort to our lips. They died for a world that is past, these men, but they did not die for this that we seem to inherit.'[2] A century onwards Scotland's war dead are still remembered, in a nation where martial tradition remains vivid. This does not happen before every single memorial, because some were raised in places where few now remain to remember. The most touching stand in remote spots, on Shetland or Skye, deserted and forgotten on 11 November too, overlooking a still loch or an empty glen. It is here the lists of dead seem longest, at least compared with the thin population living roundabout even in 1914.

Nor did the land to which the survivors returned prove to be one fit for heroes. Most Scottish recruitment had gone into territorial battalions, drawn from a single locality with men from every walk of life, so that, for example, crofters might be officered in the trenches by their lairds. Shared experience of danger and death did little to reconcile them once home. In fact, older battles at once broke out again, as if the soldiers had made no sacrifices in common. Landowners mounted a rearguard defence of their menaced position. They had before 1914 offered most of the jobs needed to supplement the proceeds of crofting, with wages generated out of the rental of sporting estates or, to less degree, the profits of tourism. By contrast the crofters blamed legal rights of property for depriving them of land to which they were, by their own reckoning, entitled. The war, so far from bringing the two sides together, deepened their ill will. In other parts of Europe such tensions produced socialism, about which the rulers of Scotland felt more paranoid than was necessary. Be that as it may, many crofters believed their military service had given them a moral title to land.

The conflict of interest was bound to take its own course in the Highlands because the crofting system, under the act of 1886, differed from anything else in Britain. Indeed, nowhere in Europe did there exist another rural society with such rigid structures. It combined archaic elements, such as the heritable possession of crofts, with more modern notions of social security, such as controls on rent. The combination was not a happy one. Zoned off under its own administration, the system remained hampered by legacies from before the war. There was a huge backlog of disputes between landowner and crofter: enough to keep officials busy for years.

They had powers of compulsory purchase that were limited, if not useless, except against a bad owner. Misdemeanours on his part could be proved only with difficulty and, more to the point, slowly. So there was never much land to dispose of – not nearly enough to satisfy demand. Highlanders complained about this shortage above all: two-thirds of their crofts were of fewer than 15 acres, and in the Western Isles more than half were of fewer than 5 acres. They did not yield a living, so incomes had to be made up by part-time work in fishing, deer forests or seasonal jobs. The people thought that, one way or another, they ought to get more land, to augment their crofts and make them economic, or to create new crofts and with them viable communities.

A modern jest has it that a croft is a piece of land surrounded by regulations. After the original Crofters Act of 1886 three more pieces of Highland legislation followed.[3] In 1897 a Conservative government created the Congested Districts Board, which handled a public fund for fifty-six parishes defined as poor or overpopulated. Here it had powers to encourage emigration or else to find land for the landless. In the latter case, it could identify uncultivated tracts they might settle. It would aid them to put up buildings, fences and other permanent fixtures. But, lacking powers of compulsory purchase, it could not take the initiative in purchasing land (unlike its Irish equivalent, which recouped the money from the owner-occupiers it had settled). The Scottish board was obliged to wait until a proprietor felt ready to sell, and then found that most of the crofters settled had no wish to become owners in their turn. Ownership in the Highlands brought penalties: they would have had to pay the high rates and lose the legal protection of the Crofters Act. So they preferred to remain tenants to the board.

Of the estates the board took over, only Glendale on Skye, a stronghold of peasant independence, saw the tenants buy their holdings. The sequel is worth pursuing. 'It was the proud boast of the parish', declares the *Third Statistical Account*, 'that there was not one man fit for service left by the time conscription was introduced in the First World War. The women kept the crofts going somehow, despite the fact that it was not only the men who went to war, but also the ponies, except the very old and white.' This made life hard for the women, 'as peat and sea-weed, manure, potatoes and hay all had to be carried or dragged by them, as was also the plough on occasion. By the end of the war, all felt it time not only for the men to come back, but to stay a while.' The condition of the British, not to say global, economy before long exerted a greater effect on the people's way of life than their own spirit of independence, however. In the 1930s they started to emigrate. In the 1940s the community ran down: the 'sheep stock had sunk to half the original number, and fences, farm cottages, shootings and fishings had all deteriorated'.[4] Nowadays Glendale is largely occupied by 'white settlers', non-natives who retire there or are seeking the good life away from modern civilization.

The Tory act of 1897 tried to tackle a problem ignored by the Liberal act of 1886.[5] The crofters on whom the reformers then lavished their favours were, if not rich, never as wretched as the cottars or squatters in and about the townships. They made up perhaps a quarter of the rural population and had no legal claim to any land. It was for them that the Conservatives sought to do something. Difficulties emerged at once on Barra, or rather on its offshore island Vatersay, let as pasture to a sheep farmer. Squatters mounted a raid there in 1901. The lessee demanded action to stop 'organized bands of cottars . . . marching hither and thither marking out for occupation ground in the lawful occupation of other people'. The board responded by acquiring some land and distributing it into sixty crofts, still not enough for all who wanted one. In 1906 the cottars landed again, 'to get possession of the whole farm of Vatersay and to remove their houses to Vatersay as soon as possible'.[6] They ferried livestock across the sound and began to build themselves homes.

By 1906 the Liberals were back in power. The Scottish Secretary, John Sinclair, sympathized with the raiders. So far from wishing to deter them, he sought to regularize their position by turning the moral rights they claimed into legal ones. He approached the proprietrix of Barra, Lady Gordon Cathcart. She was the widow of the infamous John Gordon of Cluny, but not as boneheaded as he and grudgingly respected by the islanders. She also held his lands in Aberdeenshire and wanted to apply lessons from there to the Hebrides. She thought crofting a disaster, not least in its failure to deal with congestion. She hoped to turn cottars into fishermen with a livelihood from the bountiful sea rather than from the bleak land, though they might have a plot to grow vegetables and graze a cow. She tried this out on Barra, not without success despite the uncertainty of fishing. The district clerk recalled:

> There were 40 fish-curing stations on the shores at Castlebay and a large fertilizer plant. During the fishing season hundreds of . . . boats came to sell their catches, and purchasing agents from many parts of Europe had their offices there. There was also a a large influx of girls, who were employed gutting herring. Scores of boats came from Glasgow with cargoes of salt for the industry.[7]

But congestion on the island remained severe. Lady Gordon Cathcart warned that settlement as envisaged by the legislation would not solve the problem: 'I am profoundly impressed with the view that it would be a social and economic mistake to add to the number of crofter holdings in Barra' because it 'keeps the energetic man down to the level of the least enterprising'.[8]

Sinclair at length struck a deal with her reluctant ladyship all the same. It was the prelude to extensive resettlement of Barra, then of other Outer Isles, because one official takeover of land brought demands for more. For now the board just did not have the money to meet them. Raids multiplied instead. On South Uist a hundred cottars had petitioned for holdings since 1901. 'Why be cottars or landless squatters any longer, while land in abundance is ready for instant habitation?' they cried. They wanted back the farms 'from which our forefathers were so illegally evicted' and warned that they might feel compelled to take 'forcible possession'. After two years they did occupy some grazings. Again in 1906, with flags flying and pipers at their head, they marched on to two sheep farms, 'to let the authorities see they were badly off and that more land was required'. On North Uist, too, cottars took over land to show it was fit for crofts, recalling how 'over half a century ago their forefathers were ruthlessly evicted from their homes . . . to make way for sheep'. One old man said, 'it was all very well to talk of justice and agitating on constitutional lines, but he has seen nothing come of that for 65 years'.[9]

Faced with this groundswell of raiding, Sinclair essayed the first general land reform in Scotland. It failed. The Scottish Secretary was a woolly Liberal 'with the brain of a rabbit and the temper of a pig', according to his Prime Minister, Herbert Asquith.[10] Sinclair held that, just as the peasant was morally superior to the lord, so tenancy was morally superior to ownership. In this spirit he carried the Small Landholders Act of 1911. It harked back to one or two ideas of Lord Napier spurned by William Gladstone; and it harked indeed still further back, for smallholdings had been a radical ideal in Scotland for a century. They were thought likely to erode landlords' power, create a free peasantry and offer a better life to city-dwellers sick and tired of unemployment or overcrowding. In this guise land reform seemed to be the answer to all sorts of questions, urban and social as well as rural and agricultural. But reformers blinded themselves to the fact that Scotland's biggest problems had irrevocably become problems of her cities or her industries, and could not be tackled on an assumption of common interest with the countryside.[11]

The act of 1911 in effect sought to extend crofting beyond the seven

Highland counties to the whole of Scotland.[12] The provisions were controversial: the Liberals had to have several goes at getting them through, and succeeded only after docking the powers of the House of Lords. The act set up a mechanism to create new holdings on private land and enlarge uneconomic ones, all enjoying the three Fs. It phased out the Crofters Commission and the Congested Districts Board, functions of the one being taken over by the Scottish Land Court and of the other by a Board of Agriculture for Scotland. This new board had £200,000 to spend, mostly for settlement and not least for compensation to owners, to be arbitrated by the Land Court with appeal to the Court of Session. If a proprietor refused to create or enlarge holdings on his estate, the board could ask a sheriff to make him do so. At last, it seemed, demand for redistribution might be met. In its first year of operation the board received 3370 requests for holdings, almost half from cottars in the Western Isles. But it never got much further than that.

The new board's funds turned out too small and its methods too slow. Nor could it cast off a certain deference to landowners, without whose goodwill the act was a dead letter. While some would have got rid of unprofitable land for whatever it could fetch, few wanted it settled by crofters. A MacLeod of MacLeod pointed out how the landlord had been 'at the mercy of a commission whose sympathies are entirely with the tenants, and who, if they allow any increase in rent at all, will give the very smallest increase possible, while, if prices fall, they will give the most generous increases in rent'. So certain landowners refused all co-operation. Major Duncan Matheson, proprietor of Lewis, which suffered the greatest problems of congestion and poverty, was one awkward customer. By 1916, with a war on, the board had to decide whether to postpone solicitations to him until peace came or abandon them altogether. As most applicants for land were in any case away on active service, it decided to postpone: this proved in the event to be an abandonment. But one official prophesied that 'the Lewis people, having had these farms dangled before them for some years, will break the peace if the thing is postponed more or less indefinitely'.[13]

The new board was not universally obstructed, however. In the case of the fertile island of Tiree, the owner, the duke of Argyll, readily entered into negotiations on smallholdings, with a sensible proviso that they ought to be bigger – worth up to £40 a year – than those covered by the Crofters Act, which had not produced viable units. He let plans from the board go forward unopposed and was even happy to let it set his own level of compensation. But it realized on closer inquiry that no creation of smallholdings would deal with the congestion on the island: there was nothing for it but that some cottars should leave, although this could not be said out loud. The duke of Sutherland was just as co-operative, disconcertingly so. He offered large tracts for settlement. For his pains Liberals attacked him, arguing this was not a serious offer. In the acerbic words of the duke's neighbour Lord Lovat a government that had 'harped continually' on the agricultural value of such land 'now turn round and say that it would not keep a mouse'.[14]

By 1914, when the board's work ground to a virtual halt, it had created only 500 new holdings and enlarged fewer than 300 existing ones. It had not satisfied any interested party – neither contrary cottars nor louche landlords nor patronizing politicians, none of whom helped in applying lousy legislation. When war broke out, the board more or less packed up. For example, it had just asked the Land Court to authorize thirty-two new crofts and fourteen enlargements on North Uist. It did not get round to issuing the orders until the end of 1915. The owner of the island, Sir Arthur Campbell Orde, then went to the Court of Session and asked it to appoint an arbitrator, as he was entitled to do. But this did not happen until 1918, when Sir Arthur got £5000 of the £16,000 he had asked for. Such unconscionable delay fuelled frustration all round. And Sinclair's hope of getting urban problems solved by rural measures was a chimera. Many city-dwellers lived in crowded, insanitary tenements, but before 1914 they could at least be fairly sure of wages and food. It was a better life than any to be found in some squalid, dreary back-of-beyond. Even a longer period of operation could not make the policy work, and in 1933 it was abandoned.[15]

A crux for the sequence of Highland legislation came with the soldiers' return in 1918. Men who had fought the Germans with cold steel felt no fear of landlords. Raids started up again in every crofting county but Argyll and Orkney. On South Uist thirteen ex-soldiers awaiting in vain an answer to their petition marched behind a piper to the landlord's house to let him know they were about to take over his farm. He argued, 'but we told him to go to blazes and the next morning we were on his land. We tipped over his carts, we rounded up his sheep and cattle and drove them away. It was a week after that had happened that we were served with a sheriff's interdict forbidding us to set foot on Balranald.' On North Uist raiders responded with no less confidence to the authorities' warnings: 'Please do not think we care one straw for threats of imprisonment . . . When facing the Germans we were filled with promises of getting land where and when we wanted, and now four years have elapsed but we are still left in the cold.'

On Skye raiders met similar threats with the retort that 'they were not in breach of the moral law in laying claim to cultivate some of the lands held by their forefathers for centuries'. They had served their country, and 'it was only in despair of any action being taken to apply the law that they in their suffering decided to occupy'. These men were sentenced to two months' gaol, but a public outcry forced their release in ten days. On Raasay raids were run by the island's cobbler, John MacLeod. Threatened in his turn, he turned the tables on 'the criminal negligence of the Board [of Agriculture] . . . The inaction of that incompetent body is wholly responsible for all land-seizures in Scotland, many of the applications for holdings having been sent to the Board years ago.'[16]

Such were the hopes deflated despite passage of the third piece of legislation, the Land Settlement Act of 1919.[17] This had been carried on a wave of relief at the peace and of gratitude to the soldiers, giving it a fair wind through the political cross-currents that had stranded its forerunners. Although Liberal support might be assured, it needed the Conservatives of the post-war coalition to get it on the statute book. For example, it won the backing of Lovat, whose keen interest in Highland development had just brought him the inaugural chairmanship of the Forestry Commission, which would before long be planting 20,000 acres a year on the hills, to yield a new source of livelihood in the glens beneath. The novelist John Buchan, soon to become a Tory MP, put these words into the mouth of his hero in *Mr Standfast* (1930), Richard Hannay, who in conversation with a Gael surely echoes the views of his creator: 'I told him that after the war every acre of British soil would have to be used for the men that had earned the right to it.'[18]

Against the background of a non-partisan fund of goodwill for a bold solution to Highland problems, the act of 1919 looked timid. It streamlined the procedures for creating smallholdings. It allowed powers of compulsory purchase for settlement, to landowners' alarm. In a sense this did no more than tidy up defects of the previous acts, yet it was sold as the nation's reward for the heroes, who would now breed a 'fit and healthy race' in a self-sufficient country. Ex-servicemen got preference for two years after the act came into force, and made half the applications under it. In the end 4500 profited from a right to propose a scheme of settlement by showing land was arable and available. Before long they had resettled most of the cultivable area in the crofting counties – but, as would become clear, on holdings that in the face of surging demand had been kept too small to support a family without other resources. Such resources, if not scarce from the start, certainly grew so during the slump of the 1930s. By then, though, the money to implement the act had run out and nobody else got anything.

This was the background to the most revealing episode in the Highland history of the twentieth century. It unfolded after Lord Leverhulme, a millionaire with an empire in soap, bought Lewis from the almost bankrupt Mathesons in 1918. He had ambitions as a philanthropist to round off his feats as a capitalist, and he thought the Western Isles the place to fulfil them. He expressed admiration for islanders who in exile were 'honoured and respected and filling the highest positions in Canada, Boston and New York and elsewhere throughout our colonies', yet who at home found themselves 'living under conditions of squalor and misery'. He felt driven to the conclusion that 'crofting today is entirely an impossible life for these fine people'. Lewismen already earned on average £25 a year from fishing, compared to £3 a year from sale of their crofts' produce. Leverhulme wanted to reinforce the trend with a master plan for showering his money on the island to create well-paid employment, mainly in modern fisheries based at Stornoway, where he would build processing and canning plant, reconstruct the harbour and remodel the town.[19]

He landed there at a last moment when people still looked to fisheries to counter the failures of crofting. Lord Napier had surmised that Highlanders won more income from the sea than from the land. In 1891 it was found that three out of four Gaels depended in some degree on fishing, often in combination with crofting.[20] But Mother Nature, always capricious in the Highlands, from time to time caused the shoals of herring to change their habitat and vanish without warning. Modern man in his quest for brotherhood was about to aid and abet her: the Scottish fishing industry would soon go into depression on losing its largest market as Russia was overtaken by revolution, and the Bolsheviks banned as decadent the *zakousky* of pickled herrings which lined bourgeois stomachs for vodka on festive occasions.

It was a double blow to Highlanders, who, after a slow start at fishing, now practised it in one of several ways. Either a crofter could go out by himself in a small boat, as many still do. This inshore fishery was too precarious for a living, however, and formed only one activity among others on a croft. Alternatively Gaels might find a place in the greater fishing economy, which had reached a peak before the First World War. One branch of it flourished in the Western Isles, where, as encouraged by Lady Gordon Cathcart, a new class of fisherman–farmer emerged with at last the apparent prospect of a stable future and rising income: on such an assessment, at any rate, Leverhulme also rested his master plan. Along the opposite coast of the mainland the fishing was less reliable, although

improved transport and technology overcame this handicap as it concentrated at Mallaig and Kyle of Lochalsh, with their links by road and rail to
distant markets; the relatively small numbers employed here tended to lose
any connection with crofting. The greatest fishery, on semi-industrial lines,
lured Highlanders further east. A man worked on a trawler out of Wick or
Aberdeen, or a girl as a gutter followed the fleet, which pursued the shoals
of herring from Lerwick on Shetland to Yarmouth in England, with the
migrant workers also diverted to boost their earnings from successive harvests of various crops, hoeing turnips or roaging corn or picking fruit.
Where part-time fishing turned into full-time fishing, it generated a new
workforce, however, with a different life and different ways from crofters:
the two callings separated again. In Victorian times lucrative temporary
migration had propped up remote communities, but in the twentieth century it had a corrosive effect as this separation went on. People from crofts
were exposed to an outside world more and more alluring to them. They
joined the flight off the land which, all over Scotland and Britain, quickened in the wake of the First World War. And as the fishing afterwards fell
away too, those who had followed it from smallholdings found they had
not enough to support their families. Soon rusting trawlers and rotting nets
littered ports from Stornoway to Lerwick to Wick.

Such was the evolving social and economic situation that would have to
form the matrix for Leverhulme's master plan. To put it to the people, he
spent the winter of 1920 at meetings across Lewis. Most dutifully endorsed
it, but at one place he came face to face with a deeper reality in the Gaels'
lives. As the applause for his presentation died away, a man stood up and
said: '*Seo, seo, fhiribh! Cha dèan so gnothach! Bheireadh am bodach mil-bheulach
sin chreidsinn oirnn gu'm bheil dubh geal 's geal dubh! Ciod e dhuinn na bru-
adairean brigha aige, a thig no nach tig? 'Se am fearann tha sinn ag iarraidh. Agus
'se tha mise a faighneachd: an toir thu dhuinn am fearann?*'

The audience broke out in wild cheers, to Leverhulme's bewilderment.
'I am sorry,' he said, 'it is my great misfortune that I do not understand the
Gaelic language. But perhaps my interpreter will translate for me what has
been said.'

'I am afraid, Lord Leverhulme, that it will be impossible for me to
convey to you in English what has been so forcefully said in the older
tongue. But I will do my best.' And so he did: 'Come, come, men! This
will not do! This honeymouthed man would have us believe that black is
white and white is black! We are not concerned with his fancy dreams that
may or may not come true. What we want is the land. And the question I
put to him now is: will you give us the land?'

The translation brought still louder cheers. A voice from the back was heard to say: 'Not so bad for a poor language like the English!'[21]

But Leverhulme had, for now, no mind to give them the land. When the Board of Agriculture inquired if he might co-operate in a scheme of settlement, he would not hear of it, and made clear how he altogether disapproved of crofting. It was an unhealthy, uneconomic way of life, and its deliberate extension by government 'a gross waste of public money'. It could never fill more than a fraction of a working man's day for a pitiful return, and would therefore be a millstone round the necks of his potential wage-earners. At best Leverhulme might allow them allotments to work in any spare time he left them. Otherwise there was not enough farmland on Lewis to meet the demand for smallholdings even if it should all be used for that purpose, and partial settlement would cause as many problems as it cured. Leverhulme asked the board not to proceed with any scheme until it saw the results of his master plan. The matter went to the Scottish Secretary, Robert Munro, who agreed in private that Leverhulme should go ahead for ten years without being distracted by the law; so much for the Land Settlement Act. Nothing was said publicly. Munro did not himself question the master plan but did see endless political problems from any backsliding on promises to the heroes: 'If I had chosen that moment to reverse my policy I would have lost any confidence that the islanders still had in me, and my position in the House would have become impossible.'[22]

His scruples went for nothing. Impatient Lewismen took things into their own hands. In the hinterland of Stornoway lay two farms, Coll and Gress, marked down in the master plan for dairies to supply the town. Islanders wanted them returned to crofting use. They mounted raids and staked out holdings in three successive years: 1919, 1920 and 1921. By the time of the third raid Leverhulme had had enough. He called a halt to all his projects. Munro saw this as a breach of their agreement, and proceeded to authorize settlement at Coll and Gress under the powers conferred on him. To add injury to insult, Leverhulme's business was then hit by a sharp fall in the price of fish as foreign markets shrank. Discouraged and offended, he transferred his attentions to the other end of the Long Island, turning the hamlet of Obbe into the port of Leverburgh. In Harris he spent £250,000 on works that were sold for £5000 on his death in 1925. He, too, had failed to impose reason on the weird ways of Highlanders. Yet in a final act of generosity he offered Lewis to its people as a gift. Even then, the townships declined to take the land into ownership, saying limply that they 'could not afford the augmentation of rates entailed by acceptance'.[23]

For now the intentions of the state and the aspirations of the people still appeared to march in tandem. In fact, they were proceeding on parallel lines destined not to meet. The Scottish Office, ever a timorous body, feared raids would spread into the Lowlands, so for a while it gave way to Highlanders where it thought nobody would notice. But the civil servants would, in the fulness of time, get their own back.[24]

This took place a quarter of a century later, over the sea at Knoydart, once the last fastness of the MacDonells of Glengarry. The district had since gone through a series of owners to finish up with the Barons Brocket, in origin Catholic immigrants from Ireland, with a fortune from shipping in Liverpool. The second baron, born Arthur Nall-Cain, made a career as a barrister and then a Tory MP before succeeding his father, in 1934, to 13,000 acres in England and 62,000 in Scotland. He was not so much nasty as stupid. He admired Adolf Hitler, who invited him to Germany. Back home, trying to persuade the great and good that Nazism was not so bad after all, Brocket offered them lavish hospitality at his two great houses of Brocket Hall in Hertfordshire and Bramshill Park in Hampshire. Even the Prime Minister, Neville Chamberlain, sometimes asked Brocket, as a man with access to the Führer, to convey to him thoughts of the British government that could not be aired in public. Rumour had it that the Nazi ambassador to London, Joachim von Ribbentrop, came for the shooting to Knoydart, although there is no documentation of this.

After the outbreak of the Second World War Brocket worked for an early peace with Germany but suffered a nervous breakdown because of the abuse he was attracting. The government took over his Highland estate, thought of confiscating it but decided not to, then used it to train commandoes anyway and handed it back to its legal owner after peace came. The act of 1919 still stood on the statute book, so to some locals Knoydart seemed ideal for a scheme of settlement. Who, after all, would defend the right to property of the broken Brocket? The answer was that the Labour government would, or at least its Scottish Office. Arthur Woodburn, a slow-witted Secretary of State under the thumb of his civil servants, rejected a scheme of settlement put to him in 1948. In indignation seven men of Knoydart, including the Catholic priest, Fr. Colin Macpherson, mounted a raid, occupied fields on the estate and staked out crofts. This tiny Highland rebellion provoked an over-reaction from the piqued Scottish Office. Raiders were arrested, tried and gaoled. Brocket took no further part in public life and died in 1967.[25]

The incident at least demonstrates how much the axis of state and people – as opposed to the older one of landlord and tenant, let alone of chief and clansmen – had impressed itself on the Highland mentality, even in a form of self-delusion. Perhaps it would be wrong to be too sceptical of the motives of the state expected by Highlanders to save the Highlands. That state had little idea how to do this, except by fiddling with the land laws. Settlement achieved some success. From the starting point in 1886 about 750,000 acres of pasture and more than 50,000 acres of arable land, an area getting on for double the size of Caithness, were handed over to crofters. But they had reached the limits, in a mountainous and infertile region, of the area on which they could eke out a livelihood. They merely recurred to the situation of a century before and came up against the same physical and natural bounds to their aspiration.

So, with hindsight, it is hard to see the programme of Highland legislation as anything but an economic irrelevance, even if it brought political dividends for a few. It shared the philosophy of the legislation in Ireland and brought the same sort of result. The Irish Land Acts had been vaunted by their authors as the spur to a vigorous society of small farmers, animated by security of tenure, protected from rack-renting, launched into innovation and enterprise. But Ireland remained moribund, a nation of old people from which youngsters with any gumption got out as soon as they could. Irish nationalists were amazed to find, after 1922, that political independence in itself offered no cure. They expected to see the population start rising again, but it declined for another half-century and more. Only as Ireland then embraced capitalism did much change, and the consequence was not the perpetuation of peasant agriculture.

The Highlands offered a second test of Victorian conceptions of land reform, under different conditions and without political upheaval. It still did not work. With no explanation for their failure reformers fell back on old myths. 'We are dealing with a community which has never been industrialized and resists any attempt at industrialization. Land is the basis of its existence and determines the form of social life', declared Lord Nairne, chairman of a parliamentary committee in 1928. Gaels had refused to accept the changes of the last 150 years and instead compelled governments to meet their own claims: 'The Highlander not only insists on living in the Highlands, but insists on living in his own strath or on his own island . . . He insists on being given land in his own district, and would rather have a hopeless patch of his own native heath than a fair holding in a strange glen.' Nairne was echoed by Sir Alexander MacEwen, provost of Inverness and a future founder of the Scottish National Party: 'We are suffering today not from economy, but from economists. The people who want to rationalize and centralize everything know something about industry, but they know little about the needs of a peasant population. Their calculations omit all consideration of social and spiritual values.' Sir Alexander did not expatiate on those values but confined himself to a remark that 'when these superior people visit a Highland croft and see small oats growing on the lazy beds and the cattle and the sheep seeking their scanty nourishment, they exclaim that it is impossible for people to live under such scanty conditions.'[26]

At least official Scotland felt little inclined to accept the strictures of romantics. In 1936 a mandarin, Sir William Goodchild, defined the Highlands as at once a national asset and a national problem. Usually when pundits defined them as an asset, they meant the scenery and so forth, but this was not what Sir William had in mind: 'Catering for tourists is a useful adjunct of the national economy, but is not an end in itself.' He insisted on a different point: 'Will the Scottish Highlands through time become the playground of the rich and Highlanders neglect their own industries to become a race of Swiss hotel-keepers?' If anyone should inquire what exactly these 'own industries' were, Sir William had an answer ready: 'Among the resources of that vast area there is unlimited water power, peat, stone and minerals, as well as kelp, tweed making and other rural industries.' He could not have known that a day was coming when Swiss hotel-keepers would prosper far more than any Highlander, and this not least because of the resources frittered away by the state on the Highlands' 'own industries'.[27]

What did the Highlander think of this debate going on above his head? Little coherent comment arose from outside charmed official circles, but one voice was that of Neil Gunn, a man of the people from Sutherland, who abandoned a humdrum career in HM Customs to write novels. He was an individualist, then, one of many who in the 1930s set the Scottish National Party going but stopped it getting anywhere. An egalitarian also, he could hardly help it if members of the Nazi cultural establishment took a not altogether welcome interest in him as a chronicler of *Blut und Boden* ('blood and soil'), a genre of literature they wished to promote in their own country; so his books were translated into German and he went over to promote them, finding nothing more untoward in the Munich of 1938 and 1939 than fat Bavarians slurping beer. Some of his sentiments translated well. 'I should demand a man's work,' he wrote, 'and I should demand it in my own land.' Nazis presumably overlooked it when Gunn went on to admit that work had not always been a priority of Highlanders: 'It is now a saying that the Islesman knows the Unemployment Insurance Acts better than his Bible, and there is a joke on Lewis to the effect that a man of a certain district will not go to a funeral unless he gets an insurance stamp.'[28] His real hope rested on a conviction that, so long as freedom endowed Highlanders with virility, they would not bear forever with the evils of the industrial system: 'But when this virile life is absent, then not all the deserving old women attending to the tourists of the world and prattling of the scenic beauty of empty glens can save the ancient heritage from decay and death.'

How virile were they, though? The answer is a little obscured by the fact that huge numbers of Highlanders still chose, despite attachment to their native glens, a better life in the Lowlands or abroad. The population of the crofting counties, static or at worst slowly falling in the second half of the nineteenth century, plummeted now. In 1881 it was 369,000; in 1891, 360,000; in 1901, 352,000; in 1911, 341,000; in 1921, 311,000; and in 1931, 293,000. During this last decade the population of Scotland as a whole dropped for the first time since the official census began. This happened despite novel obstacles to emigration, notably in the United States. The onset of worldwide depression would soon make life in new nations little better than in the old country – a further deterrent to emigrants, indeed a motive for some to come home. Within Scotland, too, seasonal movement died away; the harvest had by now been mechanized and merchant fleets were soon to be laid up. There also appeared some small incentives to stay put. Crofters could not be evicted anyway, and for the first time in Scotland, where the poor law had been more stingy than in England, workers might draw benefits just for being unemployed (a fuzzy concept anyway in part-time agriculture). Doles miserly in the Lowlands, let alone in London, looked princely in the isles: as an observer said of their recipients on Lewis, 'not a few prayed that "employment" would not come inconveniently soon'.[29]

Yet decline in the population quickened. Highlanders became in fact less virile, in the sense of less able to reproduce themselves. Earlier emigration had worked a selective effect in taking away a greater than average proportion of the young and fertile.[30] In 1921–31 the number of women of child-bearing age fell by 35 per cent, so the birth-rate dropped and the number of children plunged by 40 per cent. At the end of that intercensal decade pensioners outnumbered youngsters in the region. Although statistics were never collected in such a way as to confirm it, this was probably a matter of a whole Highland class, the cottars or squatters, a quarter of the rural population, melting away.

Crofters may have seen little incentive to abandon their security of tenure for the vagaries of life elsewhere, and part of the hunger for land had been sated by schemes of settlement. But what happened to men who never got on to one of the schemes? If demand for settlement faded in turn, it may have been because those who could have generated it had instead departed under their own steam. The young left, the old stayed: the life's blood drained from the Highlands. It was this, rather than any clearance of the past, that destroyed self-sufficient, often Gaelic-speaking communities whose ruined houses and byres are to be seen today all over the hills.

18

A golden wine
Modern highland culture

ON 1 JULY 1936 Hugh MacDiarmid sat down in his cottage on the
island of Whalsay, Shetland, to write a furious letter to James Whyte,
owner of a bookshop at St Andrews and editor of little magazines then
among the few outlets for the Scottish literary avant-garde. He had in fact
been good to MacDiarmid, who in return dedicated his great poem 'On
a Raised Beach' to Whyte. That did not save him now.[1]

The object of MacDiarmid's wrath was a new title Whyte had produced, *Outlook*, casting his net wider with pieces on the general cultural,
economic and political state of a Scotland just starting to recover from the
great slump. The 1930s saw the foundations laid of the country's modern
governmental structure with its reliance on bureaucrats and experts in endless quangos. MacDiarmid thought that, beside his literary business, he
might as well have a go at all this too.

For example, the shipbuilder Sir James Lithgow had just been made
chairman of an Economic Advisory Committee which survives yet,
benevolent if not always effective. To MacDiarmid it was 'playing the game
of the Anglo-Scottish authorities in forms of alleged decentralization
giving a specious pseudo-satisfaction to Scottish "interests" in lieu of genuine nationalism'.

At the University of Dundee an economist, James Bowie, was seeking
to show Scots how to move away from the shattered structure of traditional
heavy industry into the production of modern consumer goods, something
that would come about only towards the end of the century. To
MacDiarmid this had 'nothing whatever to do with the real bases of our
national economy or the masses of the workers, but is in significant and
sinister alignment with the establishment in Italy today of branch factories
by big English motor firms'.

MacDiarmid also got worked up over an article Whyte had run by Tom
Johnston, Labour politician and future Scottish Secretary, who in the
Second World War would erect consensual quangocracy in all its glory. He
called his piece 'Fascist Boards for Scotland?', a heading doubtless meant

to be mildly provocative rather than merely tasteless. It argued that if Italians could manage their economy through quangos, so could Scots.

MacDiarmid dismissed this and every other type of new politics: 'This consensus of opinion and alleged open forum business of yours are purely Fascist notions', he fumed to Whyte. But then, like progressives of a later era, he flung the Fascist tag about with abandon. Scottish nationalists had, along with Johnston, shown interest in Benito Mussolini's resurgent Italy, presumably as a model for their own country. MacDiarmid was not immune to their interest, though it came out more clearly in an aristocratic nationalist, Ruaraidh Erskine of Marr. He regretted that his party had 'still to evolve a Scottish counterpart of Fascism. One thing is certain, the Celtic myth is quite inadequate for national purposes, since it is capable of uniting only a handful of Scotsmen. We now require a leader.'[2]

By this time, however, MacDiarmid had put all such notions behind him. 'The Communist party is right in regarding the official National Party of Scotland as a Fascist organization', the poet thundered, after the SNP in his view succumbed to a plot hatched in the *Daily Record* to hand over its leadership to the duke of Montrose, Sir Alexander McEwan, sometime Provost of Inverness, Andrew Dewar Gibb, professor of Scots law at the University of Glasgow, and 'Annie S. Swan', sentimental novelist and former suffragette. MacDiarmid was expelled from their nationalist party for his communism, just as before long he would be expelled from the Communist Party for his nationalism.

To MacDiarmid every one of these personages was more or less English, if not in blood then in spirit: 'You cannot be a Scottish Nationalist without breaking with English culture, lock, stock and barrel. Continued association with England, either in the present relationship or any other, cannot but commit us to Fascism, the antithesis of the Scottish genius and the negation of its natural destiny and world-function.'[3]

Still, the bard reserved his most lethal venom for the Orcadian poet Edwin Muir, a man today regarded as MacDiarmid's fellow pioneer in the Scottish Renaissance. This term was borrowed from a French critic, Denis Saurat, who lectured for a while at the University of Glasgow, to characterize the cultural revival in a nation that had seemed doomed to destitution, desolation and dependence on its bigger neighbour.

To Whyte, MacDiarmid described Muir as – among other choice epithets – 'one of the leaders of the white mouse faction of the Anglo-Scottish literati and a noted connoisseur of buttered bread'.[4] Muir cannot be acquitted of a certain bloodlessness. Something vital was knocked out of him after an idyllic childhood on Orkney ended with his family's move to Glasgow, where they sought prosperity but found squalor, disease and ruin. The young Muir suffered a nervous breakdown on being sent out to work in a bone-processing factory and had hardly recovered by the time he left for London to try his luck teaching and writing. He underwent psychoanalysis but only marriage to his wife, Willa, also an islander by origin, restored some sanity to his shattered self. He would otherwise seek solace in a saccharine Catholicism, at its most embarrassing in the passage of his *Scottish Journey* (1935), where he visits the Marian shrine at Carfin, Lanarkshire. His early Calvinism no doubt drove him to this – not uniquely among Highland literati. Compton Mackenzie was a Catholic, but in *Whisky Galore* (1947) he brought out a more robust side to his Church's influence on those Hebridean islands which remained loyal to it. Fionn MacColla, too, converted to Romanism from Calvinism, which others besides blamed for all that was wrong with the Highlands, or indeed with Scotland in general.

As for Muir, a related reaction to the more robust aspects of the national ethos appeared in his horror of violence, even when harmlessly sublimated. In *Scottish Journey* he wrote also of his distaste for the still life, an art form he often met overnight on his fact-finding tour around the north. To him 'still life' was a misnomer, for the pictures made any dining-room look 'like a shambles, they presented such an overwhelming array of bleeding birds, beasts and fishes'. He found 'these abominations on the walls of Highland hotels, among a people of such delicacy in other things . . . peculiarly revolting'. The phenomenon rubbed in 'with superfluous force that this is a land whose main contemporary industry is the shooting down of wild creatures; not production of any kind but wholesale destruction'.[5]

MacDiarmid was never so squeamish, physically or philosophically. At one point in 'A Drunk Man Looks at the Thistle' he exposes a squalid side to the theoretical Marxist predestination of unwitting modern man:

> A means to ends he'll never ken,
> And as to michtier elements
> The slaughtered brutes he eats to him
> Or forms o' life owre sma' to see
> Wi' which his heedless body swarms,
> And a' man's thocht nae mair to them
> Than ony moosewob to a man
> His Heaven to them the blinterin' o'
> A snail-trail on their closet wa'![6]

Yet ten years earlier Muir and MacDiarmid had been close. MacDiarmid's collection of 1925, *Sangschaw*, contained such lines as:

I' the how-dumb-deid
O' the cauld hairst nicht,
The warl' like an eemis stane
Wags i' the lift.[7]

which could be understood by few Scots readers, let alone anybody else.
Muir's review yet argued that the use of synthetic Scots – the language
culled by MacDiarmid from many historical sources but never as such
spoken or written by anyone – 'may turn out to be a fact of great importance for Scottish letters. For if a Scottish literary language is possible then
a Scottish literature is possible too.' Since Muir was an older, more established, writer MacDiarmid felt grateful to him.

After MacDiarmid won renown of his own, a publishing house in
London consulted him about a series it wanted to commission from
authors of the Scottish Renaissance. Muir volunteered a volume called
Scott and Scotland, which can still be read with pleasure and profit today.
Once it was finished, Whyte carried a trailer for it in his magazine. Hence
MacDiarmid's irate letter: he smelled here a nauseating betrayal.

Muir went to some lengths in his argument to stress once again his
esteem for MacDiarmid. But he could not accept that poetry might
improve the condition of Scotland, which remained as dismal as ever. This
had little to do with individual writers and how good or bad they might
be. It was an outcome of historical forces nobody could now alter, among
them the modern prevalence of standard English, displacing for any elevated purpose the Scots language once used by the Scots people for all their
speaking and writing.

'This linguistic division', Muir insisted, 'means that Scotsmen feel in
one language, and think in another; that their emotions turn to the Scottish
tongue, with all its associations of local sentiment, and their mind to a standard of English which for them is almost bare of associations other than
those of the classroom.' That was where he made a connection with Sir
Walter Scott, a man who had been torn between his heart, devoted to the
old Scotland, and his head, counting the Union's blessings.[8]

While Scott had still been able to maintain a balance, Muir did not think
this possible a hundred years later. National culture had meanwhile not just
died but decomposed. A Scottish writer,

> if he wishes to add to an indigenous Scottish literature, and roots himself
> deliberately in Scotland, will find neither an organic community to round
> off his conceptions, nor a major literary tradition to support him, nor even
> a faith among the people themselves that a Scottish literature is possible or
> desirable. Scotland can only create a national literature by writing in English.

This last thought was the red rag to MacDiarmid's bull. Yet one premiss he and Muir agreed on: English was alien speech, in which Scots could never express all they wanted to say. Muir's cure was for them to carry on being assimilated to the English until they overcame their handicap. It was not a tactful reaction to MacDiarmid's linguistic exertions, but it had a point.

Works of the Scottish Renaissance, for all their virtues, never appealed to the people as Scott's Waverley novels had done. There were intermediaries who might have helped. Popular authors such as John Buchan and Neil Munro encouraged the work of the younger generation, who in return brought themselves to accept that good writing and commercial success were not mutually exclusive: it seemed there might yet be a little more to Scottish literary life than scratching and gouging. But somewhere along the line new writers still failed to get through as Scott had done to the essence of Scotland, whatever that was nowadays.

Some barriers between author and public obscure then appear obvious now: books by Neil Gunn or Fionn MacColla or Lewis Grassic Gibbon often seem to be histories of immaturity or elegies on vanished ways of life. The symbolism of MacDiarmid's poems is at its richest with subjects taken from the nature he knew during his boyhood in the Borders. Yet Scotland had grown into an old, urban, industrial country leading a dispiriting, laborious, unsuccessful existence: the opposite of youthful. MacDiarmid himself asked,

> Are my poems spoken in the factories and fields,
> In the streets o' town? Gin they're no,
> Then I'm failin' to dae what I ocht to ha' dune.[9]

In her tales of the kailyard (in English, the 'cabbage patch'), of that school of dialectal literature stressing the homely, local aspects of Scottish life, the despired 'Annie S. Swan' came nearer to the hearts and minds of people who read the *Sunday Post* or, at best, could recite a few lines of Robert Burns. MacDiarmid almost admitted as much when he turned during his nine years in Shetland to writing intellectual poems that he boasted were hard to understand – and in English, not Scots. Perhaps, it might be whispered, his intransigence made out of him a caricature of the modernist rebel, stereotyped into harmlessness by the élites he hated.

At any rate, MacDiarmid's programme of resurrecting the Scots language and rekindling political militancy had run out of steam by the time of his letter to Whyte from Whalsay. In other words the Scottish Renaissance, as he conceived it, was over.

It had awakened fine talents, among them Highland talents and specifically Gaelic talents. Unlike Muir, MacDiarmid gloried in the linguistic diversity thus revealed:

> These Gaelic and Scots dialect poets were products of substantially the same environment, and concerned for the most part with the same political, psychological, and practical issues, the same traditions and tendencies, the same landscapes as poets in English to whom, properly regarded, they are not only valuably complementary, but (in view of their linguistic, technical and other divergencies) corrective.[10]

Both the schools of poetry indigenous to Scotland had been 'miserably attenuated and driven underground by external factors', yet 'they have continued to complement and correct each other in the most remarkable way'. MacDiarmid held up hopes of a pan-Celtic alliance if Scots could see 'the importance of the fact that we are a Gaelic people, that Scottish anti-Irishness is a profound mistake, that we ought to be anti-English, and that we ought to play our part in a three-to-one policy of Scotland, Ireland and Wales against England'.[11]

Yet it became harder than ever for Scots to see themselves as a Gaelic people, in speech or thought or any other realm. In the Gàidhealtachd itself young men came back from the First World War after using English for four years, if they survived, often to give way to that hectic materialism which is a natural human reaction to sustained encounter with death. Anyway, they had not much time for the past. The townships abandoned Celtic customs and rituals. Those bearers of tradition who transmitted oral knowledge fell silent, for few in the next generation wanted to hear. Hector MacKinnon of Berneray was reckoned the last of *Na Daoine*, the holy laymen who wandered praying, preaching, prophesying and defending orthodoxy.[12] Before long the ceilidh houses, where Gaelic lore had been passed on for two centuries and more, stood empty. The next best thing was the *bothan*, a hovel in which men gathered to get drunk. Culture was left to professional people, migrant Gaels in the drawing-rooms of Inverness, Glasgow and Edinburgh. By now no such thing as Gaelic society existed, in the sense of communities where knowledge of the language could be taken for granted at all levels. Its upper registers, couched in terms of respect for social superiors, drifted into disuse because these people were now addressed in another tongue. As it became superfluous for non-Gaels to learn Gaelic, so it became normal for Gaels to learn English and to make sure their children had a command of it for the sake of the future. The linguistic processes mirrored a failure of collective confidence right across Gaelic Scotland.

Above all, the Gaelic-speaking population plunged. In 1901 it numbered 230,000; by 1931 it was only 130,000. The drop was most marked in the borderlands of the Gàidhealtachd. Argyll turned from a county containing a majority of Gaels, with 60 per cent of the people knowing the language at the turn of the century, to a predominantly English-speaking county, with only 33 per cent knowing Gaelic three decades later and many seldom using it. A linguistic activist, Iain Ruadh, wrote how any visitor to the Highlands 'could well be excused if he failed to observe that the inhabitants had anything to distinguish them from those of any English country district, except for a slight accent on their English speech'. He might think them

> deaf or a little slow of understanding before he discovered that the English which he saw everywhere in writing was not in fact the native language of the people at all, but a foreign idiom forced upon them by a standardized anglicizing education and the exclusion of their own tongue from every public use.[13]

The decline has not been broken to this day, but has spread out over the mainland until the Gàidhealtachd consists only of islands, and by no means every one of those, together with a fringe of the western coast.

The Churches, in practice strongholds of the language, scarcely upheld it in principle: God was more important than Gaelic. The Gaelic literary scholar Ronald Black writes that 'throughout the twentieth century, respect for the sabbath, rather than for the language, remained the principal marker of Gaelic identity'.[14] But respect for the sabbath waned too. In 1926 the Free Church protested in its *Monthly Record* at constant encroachment on the historic hush of the Highland Sunday: 'With the bait of reduced fares, railway and steamboat facilities for pleasure travelling on the Lord's Day have multiplied during the year and the scenes witnessed at some railway stations and summer resorts have been most disgraceful.' No less scandalous was 'the sale of newspapers on the Lord's Day . . . to the great annoyance of many of the community, and this is one of the many evil consequences of the Great War'. The commitment to the Lord's day of sabbatarians (lively enough even yet) outran by some distance attachment of the generality of Gaels to their language.

But not all just looked on as their mother tongue withered. One survival of its brief resurgence in the late Victorian era was an organization called An Comunn Gàidhealach, founded in 1891 to run an annual festival, the Mod, as a showcase for traditional poetry and music. At first it had also hoped to promote economic development out of the old crafts, but little came of that. After the First World War even this twee, self-satisfied body was impressed by the deep crisis in the linguistic community it sought to foster and represent. In 1923 its president, Angus Robertson, had the various poetic competitions at the Mod amalgamated into a single contest for the 'bardic crown', just as at the Eisteddfod in Wales. The appeal to participants' vanity drew them to the Mod right down into a later time when most seemed to be non-Gaels who learned their pieces by rote and at once broke into English after they came off the stage. If all this kept some popular interest alive, the muses of Gaeldom dried up. In 1974 and 1978 the bardic crown stayed on its cushion, when the judges found that no competitor had been good enough to win it. In 1979 An Comunn announced it would no longer be awarded. But Gaelic poetry had long taken new directions never imagined by the earlier worthies.[15]

Impoverishment of the spoken language went on despite the lifting of one great burden on it: its neglect in, if not exclusion from, public education. A glimpse of its standing before the war is given in a memoir of childhood on Lewis by Angus Campbell:

> A Lowlander, who had not a word of Gaelic, was the schoolmaster. I never had a Gaelic lesson in school, and the impression you got was that your language, people and tradition had come from wild, unruly and ignorant tribes and that if you wanted to make your way in the world you would be best to forget them.[16]

In 1920 a new Scottish Education Act at last gave Gaelic a statutory place in schools. This was owed largely to Iain Macpherson, MP for Ross and Cromarty, who arranged with the Secretary for Scotland, Robert Munro, to put down suitable amendments as his legislation went through. Inevitably, the Scottish Office disliked them. The act transferred everyday control of education from school boards to county councils. The civil servants said they did not want the councils' spending decisions to be dictated from outside (except, of course, by civil servants). To them the Gaels appeared just another tiresome lobby, not to be encouraged. So the act's linguistic provisions were kept permissive rather than made compulsory. It required parents and pupils to take the initiative and prompt councils into having Gaelic taught. The language was treated in the classroom as a foreign one, usually an alternative to French. Even where both master and pupils had it as their mother tongue, the instruction went on in English.

Champions of the language of Eden found not only its quantity but also its quality deteriorating. MacColla wrote in 1933 of 'an ever widening gulf between the speech of the older and younger generations'. The latter's

Gaelic was 'slovenly and illiterate'. From it had vanished 'many of the characteristic sounds which made Scottish Gaelic the most melodious language in Europe'. With them went 'a great part of a once peculiarly rich and varied vocabulary, which loss has been partially made up by the adoption of large numbers of mispronounced English words'. Young Gaels could hardly speak with 'any degree of purity on any subject not rustic and trivial. The overwhelming majority of Gaelic speakers born within this century speak only – because they know only – a colourless, impure and impoverished form of the language.'[17]

Yet on another plane a slow rehabilitation of Gaelic did start up. After 1918 the gurus of Scottish culture, seeing its stricken state, sought in Gaeldom a new heart of the nation, a means to save its soul by returning to simpler Celtic values. So MacDiarmid and others looked to the Highlands for something more spirited than any offering that had ever come from the stolid Victorian Lowlands, a region now itself a wreck. He wrote in the introduction to *The Islands of Scotland*:

> Whatever the limitations and difficulties of Scotland may be, it is necessary to insist that our great trouble (and the source of all our other troubles) is not on the material but on the spiritual plane, and that unless our idea of Scotland is deeply and truly enough laid, superficial efforts after rehabilitation can only register minor and relatively negligible successes.[18]

Something more spirited arrived with a younger Highland generation, among which there is one writer often counted as the finest of all Gaelic poets, or at the least ranking with those of the golden age in the eighteenth century. Their works had been followed by the inconsequence and mediocrity of the Victorian era. Little heralded, then, the splendid flowering that came with Sorley MacLean. He was steeped in Gaelic history and literature, and in this sense overtly traditionalist. He had no illusions about the 'very insignificant' Highland culture of his day, 'dissipated in the fogs of Celtic Twilight, a purely foreign non-Celtic development', and no time either for its prosy moralists and hymn-writers. He stood out from this tribal rabble like an Ossianic bard. While, true to that form, he often appeared obsessed with heroism or genealogy, he was also a modernist, a political poet versed in ideology, a critic conscious of other cultures. Added to this was the deep impress of a Presbyterian upbringing and the lyrical transports of his love poems, creating a potent brew indeed. He distilled from it a blend intricate yet consummate of passion, scepticism and vulnerability. With him, at one bound, Gaelic poetry moved into the modern world.

MacLean was born on Raasay in 1911, into a family bearing traditions of music, song and verse. His native island formed a stronghold of the Free Presbyterian Church, a sect of strict Calvinists that had seceded from the Free Church of Scotland in 1893. It fostered a religion of tumult and fervour, polarizing the secular and the sacred, oblivious of the resulting risk to the culture that sustained it, now disintegrating under the impact of modernity. Religion might have become a repressive force in MacLean's life and work, but his family was not so very orthodox. His parents declined to reject every worldly pleasure as vanity and corruption. He recalled: 'I think that the first great artistic impact on me was my father's mother singing some of the very greatest of Gaelic songs, and all in her own traditional versions.' He would take pride in adapting the language of the sonorous scriptures, the eloquence and colour of the sermons, to his own purposes. MacLean himself was a sceptic, repudiating dogma and priest-craft, although something in him still told him he was damned and he never got over it. In modern Scotland, Highland Calvinists are often figures of fun, yet he would have none of this. Interviewed in his old age, he thus recalled them:

> There's been an awful lot of exaggeration of a kind of self-righteousness, because those people were not self-righteous. I mean, in all fairness there might have been some cases of hypocrites and all that, but there would be in anything . . . Especially in the 1930s when a lot of people were talking and finding all the faults of Scotland in Calvinism, I was saying, 'What the devil do all these people, writers and all those, know about Calvinism?' . . . One has to be fair. Among those people, there were so many I know who were saintly, just saintly men. I didn't find those people hypocrites, because the whole business of this sinfulness, this desperate wickedness of the human heart, precluded self-righteousness.[19]

Not for MacLean the facile rejection of Calvinism, then, let alone the coy flirting with Catholicism, of lesser figures. With MacDiarmid he stood four-square on the vaunted vigour of the Scottish intellect, merely switching the theme of disputation from doctrines of grace and election to dialectical materialism (or something of the sort).

After his schooling at Portree on Skye, MacLean went to university in Edinburgh to study English, 'because it seemed economically disastrous to take Celtic'.[20] He made friends with James Caird, who in later life sought as a chief inspector of schools to diffuse the influence of the Scottish Renaissance, and the philosopher George Davie, whose book *The Democratic Intellect* (1964) would sway thinking about Scotland for the rest of the twentieth century and beyond. In 1933 Caird and Davie introduced

MacLean to MacDiarmid's work. Like others, the young Gael was at once seduced by the exquisite early Scots lyrics, which had parallels in his native literature. 'The chief reason why I think it extremely unlikely that there is a poet equal to MacDiarmid living in Europe today,' MacLean later wrote, 'is the complete originality of MacDiarmid's lyrics, their out-of-this-world quality, which rings true and hugely significant, moving in the extreme to whatever I have of sensibility.'[21] Early on, MacLean had tried writing poetry in English. He abandoned it after this vicarious encounter with MacDiarmid, perhaps because he felt his Gaelic experiments were anyway better. At all events they offered him his own literary territory. Traditional Gaelic prosody expressed feeling in a pre-modern way, by a dense virtuosity of metre, image and vocabulary. As examples in previous chapters have shown, the system could also be at times rigid, formulaic and impersonal, like the Homeric epic, though in the same way a symbol of identity. MacLean inherited and mastered the tradition, but modernized it with a radical exploration and extension of its sensuous potential.

MacLean and MacDiarmid soon met. They remained friends until MacDiarmid's death in 1978, although it helped that each worked in a different language so they could hardly be rivals. A first fruit of their amity came in collaborative translation into English of the greatest work by the Jacobite bard Alastair mac Mhaighstir Alastair. It was an odd choice for a couple of socialists, possibly explained by the fact that 'Birlinn Chlann Raghnaill', while exalting the chief of Clanranald, also stressed the dignity of the clansmen's labour. In 1935, with MacDiarmid sequestered on Whalsay, MacLean visited him. MacDiarmid returned the compliment and went in 1937 to Raasay, gathering material for *The Islands of Scotland*. The pair meant to collaborate again on a Gaelic anthology with English translations, although this never came to anything. Their ways parted in the Second World War: MacDiarmid's for conscripted labour on Clydeside, MacLean's for battle in North Africa, where he was wounded.

After the war MacDiarmid followed a yet stonier poetic path into scientific abstraction, while MacLean returned to a teaching career and eventually became headmaster at Plockton in Wester Ross. This left him little time for verse. Not until he retired in 1976 did he win wider recognition. Then, on a round of readings at home and abroad, he struck a chord with eager audiences. Few understood his words once he passed from an introductory English translation to his original text. But his vatic, distracted demeanour hinted at its depths, and his declamation could send shivers up and down the spine. That, at least, was the effect on Seamus Heaney when he first heard the mesmeric, heightened tone; the weathered voice coming in close from a far place; the swarm of the vowels; the surrender to the otherness of the poem, above all the sense of bardic dignity that was entirely without self-parade but was instead the effect of a proud self-abnegation, as much a submission as a claim to heritage.[22]

The mutual influence of MacDiarmid and MacLean endured. MacDiarmid carried on writing Highland poems, most famously 'In Scotland in the Gaidhealtachd there's a golden wine'. MacLean came to admire 'A Drunk Man . . .' as the greatest long poem of the twentieth century: 'It converted me to the belief that the long medley with lyric peaks was the form for our age.' He tried that out for himself in 'An Cuilithionn', which views the history of the world from a coign of vantage on Skye, although this is not one of his best works, not for lyric intimacy at any rate. It strains too much for effect and wanders too far afield, as he evidently had come to feel himself when he abandoned it, but it does have its moments. In the following passage a traditional bardic device, the relentless piling on of near-synonyms, finds release in a vision of Gaeldom, symbolized in the Cuillin, changeless yet potentially regenerate, redolent of history yet open to the future. It is an optimistic vision, despite what has gone before:

> Thar bochdainn, caithimh, fiabhrais, amhghair,
> thar anacothrom, eucoir, ainneart, ànraidh,
> thar truaighe, eu-dochas, gamhlas, cuilbheart,
> thar ciont is truaillidheachd; gu furachair,
> gu treunmhor chithear an Cuilithionn
> 's e 'g éirigh air taobh eile duilghe.

> Beyond poverty, consumption, fever, agony,
> beyond hardship, wrong, tyranny, distress,
> beyond misery, despair, hatred, treachery,
> beyond guilt and defilement:
> watchful, heroic, the Cuillin
> is seen rising on the other side of sorrow.[23]

For the poetry of the British Isles critics have disputed how to date the start of the twentieth century, that is, the end of Victorian sensibility and the emergence of a modern one. For Scots poetry the only answer is with MacDiarmid's 'A Drunk Man . . .'. T.S. Eliot's 'The Waste Land' stands by common critical consent as the first poem of the century in English. MacLean's equivalent for Gaelic was not the same huge set-piece, nor in the same style intellectual poetry, interested in ideas for their own sake. His less extensive oeuvre relied on a less predictable process of inspiration. He wrote:

In spite of MacDiarmid, the 'full-time' professional poet is not for me and never has been. If I have time to do it, I brood over something until a rhythm comes, as a more or less tight rope to cross the abyss of silence. I go on it, as far as I can see, unconsciously.[24]

So MacLean wrote from a metaphorical tightrope, balancing between its opposite ends as well as over the abyss. A twofold division was the arrangement he chose for the first collection he brought out while invalided home in 1943, *Dàin do Eimhir agus Dàin Eile*, with an introduction by Douglas Young, a nationalist academic at St Andrews. The 'poems to Eimhir' are about love, under a symbolic rubric from the ancient Gaelic epics for the most comely of the heroes' women; the 'other poems' are just that. According to MacLean's fellow bard Iain Crichton Smith, 'as a love poet he belongs to that small company which includes Catullus, Burns and Donne'. His emotion is enhanced with echoes of the oral sources of Gaelic song. MacDiarmid went back in his vernacular verse beyond Robert Burns to William Dunbar of the first Scottish Renaissance in the sixteenth century; MacLean also resolved to go back beyond formal or literary Gaelic poetry to sup at the flow from its wellsprings in time out of mind, which afterwards took its own course in the voices of the people. He finds there an incredible power in simplicity while able, as a sophisticated modern, to enrich it with intellectual conceit or poignant lyric. His poems have traditional virtues of passion, eloquence and intellectuality, which he puts also at the service of modern ideas, humanitarian or political. He does not so much oppose the old style with a new one as open the old style to novel topics and methods of presentation. Yet his remains a poetry of polarity, of love and hatred, of obsession and turmoil: neither of mere intellect nor of mere emotion but of a whole man and his quandaries.[25]

This was, though, not just personal poetry. MacLean set the pains of private love against his sense of public obigation amid the increasingly menacing political atmosphere of the 1930s, after the rise of Fascism and its aggression in Spain, with the prospect of a world at war not far off; he even joined the Communist Party, although it is hard to believe this helped. His poetry shows his own love life collapsing in uncertainty and doubt while Western culture and democracy sink amid the conflict of Fascism and Communism. This distracted world demands choices of the poet which only cast into relief the truth and supremacy of his love. He believes he ought to go and fight in Spain yet cannot bear parting from a woman to whom, for other reasons besides, he feels restrained from declaring his devotion. He seems helpless and remains supine, except in writing these obsessive, lacerating poems. 'It was not a case of an actual choice between the woman and Spain', he later explained. 'I was prevented from going to Spain by family circumstances. But I realized that if it were a pure choice between the woman and Spain, I'm afraid I would have chosen the woman . . . I knew that would have been my choice.'[26]

MacLean breathed new life into an ancient art, and only the weight he laid on Spain perhaps now strikes a dated note. Foreigners did go to fight and die there, but George Orwell reminded us that the stark choices they felt beforehand seldom survived experience at the front. For MacLean a deeper meaning of the Spanish Civil War may have lain in its analogy with Highland history. Now at stake was the future of Western civilization, not just of beleaguered Gaeldom – which he could accept was a forlorn little cause when set against the general advance of barbarism. General Francisco Franco and his supporters among landlords, capitalists and Catholics looked like a Hispanic version of the old chiefs, incoming proprietors and clergy of the Highlands a century before. Both form a matrix of discord for MacLean's sense of his own humiliation. He fears he is returning the same blank answer to contemporary Fascism as a previous generation of Gaelic poets returned to Victorian avarice. His irresolution betrays not only himself but also things greater than himself (for the victory of the wrong side in Spain could at length impinge on his own, and everybody's, private sphere). The choice then lies between a present love and a future terror. The poet cannot bring himself to make what he feels sure would be the right choice. All this is worked through in his poem 'Urnuigh – Prayer', in a fashion unconsoled by any resolution:

> . . . *Mo bheatha-sa a'bheatha bhàsail*
> *a chionn nach d'fhail mi cridhe mo shàth-ghaoil,*
> *a chionn gun tug mi gaol àraidh,*
> *a chionn nach sgarainn do ghràdh-sa*
> *'s gum b'fheàrr liom boireannach*
> *na'n Eachdraidh fhàsmhor . . .*

> *A chionn nach cuirear coire air diathan,*
> *nach eil ach'nam faileas iarraidh,*
> *agus a sheachnadh an duine Crìosda,*
> *chan eil mo chaomhachd ris an Nàdur*
> *a thug an tuigse shoilleir shlàn dhomh,*
> *an eanchainn shingilte 's an cridhe sgàinte.*

> . . . My life the death-like life
> because I have not flayed the heart of my fulness of love
> because I have given a particular love,

because I would not cut away the love of you,
and that I preferred a woman to crescent History . . .

Since the blame will not be put on gods,
who are only the shadow of desire,
and to avoid the man Christ,
I do not feel kindly towards Nature,
which has given me the clear whole understanding,
the single brain and the split heart.[27]

Admirers of MacLean tend to fall into two camps. 'It is a source of some perplexity to me', writes Ronald Black, 'that [the] movingly elegiac works of MacLean's maturity should be regarded as in some way superior to the poems of the 1930s, which seem so totally engaged with the present moment that they make the blood run faster.' Black adds that MacLean's *oeuvre* as a whole speaks for humanity, 'but while in the late poems he speaks for the Gael and the dead, in the early ones he speaks for the young and the living.' Yet it seems to have been the very stress on a public sphere in those later poems that made them more accessible to people in MacLean's audiences who could hardly have experienced any personal crisis as intense as his. They saw in him a social poet, moved by devotion to the Gaels and pity for their history.[28]

To these audiences at the readings the favourite poem was 'Hallaig', its title taken from a township on the eastern coast of Raasay which the people were forced to leave in the 1850s. At the time Hallaig had been full of the sound of human voices, but now it was a remote spot of eerie desolation and silence. The poem marked the passage of a century. It is a wonderful piece in its haunting, spectral atmosphere and elegiac tone. The translation here, of extracted verses, comes from Seamus Heaney:

'Tha tìm, am fiadh, an coille Hallaig'

Tha bùird is tàirnean air an uinneig
troimh 'm faca mi an Aird an Iar
's tha mo ghaol aig Allt Hallaig
'na craoibh bheithe, 's bha i riamh

eadar an t-Inbhir 's Poll a'Bhainne,
thall 's a bhos mu Bhaile-Chùirn:
tha i 'na beithe, 'na calltuinn,
'na caorunn dhireach sheang ùir.

Ann an Screapadal mo chinnidh,
far robh Tarmad 's Eachunn Mór,

tha 'n nigheanan 's am mic 'nan coille
ag gabhail suas ri taobh an lóin . . .

Tha iad fhathast ann a Hallaig,
Clann Ghill Eain's Clann Mhicleòid,
na bh'ann ri linn Mhic Ghille-Chaluim:
Chunnacas na mairbh beò.

Na fir 'nan laighe air an lianaig
aig ceann gach taighe a bh'ann,
's na h-igheanan 'nan coille bheithe,
dìreach an druim, crom an ceann . . .

's am bòidhche 'na sgleò air mo chridhe
mun tig an ciaradh air na caoil,
's nuair theàrnas grian air cùl Dhùn Cana
thig peileir dian á gunna Ghaoil;

's buailear am fiadh a tha 'na thuaineal
a' snotach nan làraichean feòir;
thig reothadh air a shùil 'sa' choille:
Chan fhaighear lorg air fhuil ri m'bheò.

'Time, the deer, is in Hallaig Wood'.

There's a board nailed across the window
I looked through to see the west
and my love is a birch forever
by Hallaig Stream, at her tryst

Between Inver and Milk Hollow,
somewhere around Baile-chuirn,
a flickering birch, a hazel,
a trim, straight, sapling rowan.

In Screapadal, where my people
hail from, the seed and breed
of Hector Mor and Norman
by the banks of the stream are a wood . . .

Hallaig is where they survive,
all the MacLeans and MacLeods
who were there in the time of Mac Gille Chaluim:
the dead have been seen alive,

The men at their length on the grass
at the gable of every house,

the girls a wood of birch trees
standing tall, with their heads bowed . . .

And their beauty a glaze on my heart.
Then as the kyles go dim
and the sun sets behind Dun Cana
Love's loaded gun will take aim.

It will bring down the lightheaded deer
as he sniffs the grass round the wallsteads
and his eye will freeze:
while I live, his blood won't be traced in the woods.[29]

The deer killed by Love's bullet is Time. At Hallaig the reality of time, of history, of what happened, is tragic. Redemption can only be achieved once the ravages of time are overcome by a love that transmutes experience into art. Yet this must still be tragic, because the overcoming is bounded by mortality. So long as the poet lives, says the last line, a vision both tragic and redemptive remains. In that sense time will be arrested, but only for a little time.

19

A great outdoor laboratory
Economic revival, 1945–1999

A T 9.58 ON the evening of 6 July 1988 an explosion rocked the oil platform known as Piper Alpha, owned by the Occidental Corporation
and sited 100 miles south-east of Orkney. There were 230 men on board.
In an hour 167 of them would be dead.[1]

An explosion on a platform was by definition a serious incident but, so
far as is known, this first one killed nobody and injured only a few. It did
shake up the huge structure, jacket and platform, which rose 600 feet from
the sea-bed, with just the last 200 feet jutting above the surface. Here,
where roughnecks and roustabouts lived and worked, the blast made walls
and ceilings buckle or collapse. It put out lights and closed down other systems: alarms, public address, pumps, extinguishers. It silenced telephone
and radio. It fractured pipes and caused leakages. It started fires. Smoke and
dust rose from falling debris and insulating material.

In the control-room it had been obvious for a good ten minutes that
something was going terribly wrong. The technicians monitoring the gas
as it rose out of the deep noticed a major disturbance in the refining system.
Yet, unable to pinpoint it, they could do nothing.

They never knew it, but the problem lay under their noses, in the platform's condensate pumps, which disposed of liquids extracted from the gas
during refinement. There a piece of routine maintenance had been left
unfinished during that day. A worker employed by sub-contractors
detached a safety valve from a pump. For some reason he could not at once
replace it. The shift changed, this detail went unrecorded and so was
overlooked.

From then on a certain volume of gas escaped instead of being refined
and, without anybody noticing, built up around the pumps. At 9.50 one
pump malfunctioned and shut down. This was the first in a series of technical failures that would eliminate the processes of production until nothing remained to control the ceaseless flow of gas. Its escape greatly
increased. A sign came in the flare on the south-western corner of the platform, which grew much larger than normal and began to roar.

While in the control-room the technicians puzzled and fiddled, many of their mates were in the cinema watching the horror film *Carrie*. Here they often spent the evening after coming off shift at six o'clock and hurrying a meal. By the sumptuous standards of the North Sea the food on Piper Alpha was thought poor; men complained it brought them out in spots. Most nights the cinematic fare seemed more alluring, although *Carrie* was bland compared to the usual diet of pornography, soft, hard or sick.

However crude, there had to be some compensation for the back-breaking labour and the absence of loved ones or home comforts. Occidental, like all operators in the North Sea, imposed an absolute ban on alcohol and, of course, on drugs: instant dismissal would be visited on anyone possessing either. Men like these were already regarded as belonging to the drug-taking classes, and had their bags searched minutely every time they came offshore. The élite were ex-servicemen, inured to hardship, discipline and loneliness. Most of the rest hailed from decaying industrial regions such as Clydeside or Tyneside. They came out to the North Sea grudgingly, but they often had no choice. On each tour of duty they worked fourteen days nonstop in shifts of twelve hours. This added up to at least 168 hours (often nearer 200) – the equivalent, squeezed into a fortnight, of more than four average weeks of forty hours which they might work onshore if they could ever find a job. At least it paid well by the standards of Govan or Jarrow. Roughnecks, employed on skilled tasks, could earn £1700 each tour, while roustabouts or labourers got £1000. These rates, in direct reflection of the market, had tumbled since the collapse in the price of oil a couple of years before.

Procedures for an emergency were drummed into the men time and time again. They cleared the cinema as soon as they heard the flare roaring. Following the drill, they hurried to their berths to fetch survival suits. They were then to muster in the galley, the large room where they all ate together, to be counted and directed to evacuate the platform.

The first explosion occurred while men were still rushing round doing this. The fires it started were not so fierce as to put them in fear of their lives; clouds of smoke meant to them that oil, not gas, was alight, and oil would soon burn up. Alarms never rang, because they were no larger functioning, so the men remained unaware of their peril. Piper Alpha had suffered a blast in 1984, when everyone got off. Accidents were perhaps to be expected on such an old crate of a platform, the longest-serving in the North Sea, dirty and cramped, noisy and rusty, where there always seemed to be something leaking somewhere.

The platform had at higher levels an adequate number of lifeboats and a helideck. Discipline among the men did not in fact hold up that well, because small groups thought it safer to start climbing aloft than go to the galley and hang about while everyone mustered. The smoke was already thick enough to turn some back. Others gathered at the north-western corner of the platform, where a light wind carried the black billows away from them. They handed round life-jackets, but showed no panic. At that hour in these northern waters it was still light, and they could see two big platforms in the same oilfield some miles away, Tartan and Claymore, together with a smaller rig, Tharos, near by. If necessary, rescue would come from there. On this warm, clear evening the explosion had indeed been observed, and boats were already setting out for Piper Alpha across calm seas.

But reassurance soon vanished. Added to the rising roar of the flare came a hair-raising screech of gas escaping somewhere else. It might ignite at any moment. Men trying to clamber up turned round to clamber down towards the tangle of gangways and gantries between the main platform and the sea. Better water than fire: from underneath they at last understood their danger, for they could see from flames licking through dense smoke that a huge blaze had become established.

Above, standby lighting flashed on and off in the living quarters. It left men to grope, at best with the help of torches, through the murk. The galley had been free of smoke at first, but now it rolled in and choked them. They sat or lay on the floor to stay below it. As the heat grew fiercer, they fumbled for coins and bought soft drinks out of slot machines to pour over their heads. Outside stood a big container full of fruit and vegetables. Men vaulted into it and passed tomatoes to their mates, who crushed them over their faces and hands. Some realized that it was now too late to muster, that it was every man for himself. They left the galley and, braving the smoke, penetrated to the helideck in the hope of being lifted off. Others shinned along metal structures sticking out from the platform, so as to be over the sea, away from the fire and ready to catch the eye of approaching boats.

Such are the last, helpless ploys of men as, without warning, death comes for them. At 10.22 a fireball of accumulated gas blasted out from below the core of the jacket, struck the sea, enveloped the platform and rose to a height of 700 feet.

Piper Alpha was also a junction of pipelines from nearby platforms carrying refined gas to be pumped ashore to Flotta in Orkney. What had happened was that one piece of equipment, the Tartan gas-import riser, burst with heat from the blaze and other breakdowns after the first explosion.

Over 11 miles of pipeline 18 inches in diameter started to free gas at a pressure of 1800 lb. per square inch. Where there had been a noxious fog, there was now a raging inferno, which would not abate for four hours.

When the riser blew, men on the platform had a split second to make a choice which meant either they were sure to perish or else they might yet be saved. For any chance of escape they had at once to jump into the sea, despite being encumbered with heavy clothing and boots. The most fortunate, on the underside of the platform, jumped as rescuers arrived in boats. For the rest it was a matter of luck, but five men jumped 175 feet from the helideck and survived. All still lost the skin of their faces and hands exposed to the fireball when it flashed over them, and suffered agony after they hit the salt water. Otherwise men aloft, if they hesitated even a moment, were incinerated where they stood or, clinging to girders and ladders, were blown away in the fireball. Those in the shelter of the galley did not die that instant, although they must have soon passed out from heat, smoke and fumes. But one had a hand-radio and at 10.33, ten minutes after in reality all was lost, he managed to send a message – the last to be heard from anyone on Piper Alpha – to the nearest rig. Out of the gates of death he spoke: 'Most people in the galley. Tharos come. Gangway. Hoses. Getting bad.'

At 10.52 the remaining pipelines attached to the platform exploded in an even more colossal fireball. Millions of cubic feet of gas in miles of pressurized tubes fed an awesome conflagration. The boats had at once to race away to avoid being destroyed: one did not make it and blew up in its own fuel. The rest were forced to stand off hundreds of yards if crews and rescued survivors were not to be burned alive. The steel of the platform glowed red-hot and the very sea steamed. At last, still wreathed in flame, Piper Alpha began to disintegrate and fell over to one side.

Red Adair, the Texan douser of fires in oilfields, had said: 'Whatever precautions are taken, there'll be a disaster in the North Sea, sooner or later. There are no proper facilities for dealing with it. The thing is time, to get trained personnel there. By then the well may have caught fire.' His words proved prophetic. But apart from any human error or technical failure the deep, wild North Sea was hostile to the oilmen. Adair arrived at Piper Alpha, still ablaze, towards the end of July, when the brief, balmy midsummer was already over. Amid winds of 80 miles an hour and waves 70 feet high he had, before starting his work, to get huge pieces of debris moved from the wellhead by cranes which tossed about like flotsam. He needed three weeks to quench the flames by pumping cement into the wells and then capping them.[2]

Exploitation of the North Sea had from the outset exacted a steady, though often avoidable, toll of deaths and injuries. Against disaster on the scale of Piper Alpha defences could only ever be limited, but other factors had raised the risk. It is odd to recall today that, when oil and gas were first discovered off Scotland in the 1960s, experts denied they could be present in profitable quantity, given the high costs of development. After the Six-Day War in 1973 the Arabs took revenge for defeat by forming a cartel, the Organization of Petroleum Exporting Countries (OPEC), and forcing up the price of oil to $40 a barrel. Overnight the North Sea became marine property so valuable as to justify any level of investment. If problems of the environment could be technically solved, money would be there.

The Seven Sisters, the multinational corporations in control of the world's oil until the Arabs barged in, now stood ready. To them this was a test. If they could create a new industry under the waves, it would show their ability to meet OPEC's challenge and regain their dominion. But nobody had ever drilled at such depths: in the other main submarine province, the Gulf of Mexico, the bed might be 60 feet down, not 600. Semi-submersible rigs in the North Sea were new technology, requiring a huge, risky injection of capital. Capital could be found, and the way to reduce risk was to recover reserves at breakneck speed.

That was the interest of the Seven Sisters, but the British government egged them on. Like other Western governments, it had its own still greater fears about OPEC, although it lacked the muscle to respond. The Arabs made global history by halting the prosperity in Europe and America which had lasted since 1945. Stability and growth gave way to deficits and inflation. For Britain in particular this short-term crisis compounded long-term problems of relative economic decline. Edward Heath's Conservative government hardly had time to face the music before it lost the general election of February 1974. Then Labour came in under Harold Wilson, carrying an additional burden of expensive promises to the electorate, which would soon force it to beg the International Monetary Fund for a loan. So Labour was even less likely to put on brakes in the North Sea. On the contrary, offering generous licences and all other conceivable incentives to rapid progress, it did just what the Seven Sisters wanted it to do. Hence the relentless, racking toil of the men on Piper Alpha. Oil and gas had to be got out, whatever the cost.[3]

Still, there were better reasons for the policy. To Scots oil seemed a godsend after every other expedient had failed to save their economy. Nobody yet dared admit it in public, but all the traditional heavy industries – coal, steel, shipbuilding – were on their last legs. Oil would without doubt transform the economy of the north of Scotland. It might also bring back factories and jobs to the central belt.

But this turned out to be another false promise. The requirement for speedy development revealed a chasm between the antiquated capabilities of the Scottish economy and the North Sea's needs for advanced technology, skilled personnel and financial resources. Such things did not exist in Scotland. Politicians thought oil would boost demand for, say, steel from Lanarkshire, but this was not what happened. The industry there made the wrong steel and had neither skills nor equipment to turn it into platforms and pipelines. The River Clyde was too narrow and too distant from the oilfields to vie with new yards that sprang up in the east of Scotland and in Norway to construct the rigs. The Seven Sisters themselves had no special interest in Scotland, any more than in Venezuela or Nigeria: unless the local economy could at once supply what was needed, they brought it in from outside. In a decade of intense development Scottish companies met under a quarter of all orders for the North Sea, although for the Highlands this still offered a third of all manufacturing jobs.[4]

This decade of development ended in 1985 with a split in OPEC, when the Saudis announced they would no longer observe the quotas for production which had kept up the price of oil. Within a year or so it plummeted to $6 a barrel. The Seven Sisters' income halved. They had to shelve future plans, slash outlays and end drilling. In Scotland visible signs of new prosperity vanished. Yards at Ardersier, Dundee, Loch Kishorn, Nigg and Stornoway suffered huge redundancies. Dozens of local firms that had grown up in the boom went bust. Production often kept going only because facilities for it were too costly and complex to abandon – such as Piper Alpha, an ageing piece of machinery which its owners might as well allow to run on until it broke down.

The death of 167 men made it bigger than a breakdown, more of an awful reckoning for ambitions reaching too high. Perhaps it even represented another defeat for Scotland. Now the euphoria was over, Scots thought they had missed their chance to muscle in on oil and create a new industry in place of those lost. The chance would never recur. A bonanza would have come and gone, leaving next to no mark on Scotland except for blights on the landscape and mourning for the dead under the sea.

Yet in the long run the gloomy predictions have not been borne out. Aberdeen and its environs flourish still, if more quietly than in the early 1980s. Scots companies have found niches in the global business of oil, although hardly ones to rival the Seven Sisters: that would never have been possible, though, for they came in as a mature industry, with which local yokels could only compete in the odd bits that were as yet immature. There have been plenty of these, however. The results are not seen in the metal-bashing extraction of raw materials from the earth by muscle-bound men pitting themselves against brute nature and sometimes losing. That had been an old Scotland, and here was a new Scotland in the making.[5]

The contribution to it of the North Sea has been to generate, where none existed before, capital, enterprise and development that owe nothing to the state. Scots had grown used to feeling miserable about themselves, but this contribution made those under its direct influence feel good about themselves and their country, as one with a future. Some feel so good as to believe Scotland could be an independent nation. It is perhaps no coincidence that these feelings have arisen at their strongest among people in the region of Scotland most affected by oil, the north-east. But Highlanders, too, reached the highest level of wealth and prosperity in their history; just as well, because the British government would no longer subsidize them as it had in the past. Indeed the psychology of the whole Scottish nation altered for the better. Nothing on earth consoles for death except the idea that it leaves room for new life.

So life and death commingled in the Highlands and islands. Oil did revive the Northern Isles, Orkney and Shetland. In these pages they have been a bit neglected, but their culture was not Celtic and their economy, if quite like the adjacent mainland's, had been more caught up in the Victorian expansion of seaborne commerce. Orkney invested the proceeds in agriculture. Cattle, fattened on sown grasses and roots, were shipped live to Aberdeen or Leith for export: to this day Orcadian calves supply juicy steaks that in Italy are turned into *vitello a la milanese*.[6] In Shetland local power passed the other way, from agricultural to mercantile interests, as in the rise of Arthur Anderson, founder of the shipping line Peninsular & Orient (P&O); today it may profit more from exotic cruises for glitterati, but it also still runs ferries for the folk of the islands. These saw depopulation too, yet their culture proved resilient enough to withstand it.[7] The years up to 1914 witnessed a Shetlandic Renaissance stressing, in reaction to modern upheavals, continuities in the way of life since Viking times. Gilbert Goudie surveyed the antiquities, right back to brochs of the Stone Age, while Lawrence Williamson collected the oral heritage of song and story, giving it a place in ethnological scholarship. Jakob Jakobsen, a Faroese, described the Norse nature of the dialect, while Haldane Burgess wrote in it a poetry of social criticism:

> Dis aristocracies is bit
> Da dokkin on da skroo [the dock in the corn].[8]

By contrast Orcadian culture remained insular until it flowered in the late twentieth century with the limpid prose and verse of George Mackay Brown, joining literature to history, lyricism to realism: an inspiration besides to the composer Peter Maxwell-Davies, who sought creative solitude on Hoy.

Orcadians and Shetlanders had always felt different from Scots, and at times not a little hostile to them. Just as the nationalist bandwagon began to roll on the mainland in the 1970s, so there arose a movement in the Northern Isles for autonomy. It was driven by a feeling that rule from Edinburgh would be no better than half as remote as rule from London (itself more remote than Oslo). In scattered settlements the islanders still lived from crofting, fisheries and knitwear, on Orkney from distilleries and stock-farming too. Oil made a bigger impact on Shetland, where the population soared and incomes one third below the Scottish average moved ahead of it. A canny local council took care to spread the benefits over the public services and to the outlying islands. It acquired powers of compulsory purchase to buy land for development, aiming to minimize the disturbance to the old way of life and maximize the return from the new one. It struck deals with the Seven Sisters and with HM Treasury. Soon 90 per cent of its revenue came in some way from oil. The islanders' sound good sense won praise in parts of Scotland where the boom was less well handled.

In crofting areas of the mainland, death in life continued. Until the oil was found, the Highland population had still been falling, from 293,000 in 1931 to 286,000 in 1951 and to 278,000 in 1961.[9] Now along the eastern seaboard the trend was reversed, with Inverness becoming an unlovely centre of private manufacturing and services for the North Sea second only to Aberdeen, as well as the seat of a new public administration for the whole region, in place of the historic counties. By 1981 the Highland population had risen 6000 to 284,000, the first increase in a century. Inverness alone accounted for 5000 of it. Growth at the centre was offset by decline at the edge. Along the western seaboard the boom spreading out coastwise from the North Sea came and went with little effect. What there was of one arrived not at an individual or social level, but in legislation and policy.

The state had guided Highland development since 1886, without solving the problems of remoteness, congestion and backwardness. From the Second World War it stepped up the effort. The appeal in any proposal for Tom Johnston, then Scottish Secretary, always waxed with its waywardness. One was for the North of Scotland Hydro-electric Board, founded in 1943. It had the task of taking Highland water in all its superfluity and turning it into electricity, which was short and could be used for economic development. But the technicians who, of necessity, then built the dams, tamed the torrents, installed the plant and generated the energy showed no concern with anything beyond that. An industrial revolution did not follow.[10]

Another commission on the crofting counties sat in 1951–4 under Thomas Taylor, Principal of the University of Aberdeen. One member was Scotland's foremost economist, Sir Alexander Cairncross, an architect of British victory during the Second World War. The Highlands proved more resistant to him than Adolf Hitler, but Cairncross raised basic questions about the merits of a regional regime applying rigid regulation to remote areas of falling population and high costs. The questions were never answered. Cairncross supposed he and his fellows would inquire how the regime might become more productive, say, by the amalgamation of crofts into larger units or the introduction of new employment: 'It was not apparent what we could usefully recommend. Our chairman was obviously anxious to report in favour of the industrial development of the Highlands as a supplement to the limited possibilities offered by crofting.' But this meant investors with money, and 'if it took a steady flow of millionaires to run factories in the Highlands, we might as well forget about industrial development.'[11]

In its report the commission bypassed the problems with ringing declarations, probably from the pen of another member, the novelist Neil Gunn: 'In the national interest the maintenance of these [crofting] communities is desirable, because they embody a free and independent way of life which in a civilization predominantly urban and industrial in character is worth preserving for its own intrinsic quality.' While people needed to work together, 'the crofter calls no man his master'. The blithe conclusion, typical of the time, was that he needed nevertheless a quango to safeguard his interests and encourage co-operation with his fellows. In 1955 Parliament passed a new act which allowed crofts to be combined and created local committees to supervise grazings. All this was to come under a resurrected Crofters Commission of non-elected officials.[12]

Only in name was it a successor to the Crofters Commission of 1886, which had spent most of its energies fixing rents before being scrapped in 1912. Residual functions then passed to a Board of Agriculture, which in turn meandered over time into the Scottish Office. There seemed, forty years on, no good reason for crofting to be supervised from Edinburgh. Policy now was to subsidize large-scale farming, and crofts did not fit into this. Better they should be corralled under a quango of their own, far away.

Policy was already causing decay in the crofting system and by extension in the society it was meant to sustain. The *Third Statistical Account* reported of Glenshiel a 'marked decline in crofting throughout the parish'. In Lochbroom the area under cultivation shrank: 'Crofting land on the Rhidorroch estate has been resumed for holiday homes and recreational purposes', while 'a large area at Braes has been decrofted to allow the building of private houses' and in Coigach crofts 'were bought by people from the south who have either settled there or use the houses as holiday homes'. A related effect was for the culture to decline. Gaels ceased to use their language in public places and reserved it for the home. In Argyll even at ceilidhs, 'old Gaelic songs in their English words are sometimes sung, but the most popular songs are those of Burns'. One minister in the county thought 'the importance of English for education, commerce and intercourse with visitors has been too much for the ancient tongue. Parents do not teach it to their children, nor do the children wish to learn it; if any did speak it, the other children would just tease them about it.'[13]

In Coigach, to take an example of a picturesque district, incomers would before long form a majority. Most, contrary to a common assumption, were not English but Scots, and did their best to fit in by boozing with the natives and learning their language, only to find that nobody would speak it back to them. But with this merest patina of assimilation they might assume local leadership from the bashful Gaels, here and elsewhere: 'The key posts are held by the incomers, both in the community and in the church', said a report from Islay. At any rate the English seemed more visible, 'affluent and arrogant . . . retiring to pleasant havens where they bid up house prices and adopt patronizing attitudes to the natives'. These were the infamous white settlers. At Duthil and Rothiemurchus, in Strathspey, 'about 10 per cent of the population are true natives, that is, they were not only born in the parish but are descended from either both or one parent who has had roots in Duthil soil for generations'. In Laggan, stretching through the middle of western Inverness-shire, 'the percentage of people born in the parish is now rather low, not more than 20 per cent at most. Indeed, it has been remarked by a present inhabitant that the reason the people of Laggan agree so well is that they are all incomers.' The English-born population grew in 1961–81 from 6 to 9 per cent in Argyll, 4 to 10 per cent in Sutherland, 2 to 9 per cent in Orkney and 3 to 12 per cent in Shetland.[14]

In places with no pretty scenery crofters were left more to themselves. But here, too, they often sub-let the croft and went off to do something useful, as at Farr in Sutherland:

The sub-tenant has many of the rights of the true crofter but lacks security of tenure and therefore, like the tenants at will prior to the Crofting Acts, has little incentive to improve the ground. This single fact accounts for the lack of effort on some of the arable ground.

On Islay things had moved an entire stage further on: in contrast to the usual Highland pattern of coastal crofts aligned in strips with no clustered settlements, 'the population is dispersed in medium to large farms round the industrial villages', where distilleries offered jobs to those not living off the land. The writer on Tongue put matters plainly: 'Crofting has now largely become a hobby or a perk.'[15]

Had it not been for that act of 1955, the evolution might have run its course and given crofting its quietus within a generation or two. The new Crofters Commission resolved to arrest the process. If nobody could be sure how it should set about the job, advice was not lacking. The writer on Gairloch in the *Third Statistical Account* said: 'The need to rehabilitate the crofts as the basis of the communal life is apparent. Early marriage must be encouraged as it implies a home and assumed secondary employment which must be part-time or piecework if the croft receives primary attention.' It is worth recalling the article on Gairloch in the *New Statistical Account* of 1836, where the minister said of distress among the soaring population of his day: 'The causes of the increase are various. Among these may be mentioned the habit of early marriage, and the system of letting lands in lots' – in other words, subdivision of crofts.[16]

Most reports written out of any expertise on the Highlands still waxed gloomy on the prospects. Farquhar Gillanders, a Gael from Wester Ross, was a forthright observer who thought the Crofters Act had been a disaster: 'The 1886 legislation heralded the death of crofting as a way of life, insulating it almost completely from normal economic trends and *legally* ensuring that crofting land could not now be developed into viable economic units.' If there was hope for the Highlands, it lay in 'the simple courage to implement proved economic principles. The Highlander must cease to regard himself as a member of a chosen race to whom normal economic laws do not apply.' A young economist from Aberdeen, Donald MacKay, concluded that the one safe bet for economic regeneration would be a big development of manufacturing industry. But its high cost demanded sacrifice of opportunities in more favoured parts of Britain, and so could not be justified on economic grounds.[17]

Other counsels prevailed, however. Among the oddballs Johnston had patronized was an English ecologist, Frank Fraser Darling.[18] The Secretary of State hauled him from his seclusion on the Tanera Isles off Wester Ross, where he meant to sit out the war while learning 'to love universally and not selfishly'. Johnston wanted his advice on better management of crofts and so made him director of the West Highland Survey, launching him on a career of bureaucratic authoritarianism that left a durable legacy to the region. Darling never went back to the simple crofting life. Once in a position of power, he spoke no longer of universal love. Instead he treated his work as 'a problem of human ecology [which] involves the state of men's minds'. He was the first to see the Highlands as a 'great, outdoor laboratory' and Highlanders as subjects of his experiments. At first they scorned his advice, while experts ignored his findings.[19] The book he published out of his research, *Natural History in the Highlands and Islands* (1947), was panned by those who knew anything of the subject, but Darling later got his own back. He exulted when in 1949 the Nature Conservancy was founded by royal charter. Now the Scots would have to do as they were told:

> The establishment of the Nature Conservancy is the most considerable event in British natural history in this century; especially so for Scotland, and most especially for the Highlands and Islands . . . [It] operates through-out Great Britain, Scotland having a headquarters in Edinburgh but with little autonomous power. Nevertheless, Scotland can have no valid grumble over the degree to which her wildlife, vegetation and land is being conserved and brought into National Nature Reserves.[20]

Arrogation of power by quangos would become a big Highland problem. For example, the Crofters Commission had managed to conquer any internal qualms about its appointed tasks by the time, in 1968, it was seeking something more than a merely administrative role. It advised Labour's Secretary of State for Scotland, William Ross, that crofters should gain complete rights of ownership. A consequent act of 1976 laid down a procedure for this, giving them the chance to buy their croft at a price equivalent to fifteen times the annual rent – rather than, for instance, at the price it would fetch on the market. They were also to be entitled to half the value of any development on land they took out of crofting. While Ross called it a 'watershed in crofting history', his modest deregulation had critics. Highland radicals wanted nationalization of land, and he was going in the opposite direction. Others feared he had given the kiss of death to crofting: the temptation to sell land for development might prove irresistible and, since no creation of new crofts was allowed for, the crofting areas would contract. Yet nothing much happened. Overall, the act failed to turn crofters into owner-occupiers capable of going into business (in North Sea oil, for example) or selling to others ready to develop their land. Take-up of the option to buy was low. Most crofters remained crofters because the balance of advantage still lay in doing so.

In the 1960s, with a romantic return to nature and the belief that politicians could run the economy better than capitalists, the Highlands had seemed ripe for attention on both courts. Labour proposed that, until the Greek kalends when local agriculture became more productive, 'a modest intermediate expansion of manufacturing employment will be necessary to ensure that the population structure of the region does not run down to an extent which would jeopardize the ultimate supply of labour on an adequate scale'.[21] To fulfil this aim Ross set up the Highlands and Islands Development Board in 1965. In it he invested personal emotion as well as public money; the one came cheaper than the other. Winding up a debate on the legislation, he said:

> If there is bitterness in my voice, I can assure the House there is bitterness in Scotland too when we recollect the history of these areas. We have nine million acres where 225,000 people live, and we are short of land. Land is the basic natural resource of the Highlands and any plan for economic and social development would be meaningless if proper use of the land were not part of it.[22]

The Highland Board, charged with making sense of nonsense, took refuge in the nostrums of regional policy, an economic sub-discipline that had only recently arisen but was now nearing the height of what intellectual influence it ever attained. On its for the moment fashionable analysis the Highlands fell into the same category as the sunny Mezzogiorno of Italy, Norway beyond the Arctic Circle, Friesland behind the Dutch dikes or the Republic of Ireland – which was still a backward European country in its entirety thanks to forty years of official favour to peasant agriculture. Yet geographic remoteness did not have to insulate these regions, it was argued. In an open economy such as Britain's the winds of the market always blew and could transform the Highlands too. The need was to diversify their economy and produce a spread of growth, with flourishing new activities able to replace faltering old ones. This would also alter the archaic mentality of the crofting counties.

In reality the Highland Board followed disparate policies during the respective terms of its early chairmen. The first was Sir Robert Grieve, promoted from chief planner at the Scottish Office. He set off by treating the Highlands as if they were the Lowlands. He adopted a programme of industrial development, new towns and what not taken straight from the Central Belt of Scotland. He decided manufacturing industries for the north would best be concentrated in 'growth points', where by achieving economies of scale they could overcome the penalties of distance from markets. This was not so different from what James Loch had tried in Sutherland 150 years earlier, and equally implied depopulation in the hinterland to 'growth points'. Grieve chose Fort William for one of them and got things going with a pulp and paper mill built at nearby Corpach. It never worked at full capacity, not least because forests planted in the surroundings had no time to mature. Its process of chemical pulping was soon superseded by mechanical pulping, which rendered its technology obsolete and unable to compete with more efficient Scandinavian factories. It closed in 1981 at a cost of 900 jobs, at the mill and in small businesses grown up in dependence on it.[23]

The second chairman in 1970–6 was the ebullient but bad-tempered Sir Andrew Gilchrist, who had made his name as defender of British fishermen while ambassador to Iceland during the Cod Wars a decade or more before. He drew the fire of Gaels, notably Professor Derick Thomson, professor of Celtic at Glasgow, for being another Lowlander, by origin a fruit farmer from Lanark. 'The revival of prosperity in the Long Island [Lewis and Harris] was the thing closest to my heart when I was chairman of the Highland Board,' Gilchrist wrote, 'and I saw no better way than the Atlantic fishery for achieving this result.'[24] How far that went will be discussed later, but meanwhile he had the privilege of opening in 1972 the aluminium smelter at Invergordon. This was another product of his predecessor's planning, meant to cut the cost of a vital but expensive import. Ever since 1905 the metal had been processed on Loch Ness by the British Aluminium Company, which thought to have found at the Falls of Foyers an equivalent to Niagara in America, where there was a similar operation. Its smelter never attained the output envisaged for the new site in Easter Ross, which boasted no waterfalls. Power still had to come cheap if British Aluminium was to compete with foreign rivals, so it could contemplate setting up at Invergordon only if supplies of electricity were subsidized. Even with subsidies, however, it never made a profit there. In 1981 a Tory government refused to subsidize the plant further and it shut.

The third chairman from 1976 was Sir Kenneth Alexander, professor of economics at the University of Strathclyde and a former Communist, though more kindly and self-questioning than that might imply. His youthful radicalism survived in a desire to make an example of bad Highland landlords. He set his sights on Dr John Green, resident of Sussex and owner of the big house on Raasay, the island of Sorley MacLean. But the Highland Board's lawyers told Alexander he had not the powers to acquire this property. A plot or strip might be bought for a school or road, but if the matter went to law no court would allow compulsory purchase of more land than was necessary for some such specific purpose. To widen his remit Alexander would have to turn to the Conservative government. George Younger, the Secretary of State and a landowner himself, refused to hear of extending the board's powers when it had not used the powers it already possessed.[25]

Too many policies always risk contradicting one another, so that they come to nothing or even do damage. Of this Scottish fisheries now offered a prime example. Highlanders had not always exploited their seas as they might have done. But after 1945 came steady if unspectacular growth in commercial fishing from northern waters, for herring in summer, for white fish all year round, then for industrial produce, Norway pout and sand-eels, to be reduced to meal and oil for fertilizer or animal fodder. This fishery required heavy investment, a burden to the individuals and communities that had to undertake it, though the Highland Board would in due course step in to offer aid. So the fishery, in expanding, also grew more confined to people or places able to equip themselves with boats and gear. While Aberdeen had a head start, Kinlochbervie and Ullapool on the Atlantic coast were among ports that underwent development, even if vessels working out of them often also arrived from the east. The number of full-time fishermen in the Highlands rose to 3000 by 1979, and many other jobs depended on them in remote spots where alternatives were rare.

On this modestly prosperous scene burst, like a bombshell, British entry to the European Community in 1973. Diplomats from the Foreign Office in London who negotiated the treaty betrayed the fishermen's interest. Existing members of the Community had, just before, cobbled together the rudiments of a Common Fisheries Policy. It enacted equal rights of access to inshore waters 'up to the beaches', as was said. Norway, faced with this demand, refused to go into Europe at all and stays out to this day, without regret. Britain, anxious to get in on other grounds, with difficulty won postponement for ten years of unrestricted access to her waters by any and every boat from the rest of the member countries. This offered a breathing space during which a less harmful common policy might have been devised, but never was. The consequence came, under feeble regulation from Brussels, in constant over-fishing of Scottish waters, most blatantly by foreign skippers. A large part both of the stocks of fish and of the local fishing fleet vanished, with dire effects not countered by the novelty of fish-farming. Now the grants came for boats and gear to be taken out of commission. A way forward for the Highland economy was barred.[26]

Compensation might have been found from European regional policy. But Highlanders, if eloquent in bemoaning their fate, no longer figured among the poorer populations of the Community, not with the boom in oil. Their economy had stopped lagging, not only on the eastern side but even on the western side, in Islay and Skye. While they suffered from remoteness and dispersal, this did not keep their incomes as low as in Calabria or Connaught. The rules had to be bent to let them within the ranks of Europe's waifs. This was congenial to the Prime Minister, Margaret Thatcher, for Britain had made the largest contribution of all the member states to the European budget: she supported anything likely to screw more out of Brussels. After her fall the British government remained eager to keep the cost of membership down. It still had, at the European summit in Edinburgh in 1992, to accept an increase in so-called structural funds, meant to reduce economic disparities. In exchange, one additional British region was to be counted among those eligible for the money. Mrs Thatcher's successor, John Major, chose the Highlands, famous for being distant, empty, windswept, mournful and so forth, even though now there were other, poorer parts of Scotland that got nothing: changed days indeed.

20

The land's for the people
The Highlands under devolution

O N THE AFTERNOON of 8 December 1992 Simon Fraser, a lawyer who specialized in crofting cases, was at work in his office overlooking the harbour at Stornoway, Lewis, when the telephone rang. The call told him of success for long, often fraught negotiations on behalf of the Assynt Crofters' Trust. He was representing it in a bid to buy North Lochinver, an estate of 21,000 acres on the Atlantic coast of Sutherland. He at once passed the good news on to John MacKenzie, an officer of the trust, who was at his home in Assynt, at the township of Culkein Drumbeg, with a television crew waiting beside him. Fraser then left by air for a meeting with the full trust. Lewis and Assynt face each other across the Minch, but the journey meant a flight to Inverness and a drive back from one side of mainland Scotland to the other, so he would arrive at his destination only after night fell.

Meanwhile the good news spread through the townships of Assynt, a peninsula 10 miles long by 4 miles wide, with a single-track road running round it. MacKenzie would recall how he at first felt a sense of anticlimax and no special elation, but the next morning he looked out from his croft and realized what had been achieved. Allan MacRae, another officer of the trust, was at work on the bridge at Lochinver when he heard. His sense of anticlimax was not so deep as to stop him ringing friends and relations to say, 'We've got the land. The word has just come through.' For their fellow officer Bill Ritchie it also took a while to sink in: 'The next day, walking out over the land, it was just awesome. To think we had actually pulled it off, that this was for the first time ever, in legal terms anyway, the crofters'. That the crofters could get up in the morning and say this is ours. That was a huge, magnificent feeling.'

Later on 8 December the trust held a meeting in the school at the village of Stoer, made an official announcement and then – with the crofters themselves, with sundry supporters and with a bevvy of journalists – set out to celebrate as only Scots can. In December the sun sets in Sutherland at about four o'clock in the afternoon, yet photographs of the jubilant revellers, bottles of whisky in hand, were taken in daylight – presumably that next morning when their new situation had at last sunk in. At the ceilidh a crofter's daughter, Isobel MacPhail, sang a song composed to the tune of 'For These are my Mountains':

> For these are my mountains
> And the crofts we all ken,
> The land's for the people,
> Not for sale yet again.
> So the crofters of Assynt
> All met in the school –
> The land's for the people
> Not for landlords to rule.

Such were the amiable sentiments being implanted in the breasts of Highland youth. But many other Scots rejoiced with the crofters of Assynt. Brian Wilson, a Labour MP and in a previous existence founder of the radical newspaper the *West Highland Free Press*, declared their success to be 'something of genuine historical importance . . . far more meaningful than all the pomp and flummery of transient summits and royal occasions' (he was presumably referring to the European Council held that year in Edinburgh and to the announcement, the following day, of the separation of the Prince and Princess of Wales).[1]

It had been six months since the owners of North Lochinver, Scandinavian Property Services UK, made known that they were going out of business and disposing of their assets. They had acquired the estate some years earlier from Lord Vestey, who came from a Liverpudlian family with a fortune made out of butchery. The company leased the shootings to wealthy Danes or Swedes, but the business had not flourished. Now the estate was to be divided and sold in seven lots: nothing novel in that, for traditional Highland estates are seldom profitable. Most struggle to break even, and many make a loss. Figures, hard to come by, are at least known for those owned by the government, which gets about £150,000 a year in rent from crofts but spends £370,000 in administration. Here was a wide gap for any commercial outfit to close.[2]

In the past crofters had always felt obliged just to put up with the operation of the free market as it affected them, being unable or unwilling to join it themselves. In more recent times they and their sympathizers have often attacked Highland landlords for stunting development by running their estates with an eye to profit out of the pleasures of plutocrats. The rights of property basic to the capitalist system were therefore held to be robbing the land of what productive uses it might ever afford, quite in line with Marxist theory. Although these productive uses are few, the controversy steadily invested the concept of communal ownership of land in Scotland with an aura of moral superiority over private ownership.

Now the people of Assynt could look for advice and support to the Scottish Crofters' Union, founded in 1985. For North Lochinver it briskly knocked together a scheme to stop the estate being partitioned and bring it into communal ownership. The Assynt Crofters' Trust was then founded to promote the idea and launch a public appeal for it. The fund-raising went well, and the trust got a grant from Highland and Islands Enterprise, successor to the Highland Board, for a modish 'pilot project to collect information on the performance of a crofting estate owned and managed by local people'. Also available was a loan of £90,000 from Highland Prospect, an investment company set up by the regional council in Inverness. Another grant of £20,000 came from a quango, Scottish National Heritage. A price for the estate of £300,000 was at length struck with the principal creditor of Scandinavian Property Services.

The trust as a legal matrix for crofters' communal ownership of the land where they lived, if a fledgeling in the Highlands, quickly took wing. It appeared to offer a golden mean between private ownership, with all its chequered history, and the nationalization that some agrarian socialists had advocated since the Second World War but which was by this time not much of a practical proposition.

The communal concept took wing on Eigg, for example. It is a small isle which had escaped the greatest historical misfortunes but still been largely depopulated by the turn of the twentieth century, and yet more so afterwards. When an American economist, Russell Kirk, visited it in 1950, he observed that 'the income of one of the poorest sharecroppers of Georgia would greatly exceed the currency the Eigg families see from one year's end to the next'.[3] Prospects brightened when Keith Schellenberg, a vegetarian businessman from Yorkshire, bought the island in 1975. He set out to improve and repopulate it. He called in the Scottish Wildlife Trust, banned all shooting, arranged for a full-time warden and encouraged the official designation of Sites of Special Scientific Interest. To every appearance he was a good Highland landlord of the sort so long lacking. But amid mounting problems he sold out in 1995 to a German sculptor, Marlin Eckhart Maruma, who reverted to the ways of the absentee. In 1996 the Scottish Wildlife Trust took matters in hand and led a public appeal for £800,000 to buy the island from him and hand it over to the islanders, claiming that 'a history of neglect at the hands of largely absentee private owners has brought Eigg to the brink of ecological collapse'. Schellenberg sued the trust for libel; it did not defend the action, admitted liability, paid all costs and published an apology. That did not impede the appeal. The biggest donor was an affiliate of Highland and Islands Enterprise, Lochaber Ltd, which gave £250,000 to, among other things, a co-operative for crafts, a mature timber study, a field study centre and a tea-room at the pier. Highlands and Islands Enterprise was also a big donor in its own right, to a business plan and to the ambition of one resident to turn his barn into boarding for backpackers. The twenty households on Eigg in effect got £20,000 a year each from the appeal. So it has gone on: the Heritage Lottery Fund gave £90,000 just to finance further proposals for grants. Meanwhile ownership passed to the Isle of Eigg Heritage Trust, controlled as to 50 per cent by the islanders and as to 25 per cent each by the Highland Regional Council and the Scottish Wildlife Trust. The trustees of Eigg possess plenary power over who may or may not live there. They have turned down more than thirty applications from would-be incomers, with the result that the population remains static, while under Schellenberg it had doubled.[4]

Prompted by Wilson, the Labour Party was now dropping broad hints that it would find means to support tenants' buy-outs of Highland estates once it came to power again. The governing Conservatives, making heavy weather as a small electoral minority in Scotland, were in their turn already inclined to accept a case for special treatment of the Highlands in defiance of the principles of capitalism. Over vast tracts of the region capitalism did not rule anyway: for example, on estates owned by the Forestry Commission under its unprofitable and subsidized regime, or in private forests used as tax havens. There was a ditty said to ring round stately homes of Scotland:

> Oh woodman, spare that tree!
> Lop not a single bough!
> From tax it sheltered me,
> So I'll protect it now.

The commission had long been buying estates and covering them in conifers. With this monoculture it altered the landscape of hill or moor in a way that many Scots found obnoxious. But, vaunting itself on its strategic national task (saving imports of timber), it seldom took local interests into account and created only meagre employment: there are, after all, few less labour-intensive activities than planting trees and watching them grow for a half a century. For instance, the commission owned much of Mull, a large, forlorn and almost deserted island, of which the final depopulation had gone on only in the twentieth century, not least because the high costs of farming there made it hard for the islanders to compete with forestry. Once again these were victims of improvement, squeezed out of a utilitarian, and now ugly, landscape. Although in the face of criticism the commission started to pay some attention to aesthetics and recreation, 'this experiment in state ownership has not been a success', wrote one academic commentator.[5] To the desperate Tories, then, there could at least be little harm in passing the Crofter Forestry Act of 1991. Grants for planting trees so far available to landlords were offered to crofters on their common grazing land too, so long as the owner of the estate agreed: this meant, however, that some tried to impose onerous conditions. The act accordingly led to another initiative in communal ownership on Skye in 1993, at the townships of Borve and Annishadder. There, again in tangled negotiations, tenants first failed to persuade the landowner, Major John Macdonald, of the merits of their proposed project of forestry, but then did reach an ageement with him to acquire the land outright.[6]

Evolution of the communal concept came in Knoydart, the history of which has been outlined above from the time when it formed a fastness for the MacDonells of Clanranald down through the Bairds and the Brockets. By the 1990s it was home to just two or three dozen people, not one of them descended from any of the hundreds who had lived there until the mid-nineteenth century. Originating in Knoydart, an obscure case was wending its way through the legal system, to end in an appeal to the Court of Session. The judgment there stood on its head one conventional interpretation of the Crofters Act of 1976, that a crofter buying his croft and then decrofting part of it for development should pay half the increase in value to the landlord. From now on, if the crofter could transfer his land to a trust, the landlord would get no more than fifteen times the annual rent. So this bypassed him to move straight on from individual crofting to communal ownership. Not surprisingly, the proprietors of Knoydart lost interest in their estate. In 1999 they sold its 17,000 acres for £850,000 to the trust set up by local people. These promptly started planting trees.[7]

Similar examples followed in Sutherland, Skye, Lewis and other districts. When Labour did come to power in 1997, the appointment of Wilson as a Minister of State at the Scottish Office assured official support for communal ownership. He asked Highland and Islands Enterprise to set up a unit to conduct experiments in the concept. Labour soon adopted it as the flagship of a general land reform. For want of any better notion the other parties tagged along – Tories too. Soon after the Scottish Parliament was set up in 1999, the Minister of Justice, James Wallace, a Liberal Democrat, produced a white paper which he forecast would portend a rapid change in the pattern of ownership in Scotland.[8]

Scots law had always been good at inhibiting rapid change, or any change at all, in ownership of land. It was drawn up expressly to protect proprietors against greedy kings or thuggish neighbours but in the long run had the effect of curbing commercial transactions too. During the last 400 years only one third of the country has ever been bought or sold, although more of the Highlands than of other regions. Wide Lowland tracts belonging for generations to a single family show the results of careful husbandry keeping rural communities alive. Now the market was to be weighted in favour of buyers, which would normally cause the already thin flow of sellers to dry up. Wallace's white paper proposed that communities in the Scottish countryside, defined as some minimal proportion of local residents, would be able to register an interest in a particular piece of land, even if this should mean nothing until its owner decided to sell it. Then the community would get first refusal, though, at a price set by an official valuer.

But there was to be a special dispensation for the Highlands. Wallace further proposed that crofting townships could at any time start the process of taking over land they lived on, so long as they met certain (in the event quite strict) conditions. At the time of writing, this provision has not yet entered into force, so it remains to be seen how, or if, it can revolutionize a region where little land is owned by the same people as owned it a hundred or even fifty years ago. What crofters acquire will still have to be paid for, albeit at a price rigged by the valuer. It seems improbable that any rapid improvement can follow on estates thus deprived of capital injections from outside, which are what private purchasers willy-nilly provide. The legislation mentions official financial aid, and a Scottish Land Fund has been set up with money from the National Lottery. Other quangos, vital in the case of Assynt, will hardly again be as generous as they were there. In that event this political experiment cannot be sustained without the fund. Yet in 2004 it announced it was about to run out of cash. The Scottish Executive said it would get no more.

Crofters' trusts are not the only ones active in devolved Scotland. There is also a more normal type known elsewhere in Britain: the charitable trust for some general purpose, including conservation. Such trusts have acquired big Highland properties. There is the Royal Society for the Protection of Birds, founded in 1889 to stop trade in the feathers of the egret. Having won that point, it sought other outlets for its zeal. Now, from a base in Bedfordshire, it runs twenty-eight Highland reserves. There is the National Trust for Scotland, founded in 1931 to save great houses from their owners' folly. Unable to separate the natural from the built environment, it has become a huge landlord too, unlike its English counterpart. It owns the islands of Berneray, Canna, Fair Isle, Iona, Mingulay, Pabbay, St Kilda, Staffa and on the mainland the estates of Kintail (18,000 acres), Torridon (16,000 acres) and Glencoe (14,000 acres), to name only the largest. There is the Scottish Wildlife Trust, already mentioned in the case of Eigg; it is the proprietor besides of Handa, Shillay and the estate of Benmore Coigach in Wester Ross. There is the John Muir Trust, named after the son of East Lothian who pioneered American conservation, established for the protection of wilderness by a circle of Scots lawyers in 1983. It has bought Ben Nevis, Schiehallion and a brace of mountains in Knoydart, together with three contiguous estates on Skye, including Strathaird, over which Sir Archibald Geikie had long ago lamented. Finally there is a quango, with a different legal status, Scottish National Heritage, formed in 1992 from the Countryside Commission for Scotland and the Nature Conservancy Council, once warmly welcomed by Frank Fraser Darling. It combines the roles of adviser to government and executive for conservatory intervention.[9]

Intervention is not universally welcomed by Highlanders, however. They often take a different idea of their interests from the one a public trust espouses. Coigach, for example, has little chance of ever becoming an idyllically self-sufficient rural community; it is a picturesque but poor wee place, scattered over a wet and windswept brae. When I went there a couple of years ago for the main attraction, the hotel at Achiltibuie and its renowned cuisine, I found my fellow guests divided into two camps.[10] The English tourists felt shocked at such a scruffy village. The weekenders from Glasgow or Aberdeen took pleasure in informing them that Scotland was a scruffy kind of country with none of the manicured hedgerows or honeysuckle they had in, say, Sussex; if they did not like it, they could always push off back to England. The division of opinion in the hotel reflected a wider one outside. Coigach, according to sociologists, follows a way of life more varied than in earlier times, yet this no longer offers any obvious social bond. Most people are manual workers, yet they share few common tasks. They mix readily, yet observe boundaries among themselves, of which the most important is not of class or occupation, but between locals and incomers. These last, having been a mere dozen or so in the 1960s, numbered 156 out of 262 inhabitants of the district by 1989.[11]

The locals led a life in common with the others in Coigach, but also a life of their own to which incomers were not admitted. This had an effect when the Scottish Wildlife Trust acquired the estate of Benmore stretching up behind Achiltibuie. Crofters enjoy the same status under a public trust as under a private landlord. Those of Coigach were not going to surrender their right to put sheep on common grazings – 97 per cent of the estate's area – without good reason or adequate compensation. The trust wanted to plant trees to restore 'the biological productivity' of the ground. Yet trees must be fenced from sheep and deer, and land from which sheep are shut out has no value to crofters. Without leave from the grazing committees of the local townships nothing could be changed. To the trust's dismay it found its rights of ownership were limited to collection of rents and sale of stalking or fishing rights. Everything else had to be done by agreement with the crofters. Doubtless all trusts are well-meaning, but the experience of this one goes to show that people who treat the land as an object of conservation have a more detached relationship to it than those who work it for a living, just as both are different again from those who treat it as a commercial asset.

Owners or managers of private estates had been the first to feel the thrust of the forces of conservation. The Highland Council patronized a Not-for-Profit Landowners' Project Group. It was made up largely of personnel from the public trusts, which had no problem of low profits because they refrained from improvement and called for aid when needing to invest. Many private estates could also be profitable if turned into trusts for native fauna and flora, with no tax owed, no crops grown, all old skills vanished, all livestock sold off and land deer-fenced – while the owners sat back to watch forests grow and collect subsidies. The trusts' staffs work as custodians of nature but can hardly avoid wielding bureaucratic power in remote communities if these do not share the aims of conservation. Usually members of the staffs, some Scots but many English, do not stay long enough in any one place to get to the bottom of its way of life, to the vexation of the natives. These have never seen the environment as inviolable, but have built a robust relationship with it that makes sure of room for its human as well as its natural elements. The modern idea of conservation as a sacred ecological duty, if it does not just fail, can only destroy an old, intimate relation between people and nature which created the paradise the incomers seek to save.[12]

So the crofters' lives have not necessarily been made easier by the trusts, of either sort. As communal owners they must still penetrate thickets of regulation, many of which were deliberately planted long ago to ensnare economic and social change. Crofters must also come to terms, like their former landlords, with the law on common grazings and the like. On top of that, and often without rules or training or experience, they are obliged to manage their resources according to priorities all of them accept. In Assynt they soon faced faction between neighbouring or even competing townships. Since one faction or another had to win, these quarrels left the losing members baffled or estranged. And nobody not registered as the tenant of a croft had any say whatever, although the townships housed such people and the decisions affected them. A price of communal ownership, subject to a majority, may be that relations worsen and townships split. Or else, if they try to reach consensus, they get stalemate and drift, just as in the past.[13]

Even if every crofting estate was turned into a trust, it would not put a single family back on the land. Were the way of life profitable, it could certainly attract more entrants to it. Instead of going for profit, however, crofters have gone for subsidy. This reduces them to pensioners of the public purse, a formula for personal and communal immobility. Today fit young Highlanders often do not specially want to follow in father's footsteps and get stuck on an isolated croft for a bare subsistence. In a more modern Scottish economy with ready mobility of labour nobody really needs security of tenure. It is certainly a mixed blessing in crofting areas where, to set against whatever good it may do, it tolerates neglect, indulges bad practice and excludes new blood. That is why people still leave these areas, prompted by economic rather than statutory laws. They leave, in other words, despite security of tenure. Absenteeism is huge. Among my best friends are three crofters: all pursue professional careers in Edinburgh and use their crofts just for holidays.

A priority of the Crofters Commission is to suppress this absenteeism. It claims that there is a bountiful supply of youngsters wishing to become crofters but frustrated by dearth of crofts or, if not, that there will be one in future. Yet it is by no means clear that demand for crofts outstrips supply. With fewer crofters, the question should be not who holds the land but whether more of it could be better organized into economic units. The question has no straightforward answer as crofting areas are never uniform, so a policy right for one could be wrong for another. The Crofters Commission itself possesses powers to expand crofts, although not to form new crofts; now a croft may run to 50 acres (formerly 30), but it usually remains much smaller. The commission still feels obliged to discourage any expansion not prompted by itself, because 'each amalgamation means the elimination of a potential crofting family'.[14]

Yet the system itself stifles the potential. One defect in it is a rigid dependence on an antique mode of allocation. An empty croft may be disposed of not on the market, by the working of supply and demand, but only through selection by the Crofters Commission, with varying involvement from landlord and local community. While the operation of the market is impersonal and shows no favouritism, this procedure is personal and judge-mental, if not arbitrary, with ample scope for plotting and intrigue. Many potential applicants are just put off: single women and ethnic minorities think they need not apply. But the commission would never dream of opening up a market. It regards the market as irrational compared to its own notion of 'realistic price', by definition one below the level of the market. The received Highland wisdom is that a free market, such as exists for private housing, debars locals. Yet if price is also a yardstick of com-mitment, the crofting community loses the advantage of entrants who would be the most committed to it. The overall effect must be to reduce supply, for few crofters will transfer their tenancy at a price below what they could obtain on a market and so in effect take a loss. The result of the commission's policy is the opposite of what it intends.

And then, although hostile to decrofting, the commission still retains the authority to hear applications for it. True, they pose but a small threat to its empire: crofters enjoy a right to buy their crofts under the act of 1976, but not many do because they would forfeit various allowances and cred-its. A crofter buying his croft is also less protected than a statutory tenant. Under the law every croft must have a tenant, and an owner-occupier is defined as being in possession of a croft with no tenant. He may be directed by the commission to instate a tenant. Then he could forfeit his croft if that tenant should use his own right to purchase.

The prejudice of the Crofters Commission is thus grounded on the letter of a law that inhibits reorganization of crofting land into viable eco-nomic units. This does still happen on the quiet, by crofters making arrangements among themselves. And where, on the Atlantic coast or in the Hebrides, thin topsoil rests on hard gneiss, crofters have also profited from the depopulation to shift from small-scale farming to small-scale ranching, to raise livestock rather than plant crops. This matched the spon-taneous effect of the market outside the crofting areas, where holdings also grew. Two-thirds of Scotland is mountain, moor or rough grazing. Such land can only sensibly be owned in large tracts. The same holds in other parts of the globe with poor soils and severe climates: the prairies, outback or steppes. So the objection often made by reformers to the gross size of Highland estates is little to the point. Also crofters who are graziers need more land than those who are farmers. Land underemployed when occupied by a farmer might seem overemployed when occupied by a pastoralist. It is another reason the land can maintain fewer of them. In the *Third Statistical Account* the minister of Daviot and Dunlichity, to the east of Loch Ness, described the process in his district, where it became common: 'In certain parts of the parish ranching has been introduced. One man runs a number of farms as a single unit, rearing large numbers of cattle and sheep on the hills and on the marginal land. The arable land is cultivated to provide silage and fodder for winter feeding.' Not far away Joseph Hobbs followed suit to become a local character after he bought the estate of Inverlochy, near Fort William: 'Until he was nearly 70, he rode in the cowboy-style annual round-up, which is a feature of the ranching year.'[15]

For most crofters the real problems meanwhile remained what they always had been: barren ground, cold climate and the impossibility of living off the croft alone. Farmers elsewhere tackle such difficulties by technology, but this is seldom worthwhile on the small, rocky plots of the Scottish glens or isles. Without a counter to diminishing returns there can be no agricultural solution to the difficulties. The reality is that peripheral land will sustain fewer and fewer crofters. Any attempt to increase their numbers without improved productivity can only push even lower the general earnings from crofts. This is all the truer now that in recent times the accent on agricultural production has been overtaken as, not only in Scotland and in Britain but in the whole European Community, dearth gives way to glut. When crofting started, the British Isles could not feed themselves and imported much of their food. Now Europeans run up such huge surpluses that they have no idea what to do with them. These surpluses are the problem, rather than any shortage. They come from industrial farming, and it is not certain small farmers will survive even in fertile regions. The chances of their doing so in the Highlands are next to nil.

So the answer to the economic problem in the Highlands cannot lie in raising agricultural production to give crofters higher earnings. By disregarding this, as the Crofters Commission does, it will create a population even less independent than that in the Victorian era of great landlords. The crofting system is, after all, the answer of the nineteenth century to a problem of the nineteenth century. In Scotland, as in every part of Europe where smallholding found favour under the philanthropy of the age, it is a recipe for poverty. Nothing in the recent Scottish reforms has cured poverty or arrested the decline in the system that went on right through the twentieth century, despite efforts at salvage. Overall, crofting has failed. Its failure becomes ever clearer with today's more rapid social change.

The Crofters Commission, when re-established in 1955, said that 'the essence of our mandate [is] to maintain the crofting population', even if 'agriculture by itself cannot support viable communities'.[16] While it has 18,500 crofts on its register, 11,000 in the Hebrides and more than 3500 on Lewis alone, it fails in this task of keeping the people on the land. The population of the whole Highlands and islands emerged as static at the census of 2001. This was the balance resulting from a rise on the mainland, especially in or around the thriving burgh of Inverness, offset by slight falls elsewhere. An exception to the general picture came in the Western Isles. Here the population took a steep plunge: 4000 people, 14 per cent of the total, had left in ten years. This is also the most heavily crofted part of Scotland. On such evidence it seems unlikely that any further fiddling with the law of the croft can produce a viable community at the heart of a healthy Highland population and culture.

Given the subdued, fairly uniform, fertility of the natives, migrants determine the general level of population. They have become a major social force – more than in any other part of Scotland – especially if they arrive from England, birthplace of 18 per cent of those enumerated in the Highlands at the census. Since Lowlanders count as incomers too, the actual proportion of people whom Highlanders see as different from themselves will be yet higher. A rough guess might be that this proportion is heading towards 40 per cent.

While white settlers are unpopular, the economic transformation of the region could hardly have taken place without them. They seem to follow the long history of anti-urbanism and idealist pastoralism in the Western intellectual tradition, something Scots themselves never much went for: witness the famous quarrel between debonair David Hume and rustic Jean-Jacques Rousseau. In truth, incomers are proving it possible to live and prosper in remote regions without lavish subsidies or cosseting legislation, something unfathomable to the locals. Their respective positions may resemble those of landless cottars and lucky crofters in Victorian times, for in crofting districts there is no land free other than crofts. Non-crofters lack the statutory rights the system confers, and the committees in the townships may take a high-handed attitude to them. Yet the white settlers are the rich ones, crofters the poor.

White settlers arrive for many reasons. Some just buy second homes, but others wish to take up permanent residence in the Highlands. Some have retired early enough to cope with the inevitable privations, cushioned by an income well above local levels. Some seek romantic retreat from the complex modern world. Some come to enjoy unspoiled wilderness and wildlife. Some are arty-crafty. Some, while continuing a busy professional life, prefer personal seclusion amid beautiful scenery now that running their business is eased by information technology, which makes a distant glen just another zone of cyberspace: in such callings as authorship, consultancy, design, programming and so on location can be irrelevant. Gaels may look on open-mouthed, but at least the enterprising Shetlanders are pursuing a scheme to lay fibre-optic cable from their islands through Orkney to the Scottish mainland and give themselves proper broadband access, since nobody else is likely to do it for them.

Where incomers produce goods, they are often of quality, in clothing, jewellery, glassware, foodstuffs. Others, defying the lessons of history, take over abandoned upland farms, perhaps to breed exotic strains of livestock. White settlers have also improved the old, abysmal standards of Highland tourism, with more visible success than the government had in the 1960s at its ghastly gulag in the skiing resort of Aviemore, a sort of Glaswegian sink estate set down in Strathspey. There are go-ahead crofters as well, who adopt the white settlers' lifestyle with 'tele-crofting', by which they sell smoked salmon or hand-knitted woollens over the internet. But the more common reaction among natives is a passive sense of being overborne, so that no recent development has left them any happier than before. They may feel like strangers in their own land, kept in crofting reservations like so many Red Indians, and like them too, afflicted by social dysfunction, by ill health, alcoholism, low expectations and feeble achievement.

As for the culture, the state's fossilizing of Victorian structures has not saved that either. The twentieth century did see a burgeoning of Highland, more especially Gaelic, cultural institutions. The Scottish Gaelic Texts Society was founded as early as 1934 to produce scholarly editions of the classical corpus of literature. The language of Eden could be heard on air about the same time; Radio Highland and Radio nan Eilean later raised the quota of Gaelic broadcasting that, from 1990, was generously supported by government. A *Historical Dictionary of Scottish Gaelic* came under the patronage of the University of Glasgow in 1966. In 1968 the Gaelic Books Council started to subsidize publications. A college of higher education, Sabhal Mòr Ostaig, was established on Skye in 1985 by Sir Iain Noble, a financier eager to have Gaels do business in their own tongue: the key, he felt sure, to much else. Gaelic has become a language of instruction in schools. A University of the Highlands and Islands is in process of formation, giving the region as a whole a centre or centres of intellectual and cultural life not seen since the bards sang at the chieftains' tables. Its headquarters will be in Inverness, but campuses are to be scattered round the region, from Scalloway on Shetland to Perth at the gateway to the

Lowlands. It will be an on-line university as well so that, as a recent report puts it, 'even in the smallest crofts . . . it should be possible to take part in a seminar or tutorial'.[17]

The catalogue of cultural achievement is impressive in this institutional sense. In terms of production, although a new school of novelists has yet to win much recognition, Gaels can be proud of Sorley MacLean and other poets of his generation or the next. It remains to be seen whether MacLean represented a glorious sunset or the bright dawn of a new day. He, a conscious traditionalist, also reinterpreted the Gaelic world so as to open the way to new literary topics and methods of presentation. With his example, the poetry of the present is also of two kinds. One derives from tradition, sometimes dealing with modern subjects to be sure, but bounded by its limitations. This tradition was tied in with old Highland society. As it eroded, the poetry became attenuated and has remained so. But there is also a school of modern poetry, related to the tradition but less directly. It differs in content, attitude and form, all of which come under outside influences, literary and cultural.[18] Unlike the traditionalist school, it reacts against, rather than merely reflecting or lamenting, decay in the culture. Most of it has been written by people transplanted from their native communities into the outside world, or else by entrants into Gaeldom – learners of the language, that is to say, but proficient enough to use it for their own poetic purposes. They are all, in short, bicultural. This creates the tension from which much of their poetry derives as, typically, it explores problems of identity. Those problems exist because modern Gaeldom has lacked a focus for the unity of its scattered communities, as well as coming face to face with the question of its very survival.

Indeed the fact remains that, for all the success in building cultural institutions and renewing cultural production, the language is not being saved as a spoken vernacular. The crofters of Assynt may have held up to fellow Highlanders a new social ideal, but they did it in English. In the *Third Statistical Account* their minister said Gaelic was dying out 'due to the fairly large number of incomers that make up the population'. Things could only get worse: 'No child can carry on a conversation in Gaelic . . . Pass a remark to them in Gaelic and they will reply in English. English is the language of the playground throughout the whole parish. In 20 years' time the old tongue will be virtually dead in Assynt.'[19] And so it has proved for much of the Highlands. The number of Gaelic-speakers fell from more than 90,000 in 1951 to fewer than 60,000 in 2001. Official figures flatter the actual state of affairs, for just 28,000 of those speakers live in the Highlands and islands. The rest are Lowland exiles or learners, neither of whom maintain Gaelic as a spoken vernacular. Only intellectuals, Lowland as well as Highland, but not many ordinary Gaels, seem truly intent on preserving the language of Eden in the new Scotland.

Yet, as remarked in a previous chapter, for Highlanders their religion was more often a marker of identity than their language. This held true up to the millennium and beyond, if in diminishing degree. In fact, the non-established Churches often take a negative view of Gaelic revival. Presbyterianism remains preponderant, but its numerical strength has declined, certainly as a single cohesive force. Its inveterate tendency to schism, more tenacious in the Highlands than elsewhere, is not least to blame. It risks becoming self-destructive in a wider Scottish society turning to all intents and purposes into a secular one. If sects now largely confined to the Highlands die out there, they are gone for ever.[20]

The established Church of Scotland is perhaps in no worse case than over the rest of the country, but the Highland Churches have suffered recurrent crises. The Free Church, with its stronghold on Lewis, is torn by tension between conservatives there and modernizers elsewhere. A messy struggle found a focus in its leading liberal, Professor Donald Macleod, principal of the Free Church College in Edinburgh, though a Lewisman by birth. It led him to court, where he won against, as his defence argued, a conspiracy among some reverend brethren to show he had had an illicit affair. The conservatives could not take their defeat, and a schism resulted. In 1989 the Free Presbyterian Church, mainly an insular denomination, had been rent by strife when its most eminent member, Lord Mackay of Clashfern, Lord Chancellor in Margaret Thatcher's Cabinet, attended the funeral of a colleague, a Catholic Scottish judge. Members of his own Church objected and, amid disputes of labyrinthine complexity, schism again followed. Among Catholics themselves, the dramatic disappearance with a woman of Roddy Wright, bishop of Argyll and the Isles, who was also a Gael, may have reduced the importance of the language in the eyes of the hierarchy, who in future are likely to look in their bishops for pastors rather than linguists.

Schism, clearly, is just one of the forces weakening the Highland Churches. Steady migration of their flocks had long sapped their influence and identity. But in recent times people have moved into the region rather than out. It has received a net immigration of Lowlanders and English people not sharing the Churches' view of what Highland life is or ought to be: the fundamentalist ministers and their congregations who lie down in front of cars off ferries violating the sabbath have done so to less and less effect. Even locals find such behaviour eccentric, if not unseemly.

The society is changing from within as well as under outside pressure. The Churches have found no means to restate their principles in modern terms. They have produced no ideas for linguistic, social or political revival. They have lost authority even among Highlanders. All they can do is stand firm for Christian purity. As they struggle to control internal dissent too, they give ground even in their own fold and lose touch with changes round it. So the new pluralist culture of the region, shared by ever more native Highlanders too, brings decline of its language and fragmentation of its religion.

Envoi

THIS HISTORY ENDS on a despondent note, yet without a tidy conclusion. An account of the Scottish Highlands could hardly do anything else. It is easy to see their last 400 years as a catalogue of catastrophe. The wonder is that anything has survived. Yet the land is eternal and the people have, come what may, shown a resilience that, beside serving them well when they go elsewhere, still stamps itself on their hills and glens and islands.

But their history is largely one of mistakes, of an almost inerrant instinct for choosing the wrong, the losing side in religion, politics, economics and society generally. Perhaps their ideals were nobler than others', although the record scarcely bears that out. Anyway, they have seldom found means to turn ideals into realities. That also strikes me as true now, when some think to see a new Highland day dawning: before the sun gets much higher, they argue, the people will have won back the land, thanks to the enlightened measures of devolved Scotland. In a bright noontide they will all live in secure and contented possession of their birthright, with lairds (and white settlers?) put to flight.

Yet this recent history is not a novel one. For over a century experiments have gone on – with crofting, with schemes of settlement, with curbs on rights of property, with quangos and with public expenditures – to give the Highlanders a stronger stake in the Highlands. Still the Highlands declined and the Highlanders fled, unless detained by some influence generated from outside, North Sea oil or the fad for back-to-nature lifestyles. It remains to be seen whether these have staying power. Meanwhile I cannot see anything in the latest craze for communal ownership to alter the course of this history. The one expedient not so far tried is for Highlanders to take their place on the same footing as everyone else – in Britain, in Europe, in North America and now in the Orient too – in the modern, liberal, individualist, capitalist order. The price of failure here can be high (though surely not higher than the price Highlanders have already paid). Yet the reward of success is huge for those who depend on themselves, not on others. In that order they cannot, under its rule of law, have their own taken away from them.

Without some such change of heart in Highlanders, one indeed greater than any before, the future for what remains of their culture is grim. Most salient are the language, religion and social order. I take no pleasure in saying so, but it seems to me that Gaelic has decayed beyond the point of being saved as a spoken vernacular. It is on its last legs everywhere but in the Western Isles, the poorest part of Scotland, still being depopulated. I asked someone in a position to make an informed guess how many children were today being brought up with Gaelic as the language of the home, that is, with both parents Gaels and the influence of the dreaded television kept at bay. He reckoned that, at best, they numbered in the low hundreds. These children can look forward to grand prospects of good jobs in a nation with a guilty conscience about Gaelic. Probably they can form a linguistic establishment able to wring the withers of anglophone Scotland, as its counterpart in Wales, the Taffia, does. They can no doubt ensure Gaelic is preserved as part of the country's heritage, just as it should be, with the learning of it encouraged and the study of its literature cultivated. But they will not be able to save it as a living language in the hills and glens and islands.

The outlook for the Highland Churches looks equally bleak. I must confess to a certain affection for that old-time religion, although it sets standards higher than I can ever aspire to. Its heart lies in individual conversion, yet it is not catholic, rather the product of a particular history and society. The history is all but over, and the society has predominantly become a secular one, seeking its salvation in a material culture. The Highland Churches have in holy horror recoiled from that culture. The inward path may be spiritually enriching, but in material terms is a stony one. It leads the Churches away from the felt needs and wants of ordinary men and women, the great majority of whom now equably, if not always blissfully, lead their lives without religion. Points of contact between the Church and the world are steadily lost. So there remain sects obsessed with themselves and with one another, in a scene unattractive even to those outside it who still have some spiritual hunger, some potential for conversion. Visitors to certain congregations, anxious as much as anything to hear the haunting liturgy in the language of Eden, may be greeted with the unfriendly question 'Have you come for God or have you come for the Gaelic?' The scene is, in fact, far along the road to dissolution in acrimony. And, as already remarked, once these Churches are gone from the Highlands they are gone for ever.

It will already be clear that I am no friend to the crofting system, erected in the nineteenth century to undergird a social order as nothing else apparently could. The original aim was to set up a safe haven for congested Victorian Highlanders by making sure each family at least had secure tenancy of a plot to eke out a bare subsistence. It seems never to have been imagined they could or would want anything else, but the system failed to keep the people on the land. From the start it excluded perhaps a quarter of the population, the landless cottars, who steadily gave up their unequal struggle for subsistence and vanished through migration. Latterly, the odd jobs needed to bulk out a crofting income have proved irksome to crofters too, who may prefer prosperous absenteeism in the Lowlands or elsewhere. (I have even met a crofter who lives in Paris, but shall say no more for fear of giving the Crofters Commission somebody else to persecute.) Finally, the late twentieth century proved, as the twenty-first century will surely prove over again, that nowadays more than a bare subsistence can be earned in the Highlands: it was for this reason that the region turned into one of net inward migration, with rising personal incomes. White settlers fill in economic gaps that crofters have no incentive to occupy. These are left indigently trailing social forces that can form the future Highlands, of technology harnessed to environment. I think crofting should be abolished, although this is not an idea likely to be entertained for a moment in politically correct, devolved Scotland. Crofting will otherwise just wither on the vine while it wastes human resources that could be put to better use. The outcome will be the same: no crofting to speak of by the turn of the twenty-second century.

But I do not want to end, with these doleful prospects for three remaining pillars of Highland society, on a wholly negative note. It strikes me there is some analogy between the relation of the Highlands to Scotland today and the relation of Scotland to Britain and the Empire in the nineteenth century. Here, as in much else, Sir Walter Scott saw and understood what had happened to the nation since the Union of 1707. He invented the historical novel to portray the process because Scottish history seemed to him exemplary. It laid out in the context of a single nation the progress of humanity, in this case more clearly because at an accelerated pace: Scotland had passed within a couple of lifetimes from slaughtering Covenanters or Jacobites to building the New Town of Edinburgh or showing how to span the world by commerce. When Scots had entered the Union, they consciously exposed themselves to the global economy. They felt they had no choice if they were not to starve in their remote, chilly corner of Europe. They took the plunge, saving what they could from the past yet knowing their country was going to be changed beyond all recognition. This indeed happened: we see it on every hand from the empty glens of Sutherland to the now silent shipyards of the River Clyde. Yet despite the transformations of those three centuries, Scotland is still Scotland, visibly separate and distinct from all other nations. In other words, Scottish experience shows it is possible for community to survive in the global economy, even against the odds: one of the nation's few achievements in the twentieth century.

Scott included the Highlanders in his grand narrative, just as in real life he brought them into the celebration of the visit by George IV in 1821, to vest his new Scotland with visible symbols. In the short run he was obviously too optimistic about the unifying power of the symbols, as about the Highlanders who furnished them. He must have known of the upheavals in the north, although he died before they had spelled utter doom to the old society there. Yet in the long run he left a legacy. His tartanry languished for over a century in the scorn of the urban, industrial Scotland that would actually overlay his ideal world of lavish lairds and picturesque peasants. But in our new Scotland today tartan is a mark of identity for all Scots, for 'a' Jock Tamson's bairns', from the Highlands to the Lowlands, from the peers to the punters.

Half a century on from Scott, while the Highlands lay at their lowest ebb, another writer who could shrewdly savour his nation, Robert Louis Stevenson, wrote this: 'The fact remains: in spite of the difference of blood and language, the Lowlander feels himself the sentimental countrymen of the Highlander. When they meet abroad they fall upon each other's neck in spirit: even at home there is a kind of clannish intimacy in their talk.'[1] Stevenson gainsays the words with which John Prebble closed his book *The Highland Clearances*: 'The Lowlander has inherited the hills, and the tartan is a shroud.'[2] Prebble can be credited with having created, almost single-handedly, the modern Highland historiography. Yet there were ways in which he, who lived his life in Canada and England, did not understand that third country on which he lavished his scholarship and his passion. The events he chronicled never created an antagonism of Highlanders and Lowlanders as such, in distinction to antagonism between one class and another, or among the several sets of participants in the various episodes of a harsh history. On the contrary, through all their troubled relations over 400 years, Highlanders and Lowlanders have not ceased to regard themselves as members of one nation, any argument having been about which were the truer members of that nation. As for the tartan shroud – well, it is not a shroud that Scots wear when today they come together at familial, sporting, social or, above all, national gatherings.

Perhaps most Scots today are of mixed Lowland and Highland ancestry.

There are more Macs in Lowland cities than in Highland glens. Although, at the time this book begins, differences between Lowlands and Highlands were stark, or at least seemed stark to contemporaries, over four centuries they have blended to create a common sense of Scottish identity. Now that process has been accomplished, however clumsily and painfully, a time ought to come when Highlanders no longer count as a special case in need of special treatment, in other words, when they stand on their own feet and not on props supplied by the rest of us.

The old independent Scotland and then Victorian Scotland consented to the transcendence of their nationality in higher political and imperial entities, but on terms ensuring it survived. In the same way Highlanders today should see the new Scotland not as a more emollient balm to their grievances but as a chance for a greater contribution to yet another renewal of its protean identity – to make the culture of the whole better reflect its unique blend of diverse origins and ensure that, in times to come too, Scotland will still be Scotland. The Gaelic inheritance is after all something only Scotland has. But it will more likely be jettisoned if it is a burden, carried in the shape of passengers harping on about what happened, not to them but to their ancestors, two centuries ago. To survive in times when identity is far from indestructible, Scotland cannot live in the past. The future of the nation is even now not secure, perhaps will never be secure: insecurity may be part of what it means to be Scottish. The ways forward will always be contested, which is no reason for not taking them. We can say with Sorley MacLean:

> *A luaidh fàire,*
> *A ghaoil nan àrd bheann,*
> *M'eudail sgàile,*
> *Mo ghradh do lì:*
> *A chearcaill mullaich*
> *Nan saoi 's nan curaidh,*
> *A bheanntan ulaidh*
> *Cha sguir bhur strì.*

> Love of the horizon,
> dear one of the high mountains,
> my treasure of shade,
> my love your beauty;
> girdling summit
> of the wise and heroic,
> treasured hills,
> your strife will not cease.[3]

Key characters

Names in the Gàidhealtachd generally consisted of a given name followed by a string of patronymics, preferably back to some forebear of distinction; alternatively, routine recitation of ancestry could be bypassed with a nick-name, often uncomplimentary. This older method of nomenclature was impoverished as the language of the Highlands changed and names had to be squeezed into the scantier system, of just first name and surname, in use in English. As a result many Highlanders found themselves sharing the same name – Alexander MacDonald being perhaps the most frequent example. The list below of persons who play some part in the book may help the reader avoid confusion.

Airlie, earls of (family name Ogilvy):
David, titular fourth earl (*d.* 1717), attainted after the '15.
John, fourth earl (1699–1761), neutral in the '45.
David, titular sixth earl (1725–1803), fought at Culloden, fled to France, formed
 Régiment Ogilvy under Louis XV.

Antrim, Ranald MacDonnell, second earl of (1609–1683), chief of Clan Donald
 in Ireland, royalist participant in Civil Wars.

Argyll, earls, marquesses and dukes of, chiefs of Clan Campbell:
Archibald, fourth earl (1498–1558), supporter of Reformation.
Archibald, fifth earl (1538–1573), supporter of Reformation.
Colin, sixth earl (1542–1584).
Archibald, seventh earl (1575–1638), converted to Catholicism and exiled.
Archibald, eighth earl and marquess (1605–1661), Convenanting leader of
 Scotland, attainted of marquessate and executed after Restoration of
 Charles II.
Archibald, ninth earl (1629–1685), forfeited 1681, executed for rebellion against
 James VII.
Archibald, tenth earl and first duke (*d.* 1703), restored to earldom, 1689, raised to
 dukedom, 1701.

John, second duke (1680–1743), supporter of Union, effective ruler of Scotland.
Archibald, third duke (1682–1761), patron of Enlightenment, effective ruler of Scotland.
John, fourth duke (1693–1770), general, helped to suppress '45.
John, fifth duke (1723–1806), first president, Highland Society.
George, sixth duke (1768–1839), fop and wastrel.
John, seventh duke (1777–1847), suffered ill-health.
George, eighth duke (1823–1900), politician and scientist, chairman of royal commission on Scottish education, 1867.
John, ninth duke (1845–1914), governor-general of Canada.

Atholl, dukes of (family name Murray):
John, first duke (1660–1724), opposed Union but supported Hanoverian succession.
Mary, wife of above (1687–1767), patroness of Adam Ferguson.
James, second duke (1690–1764), fifth son of John, first duke, vested with family's honours by Act of Parliament, 1716.
John, third duke (1729–1774), son of Lord George Murray; committed suicide.

Breadalbane, earls of (family name Campbell):
Iain Glas, first earl (1634–1717), Jacobite, but reconciled clans to William of Orange.
John, second earl (1662–1752), pacified his clansmen.
John, third earl (1696–1782), 'a warm Old Whig'.

Cameron, Alexander (1827–1888), collector of *Reliquiae Celticae*.

Cameron, Daniel (*fl. c.* 1700), schoolmaster at Abertarff, Inverness-shire.

Cameron of Corrychoillie (*fl.* 1792), John, sheep farmer.

Cameron of Erracht, Alan (1750–1828), first colonel of Cameron Highlanders.

Cameron of Invercaddle (*fl.* 1792), Allan, sheep farmer.

Cameron of Kildermorie, Alexander and Allan (*fl.* 1792), sheep farmers.

Cameron of Lochiel, chiefs of Clan Cameron:
Ewen, 17th chief (1629–1719), Jacobite, fought at Killiecrankie, 1689.
John, 18th chief (*d.* 1748), died in exile.
Donald, 19th chief, 'Gentle Lochiel' (1695–1748), Jacobite, commander at Culloden, attainted, died in exile.
John, 20th chief (*d.* 1782), attainted.

Charles, 21st chief (*d.* 1776).
Donald, 22nd chief (1769–1832), had estates restored in 1784.
Donald, 23rd chief (1796–1858).
Donald, 24th chief (1835–1905), member of Napier Commission.

Cameron, Richard (*d.* 1680), Covenanter, killed in battle.

Campbell, Angus (1903–1982), Gaelic poet.

Campbell, Colin (1792–1863), Scottish general in the Indian Mutiny.

Campbell, John (*d.* 1771), cashier of Royal Bank of Scotland.

Campbell, John (*d.* 1776), loyalist in North Carolina.

Campbell of Ardkinglas, Sir Colin (1640–1709), sheriff of Argyll.

Campbell of Auchinbreck, Sir Duncan (*d.* 1645), general.

Campbell of Fonab, Alexander (1660–1724), military commander, survivor of Darien.

Campbell of Glenlyon, Robert (*fl.* 1692), military officer at Massacre of Glencoe.

Campbell of Glenorchy, Sir John (*d.* 1696), expansionist chief.

Campbell of Glenure, Colin (*d.* 1752), victim of Appin murder.

Campbell of Islay, John Francis (1821–1885), son of Walter Frederick Campbell of Islay and compiler of *Popular Tales of the West Highlands*.

Campbell of Islay, Walter Frederick (1798–1855), MP for Argyll, bankrupt 1848.

Cromartie, earls of (family name Mackenzie):
George, first earl (1630–1714), judge, Secretary of State 1702–4, Unionist.
John, second earl (1656–1731), bankrupt 1724.
George, third earl (1702–1766), Jacobite, joined '45, convicted of treason but reprieved.

Gordon, dukes of (family name Gordon):
Alexander, fourth duke (1743–1827), raised Gordon Highlanders.
George, fifth duke (1770–1836), sold estates to pay debts; title extinct with his death.

Gordon, Ann (*d.* 1797), daughter of Sir William Gordon of Invergordon, wife of Henry Dundas.

Gordon, Lord Adam (1726–1801), soldier, served in West Indies and American colonies; commander-in-chief, Scotland, from 1782.

Gordon, Lady Elizabeth, *m.* 1685–98 to John, second earl of Cromartie; divorced for extravagance.

Gordon, Sir Robert (1580–1656), tutor of Sutherland.

Gordon of Cluny, Cosmo (1736–1800), patron of Adam Ferguson.

Gordon of Cluny, John (*d.* 1878), proprietor of Outer Isles, which he cleared.

Gordon of Gordonstown, Robert (1696–1772), MP, Jacobite.

Loudoun, earls of, sept of Clan Campbell:
John, first earl (1598–1662), chancellor of Scotland, proclaimed Charles II in 1649.
John, fourth earl (1705–1782), general, Hanoverian commander against Jacobite rising of 1745.

Lovat, lords, chiefs of clan Fraser:
Simon, eleventh lord (1667–1747), Jacobite conspirator.
Simon, master of Lovat (1726–1782), military officer, MP, had forfeited lands restored, died childless.
Thomas, twelfth lord (1802–1875), distant cousin, had attainder reversed.
Simon, thirteenth lord (1828–1887).
Simon, fourteenth lord (1871–1933), raised Lovat Scouts, inaugural chairman of Forestry Commission.

MacCrimmon, Donald Mòr (*fl.* 1600–1614), hereditary piper to MacLeod of MacLeod, originator of pibroch.

MacCrimmon, Patrick Mòr (*fl.* 1640–1670), hereditary piper to MacLeod of MacLeod.

MacDonald, Alasdair MacColla (*d.* 1647), royalist chieftain in Civil Wars.

MacDonald, Donald, officer at Quebec, 1759.

MacDonald, Flora (1722–1790), Jacobite heroine who helped Prince Charles to escape pursuit after Culloden.

MacDonald, Michael (*fl.* 1772), poet and emigrant to Canada.

MacDonald of Castle Camus, Donald MacIain (*d.* 1650), first Highland cattle dealer.

MacDonalds of Clanranald:
Allan, fourteenth chief (*d.* 1715), fought at Battle of Killiecrankie, fell at Battle of Sheriffmuir.
Ranald, fifteenth chief (*d.* 1725), died in France.
Donald, sixteenth chief (*d.* 1730).
Ranald, seventeenth chief (*d.* 1766), declined to join '45.
Ranald, eighteenth chief (*d.* 1776) fought at Battle of Culloden but escaped attainder.
John, nineteenth chief (*d.* 1794).
Ranald, twentieth chief (1788–1873), MP, sold all property except one castle.

MacDonald of Glenaladale, John (*d.* 1811), tacksman.

MacDonalds of Glencoe:
Alasdair MacIain, eleventh chief (*d.* 1692), victim of Massacre of Glencoe.
Iain, twelfth chief (*d.* 1714), survived massacre.
Alasdair, thirteenth chief (*d.* 1750), survived massacre, forfeited 1715.
John, fourteenth chief (*d.* 1785).
Alexander, fifteenth chief (*d.* 1817), sheep farmer in Lochaber and Easter Ross.

MacDonalds of Keppoch:
Alasdair and Raghnall (*d.* 1663), victims of Keppoch murder.
Alasdair Buidhe, tutor of Keppoch (*d.* 1670), murderer of the above, his nephews.
Archibald (*d.* 1682), poet.
Sileas (1660–1729), poetess, daughter of above.
Alexander (*d.* 1746), fought in '15, fell at Culloden.

MacDonald of Kingsburgh, Allan (1722–1792), farmer, husband of Flora MacDonald.

MacDonalds of Sleat, lords:
Alexander, first lord (1745–1795), ennobled 1776, host of Johnson and Boswell.
Alexander, second lord (1773–1825), MP, improver.
Godfrey, third lord (1775–1833), improver.
Godfrey, fourth lord (1809–1863), saw estate put under trust.
Somerled, fifth lord (1849–1874).
Ronald, sixth lord (1853–1947), in conflict with crofters.

MacDonells of Glengarry:
Angus, ninth chief (*d.* 1680), fought under Montrose, rebelled against Cromwellian regime, 1654.
Raghnall, tenth chief.
Alastair, eleventh chief, fought at Battle of Sheriffmuir.
Ian, twelfth chief (*d.* 1754), said to have been first to wear kilt, out in '45.
Alastair, thirteenth chief (*d.* 1761).
Duncan, fourteenth chief (*d.* 1788).
Alastair, fifteenth chief (1771–1828), leader of tartan cult.
Aeneas, sixteenth chief (1818–1842), emigrated to Australia but returned broken.
Josephine (*d.* 1857), wife of above, cleared Knoydart.

MacDonnell, Father Alexander (1762–1840), leader of emigration to Canada from Glengarry.

MacDonnell of Barrisdale, Alexander (*d.* 1759), officer killed at Quebec.

MacKay, Sir Donald (*b.* 1937), economist, chairman of Scottish Enterprise.

Mackay of Clashfern, James, Lord (*b.* 1927), Lord Chancellor under Margaret Thatcher, member of Free Presbyterian Church.

Mackay of Scourie, Hugh (*d.* 1692), Williamite general defeated at Battle of Killicrankie.

Mackenzie, Alexander (1764–1820), Canadian explorer, first to traverse North America overland.

Mackenzie, Alexander (1838–1898), author of clan histories.

Mackenzie, Alexander (*fl.* 1883), crofters' spokesman on Skye.

Mackenzie, Sir Compton (1883–1972), novelist.

Mackenzie, Henry (1745–1831), of Highland descent, lawyer, novelist, chief collector of taxes in Scotland; wrote report on Highlands.

Mackenzie, Roderick (1761–1844), cousin of Alexander Mackenzie (explorer), above.

Mackenzie, Rory Roy (*fl.* 1770), emigrant to Canada and poet.

Mackenzie, Revd William (1734–1816), minister of Assynt.

Mackenzie of Cromarty, George (1702–1748), MP, bankrupt 1741.

Mackenzie of Gairloch, Sir Kenneth (1832–1900), member of Napier Commission.

Mackenzie of Rosehaugh, Sir George, Bluidy Mackenzie (1637–1691), Lord Advocate.

Mackinnon, Revd Donald (1816–1888), minister of Strath, Skye, succeeded his father, John Mackinnon, below.

Mackinnon, Donald (1839–1914), first professor of Celtic at Edinburgh.

MacKinnon, Hector (1886–1954), religious poet, reckoned last of *Na Daoine*, the Men.

Mackinnon, Revd John (1786–1856), minister of Strath, Skye.

Mackintosh, Charles Fraser (1828–1901), MP, champion of Gaelic, member of Napier Commission.

Mackintosh of Moy, Angus (*d.* 1770), Hanoverian military officer.

Mackintosh, Anne (1723–1784), Jacobite, wife of above.

MacLean, Alexander (*fl.* 1776), loyalist in North Carolina.

MacLean, Sorley (1911–1996), greatest Gaelic poet of twentieth century.

MacLean of Coll, Florence, *née* Campbell (*fl.* 1645), poetess.

MacLean of Duart, Sir Lachlann (*d.* 1649), chieftain.

MacLeod, Donald (*d.* 1776), loyalist in North Carolina.

Macleod, Donald (*fl. c.* 1800–1850), stonemason, author of *Gloomy Memories in the Highlands of Scotland*.

Macleod, Professor Donald (*b.* 1940), principal of Free Church College, Edinburgh.

Macleod, John (*fl.* 1822), teacher and leader of religious revival on Skye.

MacLeod, John (*fl.* 1925), cobbler on Raasay, organizer of land raids.

Macleod, Revd Kenneth (1871–1955), minister of Gigha, Gaelic poet.

Macleod, Revd Norman (1780–1866), separatist minister in Assynt, Nova Scotia and New Zealand.

Macleod of Geanies, Donald (1745–1834), sheriff of Ross.

MacLeod of Glendale, Alexander (*fl.* 1771), factor to MacLeod of MacLeod.

MacLeod of MacLeod, Iain Breac (*d.* 1693), chieftain.

MacLeod of MacLeod, Norman (1706–1772), MP, drunkard, gambler, double agent; Jacobite conspirator but did not join rising of 1745.

MacLeod of Raasay, Malcolm (*d.* 1786), chieftain.

MacMhuirich, Cathal (*fl.* 1650), Gaelic bard.

MacMhuirich, Niall (1550–1630), bard of Clanranald.

MacMhuirich, Ruaidhri (1656–1714), the Blind Harper, bard to MacLeod of MacLeod.

McNeill, Sir John (1795–1883), chairman of board of supervision (in charge of Scots poor law).

MacNeills of Barra:
Roderick (*d.* 1759), killed at Quebec.
Roderick (*d.* 1822).
Roderick (*d.* 1863), sold island.

Macpherson, Father Colin (1919–1990), priest of Kintail; aided land raid there.

Macpherson, Iain (1880–1937), MP, largely responsible for introduction of Gaelic to school curriculum in Education Act (1918).

Macpherson, James (1736–1796), writer and editor of poems of Ossian.

MacPherson, Mary (1740–1815), religious poetess in Gaelic.

Macpherson, Mary, Màiri Mhòr nan Oran, Big Mary of the Songs (1821–1898), Gaelic poetess.

Macpherson, William (*fl.* 1883), emigrant to Canada.

MacPherson of Cluny, Ewen (1706–1764), chieftain, Jacobite, sheltered fugitive Prince Charles.

MacPherson, John (1709–1770), brother of above, soldier exiled after '45.

MacPherson of Phoiness, Malcolm, soldier at Quebec, 1759, renowned as swordsman.

Martin, Abraham (1589–1644), known as 'l'Ecossais'; Plains of Abraham at Quebec are named after him.

Martin, Martin (*d.* 1718), early writer on Highlands.

Matheson, Sir Alexander (1805–1886), taipan of Jardine Matheson 1842–52; MP 1852–84; purchased Lochalsh, 1851.

Matheson, Duncan (1850–1930), succeeded kinsman Sir James (below) as proprietor of Lewis and sold estate, 1918.

Matheson, Sir James (1796–1878), co-founder of Jardine Matheson trading house in Hong Kong; Liberal MP 1843–68; purchased Lewis from earl of Seaforth, 1844.

Matheson, Murdoch (1670–1757), bard to earls of Seaforth.

Muir, Edwin (1887–1959), Orcadian poet and literary critic.

Muir, John (1838–1914), pioneer of American conservation.

Munro, Neil (1863–1930), novelist and journalist.

Munro, Robert (1868–1955), Scottish Secretary.

Munro, William (*fl.* 1857–1887), soldier of Sutherland Highlanders.

Munro of Culcairn, George (*d.* 1746), commander of Hanoverian militia in '45.

Munro of Novar, Sir Hector (1725–1806), MP, Indian general, Highland landlord.

Munro of Novar, Hugh (1797–1864), nephew of above, cleared Culrain, 1820.

Murray, Lord Charles (1691–1720), son of first duke of Atholl, Jacobite.

Murray, Lord George (1694–1760), son of first duke of Atholl, Jacobite commander in rising of 1745.

Murray, James (*fl.* 1714–1719), teacher at Blair Atholl.

Murray, Lord John (*d.* 1709), son of duke of Atholl, killed at Battle of Malplaquet.

Murray, Lord John (1711–1787), colonel of Black Watch.

Seaforth, earls of, chiefs of Clan Mackenzie:
Colin, first earl (1597–1633), ennobled by James VI.
George, second earl (*d.* 1651), Covenanter.
Kenneth, Coinneach Mòr, third earl (1635–1678), persecutor of Covenanters.
Kenneth, Coinneach Beag, fourth earl (1661–1701), Jacobite.
William, fifth earl (*d.* 1740), Jacobite, attainted 1715.
Francis, Lord Seaforth (1754–1815), in whom family's noble rank was restored, 1797, after he raised Seaforth Highlanders.
Mary Elizabeth (1783–1862), eldest surviving child of above, succeeded him as chieftain but sold estates in 1844.

Sinclair, James (1688–1762), brother of John, Lord Sinclair, below; inherited estates, MP, general, patron of philosopher David Hume.

Sinclair, John, Lord (1683–1750), Jacobite, attainted.

Sinclair, Sir John (1754–1835), MP, Highland landowner, organizer of *Old Statistical Account of Scotland*.

Sinclair, John (1860–1925), Scottish Secretary, land reformer.

Sinclair of Lochaline, John (1751–1844), proprietor of Ardnamurchan.

Stewart, Dugald (1753–1828), professor of moral philosophy at Edinburgh.

Stewart, James (1701–1789), minister of Killin; translated New Testament into Gaelic.

Stewart of Ardshiel, Charles (*d.* 1757), Jacobite.

Stewart of Garth, David (1768–1829), colonel of Black Watch, author of *Sketches of the Highlanders*.

Stewart of the Glen, James (1700–1752), convicted of Appin murder and hanged.

Sutherland, Elizabeth, countess of (1765–1839), landowner; married marquess of Stafford, later duke of Sutherland.

Sutherland, dukes of (family name Leveson-Gower):
George, first duke (1758–1833), marquess of Stafford; raised to ducal rank 1833, husband of countess of Sutherland.
George, second duke (1786–1861).
George, third duke (1828–1892).
Cromartie, fourth duke (1851–1913).
George, fifth duke (1888–1963).

Urquhart of Cromarty, Sir Thomas (1611–1660), author, wit.

Urquhart of Newhall, Alexander (*d.* 1727), MP, Jacobite, bankrupt.

Chronology

1603   Union of Crowns: James VI of Scotland ascends English throne as James I.

1609   Statutes of Iona.

1616   Scottish Parliament provides for a school in every parish.

1625   James VI and I dies; Charles I succeeds.

1638   National Covenant.

1639   Civil War breaks out.

1641   Irish rising against Charles I, aided by Scottish Catholics.

1644   Irish invasion of Highlands under Montrose.

1645   Battle of Inverlochy: Montrose defeats Campbells.

1649   Execution of Charles I.

1650   Montrose again invades Scotland; defeated and executed.

1651   Charles II crowned at Scone; defeated at Battle of Worcester. Cromwell conquers Scotland.

1653   Cromwellian Union of Scotland with England. Publication of *Shorter Catechism* in Gaelic.

1660   Charles II restored. Union of Scotland and England ends.

1684   Robert Kirk publishes complete Gaelic psalter.

1685   Death of Charles II; accession of James VII and II.

1688   Revolution overthrows James VII and II, succeeded by his daughter Mary and her husband, William of Orange.

1689   Claverhouse leads first Jacobite revolt but is killed after victory at Battle of Killiecrankie.

1690   Presbyterianism re-established in Church of Scotland. Gaelic Bible published.

1692   Massacre of Glencoe.

1696   Scottish Parliament legislates for universal education.

1701   James VII and II dies in exile; the Old Pretender, James VIII and III, succeeds as Jacobite claimant to throne.

1702   William of Orange dies, succeeded by Queen Anne.

1707   Union of Parliaments between Scotland and England.

1709   Foundation of Society in Scotland for Propagating Christian Knowledge.

1714   Queen Anne dies, succeeded by Elector of Hanover, George I.

1715   Jacobite rising. Battle of Sheriffmuir.

1725   George Wade, road-building in Highlands, raises Independent Companies.

1727   Last witch burned at Dornoch.

1739   Black Watch formed as regular regiment.

1743   Highland cultivation of potato begins.

1745   Jacobite rising under Young Pretender, Prince Charles.

1746   Battle of Culloden: Jacobites crushed. Legislation to disarm Highlanders and ban kilt.

1752   Annexing Act for forfeiture of Jacobite estates.

1755   Dr Alexander Webster's census of Scotland.

1760 James Macpherson publishes first volume of Ossianic poetry.

1766 Old Pretender dies; Young Pretender, Charles III, succeeds as Jacobite claimant to throne.

1767 Publication of Gaelic New Testament.

1773 Highland tour by Samuel Johnson and James Boswell.

1784 Forfeited estates returned to Jacobite families. Highland Society founded to encourage private schemes of improvement.

1786 British Fisheries Society founded. Commissioners for Northern Lighthouses appointed.

1788 Young Pretender dies in Rome.

1792 *Bliadhna nan Caorach*, the Year of the Sheep: resistance to evictions in Easter Ross.

1793 War with revolutionary France. Emigrant traffic halted.

1803 Highland Society publishes Old Testament in Gaelic.

1813 Troops suppress unrest over clearances in Sutherland.

1814 Patrick Sellar clears Strathnaver. Walter Scott anonymously publishes his novel *Waverley*, on the '45.

1815 End of Napoleonic Wars brings economic crisis in Highlands.

1816 Sellar tried and acquitted at Inverness.

1822 George IV makes visit to Scotland, stage-managed by Scott.

1823 Whisky stills legalized.

1828 Highland Society publishes Gaelic dictionary.

1841 At census, Highland population reaches peak of 400,000.

1843 Disruption of Church of Scotland, most extensive in Highlands. Formation of Free Church of Scotland.

1846   Failure of potatoes in Highlands.

1851   Census shows first fall in Highland population.

1852   Highland Emigration Society formed, under Prince Albert as patron. He buys Balmoral for Queen Victoria.

1861   Railway reaches Inverness.

1872   Education Act establishes universal system of schools, without provision for Gaelic.

1882   Battle of the Braes on Skye. Chair of Celtic founded at Edinburgh University.

1884   Napier commission recommends statutory basis for crofting.

1885   Scottish Office established.

1886   Crofters Act. Crofters Commission established. Widespread disturbances in Highlands: gunboats restore order.

1893   Formation of Free Presbyterian Church.

1911   Small Landholders Act provides for extension of crofting.

1912   Crofters Commission abolished.

1918   Lord Leverhulme buys Lewis. Education Act provides for teaching of Gaelic.

1919   Land Settlement Act allows new crofting areas to be identified. Widespread raids, or seizures of land, follow.

1920   *Iolaire* sinks off Stornoway with loss of 205 servicemen.

1931   National Trust for Scotland founded.

1943   Sorley MacLean publishes first collection of poetry, *Dain do Eimhir*. North of Scotland Hydro-electric Board set up.

1955   Crofters Commission restored.

1965   Highlands and Islands Development Board set up.

1966   *Historical Dictionary of Scottish Gaelic* initiated.

1967   Exploration for oil in North Sea begins.

1972   Scottish counties organized into regions. Mainland Highlands (except Argyll) form one region, with Western Isles, Orkney and Shetland under separate authorities.

1973   British entry into European Economic Community heralds ruin of Scottish fisheries.

1976   First North Sea oil comes ashore. New Crofters Act offers rights of ownership, mostly spurned by crofters.

1981   Census shows first rise in Highland population for a century.

1985   Foundation of Sabhal Mòr Ostaig, Gaelic college of higher education. Scottish Crofters' Union formed.

1988   Explosion on Piper Alpha oil platform causes 167 deaths.

1989   Free Presbyterian Church splits.

1992   First crofters' trust established for Assynt. Scottish National Heritage formed for conservation.

1999   Scottish Parliament re-established. Land reform initiated.

Scots and Gaelic glossary

abulziments	outer garments
airth	direction, compass point
aois dàna (Gaelic)	learned orders in traditional Highland society, of bards, musicians and so on
bairn	baby, child
bere	inferior variety of barley
Bliadhna an Aomaidh (Gaelic)	Year of the Swooning, 1820
Bliadhna nan Caorach (Gaelic)	Year of the Sheep, 1792
blintering	glistening
Bluidy Clavers and Bluidy Mackenzie	epithets respectively of John Graham of Claverhouse and Sir George Mackenzie of Rosehaugh, persecutors of the Covenanters
breacan (Gaelic)	tartan
broch	prehistoric fortress
broken men	ex-clansmen displaced from their original territory
Caledonian antisyzygy	Scottish genius for reconciling opposites
Cameronians	sect of extreme Presbyterians, named after their martyred leader Richard Cameron, in revolt against King Charles II
caterans	bands of marauders, often broken men (q.v.)

ceòl-mòr (Gaelic)	classical music for the bagpipes, including the form known as pibroch.
clachan (Gaelic)	township
clann (Gaelic)	literally children, by extension a clan
clàrsach (Gaelic)	harp
claymore	large double-edged sword of the Highland warrior
common grazings	land held jointly by crofting townships for cattle and sheep
cott	home of a cottar
cottar	landless agricultural labourer
Covenanters	adherents of the National Covenant of 1638, by which Scots pledged themselves to defend the Calvinist Reformation; after 1660, reduced to small, extreme sects, such as the Cameronians
crawdoun	cowardly
croft	a Highland agricultural smallholding, since 1886 legally defined (see p. 252)
crofter	tenant of a croft
Cuillins, *An Cuilithionn* (Gaelic)	highest mountains on Skye
dàn (plural: *dàin*) (Gaelic)	song
Daoine, Na (Gaelic)	The Men, lay evangelists in the Gàidhealtachd
daoine uaisle (Gaelic)	gentlemen of the clan, usually kinsmen of the chief
deborden	exile
decroft	take out of crofting tenure
dreich	dreary, depressing (of weather)
drouthy	thirsty
droving	driving Highland cattle to Lowland markets

drystone dyke	stone wall built without mortar
eemis	unsteady
fencible	pertaining to military service
flyting	formal abuse, usually in poetry
Foirm na h-Urrnuidheach (Gaelic)	literally form of prayers, translation of the Book of Common Order in the Church of Scotland
Freiceadan Dubh, Am (Gaelic)	the Black Watch, the first Highland regiment
Gàidhealtachd or Gaeldom	Gaelic-speaking area of Scotland, often in modern usage the Highlands generally, even where English-speaking
gin	if
glebe	farmland reserved for the minister of a parish, in the Highlands often in lieu of stipend
glen	narrow valley
Glengarry	round cap, creased on top, with ribbons behind
graip	pitchfork
hairst	harvest
heritable jurisdictions	areas in which feudal superiors enjoyed judicial powers, abolished in 1747
heritor	landowner
hirple	hobble
how-dumb-deid	deep silent depth
Jacobites	adherents of the legitimate line of the House of Stewart, overthrown by the Revolution of 1688
Jock Tamson	mythical figure of the typical Scot

kailyard	literally, a cabbage patch; applied metaphorically to a school of literature in the nineteenth and early twentieth centuries, often written in Scots, which stressed the homely, local aspects of Scottish life
kelp	variety of seaweed harvested and burned for fertilizer
ken	know
kist	chest
kyle	strait
Latha na Ceiste (Gaelic)	day of questions, part of the celebration of evangelical Presbyterian communions
lazy bed	patch or terrace of poor land artificially fertilized for cultivation
lift	sky
linn nan creach (Gaelic)	time of forays, period of disorder after the forfeiture of the Lordship of the Isles in 1493
Long Island	Lewis and Harris
MacChailein Mòr	great son of Colin, epithet of the dukes of Argyll
mair	more
Makars	school of medieval poets in Scots
midden	dungheap
mirls	measles
moosewob	spider's web
ocht	ought
owre	over, excessively
paroch	parish
philibeg	kind of kilt
piobaireachd (Gaelic, anglicized as pibroch)	see *ceòl-mòr*

poind	legally confiscate
roag	strip stalks of corn (after harvest)
runrig	Scottish system of communal agriculture in cultivable strips
Sasunnach	Englishman
Seachdaran Dearg (Gaelic)	redcoated soldiers
sept	subdivision of a clan, often differentiated by an English or anglicized surname
sgian dubh (Gaelic)	black knife, dagger worn in the stocking as part of Highland dress
sheilings	high pastures for grazing cattle in summer
Sìol Tòrcail	seed of Torquil, epithet of the MacLeods of Lewis
sorning	chief's right to quarter armed retinue on clansmen
steading	farm buildings
strath	broad valley
strynd	strain, sound
sunways	clockwise
tack	lease
tacksman	principal tenant to the chief of a clan, often his kinsman
targe	small circular shield of the Highland warrior
thocht	thought
tolbooth	prison of a burgh
trechour	treacherous
tutor	in Scots law, guardian of minors
Union of the Crowns	Union of Scotland and England by the accession of James VI to the English crown, as James I, in 1603

Union of the Parliaments	political union of Scotland and England by the Treaty of Union of 1707
wadset	mortgage
widdie	short length of rope
wynd	narrow street

Notes

1 BANG IT OUT BRAVELY

1. 'The language of Eden' seems to have been first used as an epithet for Gaelic by the Revd David Malcolm, minister of Duddington (1705–43), although he may have owed it to an earlier tradition. I am grateful for this information to William Gillies, Professor of Celtic at the University of Edinburgh.
2. A.-M. Schmidt (ed.), *Poètes du XVIe siècle*, Bibliothèque de la Pléiade (Paris, 1953), 449.
3. *Basilikon Doron*, I, 70.
4. A.J. Otway-Ruthven, *A History of Medieval Ireland* (London, 1968), 224–30; G.W.S. Barrow, *Robert Bruce and the Community of the Realm of Scotland* (Edinburgh, 1988), 316.
5. K. Brown, *Bloodfeud in Scotland* (Edinburgh, 1986), *passim*.
6. *Basilikon Doran*, I, 24.
7. F. Collinson, *The Bagpipe* (London, 1975), 90, 140–1.
8. J. Templeton, 'Scots: An Outline History', in A.J. Aitken (ed.), *Lowland Scots* (Edinburgh, 1978), 4–19; D. Murison, *The Guid Scots Tongue* (Edinburgh, 1977) 4–5; 'The Historical Background', in A.J. Aitken and T. MacArthur (eds.), *The Languages of Scotland* (Edinburgh, 1979), 2–13.
9. M.A. Mackay, 'The Scots of the Makars', in Aitken and MacArthur, op. cit., 20–37; R. Crawford and M. Imlah (eds.), *The New Penguin Book of Scottish Verse* (London, 2000), 87–91.
10. D. Hay (ed.), *Letters of James V* (Edinburgh, 1954), 162, 364.
11. M. Lee, *Government by Pen: Scotland under James VI and I* (Chicago, 1980), *passim*.
12. D. Laing (ed.), *Original Letters Relating to the Ecclesiastical Affairs of Scotland . . . 1603–1625*, Bannatyne Club (Edinburgh, 1851), I, 152–3.
13. T. Thomson and C. Innes (eds.), *Acts of the Parliament of Scotland*, 12 vols. (Edinburgh, 1814–75), IV, 625.
14. So called by Henry IV of France.

2 JESUS AND NO QUARTER

1. 'Oran air Latha Blàir Inbhir Lòchaidh eadar Clann Dòmhnaill agus na Caimbeulaich', in C. Ò'Baoill (ed.), *Gàir nan Clàrsach* (Edinburgh, 1994), 106–13; the translation is by M. Bateman.
2. David Laing (ed.), *Royal Letters, Charters and Tracts Relating to the Colonisation of New Scotland* (Edinburgh, 1869), 48.
3. 'Iorram do Shir Lachlann', *Gàir nan Clàrsach*, 88–9.
4. E. Hyde, Earl of Clarendon, *History of the Rebellion and Civil Wars in England* (Oxford, 1807), I, 384.
5. Montrose is far and away the favourite of biographers. For opposing views, see J. Buchan, *Montrose* (London, 1931), and E.J. Cowan, *Montrose: For Covenant and King* (London, 1977).
6. See D. Stevenson, 'The Way of the Warrior: Alasdair MacColla', *King or Covenant? Voices from the Civil War* (East Linton, 1996), 137–9.
7. 'Turas mo chreiche thug mi Colla', *Gàir nan Clàrsach*, 112–7.
8. R. Bell (ed.), *Collected Poems of James Graham, First Marquis of Montrose* (Hitchin, 1990), 18.
9. 'Oran Cumhaidh air Cor na Rioghachd', *Gàir nan Clàrsach*, 132–3.
10. S. Firth (ed.), *Scotland and the Commonwealth*, Scottish History Society (Edinburgh, 1895), 50.
11. Ibid., 152–3.
12. G. Burnet, *History of his Own Time* (London, 1979), 56–7.
13. Ibid., 59.
14. Archibald, late Marquiss of Argyle (*sic*), *Instructions to a Son* (Edinburgh, 1661), 85.

3 POWERLESS BEFORE THE CAMPBELLS

1. The most dramatic account is J. Prebble, *Glencoe* (London, 1966), and the most scholarly P. Hopkins, *Glencoe and the End of the Highland War* (Edinburgh, 1986), which has become still better in subsequent editions.
2. I.F. Grant, *The Macleods: The History of a Clan, 1200–1956* (London, 1959), 345–8, 358–77; An Clàsair Dall, 'Oran do Mhac Leòid Dhùn Bheagain', in C. Ò'Baoill (ed.), *Gàir nan Clàrsach* (Edinburgh, 1994), 206–7.
3. Mairghread nighean Lachlainn, 'Do Chlainn Ghill-Eain', ibid., 214–5.
4. Sir J. Lauder of Fountainhall, *Historical Observes of Memorable Occurrents . . .*, 2 vols., Bannatyne Club (Edinburgh, 1848), I, 108.
5. National Archives of Scotland, GD 112/39/940, Glenorchy to Earl of Glencairn, 12 September 1660.
6. *Biobla Naobhtha . . .* (Lunnduin [London], 1690).
7. E.W.M. Balfour-Melville (ed.), *An Account of the Proceedings of the Estates*

in Scotland 1689–90, 2 vols., Scottish History Society (Edinburgh, 1954), I, 5 ff.

8. R. Bell (ed.), *The Siege of the Castle of Edinburgh*, Bannatyne Club (Edinburgh, 1828); Colin, Earl of Balcarres, *Memoirs Touching the Revolution in Scotland*, Bannatyne Club (Edinburgh, 1841), 25–30; 'An Officer of the Army', *Memoirs of Dundee* (London, 1714), 22.

9. Hopkins, op. cit., 120–98.

10. Ibid., 263–86.

11. J.R.N. McPhail (ed.), *Highland Papers*, Scottish History Society (Edinburgh, 1914), 57–8.

12. Ibid., 65.

13. Ibid., 90.

14. Ibid., 108.

4   'I AM NO STRANGER TO MISFORTUNE'

1. R. Wodrow, *Analecta, or Materials for a History of Remarkable Providences*, Maitland Club, 4 vols. (Edinburgh, 1842–3), II, 308.

2. B. Lenman, *The Jacobite Risings in Britain, 1689–1746* (London, 1980), 126–54. This is the best modern book on the '15 (and the '45).

3. Sir J. Lauder of Fountainhall, *Historical Observes of Memorable Occurrents . . .* 2 vols., Bannatyne Club (Edinburgh, 1848), II, 692.

4. J.G. Michie (ed.), *Records of Invercauld*, New Spalding Club (Aberdeen, 1901), 324–5.

5. G.D. Henderson (ed.), *Mystics of the North-east*, Third Spalding Club (Aberdeen, 1934), introduction.

6. R. Black (ed.), *An Lasair* (Edinburgh, 2001), 94–9.

7. A. Mackenzie, *History of the Camerons* (Inverness, 1884), 214.

8. John, Master of Sinclair, *Memoirs of the Insurrection in Scotland in 1715*, Abbotsford Club (Edinburgh, 1858), 4–7, 95–102, 142, 264, 270, 326–8.

9. J. Baynes, *The Jacobite Rising of 1715* (London, 1970), 61–2.

10. A. Mackenzie, *History of the Chisholms* (Inverness, 1891), 61.

11. Sir J.B. Paul (ed.), *Scots Peerage* (Edinburgh, 1914), III, 318.

12. W.C. Mackenzie, *Western Isles* (Paisley, 1932), 45–8; I.F. Grant, *Clan Macleod* (Edinburgh, 1953), 404–9; D. Warrand (ed.), *More Culloden Papers*, 5 vols. (Inverness, 1927–30), III, 141.

5   THE LITTLE FIRE

1. D.J. Withrington and I.R. Grant (eds.), *The Statistical Account of Scotland*, XVIII, *Caithness and Sutherland* (Wakefield, 1991; first published, 1790–9), IV, 353 ff.

2. E. Burt, *Letters from the North of Scotland* (London, 1876), I, 242–3.

3. M. Martin, *A Description of the Western Isles of Scotland* (Edinburgh, 1999; first published, 1703), 80–1.

4. Exodus II: 18.

5. G.F. Black, *A Calendar of Cases of Witchcraft in Scotland, 1510–1727* (New York, 1938), 30.

6. National Archives of Scotland, Melville Papers, GD 235/4/3/2.

7. R. Wodrow, *History of the Sufferings of the Church of Scotland from the Restoration to the Revolution*, 2 vols. (Edinburgh, 1721–2), II, 154.

8. R. Wodrow, *Analecta, or Materials for a History of Remarkable Providences*, Maitland Club, 4 vols. (Edinburgh, 1842–3), IV, 156.

9. Ibid., IV, 323.

10. T. M'Crie, *Correspondence of the Rev. Robert Wodrow*, 3 vols. (Edinburgh, 1842–3), III, 275.

11. D.J. Withrington and I.R. Grant (eds.), *The Statistical Account of Scotland*, XVIII, *Caithness and Sutherland* (Wakefield, 1991), IV, 465.

12. C. Larner, *Enemies of God* (Edinburgh, 2000), 192–203.

13. Martin, op. cit., 63, 123–4.

14. A. Carmichael, *Carmina Gadelica*, 2 vols (Edinburgh, 1900), I, xxii–xxiii.

15. Martin, op. cit., 201.

16. Ibid., 20.

17. R. Black (ed.), *An Lasair* (Edinburgh, 2001), 485–6.

18. J. Macinnes, *The Evangelical Movement in the Highlands of Scotland* (Aberdeen, 1951), 59, 103; Black, op. cit., xii.

19. Withrington and Grant, *Caithness and Sutherland*, IV, 465.

20. J. Macleod, *Highlanders* (London, 1996), 222.

21. V.E. Durkacz, *The Decline of the Celtic Languages* (Edinburgh, 1983), 45 ff.

22. National Library of Scotland, Minutes of the Society for the Reformation of Manners, MS 1854, 23 (4 April 1702).

23. National Archives of Scotland, Minutes of the Society in Scotland for Propagating Christian Knowledge, GD 95/1/1/2.

24. Anon., *An Account of the Society in Scotland for Propagating Christian Knowledge from its Commencement in 1709* (Edinburgh, 1774), 54.

25. J. Rose (ed.), *Metrical Reliques of 'The Men' in the Highlands* (Inverness, 1851), 101.

6 RUN, YOU COWARDLY ITALIAN

1. Good modern accounts of the battle are in: F. Buist and K. Tomasson, *Battles of the '45* (London, 1962); D. Daiches, *Prince Charles Edward Stuart* (London, 1973); W. Duke, *Prince Charles Edward and the Forty-five* (London, 1938); J. Prebble, *Culloden* (London, 1961); and W. Speck, *The Butcher: The Duke of Cumberland and the Suppression of the '45* (London, 1981).

2. A. Tayler and H. Tayler, *The Stuart Papers at Windsor* (London, 1939), 26; J. Browne, *History of the Highlands and of the Highland Clans*, 4 vols. (Glasgow, 1838), II, 484–5.

3. J. Murray of Broughton, *Memorials*, Scottish History Society (Edinburgh, 1898), 108–12, 143–5, 423–8, 466; David, Lord Elcho, *Short Account of the Affairs of Scotland, 1744–1746* (Edinburgh, 1907), 63; D. Warrand (ed.), *More Culloden Papers*, 5 vols. (Inverness, 1927–30), IV, 10–12; A. Tayler and H. Tayler, *The Stuart Papers at Windsor*, 138–9.

4. See the discussion and account in Speck, op. cit., 148–56.

5. Ibid., 164.

6. Ibid., 168.

7. Ibid., 169.

8. Prebble, op. cit., 208–9.

9. Ibid., 207–8.

10. Ibid., 215–6.

11. Ibid., 301–2.

12. A.I. Macinnes, *Clanship, Commerce and the House of Stuart* (East Linton, 1996), 211–3.

13. Speck, op. cit., 171–3.

14. R. Black (ed.), *An Lasair* (Edinburgh, 2001), 174–9.

7   LIKE SO MANY INFURIATED DEMONS

1. G. Doughty, *The Siege of Quebec and the Battle of the Plains of Abraham*, 6 vols. (Quebec, 1901), V, 40 ff.

2. 'John Robison', *Transactions of the Royal Society of Edinburgh*, VII (1815), 207.

3. M. Fraser, *Extracts from a Manuscript Journal . . . kept by Colonel Malcolm Fraser* (Quebec, 1868), 21–3.

4. W. Mackay (ed.), 'Unpublished Letters by Simon Lord Lovat', *Transactions of the Gaelic Society of Inverness*, XIII (1886–7), 142–3, 169–70.

5. D.M. Mackay (ed.), *Trial of James Stewart (The Appin Murder)* (Edinburgh, 1931), *passim*.

6. British Library, Newcastle Papers, Add. MS 32733, fol.28.

7. *Hansard's Parliamentary History, 1766* (London, 1813), XVI, 98.

8. C.S. Terry, *The Albemarle Papers* (Aberdeen, 1902), II, 480–4.

9. A.M. Smith, 'The Administration of the Forfeited Estates, 1752–1754', in G.W.S. Barrow (ed.), *The Scottish Tradition: Essays in Honour of Ronald Gordon Cant* (Edinburgh, 1974), 198–210.

10. Technically it became the 42nd only in 1749, but for convenience that numbering will be used here throughout.

11. D. Stewart of Garth, *Sketches of the Character, Manners and Present State of the Highlanders of Scotland*, 2 vols. (Edinburgh, 1822), II, 14–16.

12. British Library, Hardwicke Papers, Add. MS 35450, fol. 262.
13. Quoted in J. Brooke and Sir L. Namier, *The House of Commons, 1754–90*, 2 vols. (London, 1985), II, 471.
14. British Library, Newcastle Papers, Add. MS 32923, fol. 70; Sir J. Fortescue, *Correspondence of King George III*, 6 vols. (London, 1927–8), II, 454.
15. J. Almon, *Parliamentary Register* (1776), III, 206–7.
16. J. Ramsay, *Scotland and Scotsmen in the Eighteenth Century*, 2 vols. (Edinburgh and London, 1888), I, 198; Smith, op. cit., 198 ff.; A. Macinnes, 'Scottish Gaeldom: The First Phase of Clearance', in T.M. Devine and R. Mitchison (eds.), *People and Society in Scotland, 1760–1830* (Edinburgh, 1988), 82.
17. *Parliamentary History* (1782), XXIV, cols. 1316 ff. Edinburgh University Library Papers, DC I. 77, no. 71.
18. V. Merolle (ed.), *Correspondence of Adam Ferguson*, 2 vols. (London, 1995), II, 306–7.
19. National Library of Scotland, Melville Papers, MS 9370, fol.3; National Archives of Scotland, GD 51/5/363; William L. Clements Library, University of Michigan, Ann Arbor (2 Nov 1782).
20. British Library, Auckland Papers, Add. MS 34412, fols. 352 ff.; B. Bailyn, *Voyagers to the West* (New York, 1986) 9, 26, 41–54, 57–70, 92, 394–9.

8 LOVE SCOTLAND BETTER THAN TRUTH

1. R.W. Chapman (ed.), *Johnson's 'Journey to the Western Isles of Scotland' and Boswell's 'Journal of a Tour to the Hebrides with Samuel Johnson, LL.D.'* (Oxford, 1924), 254.
2. Ibid., 259.
3. Ibid., 50, 265.
4. Ibid., 320–1.
5. Ibid., 279–80.
6. Ibid., 108, 320–1.
7. R. Black (ed.), *An Lasair* (Edinburgh, 2001), 425–7.
8. J.H. Burton (ed.), *The Autobiography of Dr Alexander Carlyle* (Edinburgh and London, 1861), 282.
9. Sir W. Scott, review of H. Mackenzie, *The Works of John Home*, in *Quarterly Review*, XXXVI (1827), 196.
10. *A Sermon Preached in the Ersh Language to His Majesty's Regiment of Foot, Commanded by Lord John Murray . . .* (London, 1746), 23.
11. V. Merolle (ed.), *Correspondence of Adam Ferguson*, 2 vols. (London, 1995), I, 10.
12. Ibid., xxix.
13. R. Klibansky and E.C. Mossner (eds.), *New Letters of David Hume* (Oxford, 1954), 55–8; A. Dalzel, *History of the University of Edinburgh*, 2 vols. (Edinburgh, 1862), 428.

14. H. Mackenzie (ed.), *Report of the Committee of the Highland Society of Scotland, appointed to inquire into the nature and authenticity of the poems of Ossian* (Edinburgh, 1805), appendix 4; H. Mackenzie, 'Account of the Life of Mr John Home', in *The Works of John Home* (Edinburgh, 1822); D.S. Thomson, 'Ossian Macpherson and the Gaelic World of the Eighteenth Century', *Aberdeen University Review*, XL (1963).

15. F.J. Stafford, *Sublime Savage: A Study of James Macpherson and the Poems of Ossian* (Edinburgh, 1986), 122–8.

16. D.S. Thomson, 'James Macpherson: The Gaelic Dimension', in H. Gaskill and F. Stafford (eds.), *From Gaelic to Romantic: Ossianic translations* (Amsterdam and Atlanta, GA, 1998), 23.

17. J. Boswell, *Life of Samuel Johnson*, 2 vols. (London, 1792), II, 297; W.S. Lewis (ed.), *Horace Walpole's Correspondence*, 30 vols. (New Haven, 1955), XXIX, 239–40.

18. *Fingal* (London, 1762), xiv and preface; J.H. Burton, *Life and Correspondence of David Hume*, 2 vols. (Edinburgh, 1846), I, 468.

19. R.B. Sher, *Church and University in the Scottish Enlightenment* (Edinburgh, 1985), chapter 6.

20. J. Macpherson, *Works of Ossian*, 2 vols. (London, 1765), I, 109, 111, 279, 288.

21. A. Ferguson, *Essay in the History of Civil Society* (Edinburgh, 1767), 88.

22. Ibid., 91.

23. Ibid., 135.

24. National Archives of Scotland, MSS Society in Scotland for Propagating Christian Knowledge, GD 95/2/2/95.

25. Ibid., GD 95/2/103.

26. Ibid., GD 95/2/2/259 and 342.

27. Ibid., GD 95/2/3/189–90.

28. M. Maclean, *The Literature of the Highlands* (London, 1925), 26–37.

29. National Archives of Scotland, GD 95/2/7/30–1.

30. R.W. Chapman (ed.), *Letters of Samuel Johnson*, 2 vols. (Oxford, 1952), I, 189.

9   A NATION NO LONGER

1. See ch. 8, n. 30 above.

2. H.F. Rankin, *The Moores Creek Bridge Campaign, 1776* (Conhoshocken, PA, 1986), *passim*.

3. R.W. Chapman (ed.), *Johnsons's 'Journey to the Western Islands of Scotland' and Boswell's 'Journal of a Tour to the Hebrides with Samuel Johnson, LL.D.'* (Oxford, 1924), 279–80.

4. National Library of Scotland, Mackenzie of Delvine Papers, MS 1306, fol. 67.

5. Chapman, op. cit., 345.

6. Ibid., 295.

7. Ibid., 120.
8. Ibid., 86–90.
9. E.R. Cregeen (ed.), *Argyll Estate Instructions, 1771–1805* (Edinburgh, 1964), xxi–xxiv.
10. E. Burt, *Letters from the North of Scotland* (Edinburgh, 1998; first published, 1754), 201.
11. Ibid., 193–4.
12. Ballindalloch, Macpherson–Grant Papers, Atholl to Sir James Grant, 22 May 1772.
13. For the counties of Argyll, Caithness, Inverness, Perth, Ross and Cromarty, Sutherland.
14. R.W. Chapman (ed.), *Johnson's 'Journey'*, 279.
15. W. Gilpin, *Observations, Relative to Picturesque Beauty, Made in the Year 1776* (London, 1789), 170–1.
16. G. Patterson, *A History of the County of Pictou, Nova Scotia* (Montreal, 1877), 82.
17. Scottish Catholic Archive, Blairs Letters, BL3/451/10.
18. Public Record Office, Colonial Office series, 5/82.
19. W.S. Wallace, *Documents Relating to the North-West Company* (Toronto, 1934), 1–10; M.W. Campbell, *The North West Company* (Toronto, 1957), 19, 52–6, 67, 195; M.W. Campbell, *McGillivray, Lord of the North West* (Toronto, 1962), 11, 27–9, 45, 95; W.K. Lamb (ed.), *The Letters and Journals of Simon Fraser* (Toronto, 1960), 11; *The Journals and Letters of Sir Alexander Mackenzie* (Cambridge, 1970), 6 ff.; D.S. Macmillan (ed.), *Canadian Business History: Selected Studies* (Toronto, 1972), 62; J. Calder (ed.), *The Enterprising Scot* (Edinburgh, 1986), 97.
20. P.L. Brown (ed.), *Clyde Company Papers* (Oxford, 1940), II, 190–1; III, xxv, 159; IV, xvii; P. de Serville, *Port Philip Gentlemen* (Melbourne, 1980), 171 ff.; P. de Serville, *Pounds and Pedigrees: The Upper Class in Victoria, 1850–1880* (Oxford, 1991), 164.
21. Dunvegan Castle Archives, MSS section 4/1113.
22. M. Macdonnell, *The Emigrant Experience: Songs of Highland Emigrants in North America* (Buffalo, NY, and Toronto, 1982).

10   SEATS OF OPPRESSION

1. National Archives of Scotland, Home Office Papers, RH2/4/64/260–2.
2. National Archives of Scotland, Home Office Papers, RH 2/4/63/79; National Archives of Scotland, Melville Papers, GD 235/10/2/4; Blairquhan, Ayrshire, Hunter Blair Papers, 5 June 1784.
3. National Archives of Scotland, Home Office Papers, RH/2/4/141.
4. I.S. Macdonald, 'Alexander Macdonald Esq. of Glencoe: Insights into Early Highland Sheep-farming', *Review of Scottish Culture*, X (1996–7).

5. National Archives of Scotland, Home Office Papers, RH 2/4/218 and 271.

6. J. Knox, *View of the British Empire* . . . (Edinburgh, 1784), 122, 127.

7. V. Durkacz, *The Decline of the Celtic Languages* (Edinburgh, 1983), 117.

8. R. Black (ed.), *An Lasair* (Edinburgh, 2001), 248–9.

9. National Library of Scotland, Dep. 313, Sutherland Papers, MS 1578.

10. National Archives of Scotland, Home Office Papers, RH 2/4/64/2544.

11. Ibid., RH/2/4/218.

12. Revd George Balfour of Tarbat, in D.J. Withrington and I.R. Grant (eds.), *Statistical Account of Scotland*, 20 vols. (Wakefield, 1991; first published 1791–9), XVII, 634, 649.

13. Cited in E. Richards, *The Highland Clearances* (Edinburgh, 2000), 105 ff.

14. Revd James Goldie of Temple, in Withrington and Grant, op. cit., X, 497.

15. A. Smith, *The Wealth of Nations*, ed. R.H. Campbell and A.S. Skinner (Cambridge, 1976), I, ch. 8.

16. E. Burt, *Letters from the North of Scotland* (Edinburgh, 1998; first published, 1754), 51–2, 237–8.

17. M. Flinn *et al., Scottish Population History* (Cambridge, 1977), 291.

18. J. Ramsay, *Scotland and Scotsmen in the Eighteenth Century*, 2 vols. (Edinburgh and London, 1881), II, 257.

19. National Archives of Scotland, Home Office Papers, RH 2/4/87/53, 2/4/89/140.

20. T. Royle, 'The Scottish Military Tradition', unpublished paper given at The Citadel, Charleston, SC, 10 April 2003. I am grateful to the author for permission to use material from his paper.

21. J. Dunlop, *The British Fisheries Society, 1786–1893* (Edinburgh, 1978); M. Gray, *The Fishing Industries of Scotland, 1790–1814* (Oxford, 1978), *passim*.

22. J.M. Bumsted, *The People's Clearance: Highland Emigration to British North America, 1770–1815* (Edinburgh and Winnipeg, 1982), 41 ff.

23. 'Scotch Drink', in J.A. Mackay (ed.), *Robert Burns: The Complete Poetical Works* (Darvel, 1993), 167.

24. D. Daiches, *Scotch Whisky: Its Past and Present* (Edinburgh, 1969), 39.

11   THE RAGE OF IMPROVEMENTS

1. Stafford County Record Office, Stafford Papers, D593/K.

2. R.J. Adam (ed.), *Papers on Sutherland Estate Management, 1802–1816* (Scottish History Society, 1972), 239.

3. E. Richards, *The Leviathan of Wealth* (London and Toronto, 1973), 7.

4. Ibid., 8.

5. Library of Political and Economic Science, London School of Economics, Melville Papers, HE 151 (41), Coll. F, II, 3, i; J. Dunlop, *The British Fisheries Society, 1786–1893* (Edinburgh, 1978), 4, 20, 100, 128–9; E.B. Kapstein, 'The

Improvement of the West Highlands Fisheries', *Mariner's Mirror*, LXVI (1980).

6. D.J. Withrington and I.R. Grant (eds.), *The Statistical Account of Scotland*, VIII, *Argyll (Mainland)* (Wakefield, 1983; first published 1790–90), 66, 72, 212, 352.

7. Ibid., 94, 167, 294.

8. National Archives of Scotland, Melville Papers, GD 51/5/52/4.

9. A. Chitnis, 'Agricultural Improvement, Political Management and Civic Virtue in Enlightened Scotland: An Historiographical Critique', *Studies on Voltaire and the Eighteenth Century*, CCLXV (1986).

10. *Edinburgh Review*, V (October 1804), 16.

11. Adam, op. cit., 16, 26.

12. Ibid., 245.

13. Stafford County Record Office, Stafford Collection, Estate Corr D593K.

14. Adam, op. cit., 229, 237.

15. R. Black, *An Lasair* (Edinburgh, 2001), 430.

16. G. Rosie, *Hugh Miller: Outrage and Order* (Edinburgh, 1981), 100.

17. H. Miller, *Sutherland as It Was and as It Is . . .* (Edinburgh, 1843), 15, 24.

18. Ibid., 5, 7, 31.

19. R.J. Adam (ed.), *John Home's Survey of Assynt* (Edinburgh, 1960), xxiv–xxxi.

20. D.J. Withrington and I.R. Grant (eds.), *The Statistical Account of Scotland*, XVIII, *Caithness and Sutherland* (Wakefield, 1991; first published 1790–9), 303, 324, 357–8, 391, 413, 435, 470.

21. J. Loch, *An Account of the Improvements on the Estate of Sutherland* (London, 1815), 11.

22. Adam, *Sutherland Estate Management*, 221.

23. National Archives of Scotland, Sutherland Papers, GD 258/215.

24. J. Halkett, *Statement Respecting the Earl of Selkirk's Settlement upon the Red River* (London, 1817).

25. P. Robertson, *Report of the Trial of Patrick Sellar . . .* (Edinburgh, 1816), especially 8, 11, 13–14.

12 VERY VULGAR AND GAUDY

1. J. Prebble, *The King's Jaunt* (London, 1988), 237–47.

2. Ibid., 263–80.

3. National Archives of Scotland, Melville Papers, GD 51/5/749/2.

4. Ibid., GD 51/5/749/40; Lady E. Grant of Rothiemurchus, *Memoirs of a Highland Lady*, 2 vols. (Edinburgh, 1988), II, 166.

5. National Archives of Scotland, Melville Papers, GD 51/5/749/67.

6. Sir J.G. Dalyell, *Musical Memoirs of Scotland* (Edinburgh, 1849), 198.

7. National Archives of Scotland, Stewart of Garth transcripts, GD 1/53, 8 and 18 January, 14 February, 5 December 1815.

8. A. Macdonald (ed.), *Poems of Alexander Macdonald (Mac Mhaighstir Alastair)* (Inverness, 1924), 204.

9. G. Buchanan, *History of Scotland*, 2 vols. (Edinburgh, 1751–2), II, 82.

10. A. Mudie, *The Present State of Scotland* (Edinburgh, 1711), 81.

11. J. Philp, *The Grameid*, Scottish History Society (Edinburgh, 1888), 143; Sir T. Innes of Learney, *Scottish Clans and their Tartans* (Edinburgh, 1938), xx, 59; M. Martin, *A Description of the Western Isles of Scotland* (Edinburgh, 1999), 63.

12. J. Allardyce, *Historical Papers Relating to the Jacobite Period*, 2 vols. (Aberdeen, 1895–6), I, 288.

13. E. Burt, *Letters from the North of Scotland* (Edinburgh, 1998; first published, 1754), 51.

14. T. Royle, 'The Scottish Military Tradition', unpublished paper given at The Citadel, Charleston, SC, 10 April 2003. I am grateful to the author for permission to use material from his paper.

15. T. Garnett, *Observations on a Tour through the Highlands* (London, 1800), 90; E.I. Spence, *Letters from the Northern Highlands* (London, 1817), 98; H. Cockburn, *Circuit Journeys* (Edinburgh, 1888), 202.

16. J.P. Eckermann, *Gespräche mit Goethe* (Wiesbaden, 1955), 638.

17. T. Nairn, *The Break-up of Britain* (London, 1977), 162.

18. Ibid., 114–6; *Sunday Herald* (12 October 2003).

19. D. Stewart of Garth, *Sketches of the Character, Manners and Present State of the Highlanders of Scotland . . .*, 4 vols. (Edinburgh, 1822), II, 418n.

20. Central Regional Archive, Stirling, McGregor of Macgregor MSS, letters of 27 March, 19 and 30 April, 9 May, 5 July 1820; D. Stewart of Garth, *Sketches*, I, 174–6.

21. D. Stewart of Garth, *Sketches*, I, 92.

22. Public Record Office, Colonial Office series, CO 253/26 35545, letters of 23, 27, 29 and 31 July 1829.

23. National Archives of Scotland, David Stewart of Garth Transcripts, GD 1/53, letter of 8 March 1821.

24. Cited in E. Richards, *A History of the Highland Clearances*, 2 vols. (London, 1982), 117, 403.

25. J. Prebble, *The Highland Clearances* (London, 1963), 125.

26. Ibid., 145.

13   'I'M PROUD OF MY COUNTRY'

1. T. Brown (ed.), *Annals of the Disruption* (Edinburgh, 1893), 411–2.
2. Ibid., 413.
3. Ibid., 416.
4. Ibid., 424.
5. Ibid., 427.

6. Ibid., 420.

7. H. Miller, *Sutherland As it Was and As It Is* . . . (Edinburgh, 1843), 7, 12, 28.

8. S.J. Brown and M.R.G. Fry (eds.), *Scotland in the Age of the Disruption* (Edinburgh, 1993), 21.

9. T. Brown, op. cit., 95.

10. M.R.G. Fry, 'The Disruption and the Union', in S.J. Brown and M.R.G. Fry, *Scotland in the Age of the Disruption*, 31–43.

11. Figures compiled from T. Brown, op. cit., 797–812.

12. op. cit., 11.

13. D. Ansdell, *The People of the Great Faith: The Highland Church, 1690–1900* (Stornoway, 1998), 63–5.

14. National Archives of Scotland, Records of the Church of Scotland, CH 2/567/3.

15. G. Brown, *Remarks on the Earl of Selkirk's Observations on the Highlands* (Edinburgh, 1806), 39–40.

16. National Library of Scotland, Melville Papers, MS 8, fol. 21.

17. *Memoirs of Mrs William Veitch, Mr Thomas Hog of Kiltearn, Mr Henry Erskine and Mr John Carstairs* (Edinburgh, 1846), 38 ff.

18. Ansdell, op. cit., 123–4.

19. Quoted in J. Hunter, 'The Emergence of the Crofting Community: The Religious Contribution, 1798–1843', *Scottish Studies*, XVIII, 1977, 106.

20. John Kennedy, *The Days of the Fathers in Ross-shire* (Inverness, 1861), 80.

21. F. McPherson, *Watchman against the World: Norman McLeod and his People* (London, 1962), 71, 108.

22. Cited in D. Ansdell, *The People of the Great Faith*, 47–8.

23. Quoted in A.A. Auld, *Ministers and Men in the Far North* (Wick, 1868), 81.

24. Quoted in C. Brown, *The Social History of Religion in Scotland since 1730* (London and New York, 1987), 125.

25. R. Black (ed.), *An Tuil* (Edinburgh, 1999), 2–3.

26. J.S. Black and G. Chrystal, *The Life of William Robertson Smith* (London, 1912), passim.

14   ONE PROLONGED NOTE OF DESOLATION

1. A. Geikie, *Scottish Reminiscences* (Glasgow, 1906), 224–7.

2. *New Statistical Account of Scotland*, XIV, *Inverness, Ross and Cromarty* (Edinburgh, 1845), 308.

3. Ibid., 166–9.

4. *New Statistical Account of Scotland*, VII, *Renfrew and Argyll*, 77; XIV, *Inverness, Ross and Cromarty*, 190, 208.

5. *Parliamentary Papers*, 1884, XXXII, Report of the Commissioners of Inquiry into the Condition of the Crofters and Cottars in the Highlands and Islands of Scotland [Napier Commission], 28.

6. *Parliamentary Papers*, 1841, XXVI, Report of the Agent General for Emigration, 697.
7. *New Statistical Account of Scotland*, XV, *Caithness, Sutherland, Orkney, Shetland*, 185.
8. Karl Marx, *Capital*, ch. 31.
9. National Archives of Scotland, Macdonald of Sleat Papers, GD 221/160/4.
10. *The Scotsman* (25 August 1849); J. Mitchell, *Reminiscences of my Life in the Highlands*, 2 vols. (London, 1883), I, 212–3.
11. National Archives of Scotland, Macdonald of Sleat Papers, GD 221/38.
12. H. Cockburn, *Circuit Journeys* (Edinburgh, 1888), 221; H. Cockburn, *Journal*, 2 vols. (Edinburgh, 1874), II, 247.
13. National Archives of Scotland, Macdonald of Sleat Papers, GD221/51.
14. H. Barron (ed.), *Third Statistical Account: The County of Inverness* (Edinburgh, 1985), 485.
15. C. Fraser-Mackintosh, *Letters* (Inverness, 1890), 311–2.
16. *Parliamentary Papers*, XLVI, Papers Relative to the Emigration to the North American Colonies (1854), 79.
17. National Archives of Scotland, Seaforth Papers, GD 46/L/294.
18. P. Gaskell, *Morvern Transformed* (Cambridge, 1968), 29.
19. *Parliamentary Papers*, VI, Report from the Select Committee appointed to inquire into the condition of the population of the Highlands and islands of Scotland, and into the practicability of affording the people relief by means of emigration, 1841, 71.
20. National Library of Scotland, *Lamplight and Storyteller* (1985), 10 [catalogue of exhibition on John Francis Campbell].
21. *Parliamentary Papers*, 1884, XXXV, Report and Evidence of the Commissioners of Inquiry into the Condition of the Crofters and Cottars in the Highlands and Islands of Scotland [Napier Commission], Q41864.
22. *New Statistical Account of Scotland*, XIV, *Inverness, Ross and Cromarty*, 12–13.
23. Napier Commission, Q426.
24. E. Richards, 'St Kilda and Australia: Emigrants in Peril, 1852–1853', *Scottish Historical Review*, LXXI (1993), 129–55.
25. H. Cockburn, *Journal*, 136; H. Cockburn, *Circuit Journeys*, 67–8.
26. 'Edward Ellice', *Dictionary of National Biography*, VI, 665–6.
27. J.M. Bulloch, *The Gordons of Cluny* (Buckie, 1911); *Parliamentary Papers*, 1841, XXVI, Report of the Agent-General for Emigration, QQ184, 2687.
28. Quoted in D. MacLeod, *Gloomy Memories of the Highlands of Scotland* (Glasgow, 1852), 135.
29. Napier Commission, Q1680.
30. Napier Commission, Q4214; R. Somers, *Letters from the Highlands* (London, 1848), 92, 119.
31. C.N. Crisswell, *The Taipans* (Hong Kong, 1981), 66; M. Keswick, *The Thistle and the Jade: A Celebration of 150 Years of Jardine, Matheson & Co.* (London, 1982), 27.

32. J. Prebble, *The Highland Clearances* (London, 1963), 246.

33. Napier Commission, Q3786.

15 DON'T LIVE STARVING WHERE YOU ARE

1. W.G. Alexander, *Recollections of a Highland Subaltern* (London, 1898), 104; L. Sykes, *Calcutta through British Eyes* (Madras, 1992), 47.

2. Sir W.W. Hunter, *The Marquess of Dalhousie* (Oxford, 1890), 76–92.

3. *The Scotsman* (8 April, 11 May, 25 May 1854).

4. Queen Victoria, *Leaves from the Journal of Our Life in the Highlands* (London, 1973), 100.

5. Sir A. Quiller-Couch (ed.), *The Oxford Book of English Verse* (Oxford, 1919), 528.

6. J. Prebble, *The Highland Clearances* (London, 1963), 303; E. Richards, *The Highland Clearances* (Edinburgh, 2000), 279.

7. M. Flinn *et al.*, *Scottish Population History* (Cambridge, 1977), 464 ff.

8. *Parliamentary Papers*, 1884, XXXV, Report and Evidence of the Commissioners of Inquiry into the Condition of the Crofters and Cottars in the Highlands and Islands of Scotland [Napier Commission], Q41318.

9. G. Patterson, *A History of the County of Pictou, Nova Scotia* (Montreal, 1877), 82.

10. Napier Commission, Appendix A, 125, 164.

11. F. Ramsay, *John Ramsay of Kildalton* (Toronto, 1971), ix, 96–7, 133.

12. D. Craig, *On the Crofters' Trail* (London, 1990), 88, 102, 190–1, 272.

13. D.E. Meek, ' "Falling Down as if Dead": Attitudes to Unusual Phenomena in the Skye Revival of 1841–2', *Scottish Bulletin of Evangelical Theology* (1995), 118.

14. J. Hunter, *The Making of the Crofting Community* (Edinburgh, 1976), 94–106.

15. A. Mackenzie, *Isle of Skye in 1882* (Inverness, 1883), appendix.

16. J. Hunter (ed.), *For the People's Cause, from the Writings of John Murdoch* (Edinburgh, 1986), 9–39.

17. J.S. Blackie, *Scottish Highlanders and the Land Laws* (London, 1885), introduction, 15, 129; W. Gillies, *Gaelic and Scotland – Alba agus a'Ghàilig* (Edinburgh, 1989), 5–14.

18. National Archives of Scotland, Skene–Trevelyan Correspondence, HD 7/46.

19. V.E. Durkacz, *The Decline of the Celtic Languages* (Edinburgh, 1983), 133.

20. *Parliamentary Papers*, 1867, XXV, Education (Scotland) Commission, Report on the State of Education in the Hebrides, by Alexander Nicolson, especially 193 ff.

21. J.L. Campbell, *Gaelic in Scottish Education and Life* (Edinburgh, 1950), 66–7; M. Macleod, 'Gaelic in Highland Education', *Transactions of the Gaelic Society of Inverness*, XLIII (1963), 319. See also B. Lenman and J. Stocks, 'The Beginnings of State Education in Scotland', *Scottish Educational Studies*, IV (1972).

22. S.J. Blackie, *The Gaelic Language* (Edinburgh, 1864), 30.
23. Gillies, op. cit., 6.
24. J.F. Campbell, *Popular Tales of the West Highlands*, 4 vols. (Paisley, 1890), II, i.
25. E. Renan, *L'Ame bretonne* (Maulévrier, 1982), 11.
26. M. Arnold, *On the Study of Celtic Literature* (London, 1867), 115, 180–1.
27. W. Sharp, *Lyra Celtica* (Edinburgh, 1896), li.

16   THE GREAT GRIEVANCE

1. H.J. Hanham, 'The Creation of the Scottish Office', *Juridical Review*, X (1965); S.H. Zebel, *Balfour: A Political Biography* (Cambridge, 1973), 75.
2. *Parliamentary Papers*, 1884, XXIV, Report and Evidence of the Commissioners of Inquiry into the Condition of the Crofters and Cottars in the Highlands and Islands of Scotland [Napier Commission], QQ5320–39; B.E. Dugdale, *Arthur James Balfour*, 2 vols. (London, 1939), 64–5.
3. National Archives of Scotland, Home Office Papers, HH1/3.
4. Ibid., 1/842.
5. Ibid., 1/816.
6. S. MacLean, *Ris a'Bhruthaich* (Stornoway, 1985), 70–2; D.E. Meek (ed.), *Màiri Mhòr nan Oran, taghadh de a h-òrain le eachdraidh a beatha is notaichean* (Glasgow, 1977), 91. I am grateful to Farquhar Mackintosh for the translation.
7. I.M.M. Macphail, 'The Skye Military Expedition of 1884–5', *Transactions of the Gaelic Society of Inverness*, XLVIII (1972–4), 62–94; National Archives of Scotland, Macdonald Papers, GD 221/148/1; National Archives of Scotland, Ivory Papers, GD 1/36/1; National Archives of Scotland, Home Office Papers, HH 22/4; Napier Commission, QQ9385, 9470–6, 9924.
8. National Archives of Scotland, Crofting Files, AF 35–8.
9. Ibid., AF 38–40; D. MacDonald, *Lewis: A History of the Island* (Edinburgh, 1978), 174.
10. D.W. Crowley, 'The Crofters' Party 1885–1892', *Scottish Historical Review*, XXV (1956).
11. Napier Commission, Q2804.
12. Napier Commission, Appendix A, 14.
13. M. Barker, *Gladstone and Radicalism* (Hassocks, 1975), 14.
14. George Campbell, duke of Argyll, *The Unseen Foundations of Society* (London, 1883), 230; *Scotland as It Was and as It Is* (Edinburgh, 1883), I, 49.
15. Barker, *Gladstone and Radicalism*, 28.
16. Quoted in I.M.M. Macphail, *The Crofters' War* (Stornoway, 1989), 72.
17. Lord Napier and Ettrick, 'The Highland Crofters', *Nineteenth Century*, XVII (1885), 448.
18. Napier Commission, QQ8602–4.
19. Ibid., QQ8951, 13326, 29209–17.

20. Ibid., QQ13380–1, 27253.
21. Ibid., QQ44504–6.
22. Napier Commission, Report, 108.
23. Ibid., 111.
24. H. George, *Poverty and Progress* (London, 1880), 91.
25. Napier Commission, Report, 118, 124.
26. J.P. Day, *Public Administration in the Highlands and Islands of Scotland* (London, 1918), 192.
27. J. Ridley, *Garibaldi* (London, 1974), 549–51; Stafford Country Record Office, Stafford Papers, D593/K/1/7/23.
28. Cited in E. Richards, *The Highland Clearances* (Edinburgh, 2000), 305.
29. Napier Commission, Report, 136.

17   FANCY DREAMS

1. Anonymous, *Sea Sorrow: The Story of the Iolaire Disaster* (Stornoway, 1972).
2. L.G. Gibbon, *A Scots Quair* (London, 1946), 193.
3. Surveyed in E. Cameron, *Land for the People? The British Government and the Scottish Highlands, 1880–1925* (East Linton, 1996).
4. H. Barron (ed.), *Third Statistical Account of Scotland: The County of Inverness* (Edinburgh, 1985), 454–60.
5. Cameron, op. cit., 83 ff.
6. National Archives of Scotland, Crofting Files, AF 67/120, 121.
7. H. Barron (ed.), *Third Statistical Account, County of Inverness*, 548 ff.
8. National Archives of Scotland, Crofters Files, AF 67/126.
9. Ibid., AF 67/125.
10. E. David, *Inside Asquith's Cabinet* (London, 1977), 79–80.
11. J. Brown, 'Scottish and English Land Legislation', *Scottish Historical Review*, XLVII (1968).
12. Cameron, op. cit., 147 ff.
13. R.C. Macleod, *Book of Dunvegan*, 2 vols., Third Spalding Club (Aberdeen, 1938–9) II, 100; National Archives of Scotland, Crofting Files, AF 67/57, 61, 62, 142, 145.
14. Quoted in Cameron, op. cit., 159.
15. National Archives of Scotland, Crofting Files, AF 67/61.
16. Ibid., AF 67/49, 146–9, 151–2, 175, 238, 254, 329.
17. Cameron, op. cit., 167 ff.
18. J. Buchan, *The Four Adventures of Richard Hannay* (London, 1930), 550.
19. Nigel Nicolson, *Lord of the Isles* (London, 1960), 76–7.
20. *Parliamentary Papers*, XLIV, 1890–1, Reports of the Committee appointed to Inquire into Certain Matters Affecting the Interests of the Population of the Western Highlands and Islands of Scotland, 219.
21. Nicolson, op. cit., 158.

22. Ibid., 151.
23. A. Geddes, *The Isle of Lewis and Harris* (Edinburgh, 1955), 275.
24. Barron, op. cit., 23.
25. I.F. Grigor, *Highland Resistance* (Edinburgh and London, 2000), 209 ff.
26. Quoted in R. Finlay, *Scotland, 1914–2000* (London, 2004), 159–60.
27. Quoted in M.P. McCulloch (ed.), *Modernism and Nationalism* (Glasgow, 2004), 304–5.
28. *Scots Magazine*, XXXVIII (October 1937), 13–20.
29. Geddes, op. cit., 84–5.
30. A. Collier, *The Crofting Problem* (Cambridge, 1953), 133–41.

18   A GOLDEN WINE

1. H. MacDiarmid, *Letters* (London, 1984), 303.
2. M.P. McCulloch, *Modernism and Nationalism* (Glasgow, 2004), 288.
3. MacDiarmid, op. cit., 202.
4. Ibid.
5. E. Muir, *Scottish Journey* (London, 1936), 195–6.
6. M. Grieve and A. Scott (eds.), *The Hugh MacDiarmid Anthology* (London, 1976), 64.
7. Ibid., 8.
8. E. Muir, *Scott and Scotland* (London, 1936), 110 ff.
9. Grieve and Scott, op. cit., 191.
10. Quoted in McCulloch, op. cit., 210 ff.
11. 'The Caledonian Antisyzygy and the Gaelic Idea', in D. Glen (ed.), *Selected Essays of Hugh MacDiarmid* (London, 1969), 71.
12. R. Black (ed.), *An Tuil* (Edinburgh, 1999), 738.
13. McCulloch, op. cit., 298 ff.
14. Black, op. cit., 719.
15. F. Thompson, *History of An Comunn Gàidhealach* (Inverness, 1992).
16. Black, op. cit., 757.
17. McCulloch, op. cit., 290–1.
18. H. MacDiarmid, *The Islands of Scotland* (London, 1939), 44.
19. J. Hendry and R.J. Ross (eds.), *Sorley MacLean: Critical Essays* (Edinburgh, 1986), 217–8.
20. S. MacLean, *Ris a'Bhruthaich: The Criticism and Prose Writing of Sorley MacLean* (Stornoway, 1985), 10.
21. Ibid., 9.
22. S. Heaney, 'Introduction', in Hendry and Ross, op. cit., 2.
23. S. MacLean, *O Choille gu Bearradh* (Manchester, 1989), 130–1.
24. Hendry and Ross, op. cit., 17.
25. D. Macaulay (ed.), *Modern Scottish Gaelic Poems* (Edinburgh, 1986), 54.

26. Quoted in C. Nicholson, *Poem, Purpose and Place: Shaping Identity in Contemporary Scottish Verse* (Edinburgh, 1992), 6.
27. S. MacLean, *O Choille gu Bearradh*, 16–17.
28. Black, op. cit., 764–8.
29. *The Guardian* (30 November 2002).

19   A GREAT OUTDOOR LABORATORY

1. E. Pinchard, *Piper Alpha: A Survivor's Story* (London, 1986).
2. P. Singerman, *Red Adair: An American Hero* (London, 1989), 156, 204.
3. A. Sampson, *The Seven Sisters, the Great Oil Companies and the World they Made* (London, 1975), 256 ff.
4. P. Payne, 'The Decline of the Scottish Heavy Industries 1945–1983', in R. Saville (ed.), *The Economic Development of Modern Scotland* (Edinburgh, 1985), 79–113.
5. I am grateful to Ross Leckie, roustabout and financier, for advice on several points in this discussion.
6. G. Schrank, *An Orkney Estate* (East Linton, 1995), 4–8.
7. H.D. Smith, *Shetland Life and Trade, 1550–1914* (Edinburgh, 1984), 287–8.
8. J.J.H. Burgess, *Rasmie's Büddie Poems in the Shetlandic* (Lerwick, 1979).
9. I. Carter, 'The Highlands of Scotland as an Underdeveloped Region', in E. De Kadt and G. Williams (eds.), *Sociology and Development* (London, 1974), 280 ff.
10. T. Johnston, *Memories* (London, 1952), 122.
11. Sir A. Cairncross, *Living with the Century* (Kirkcaldy, 1998), 161.
12. *A Programme for Highland Development* [report of the commission of inquiry into crofting conditions, Command Paper 9091].
13. A.S. Mather (ed.), *Third Statistical Account of Scotland: The County of Ross and Cromarty* (Edinburgh, 1987), 297–8, 378.
14. A. MacLeod and G. Payne, 'Locals and Incomers: Social and Cultural Identity in Late Twentieth-century Coigach', in J. Baldin (ed.), *People and Settlement in North-west Ross* (Edinburgh, 1994), 392–5; H. Barron (ed.), *Third Statistical Account: The County of Inverness* (Edinburgh, 1987), 272 ff., 314 ff.
15. J.S. Smith (ed.), *Third Statistical Account of Scotland: The County of Sutherland* (Edinburgh, 1988), 180, 271.
16. Mather, op. cit., 310; *New Statistical Account*, XIV, *Ross and Cromarty* (Edinburgh, 1845), 95.
17. Carter, op. cit., 282; F. Gillanders, 'The Economic Life of Gaelic Scotland Today', in D.S. Thomson and I. Grimble (eds.), *The Future of the Highlands* (London, 1968), 148 ff.
18. I. Mitchell, *Isles of the West* (Edinburgh, 1999), 22–4.

19. J.M. Boyd, *Fraser Darling's Islands* (Edinburgh, 1986), 19, 233–4; F.M. Darling, *Island Years*, 114.

20. J.M. Boyd and F.F. Darling, *Highlands and Islands* (London, 1964), 291–2.

21. *The Scottish Economy 1965–70: A Plan for Expansion*, Command Paper 2864 (1966), 47.

22. *Hansard* (5 July 1965), col. 1044.

23. M.A. Greig, 'The Regional Income and Employment Multiplier Effects of a Pulp Mill and Paper Mill', *Scottish Journal of Political Economy*, XVIII (1971).

24. Sir A. Gilchrist, *Cod Wars and How to Lose Them* (Edinburgh, 1977), 115.

25. Sir K. Alexander, 'The Highlands and Islands Development Board', in Saville, op. cit., 214 ff.

26. J. Dunlop, *The British Fisheries Society, 1786–1893* (Edinburgh, 1978), 205 ff.; J.R. Coull (ed.), *Third Statistical Account of Scotland: The County of Shetland* (Edinburgh, 1985), xiv, 55; D. Thomson, 'Highland Fisheries', in *The Companion to Gaelic Scotland* (Glasgow, 1984), 76.

20   THE LAND'S FOR THE PEOPLE

1. J. MacAskill, *We Have Won the Land* (Stornoway, 1999), 15 ff.

2. I.F. Grigor, *Highland Resistance* (Edinburgh, 2000), 227 ff.

3. C. Dressler, *Eigg: The Story of an Island* (Edinburgh, 1988), 140 and *passim*.

4. *The Herald* (28 May 1999).

5. W. Orr, *Deer Forests, Landlord and Crofters* (Edinburgh, 1982), 148.

6. Grigor, op. cit., 231

7. See www.knoydart-foundation.com

8. This became the Land Reform (Scotland) Act 2003.

9. I. Mitchell, *Isles of the West* (Edinburgh, 1999), ix.

10. The Summer Isles Hotel.

11. A. Macleod and G. Payne, 'Locals and Incomers: Social and Cultural Identity in Late Twentieth-century Coigach', in J. Baldwin (ed.), *People and Settlement in North-west Ross* (Edinburgh, 1994), 392–5.

12. Mitchell, op. cit., 126, 146, 195.

13. W.G. Berry, J.B Caird, N.J. Ford and H.R. Jones, 'Counter-urbanisation, English Migration to the Scottish Highlands and Islands', in H.R. Jones (ed.), *Population Change in Contemporary Scotland* (Norwich, 1984), 73 ff.

14. Cited in D. Turnock, *Patterns of Highland Development* (London, 1970), 115.

15. H. Barron (ed.), *Third Statistical Account of Scotland: County of Inverness* (Edinburgh, 1985), 38 ff., 420.

16. D. Turnock, *Patterns of Highland Development*.

17. D. Thomson, *The Companion to Gaelic Scotland* (Glasgow, 1984), 27; D. Thomson, *Why Gaelic Matters* (Edinburgh, 1984), 27–8.

18. D. Macaulay (ed.), *Modern Scottish Gaelic Poems* (Edinburgh, 1976), 46 ff.

19. J.S. Smith, *Third Statistical Account of Scotland: The County of Sutherland* (Edinburgh, 1988), 38.
20. D.E. Meek, 'The Language of Heaven? The Highland Churches, Culture Shift and the Erosion of Gaelic Identity in the Twentieth Century', in R. Pope (ed.), *Religion and National Identity: Wales and Scotland, 1700–2000* (Cardiff, 2001), 307 ff.

ENVOI

1. R.L. Stevenson, 'The Foreigner at Home', *Miscellanies* (Edinburgh, 1894), 98–9.
2. J. Prebble, *The Highland Clearances* (London, 1963), 304.
3. S. MacLean, *O Choille gu Bearradh* (Manchester, 1989), 100–01.

Index

In general, names of persons, places and subjects mentioned only once in the text have not been included in the index, but exceptions are made for longer references and occasionally for other reasons.

Assynt, 171, 203, 304–5, 306, 309, 312, 317

Atholl (district), 23, 83, 84, 85, 87

Atholl, James Murray, 2nd duke of, 52, 326

Atholl, John Murray, 1st duke of, 52, 104, 326

Atholl, John Murray, 3rd duke of, 116, 117, 134–5, 326

Atholl, John Murray, 4th duke of, 178, 186, 188

Atholl, Mary Murray, duchess of, 116, 117, 326

Australia, 140, 203, 209, 215, 218, 230

Bacach, Eachann, 19–20

Badenoch, 78, 114, 119

Balfour, Arthur James, 240, 241, 243

Balmoral, 185, 225

Barra, 91, 211, 219, 220, 222, 229, 258–9

Beaton, Fergus and Neil, 71

Bedell, William, bishop of Kilmore, 40, 41, 76

Bellay, Joachim du, 2, 3

Benbecula, 119, 219

Ben Nevis, 16, 310

Bethune, Revd John, 64, 172

Bettyhill, 160, 175

Bible, Gaelic, 40, 41, 74, 76, 78, 126–7, 149, 198, 231, 247

Black, Ronald, 169, 277, 285

Black Isle, 153, 217

Black Watch, 87, 104–5, 116–17, 123, 146, 180, 183

Blackie, John Stuart, 185, 231, 232, 235–6, 237

Blair, Hugh, Revd, 115, 118–19, 121

Board of Agriculture, 260, 262, 265, 296

Boswell, James, 112–14, 130, 131, 134, 140, 143, 212

Braemar, 42, 50, 232

Braes, the (Skye), 214, 244. 247, 248

Breadalbane, Iain Glas Campbell, 1st earl of, 35, 37, 40, 43, 45–6, 52, 53, 59, 61, 326

Breadalbane, John Campbell, 2nd earl of, 326

Breadalbane, John Campbell, 3rd earl of, 105, 210–11, 326

Brougham, Henry, Lord, 167, 169

Buchan, Alexander, 124–5

Buchan, John, 262, 275

Buchanan, Dugald, 149, 231

Buchanan, George, 2, 7, 181

Burns, Robert, 157, 216, 275, 283, 297

Burt, Edmund, 134, 154, 183

Bute, John Stuart, earl of, 107, 108, 115, 117, 118, 120, 148

Caird, James, 280–1

Caithness, 57, 67, 75, 197, 201, 205, 245, 252, 267

Caledonian Canal, 165, 199

Calvin, John, 29, 198

Cameron, Alexander, 237, 326

Cameron, Daniel, 76, 326

Cameron, Richard, 41, 326

Cameron Highlanders, 155, 183

Cameron of Corrychoillie, John, 146, 326

Cameron of Erracht, Allan, 183, 326

Cameron of Invercaddle, Allan, 146, 326

Cameron of Kildermorie, Alexander and Alan, 144, 150–1, 155–6, 158, 326

Cameron of Lochiel, Charles, 21st chief, 327

Cameron of Lochiel, Donald, 19th chief, 81, 165, 326

Cameron of Lochiel, Donald, 22nd chief, 327

Cameron of Lochiel, Donald, 23rd chief, 327

Cameron of Lochiel, Donald, 24th chief, 247, 251, 327

Cameron of Lochiel, Ewen, 17th chief, 29, 52, 56, 326
Cameron of Lochiel, John, 18th chief, 326
Cameron of Lochiel, John, 20th chief, 326
Campbell, Angus, 278, 327
Campbell, Colin, 223–4, 327
Campbell, John (banker), 61, 94, 327
Campbell, John (loyalist), 129, 327
Campbell of Ardkinglas, Sir Colin, 46, 47, 327
Campbell of Auchinbreck, Sir Duncan, 17, 24, 327
Campbell of Fonab, Alexander, 59, 327
Campbell of Glenlyon, Robert, 33, 59, 327
Campbell of Glenorchy, Sir John, 327
Campbell of Glenure, Colin, 99, 327
Campbell of Islay, John Francis, 216, 236–7, 327
Campbell of Islay, Walter Frederick, 216, 327
Canada, 96–8, 106, 137, 138, 139, 140, 141–3, 155, 173–4, 203, 209, 210, 215, 221, 224, 228–9, 230, 263, 323
Cape Wrath, 169, 170
Carey, Sir Robert, 1–2
Carlyle, Alexander 'Jupiter', 115, 119
Carmichael, Alexander, 71, 237
Carrick, 3, 9
Carswell, Revd John, 11, 29, 40
Cathcart, Lady Gordon (née Emily Pringle), 258, 259, 263
Catholics and Catholicism, xii, 2, 21, 22, 23, 28, 42, 60, 65, 71, 76, 216, 220, 273, 284, 318
Ceilidhs, 71–4, 206
Charles I, King, 14, 16, 18, 19, 20, 21, 22, 25, 26, 27, 31, 38, 53
Charles II, King, 26, 28, 30, 34, 35, 38, 41, 57, 200
Charles Edward Stewart, Prince, the Young Pretender, 'Bonnie Prince

Charlie': character, 94–5; in rebellion, 63, 83, 98, 99, 106, 116; at Culloden, 53, 80–2, 84–5, 86, 87; in flight, 90, 91, 92, 113; death, 43; cult, 185
Church of Scotland: as establishment, 42, 65, 70, 74, 75–6, 81, 185, 200, 201–2, 203, 204, 216, 224, 318; under James VI, 18; under Charles I, 20, 21; under Cromwell, 29; in Revolution, 40–1, 54, 64, 69; and Union, 67, 68; and Disruption, 193, 194, 195, 196, 197–8, 205, 209, 230, 234; and Gaelic, 113, 117, 233
Clans and septs, with some Lowland names: 4, 6, 132–5, 165, 178, 180, 182, 206, 231, 246
Armstrong, 5
Beaton, 6
Buchanan, 93
Cameron, 38, 43, 44, 59, 61, 85, 90, 91, 92
Campbell: political role, 2, 107; and Reformation, 11, 20; expansion and feuds, 10, 12, 16–7, 21, 22, 23, 24, 25, 26, 34, 212; divisions, 51–2, 53, 59, 60; and improvement, 35, 134, 156, 157, 158, 183, 246; tartan, 183
Chattan, 10, 57, 93, 134
Chisholm, 42, 61, 93
Erskine, 53, 140
Farquharson, 42, 53
Fraser, 62, 83, 85, 88, 93, 107
Gordon, 2, 10, 53, 183
Grant, 89, 104, 107, 182
Johnston, 5
MacDonald, 10, 13, 17, 21, 23, 24, 33–4, 37, 42, 43, 45, 46, 47, 53, 62, 71, 85, 92, 93, 106, 112, 132, 138, 183, 212, 214, 222
Macdonnell, 12, 140, 266
McGillivray, 138, 139–40
MacGregor, 12, 38
MacKay, 44, 57, 169, 212, 222

Edinburgh: as capital of Scotland, 1, 3,
6, 173, 296, 303, 305; Reformation
in, 11; under Charles I , 18, 22, 23,
26; under Charles II, 27, 31, 34, 36;
at Revolution, 43, 47; Church of
Scotland in, 68, 76, 194–5; Jacobites
in, 80, 82; Enlightenment in, 39, 71,
115–16, 119, 123, 169, 232, 322;
George IV in, 176, 177, 178, 179,
180; relations with Highlands, 8, 11,
14, 40, 100, 102, 146, 147, 148, 152,
218, 220, 226, 276, 295, 312
Edinburgh, University of, xi, xii, 65,
97, 122, 166, 167, 185, 208, 231,
234, 237, 247, 280
Edinburgh Review, 167, 168, 173, 175, 195
Education Acts: 1872, 234–5; 1918,
235, 278
Eigg, 91, 193, 306–7, 310
Emigration, 96–8, 106, 131–5, 137, 138,
139, 140, 141–3, 155, 171, 173, 174,
203, 209, 210, 215, 218, 221, 221,
228–9, 230, 254, 258
Empire, British, 96–7, 106, 108, 148,
155, 177, 185, 188, 199, 212, 229,
255, 310
English language, v, xix, 2, 8, 14–15,
64, 76, 77, 78, 119, 124, 125–6, 198,
204, 233, 234, 265, 274, 275, 276,
277, 280, 281, 297, 317
Enlightenment, Scottish, 39, 55, 122,
166, 206, 233, 236
Erskine of Grange, James, 53, 63, 81–2
Erskine, Rachel, 53, 81
European Community, 305, 314

Ferguson, Adam, 8, 109, 115, 116–17,
118, 122, 152, 187
Fergusson, John, 90–1
Fianna, 72–3, 119
Finlayson, Revd Robert, 210
Fingal, 113, 114, 119, 120, 121, 124
Finn MacCool, 7, 73
First World War, 255, 257, 260, 261,
263, 276, 277, 278

Fletcher, Andrew, Lord Milton, 101,
111, 117, 118
Fletcher of Saltoun, Andrew, the
Patriot, 101, 117
Fontenoy, Battle of, 104, 116
Forbes of Culloden, Duncan, 63, 82,
83, 87, 88, 93, 101, 140, 157
Forestry Commission, 262, 307–8
Fort Augustus, 87, 88, 89, 91
Fort William, 16, 46, 47, 63, 89, 301,
314
Fox, Charles James, 98, 108
Fraser, Simon, Master of Lovat, 82,
98–100, 106, 107, 328
Fraser's Highlanders, 96, 97, 98
Free Church of Scotland, 11, 158, 192,
193, 195, 196, 204, 206, 207, 210,
216, 224, 233–4, 240, 277, 289, 318
Free Presbyterian Church, 207, 280, 318

Gaelic culture, general, 3, 36, 53, 71,
77, 112–13, 149, 206, 214, 230, 245,
276, 316
language: outline, xix–xx; Common
Classical Gaelic, 7, 11; as
language of religion and
education, 42, 75, 77, 78, 116,
117, 127, 160, 198, 199, 204, 205,
207, 216; in America, 128, 138,
230; other varieties of, 64, 120;
translations into, 29, 40, 76; status
of, 113, 114, 149, 156; relation to
Scots, 39; relation to English,
8–9, 14–15, 70; revival of, 232,
233, 234–5; decline of, 124, 270,
276–7, 297, 317–18, 321
literature, of the seventeenth
century, 7, 13, 14, 17, 20, 24–5,
29, 34, 36, 37, 40, 41, 54; of the
eighteenth century, 71, 95, 114,
115, 118, 120, 121, 126, 141–3,
149, 170; of the twentieth
century, 205–6, 231, 242–3, 276,
278, 279–87, 317, 324
society, 4, 101, 135, 166, 216, 276